Constructing Democratic Governance:
South America in the 1990s

An Inter-American Dialogue Book

Constructing Democratic Governance: Latin America and the Caribbean in the 1990s
edited by Jorge I. Domínguez and Abraham F. Lowenthal

Available in separate paperback editions:

Constructing Democratic Governance: Latin America and the Caribbean in the 1990s—Themes and Issues
edited by Jorge I. Domínguez and Abraham F. Lowenthal

Constructing Democratic Governance: South America in the 1990s
edited by Jorge I. Domínguez and Abraham F. Lowenthal

Constructing Democratic Governance: Mexico, Central America, and the Caribbean in the 1990s
edited by Jorge I. Domínguez and Abraham F. Lowenthal

Constructing Democratic Governance

South America in the 1990s

edited by
Jorge I. Domínguez and
Abraham F. Lowenthal

The Johns Hopkins University Press
Baltimore and London

© 1996 The Johns Hopkins University Press
All rights reserved. Published 1996
Printed in the United States of America on acid-free paper
05 04 03 02 01 00 99 98 97 96 5 4 3 2 1

The Johns Hopkins University Press
2715 North Charles Street
Baltimore, Maryland 21218-4319
The Johns Hopkins Press Ltd., London

The Library of Congress has cataloged the hardcover edition as follows:

Constructing democratic governance: Latin America and the Caribbean
  in the 1990s / edited by Jorge I. Domínguez and Abraham F. Lowenthal
    p.   cm.—(An Inter-American dialogue book)
  Includes bibliographical references and index.
  ISBN 0-8018-5385-0 (alk. paper)
    1. Latin America—Politics and government—1980– . 2. Democracy—
  Latin America. 3. Caribbean Area—Politics and government—1945– .
  4. Democracy—Caribbean Area. I. Domínguez, Jorge I., 1945– .
  II. Lowenthal, Abraham F. III. Series.
  JL966.C677   1996
  321.8′098—dc20   96-12421
                                                                        CIP

A catalog record for this book is available from the British Library.

ISBN 0-8018-5403-2 (pbk.)

Contents

Foreword • ix
Contributors • xi
Acronyms and Abbreviations • xiii

I

Introduction: Constructing Democratic Governance
Abraham F. Lowenthal and Jorge I. Domínguez • 3

II

1. Venezuela: The Rise and Fall of Partyarchy
Michael Coppedge • 3

2. Colombia: Building Democracy in the Midst of
Violence and Drugs
Harvey F. Kline • 20

3. Ecuador: Democracy Standing the Test of Time?
Anita Isaacs • 42

4. Peru: The Rupture of Democratic Rule
Susan Stokes • 58

5. Bolivia: Managing Democracy in the 1990s
Eduardo A. Gamarra • 72

6. Chile: The Political Underpinnings of Economic Liberalization
Timothy R. Scully, C.S.C. • 99

7. Paraguay: Transition from *Caudillo* Rule
Diego Abente Brun • 118

8. Uruguay: From Restoration to the Crisis of Governability
Juan Rial • 133

9. Argentina: Democracy in Turmoil
Liliana De Riz • 147

10. Brazil: The Hyperactive Paralysis Syndrome
Bolívar Lamounier • 166

Notes to Part II • 189
Index to Part II • 215

III

Conclusion: Parties, Institutions, and Market Reforms in
Constructing Democracies
Jorge I. Domínguez and Jeanne Kinney Giraldo • 3

Foreword

There is no more important challenge in the hemisphere today than building effective democratic governance. The understandable celebrations associated with the transition to constitutional, elected governments in Latin America over the past fifteen years have now yielded to growing concern that persistent obstacles stand in the way of constructing and consolidating genuine democracies. Free and competitive elections are no longer noteworthy events in the region. Yet progress is lagging behind in other key areas such as establishing civilian control over armed forces, fully protecting human rights, advancing the rule of law, strengthening the role of the legislature and the judiciary, fostering citizen participation, improving the performance of political parties, and redressing sharp social inequalities and ethnic divisions.

Analysts make many claims about the state of democracy in the hemisphere—and policymakers make decisions based on such assessments—but there have been few, if any, systematic attempts to understand and explain prevailing conditions in Latin America and the Caribbean. This volume is just such an effort. The editors commissioned twenty-one country studies and five chapters on crosscutting issues relevant to a number of the national cases. Abraham F. Lowenthal, the Inter-American Dialogue's founding executive director and currently a board member, and Jorge I. Domínguez, who is a member and associated fellow of the Dialogue, succeeded in attracting first-rate analysts from Latin America, the Caribbean, Canada, and the United States to prepare these studies.

The chapters went through several drafts. They benefited from the comments of the editors as well as from a major, two-day conference held in Washington, D.C., in September 1994 that brought together U.S. and Latin American senior government officials, representatives of multilateral institutions, congressional staff, policy analysts, and key leaders from many nongovernmental organizations. The conference prompted rich discussion on both the country and the thematic papers and helped bridge the worlds of policy and academia.

Many others deserve credit for their role in this project. Jeanne Kinney Giraldo, a doctoral student in political science at Harvard University, provided detailed, critical commentary on all the chapters. We would also like to extend our appreciation to Javier Corrales and Robert Hemmer for their fine translations and to the Dialogue interns who contributed to this project: Robert Bettman, Corrine Castagnet, Sarah Connelly, Cindy Garret, Alex Gross, Robyn Prinz, James Rogan, Eduardo

Romo, and John White. Special thanks are in order for Nicola Lowther, who skillfully performed the countless editing and other tasks that finishing such a volume entails, and to Jenny Pilling, for her unfailing patience and dedication in coordinating the project.

The Inter-American Dialogue's research and publications are designed to improve the quality of public debate and decision on key issues in western hemisphere affairs. The Dialogue is both a forum for sustained exchange among leaders and an independent, nonpartisan center for policy analysis on U.S.–Latin American economic and political relations. The Dialogue's one hundred members—from the United States, Canada, Latin America, and the Caribbean—include prominent political, business, labor, academic, media, military, and religious leaders. At periodic plenary sessions, members analyze key hemispheric issues and formulate recommendations for policy and action. The Dialogue presents its findings in comprehensive reports circulated throughout the Americas. Its research agenda focuses on four broad themes: democratic governance, inter-American cooperation, economic integration, and social equity.

The Inter-American Dialogue wishes to express its gratitude to the National Endowment for Democracy and the A. W. Mellon Foundation for their support for commissioning the papers, the September 1994 international conference in Washington, and the publication of this volume. Mead Data Central–Lexis/Nexus Research Information Services gave us crucial research assistance. We are also pleased to acknowledge the broader support that the Dialogue has obtained from the Ford, A. W. Mellon, and William and Flora Hewlett foundations and the Carnegie Corporation of New York.

Michael Shifter
Program Director, Democratic Governance
Inter-American Dialogue

Peter Hakim
President
Inter-American Dialogue

Contributors

Diego Abente Brun is professor of political science at the National University of Asunción and the Catholic University of Asunción, Paraguay, and was formerly professor of political science at Miami University in Ohio. He has written various articles and books on Paraguay and the democratic transition in Latin America such as *Paraguay en transición* (1993). Dr. Abente Brun received his Ph.D. in political science from the University of New Mexico and in 1993 was elected senator to the Paraguayan National Congress.

Michael Coppedge is associate professor in the department of government at the University of Notre Dame. He previously taught at the Nitze School of Advanced International Studies of Johns Hopkins University and at Princeton University. His research interests include the governability and performance of democratic regimes, the evolution of Latin American party systems, politics in Venezuela and Mexico, and the measurement of democracy. His latest book is *Strong Parties and Lame Ducks: Presidential Partyarchy and Factionalism in Venezuela* (1994). Dr. Coppedge received his Ph.D. from Yale University.

Liliana De Riz is currently a senior researcher at the Instituto de Investigaciones de la Facultad de Ciencias Sociales of the Universidad de Buenos Aires, where she is a professor of political science. In addition to writing numerous articles on Argentina and comparative politics, Dr. De Riz has edited *Retorno y derrumbe: El último gobierno peronista*, in its second edition (1987); *Radicales y Peronistas: El Congreso Argentino entre 1983 y 1989* (1994); and *Argentina since 1946*, which she co-authored. She holds a Ph.D. in sociology from the

Ecole Pratique des Hautes Etudes, Université de Paris.

Jorge I. Domínguez is Frank G. Thomson Professor of Government at Harvard University. Previously he was visiting senior fellow at the Inter-American Dialogue, of which he is a founding member. A past president of the Latin American Studies Association and member of the Council on Foreign Relations, he is a member of the editorial boards of *Mexican Studies, Cuban Studies, Political Science Quarterly*, and the *Journal of Inter-American Studies and World Affairs*. Dr. Domínguez is a leading authority on Cuban and Latin American politics and is widely published on these topics. With James McCann, he recently co-authored *Democratizing Mexico: Public Opinions and Electoral Choice*.

Eduardo A. Gamarra is acting director of the Latin American and Caribbean Center and associate professor of political science at Florida International University. His research interests include civil-military relations, democratization, legislatures and political parties in Latin America, narcotics trafficking, and U.S.–Latin American relations. His recent publications include *Entre la Droga y la Democracia* (1994); *Democracy, Markets, and Structural Reform in Latin America: Argentina, Bolivia, Brazil, Chile, and Mexico* (1994); and *The Administration of Justice in Bolivia: An Institutional Analysis* (1991). He holds a Ph.D. in political science from the University of Pittsburgh.

Jeanne Kinney Giraldo is a Ph.D. candidate and has been a teaching fellow in the department of government at Harvard University. Her papers include "Democracy and Development in Chile: Alejandro Foxley and the Concertación's Economic Policy," which she presented to the Latin American Studies Association in March 1994.

Anita Isaacs is associate professor of political science at Haverford College in Pennsylvania and previously taught at Oxford University and New York University. She has served as program officer for the Ford Foundation and as a consultant to the Canadian International Development Research Centre (IDRC). Her publications include *The Politics of Military Rule and Transition in Ecuador* (1993); "Ecuador," in *Oxford Companion to World Politics* (1993); and "Problems of Democratic Consolidation in Ecuador," *Bulletin of Latin American Research* (1991). Dr. Isaacs holds a Ph.D. in politics from Oxford University.

Harvey F. Kline is the director of the Latin American Studies Program at the University of Alabama, where he is professor of political science. Previously he taught at the University of Massachusetts-Amherst and the Universidad de los Andes. Among his many publications are *Colombia: Portrait of Unity and Diversity* (1983); *The Coal of El Cerrejón: Dependent Bargaining and Colombian Policy Making* (1987); and *Colombia: Democracy under Assault* (1995). A Phi Beta Kappa graduate of the University of North Carolina, Dr. Kline received his Ph.D. from the University of Texas.

Bolívar Lamounier founded and was first director of the São Paulo Institute of Social, Economic, and Political Research (IDESP), where he remains a senior researcher. He was previously a member of the Brazilian Presidential Commission for Constitutional Studies (the Arinos Commission) and a member of the Academic Council of the Woodrow Wilson International Center for Scholars Latin American Program. Dr. Lamounier has written extensively on Brazilian and comparative politics for both academic and journalistic publications. He received

his Ph.D. from the University of California, Los Angeles.

Abraham F. Lowenthal is president of the Pacific Council on International Policy and director of the Center for International Studies at the University of Southern California. From 1982 to 1992 he was the Inter-American Dialogue's founding executive director. He was previously the founding director of the Latin American Program at the Woodrow Wilson International Center for Scholars and director of studies at the Council on Foreign Relations. He is widely published.

Juan Rial is senior researcher at the *Peitho* Society for Political Analysis in Montevideo, Uruguay, and currently works as a consultant for electoral processes in Latin America and Africa. He has published extensively in his fields of expertise. He was one of the editors of *The Military and Democracy* (1990) and *Elecciones y democracia en América Latina* (1992).

Timothy R. Scully, C.S.C, is senior faculty fellow and associate professor of government and international studies at the University of Notre Dame, where he directs the Latin American Studies Program. He also serves as the university's vice-president and associate provost. Among his many publications are *Rethinking the Center: Party Politics in Nineteenth and Twentieth Century Chile* (1992) and *Building Democratic Institutions: Party Systems in Latin America* (1995), which he co-authored and co-edited. Father Scully holds a Ph.D. from the University of California, Berkeley.

Susan Stokes is assistant professor of political science at the University of Chicago, where she concentrates on comparative politics and the political economy and development of Latin America. She previously taught at the University of Washington. Dr. Stokes is widely published and serves on the editorial board of *Politics and Society*. She holds a Ph.D. from Stanford University.

Acronyms and Abbreviations

General

CEPAL • Economic Commission for Latin America

EC • European Community

ECLA • Economic Commission for Latin America

ELG • export-led growth

FBIS • Foreign Broadcast Information Service

FDIC • Federal Deposit Insurance Corporation

GATT • General Agreement on Tariffs and Trade

GDP • gross domestic product

GNP • gross national product

ISI • import-substituting industrialization

LDCs • lesser developed countries

MDCs • more developed countries

MERCOSUL/R • Southern Cone Common Market

NAFTA • North American Free Trade Agreement

NGOs • nongovernmental organizations

OPEC • Organization of Petroleum Exporting Countries

PSOE • Socialist Workers Party of Spain

SOFRES • French Polling Association

VAT • Value Added Tax

International Organizations

IDB • Inter-American Development Bank

IMF • International Monetary Fund

NACLA • North American Congress on Latin America

OAS • Organization of American States

UN • United Nations

UNDP • United Nations Development Program

USAID • United States Agency for International Development

Anglophone Caribbean

CARICOM • Caribbean Common Market

JCF • Jamaican Constabulary Force

OECS • Organization of Eastern Caribbean States

PNP • People's National Party (Jamaica)

Argentina

CGT • General Confederation of Labor

FG • Left-of-center political organization

FREPASO • Center-Left coalition

MID • Movement for Integration and Development

MODIN • Movement for National Dignity and Independence

PJ • Peronists

UCEDE • Union of the Democratic Center

UCR • Radical Civic Union

Bolivia

ADN • Democratic and Nationalist Action

AP • Patriotic Accord

CBN • Bolivian National Brewery

COB • Bolivian Worker Central

COMSUR • Mineral Company of the South

CONDEPA • Conscience of the Fatherland

COPAP • Political Council of the Patriotic Accord

ENAF • National Smelting Company

ENDE • National Electricity Company

ENFE • National Railroad Enterprises

ENTEL • National Telecom Enterprises

FELCN • Special Counternarcotics Force

LAB • National Airways

MBL • Free Bolivia Movement

MIR • Revolutionary Movement of the Left

MNR • National Revolutionary Movement

MRTK • Tupac Katari Revolutionary Movement

NPE • New Economic Policy

RTP • Popular Radio and Television

UCS • Solidarity Civic Union

YPFB • National Hydrocarbons Enterprises of Bolivia

Brazil

ARENA • National Renovating Alliance

"Diretas-Já" • Direct Elections Now campaign

IBOPE • Brazilian Institute of Public Opinion

IDESP • Institute of Social Economic and Political Research

MDB • Brazilian Democratic Movement

OAB • Brazilian Bar Association

PCB • Brazilian Communist Party

PDS • Democratic Social Party

PDT • Democratic Labor Party

PFL • Liberal Front Party

PMDB • Brazilian Democratic Movement Party

PMDB+PFL • Democratic Alliance

PRN • Party of National Renovation

PSDB • Brazilian Social Democratic Party

PT • Workers' Party

PTB • Brazilian Workers Party

Chile

CD • Concertation for Demoncracy

CODELCO • National Copper Corporation

MIDA • Communist Party

PPD • Party for Democracy

RN • National Renovation

UCC • Center-Center Union

UDI • Independent Democratic Union

Colombia

AD M-19 • Democratic Alliance M-19

ANAPO • National Popular Alliance

ANDI • National Association of Industrialists

ANIF • National Association of Financial Institutions

CAMACOL • Colombian Chamber of Construction

CGT • General Confederation of Labor

CRIC • Regional Indigenous Council of the Cauca

CSTC • Syndical Confederation of Workers of Colombia

CTC • Confederation of Colombian Workers

ELN • National Liberation Army

ELP • Popular Liberation Army

EPL • Popular Army of National Liberation

FARC • Armed Forces of the Colombian Revolution

FEDECAFE • National Federation of Coffee Growers

FEDEMETAL • Colombian Federation of Metallurgical Industries

FEDESARROLLO • Foundation for Higher Education and Development

FENALCO • National Federation of Merchants

M-19 • Nineteenth of April Movement; *see also* AD M-19

MSN • National Salvation Movement

NFD • New Democratic Force

PEPES • Persecuted by Pablo Escobar

SAC • Colombian Agricultural Society

UP • Patriotic Union

UTC • Union of Colombian Workers

Costa Rica

CBI • Caribbean Basin Initiative

OIJ • Judicial Police

PLN • National Liberation Party

PUSC • Social Christian Unity Party

TSE • Supreme Electoral Tribunal

Cuba

CCD • Cuban Committee for Democracy

CODEHU • Human Rights Organizations Coordinating Committee

PCC • Cuban Communist Party

Dominican Republic

PLD • Dominican Liberation Party

PRD • Dominican Revolutionary Party

PRI • Independent Revolutionary Party

PRSC • Social Christian Reformist Party

PUCMM • Pontifical Catholic University"Madre y Maestra"

Ecuador

CONAIE • National Confederation of Indigenous Nationalities of Ecuador

FUT • United Federation of Workers

PSC • Social Christian Party

PUR • United Republican Party

El Salvador

ABECAFE • Salvadoran Association of Coffee Cultivators and Exporters

ASCAFE • Salvadoran Coffee Association

ANSP • National Academy of Public Security

ARENA • Nationalist Republican Alliance

CD • Democratic Convergence

COPAZ • Commission for the Consolidation of Peace

FAES • Armed Forces of El Salvador

FMLN • Farabundo Martí National Liberation Front

FPL • Popular Liberation Forces

ILO • International Labor Organization

IUDOP • University Institute for Public Opinion

MAC • Christian Authentic Movement

MNR • National Revolutionary Movement

MSN • National Solidarity Movement

MU • Unity Movement

PCN • Party of National Conciliation

PDC • Christian Democratic Party

PN • National Police

PNC • National Civilian Police

ONUSAL • United Nations Mission in El Salvador

SIRES • Application for identification an card

TSE • Supreme Electoral Board

Guatemala

CACIF • Chambers of Commerce Industry and Finance

CERJ • Council of Ethnic Communities "We Are All Equal"

CONAVIGUA • National Steering Group of Guatemalan Widows

FDG • Guatemalan Republican Front

GAM • Mutual Help Group

INC • National Instance for Consensus

MLN • Movement of National Liberation

PID • Institutional Democratic Party

UCN • National Center Union

URNG • Guatemalan National Revolutionary Unity

Haiti

CEP • Provisional Electoral Commission

FNCD • National Front for Democratic Convergence

KID • Convention for Democratic Initiatives

KONAKOM • National Committee of the Congress of Democratic Movements

MOP • Organizing Movement of the Nation

OPL • Popular Organization Lavalas

PLB • Barye Workers Party

VSN • Volunteers for National Security

Honduras

BANFAA • Armed Forces Bank

CCIC • Chamber of Commerce and Industry of Cortes

DNI • National Investigative Directorate

FPM • Morazanista Patriotic Front

HONDUTEL • Telecommunications monopoly

IPM • Military Pensions Institute

PDC • Christian Democratic Party

PINU • Innovation and Unity Party

PL • Liberal Party

PN • National Party

Mexico

AC • Civic Alliance

EZLN • Zapatista National Liberation Army

FDN • National Democratic Front

IFE • Federal Electoral Institute

ISI • Import-substituting industrialization

IVA • Value Added Tax

PAN • National Action Party

PARM • Authentic Party of the Mexican Revolution

PPC • Popular Christian Party

PPS • Popular Socialist Party

PRD • Democratic Revolutionary Party

PRI • Institutional Revolutionary Party

PRONASOL • National Solidarity Program

Nicaragua

AMNLAE • Nicaraguan Women's Association Luisa Amanda Espinosa

ATC • Farmworkers Association

COSEP • Superior Council of Private Enterprise

CST • Sandinista Workers Federation

EPS • Sandinista Popular Army

ESAF • Enhanced Structural Adjustment Facility

FISE • Emergency Social Investment Fund

FNT • National Workers' Front

FSLN • Sandinista Front for National Liberation

IEN • Institute of Nicaraguan Studies

MRS • Sandinista Renewal Movement

PALI • Authentic Liberal Party

PLC • Liberal Constitutionalist Party

PLI • Independent Liberal Party

PLIUN • Liberal Party for National Unity

PLN • National Liberal Party

UNAG • National Union of Farmers and Ranchers

UNO • National Opposition Union

Panama

ARI • Inter-Oceanic Regional Authority

FP • Public Force (national police)

MOLIRENA • National Liberal Republican Movement

PDF • Panamanian Defense Forces

PRD • Democratic Revolutionary Party

Paraguay

ANR • Colorado Party

EN • National Encounter

PLRA • Liberal Radical Authentic Party

Peru

APRA • American Popular Revolutionary Alliance

CCD • Democratic Constitutional Congress

FREDEMO • Democratic Front

IFI • International financial institutions

IU • United Left

PPC • Popular Christian Party

SIN • National Intelligence Service

Uruguay

FA • Broad Front

PIT–CNT • Interunion Workers Council–Workers National Caucus

Venezuela

AD • Social Democratic Party

Causa R • Cause R (a new unionist party)

CN • A personal vehicle for Rafael Caldera

CONINDUSTRIA • Council of Industrial Producers

CONSECOMERCIO • Council of Commercial Enterprises

COPEI • Christian Democratic Party

CTV • Venezuelan Workers Confederation

FEDECAMARAS • Federation of Chambers of Commerce and Production

MAS • A democratic party of the Left

MEP • People's Electoral Movement

RECADI • Foreign Exchange Agency

UNO • Odríist National Union

URD • A personal vehicle for Jóvito Villalba

I

Introduction: Constructing Democratic Governance

Abraham F. Lowenthal and Jorge I. Domínguez

Democratic political norms and procedures are increasingly common throughout Latin America and the Caribbean. But effective democratic governance—the daily practice of constitutional rule under law with stable political institutions that mediate among power contenders, restrain the dominant, and protect the weak—is far from consolidated; in many countries it is not even gaining strength. In fact, effective democratic governance has yet to be constructed in most countries of the region.

That mixed message is the main finding of this project on the state of democracy in the Americas in the mid-1990s. We aim neither to celebrate democracy's recent progress in the hemisphere nor to lament its continuing shortfalls. Rather we seek to analyze the sources of Latin America's current democratizing tendency as well as the remaining obstacles to democratic governance, to understand what has been achieved and how, and to illuminate what remains to be done.

In commissioning essays for what we hope will be a benchmark survey for the mid-1990s, we turned primarily to specialists on the politics of individual countries of Latin America and the Caribbean, often na-

This introduction draws on points made in various chapters of *Constructing Democratic Governance*. It also draws on a vast literature about democratic transitions, consolidation, and construction. We have been influenced by many other authors of whom we would cite the following, in alphabetical order, as particularly helpful: Giorgio Alberti, Nancy Bermeo, Catherine Conaghan, Robert Dahl, Larry Diamond, Jonathan Fox, Manuel Antonio Garretón, Jonathan Hartlyn, Samuel P. Huntington, Terry Karl, Juan Linz, Scott Mainwaring, Guillermo O'Donnell, Robert Putnam, Adam Przeworski, Karen Remmer, Aníbal Romero, Philippe Schmitter, Ben Ross Schneider, Alfred Stepan, J. Samuel Valenzuela, and Laurence Whitehead. We are especially grateful to Michael Shifter for his comments on this and several other chapters in this collection. We would like to express our special appreciation to those at Harvard's Center for International Affairs and David Rockefeller Center of Latin American Studies and at the Center for International Studies of the University of Southern California who help us try to keep up, in both cases, with too many projects. We are also very grateful to all those mentioned in the Foreword by Peter Hakim and Michael Shifter.

tionals of these countries. In order to facilitate comparability, we asked the authors of country chapters to address a common set of issues. Among the topics we posed were the nature of the electoral process; the condition of parties and other political institutions; executive-legislative, civil-military, and church-state relations; the rule of law and the state of the judiciary; the roles of civic, professional, business, and labor organizations and of the media; the treatment of minorities and women; the impact of socioeconomic inequities; and the challenge (when relevant) of incorporating into politics those who until recently had employed violence to secure their objectives. We also asked contributors to highlight special issues salient in particular countries, such as the impact of ethnic movements, the narcotics trade, or gross corruption. No one chapter in this collection addresses all these questions in detail, but most of them take up many of the topics, with the result that the collection as a whole provides a nuanced set of appraisals.

To capture some of the important insights to be gained from crossnational analysis, we invited essays on central issues faced in several countries: the challenge for constructing democracy of incorporating the formerly extraconstitutional Left and the equally thorny task of taming the extraconstitutional Right; the difficulties of building effective democratic governance in fundamentally unjust societies; the issues posed by the growing and more active indigenous movements; and the tension between traditional power structures and the modern political forms they still sometimes dominate. Because our project permitted the exchange of drafts over many months, authors of these crosscutting chapters were able to draw on evidence from the country studies, and many of the authors of country studies, in turn, were able to incorporate insights from the topical essays into their final drafts; we believe these "conversations" among contributors have considerably enriched our efforts.

The positive side of our mixed message should not be underestimated or taken for granted. It is noteworthy that politics throughout Latin America and the Caribbean has moved unevenly but steadily toward electoral democracy. U.S. president George Bush surely overstated matters in 1992 when he proclaimed the western hemisphere, apart from Cuba, as the "first completely democratic hemisphere in human history," and Clinton administration officials engaged in similar hyperbole at the December 1994 Miami summit of democratically elected heads of governments. But, such flights of politically motivated rhetoric aside, it is undeniable that one Latin American nation after another has moved from authoritarian rule toward democratic politics.

In 1975 only two countries in all of South America had elected presidents, while Central America was still governed by praetorian dictators in every nation but Costa Rica. Since that time, governments of force have almost everywhere given way to regimes chosen in national elections, most of them reasonably free and fair, and the elected authorities have almost without exception served out their constitutionally stipulated terms. Whenever an internal attempt has been made to overthrow an elected government during the past decade, the attempted coup has been put down immediately or soon thereafter reversed. In the more ambiguous case of Peru, where an elected government itself closed down democratic institutions to rule by decree, internal and external pressures combined to produce a gradual restoration of democratic legitimacy; a similar *autogolpe* (auto-coup) in Guatemala was reversed even more quickly.

Acting through the regional organization the Organization of American States, Latin American governments have reduced strict doctrinal adherence to the norm of nonintervention in order to make a meaningful regional commitment to collective action in defense of democracy. The internationally endorsed multilateral effort to restore President Jean-Bertrand Aristide to office in Haiti was a stunning display of the new regional consensus. If Cuba's personal autocracy still persists in the mid-1990s, it is ever more conspicuous as an anachronistic exception. And even Cuba has undertaken some political reforms in a democratic direction, albeit modest ones.

The core democratic idea—that, to be legitimate, government authority must derive from periodic free, fair, broadly participatory, and genuinely contested elections—has gained broad acceptance throughout the Americas. Both elites and masses from many different perspectives and ideological backgrounds have come to support the fundamental democratic notion of popular sovereignty as well as the understanding that, for democratic elections to be legitimate, there must be freedom of opinion and of association and a free press to which all competitors have access. People from across the political spectrum—military officers and former guerrillas, peasants and industrial workers, intellectuals and industrialists—agree on the desirability and feasibility of democratic governance.

It was not always thus. Just thirty years ago, even twenty-five years ago, vanguards on the Left and guardians on the Right openly proclaimed their disdain for democratic institutions, and each current had considerable support. It was often argued that cultural and religious traditions predisposed Latin Americans toward authoritarian rule and that democracy was a foreign transplant, bound to be rejected by the body politic.

Throughout the chapters of this collection, there is ample evidence that Latin Americans today want democratic governance and are trying to build it. Perhaps the most dramatic illustration of this transformation came in Chile and Nicaragua, where entrenched rulers let power be taken from them as a result of internationally observed elections they certainly could have prevented. But less dramatic examples abound. The presidency has been turned over from incumbents to oppositions in numerous countries. Where that has not yet occurred, it has become imaginable. Elected civilian presidents have survived military coup attempts in half a dozen nations during the past few years. And military coups have become unlikely in several other countries where it was still a ready option, frequently invoked, just a generation ago. Even in Central America, where military officers have for so long dominated politics, the growth of civilian institutions is clearly taking place.

All this is true and important. Latin America's broad and forceful transition toward democratic governance is a paradigm shift of historic dimensions. Whatever the shortfalls of performance or the detours and reversals along the way, these chapters emphasize the significance of Latin America's turn toward democracy. That this turn has occurred and been sustained during a period of major economic stress and structural change is all the more impressive.

But what is equally evident in these chapters and just as significant is that holding fair elections and avoiding successful coups are not by themselves sufficient to produce effective and enduring democratic governance. Effective democratic governance requires not only that the governing authorities be freely and fairly elected but that the public share the expectation that the rulers will remain subject to periodic popular review and that they can be replaced through equally fair elections. It also implies that executive authority is otherwise constrained and held accountable by law, by an independent and autonomous judiciary, and by additional countervailing powers.

Effective democratic governance involves clear and consistent subordination of the military and the police to civilian political institutions, especially parties, that are autonomous, stable, and powerful enough to express and aggregate social interests and also to constrain self-aggrandizing power grabs by the executive. It implies the organizations and procedures of civil society, of intermediary institutions engaging in the interests and values of diverse individuals and groups. Yet for democratic governance to work well, government officials must also have enough authority and legitimacy to take and implement decisions that are intended to privilege public and national interests over those of sectors, classes, regions, or private actors. The tension between effective authority and accountability is built into democratic governance and provides a constant challenge, even in those societies where democracy has been most fully achieved.

These chapters suggest that it is premature and indeed misleading to talk about "consolidating" democratic governance in Latin America and the Caribbean. Electoral procedures are being institutionalized in a number of countries, to be sure, but all too often these coexist with pervasive clientelism, imbedded injustice, massive corruption, flagrant impunity, and reserved domains beyond the authority of government or the rule of law. Throughout much of the region, the frustrations in advancing effective democratic governance have at times shaken Latin Americans' confidence in and commitment to democracy itself.

In most nations, effective democratic governance is still incipient, inchoate, fragile, highly uneven, incomplete, and often contradicted. Democratic governance in Latin America needs to be nurtured, constructed, and reinforced, bit by bit and country by country. In their assessment of Latin America's progress toward democracy, these essays underline that a great deal remains to be accomplished.

How hard it is to build effective and enduring democratic governance is highlighted by considering the United States, the hemisphere's most established democracy. Effective democratic governance in the United States has been deteriorating in recent years with the marked decline in public respect for parties and virtually all other political institutions; the deep rejection of professional politicians and incumbents; the decline of interconnectedness among citizens in the communities where they live; growing struggle over identity, culture, and values that cannot be resolved by compromises over "more or less"; consistently high levels of violent crime; the privatization of security and the use of deadly force; and an erosion of confidence in law, courts, and access to equal justice. Any inclination to think that democracy in the western hemisphere is close to being consolidated must be challenged throughout the Americas, North and South.

This is not the place for extended comments on what can be done to strengthen the prospects of constructing democratic governance.[1] But one strong implication of these essays is that we should rethink the sharply dichotomous categorization of "democracies" and "non-democracies." The tendency to think about democracy in "on-off" terms focuses too much international policy attention on holding and monitoring elections and on preventing or reversing coups. Elections and attempted coups are clearly defined moments of decision, and the steady reinforcement of international norms in favor of free elections and against coups has certainly been important in making democratic governance possible.

But effective democratic governance depends fundamentally on the quotidian building, exercise, and maintenance of democratic political

---

1. We have dealt with this issue in an Inter-American Dialogue Policy Brief, *The Challenges of Democratic Governance in Latin America and the Caribbean: Sounding the Alarm,* and the Dialogue has recently published an entire volume on international efforts to promote Latin American democracy: Tom Farer, ed., *Beyond Sovereignty: Collectively Defending Democracy in the Americas* (Baltimore: Johns Hopkins University Press, 1996).

practice. The most urgent and important task today is to help make democracy in the Americas work day to day: to maintain order peacefully with the consent of the governed, to represent the interests of all citizens fairly and effectively, and to extend the rule of law to all corners and all issues in the hemisphere. These are the challenges all true democrats must confront.

II

1

Venezuela: The Rise and Fall of Partyarchy

Michael Coppedge

Venezuela, once the most governable democracy in Latin America, is now a very fragile one. This chapter describes the formula that made Venezuela governable in the 1970s, traces that formula's emergence in the 1960s, and explains why it broke down in the 1980s, leaving the democratic regime in danger in the 1990s. This historical perspective is necessary for anyone seeking to understand the prospects for democratic governability in the Caldera government, for it will be expected to provide an alternative to the old formula but will also be judged by comparison with the old formula's achievements. If Caldera's democratic alternative is judged a failure, many Venezuelans will be inclined to give the nondemocratic alternative a second look.

The historical perspective is also useful for generating several lessons for other Latin American democracies. First, because Venezuela's formula worked well for a while, it helps identify the elements of democratic governability. Second, the crisis of governability yields insights into the strengths and weaknesses of one formula that is often held up as a model for other countries. Finally, only the long-term view can provide an appreciation of the challenges faced by any formula in a dynamic social and economic context. Even successful formulas for governability must adapt to survive. The guardians of Venezuela's formula adapted too little at first, but perhaps not too late.

Elements of Democratic Governability

Governability is best understood by analyzing the relationships among strategic actors, that is, organized interests with sufficient control of some power resource—factors of production, mass membership, public office, armed force, moral authority, or ideas and information—to disturb public order or economic development.[1] Whether they actually cause disturbances, merely threaten to do so, or take advantage of an implicit understanding of their potential for disturbance, they are the only actors whose behavior is relevant for governability. In Latin American democratic regimes there are generally three kinds of strategic actors. Some are state actors, specifically the military (and police), the permanent bureaucracy, and the government (those temporarily holding public office and providing direction to the state). Some are social actors: the church, private sector associations, labor unions, the media, organized peasants, indigenous movements, even guerrillas and terrorists. Finally, political parties are usually strategic actors as well, not acting exclusively in the state or society, but attempting to mediate between them by contesting elections, staffing the government, and representing civil society in the legislature.

Governability is the degree to which relations among these strategic actors obey formulas that are stable and mutually acceptable. Some formulas are formalized in law, such as constitutions, labor codes, or provisions for tripartite representation on the boards of state enterprises. Many other formulas are informal, such as coalitions, party pacts, or the tendency of policymakers to consult with private sector associations. When the formulas are stable and mutually acceptable, violence is minimized, conflicts are resolved peacefully, actors "play by the rules of the game," and interactions build trust. In short, governability reigns. When the formulas that govern relations among strategic actors are not stable and mutually acceptable, manifestations of ungovernability occur as some actors reject old formulas, try to impose new ones, or withhold consent from any formula while they build up their own power or attempt to undermine the power of other actors. Examples of such manifestations range from cabinet crises, stalemate, and electoral fraud to violent protest, terrorism, and military coups.

Venezuela's Formula: Partyarchy

Venezuela practiced a formula for governability that worked exceptionally well in the 1970s. It was a formula that gave a central role to the two largest political parties, the social democratic Acción Democrática (AD) and the Christian democratic COPEI (Comité de Organización Política Electoral Independiente). Many Venezuelans came to call this formula *partidocracia* (from *partido* and *democracia*), which I translate as "partyarchy."[2] The guardians of the formula, so to speak, were the leading *adecos* and *copeyanos*, whom some Venezuelans called the "*status*" *adecopeyano* and I will call the Adecopeyano establishment, or simply the establishment.

The terms of the partyarchy formula were as follows:

1. *Inclusive representation.* AD and COPEI represented almost all groups in society. The card-carrying membership of these two parties was larger (up to 31% of total voters) than party membership in any other democratic country in the world, with the possible exceptions of Costa Rica and Chile. Because most nonmembers were at least sympa-

thizers, these two parties also shared about 80 percent of the legislative vote and 90 percent of the presidential vote from 1973 to 1988, even though dozens of other parties appeared on the ballot. Party organization was extensive: every small town in Venezuela had a party headquarters for AD and COPEI. Moreover, the leadership of practically all organizations of civil society (other than the church and private sector associations) was chosen in elections using slates identified with AD and COPEI. About 80 percent of the peasant federations and at least 60 percent of the labor unions were controlled by leaders affiliated with AD.

2. *Electoral competition.* Citizens and social actors not affiliated with the Adecopeyano establishment at least recognized elections, whose fairness was a source of pride, as the legitimate mechanism for deciding who would occupy public office. Election campaigns were civic festivals lasting nearly a year, mobilizing millions in canvassing, parades, car caravans, and open-air mass meetings, always flooded with campaign paraphernalia. Abstention never exceeded 12.4 percent before 1988.

3. *Party discipline.* AD and COPEI practiced iron discipline: militants at all levels of the party organization risked expulsion if they disobeyed decisions made by the small inner circle of leaders, or *cogollo*, at the head of each party. The Leninist principle of democratic centralism was even explicitly endorsed by AD party statutes. Consequently, senators and deputies, state legislators, and municipal council members strayed from the party line so infrequently that congressional leaders did not even bother to tally or record votes; only the relative sizes of the parties mattered. Labor leaders usually refrained from holding strikes when their party was in power, and the politicized officers of professional associations, student governments, peasant federations, state enterprises, foundations, and most other organizations used their positions to further their party's interests. The two parties therefore acted as powerful and readily mobilized blocs.

4. *Concertación (consensus-seeking).* The leaders of AD and COPEI made a habit of consulting one another, and usually leaders of other parties and social organizations as well, whenever controversial issues arose.[3] Policies concerning defense, foreign affairs, and the oil industry were usually made by consensus, and even when consensus proved impossible, the attempt to reach it mollified the opposition. Party leaders were openly committed to the principle that no conflict could be allowed to escalate to the point of threatening the democratic regime. Although conflicts did occur, the leadership always stepped back from the brink in time to save the regime.[4]

5. *Wider relations.* The parties also hammered out good working relations with other strategic actors—the military and the private sector.[5] In exchange for noninterference in political questions, AD and COPEI

governments rewarded the armed forces with high salaries, ambitious educational programs, frequent promotions, and expensive equipment. The private sector associations FEDECAMARAS (Federation of Chambers of Commerce and Industry), CONSECOMERCIO (Commercial Council), and CONINDUSTRIA (Confederation of Industry), while often critical of government policies, also became dependent on high subsidies, low taxes, and protectionist tariffs. These associations were often included in the concertación process, and it was understood that the finance minister would be designated in consultation with one or more of the huge holding companies owned by the wealthiest families.

Governability was therefore ensured by the Adecopeyano establishment which, because it controlled large, popular, and tightly disciplined parties with influence over most other organizations, had the authority to bargain with other parties and other strategic actors and the power to enforce the deals that it made.

The Rise and Decline of Partyarchy

The formula just described was typical of the 1970s in Venezuela but existed only in a much weakened form by 1990. While the leaders of the democratic transition in 1958 benefited greatly from many aspects of their emerging partyarchy, the formula did not become fully consolidated until about 1970. Therefore, the 1970s represent a peak in the rising and declining life cycle of Venezuelan partyarchy.

Challenges and Consolidation in the 1960s

Acción Democrática had been a large, broad-based, and tightly disciplined party since its founding in 1941, but the other elements of partyarchy were missing before 1958.[6] Only two fair, full-suffrage national elections had been held before that year, and they were in 1946 and 1948, long since interrupted by the military dictatorship of Marcos Pérez Jiménez. COPEI had come into existence during the 1945–48 Trienio but was not a likely partner for *concertación* with AD; indeed, the Copeyanos and the church hierarchy had supported the coup that ended the first AD government in 1948.[7] The military had been persecuting AD for the last decade, and some business leaders were wary of a return to AD rule because of its left-of-center orientation. When Pérez Jiménez was overthrown in an internal coup, negotiations among AD, COPEI, Unión Republicana Democrática, (URD, Democratic Republican Union), and a business leader culminated in the 1958 Pact of Punto Fijo, which first put the other elements of partyarchy in place. Under the leadership of Rómulo Betancourt and Rafael Caldera, AD and COPEI formed a united front to demand elections, thus beginning a long tradition of *concertación*. Relying on its party discipline, AD promised labor pervasive clientelism, imbedded injustice, massive corruption, flagrant impunity, and reserved domains beyond the authority of government or the rule of law. Throughout much of the region, the frustrations in advancing effective democratic governance have at times shaken Latin Americans' confidence in and commitment to democracy itself.

In most nations, effective democratic governance is still incipient, inchoate, fragile, highly uneven, incomplete, and often contradicted. Democratic governance in Latin America needs to be nurtured, constructed, and reinforced, bit by bit and country by country. In their assessment of Latin America's progress toward democracy, these essays underline that a great deal remains to be accomplished.

How hard it is to build effective and enduring democratic governance is highlighted by considering the United States, the hemisphere's most established democracy. Effective democratic governance in the United States has been deteriorating in recent years with the marked decline in public respect for parties and virtually all other political institutions; the deep rejection of professional politicians and incumbents; the decline of interconnectedness among citizens in the communities where they live; growing struggle over identity, culture, and values that cannot be resolved by compromises over "more or less"; consistently high levels of violent crime; the privatization of security and the use of deadly force; and an erosion of confidence in law, courts, and access to equal justice. Any inclination to think that democracy in the western hemisphere is close to being consolidated must be challenged throughout the Americas, North and South.

This is not the place for extended comments on what can be done to strengthen the prospects of constructing democratic governance.[1] But one strong implication of these essays is that we should rethink the sharply dichotomous categorization of "democracies" and "non-democracies." The tendency to think about democracy in "on-off" terms focuses too much international policy attention on holding and monitoring elections and on preventing or reversing coups. Elections and attempted coups are clearly defined moments of decision, and the steady reinforcement of international norms in favor of free elections and against coups has certainly been important in making democratic governance possible.

But effective democratic governance depends fundamentally on the quotidian building, exercise, and maintenance of democratic political

1. We have dealt with this issue in an Inter-American Dialogue Policy Brief, *The Challenges of Democratic Governance in Latin America and the Caribbean: Sounding the Alarm*, and the Dialogue has recently published an entire volume on international efforts to promote Latin American democracy: Tom Farer, ed., *Beyond Sovereignty: Collectively Defending Democracy in the Americas* (Baltimore: Johns Hopkins University Press, 1996).

The Emergence of New Challenges in the 1980s

Over the next decade, however, Venezuela's partyarchy developed pathological tendencies: a loss of direction, corruption, and obsession with control. It was as though new terms had been added to the formula for governability, too shameful to acknowledge, but nevertheless very real.

Loss of Direction. In the twenty years following the Pact of Punto Fijo, AD and COPEI governments had accomplished most of the policy goals their parties had discussed in the early 1960s: land reform, nationalization of the oil industry, expansion of public education, job creation, and the consolidation of democracy. If debate over policy had continued within or among the parties during those two decades, they would have set new goals for themselves, but such was not the case: AD's *Tesis Política* has not been updated since 1964. Party discipline stifled the expression of controversial ideas within each party, and *concertación* filtered the controversy out of interparty debate.

With the threat of expulsion, made credible by a series of party splits in the 1960s, and therefore the end of one's political career hanging over every militant's head, few party leaders were willing to suggest new ideas that might turn out to be controversial. The most daring leaders had already been expelled; those remaining in the party were the ones who had learned to keep quiet and wait for the national leadership to tell them what to think.

Furthermore, AD and COPEI both drifted toward the center, and the more similar they became, the fewer questions of substance they found to debate. Presidential campaigns relied more and more on personal attacks, mudslinging, and nice-sounding but meaningless slogans. It became hard for voters to support parties as a means to some honorable end; increasingly, they came to be seen as ends in themselves.

Corruption. Venezuela had never been entirely free of corruption, not even during the early years of the democratic regime when the government was prosecuting the former dictator for corruption. But two developments caused an increase in corruption in the late 1970s—the oil bonanza and partyarchy. As Terry Karl has reported, oil revenues earned during the Pérez government (1974–79) were 54 percent greater, in real terms, than those received by all previous Venezuelan governments since 1917 combined.[12] In this incredible deluge of wealth, it was inevitable that some public officials would divert part of the flow into their own pockets and that financial accountability would grow lax.

What is harder to understand is why corrupt practices continued to flourish even after the country went deeply into debt and oil prices fell, plunging the country into economic crisis. The continuation of corruption required a climate of impunity, which was a by-product of partyarchy. The courts, like the bureaucracy, the universities, and most other institutions, were thoroughly politicized along party lines and seemed never to find sufficient evidence to justify a trial or a conviction. There had to have been complicity between AD and COPEI as well, because they behaved as though there were a secret clause of the Pact of Punto Fijo prohibiting prosecution for corruption. The practice of *concertación,* intended to moderate political conflict, served equally well to conceal abuses of power by the Adecopeyano establishment. The practitioners of impunity no doubt rationalized their actions on the grounds that full disclosure of the magnitude of corruption would endanger the democratic regime; in retrospect, ironically, they appear to have been correct.

Obsession with Control. In the hands of increasingly unprincipled party militants, the party founders' dedication to the moderation of conflict was transmogrified into an obsession with controlling other actors in civil society. Governments by and large respected the freedom of organization; but to the parties, the founding of any new independent organization was a call to arms. Efforts would be made to co-opt its leadership. If this tactic was successful, the organization would be subject to party discipline. If unsuccessful, party activists would sometimes secretly infiltrate the organization, win control of it, and then hand it over to their party. If all else failed, they would create a parallel organization with the same mission and outcompete the independent organization with the assistance of fellow partisans in the local government, eventually causing the independents to fail. This tactic was employed so commonly that the word *paralelismo* gained currency to describe it.

At first the parties were successful in preserving their control, but here and there independent organizations gained a foothold—unions in the state of Bolívar, some neighborhood associations in the cities, and in the late 1980s, human rights and ecology nongovernmental organizations (NGOs).[13] Such social movements should have been welcomed because they represented a strengthening of civil society and posed no more threat to governability than Christian base communities did in Brazil, or peasant *coordinadoras* in Mexico, or the mothers of the Plaza de Mayo in Argentina. But rather than welcoming and encouraging this newly flourishing civil society and opening the system to more genuine participation, the parties treated independent groups as threats to party control. An opportunity to deepen Venezuelan democracy was thus lost, and the independent organizations responded by linking their aims to an antiparty, anti-establishment agenda.

During the 1980s the new challenges to partyarchy gained enough strength to harm governability. The economic decline of 1979–90 acted as a catalyst for the opposition to the establishment.[14] When the debt crisis hit in 1983 and when oil prices fell, particularly after 1985, the parties' capacity to control civil society diminished. Fewer resources were available for patronage or for simply meeting the state's routine obligations; public services declined, and infrastructure was allowed to deteriorate. The parties lost some of their ability to fulfill their promises, to co-opt new organizations—particularly the neighborhood associations that sprang up to clamor for better public services—and to provide government jobs for friends and (former) enemies.[15] As living standards declined, disenchantment grew, made bitter by the knowledge that the country had seen tremendous wealth and let it slip away. For most of the decade, however, most Venezuelans were willing to channel their discontent into the electoral process just as they had for years, driving the alternation of AD and COPEI in power.

Two developments during the second Pérez government (1989–93) transformed the anti-incumbent anger into an anti-establishment anger. First, the economic policies of the Pérez government were powerfully disillusioning. Many people voted for Pérez in 1988 hoping that he would somehow return Venezuela to the boom it had enjoyed during his first government, and Pérez' campaign did little to discourage that hope. For example, a poll taken in January 1989, just before the inauguration, showed that 45 percent of Venezuelans believed that their own situation would be better by the end of the Pérez government, and the president-elect's approval rating was 79 percent favorable.[16]

One of Pérez' first acts as president, however, was to announce a drastic *paquete* of structural adjustment measures, including many price increases, with insufficient explanation of their necessity. The day they took effect, the widespread feeling of betrayal and desperation exploded in the three days of looting and riots known as the *Caracazo*. People had pinned their hopes on an election and a change of government, and it seemed only to make things worse. In the short term, that was true: 1989 gave Venezuela its worst economic performance since the Depression, with an 8.3 percent drop in production and inflation topping 80 percent. By May 1992, between the two coup attempts, only 28 percent believed their situation would improve by the end of the Pérez government, and the president's approval rating had plunged to 69 percent unfavorable.[17]

In the long run, these policies were responsible for a dramatic economic recovery beginning in 1991, but before that could happen a second development turned the popular anger against the entire political class. In 1989–90 the increasingly independent press gave constant, high-profile coverage to corrupt activities that had taken place during the previous administration. There were frequent revelations about how the foreign exchange agency RECADI had been used to manufacture illegal profits for politicians and businessmen with connections to former president Jaime Lusinchi (1984–89) and his secretary and mistress, Bianca Ibáñez (whom he later married). When Venezuelans, in the depths of economic crisis, were bombarded with reports of millions of dollars being spirited away, they drew the understandable (though certainly exaggerated) conclusion that they were suffering because the politicians had stolen their country's riches.[18]

For example, when a 1984 poll asked Venezuelans what factor contributed most to the country's large foreign debt, the top two responses were "bad administration of the nation's funds" (36%) and "administrative corruption" (33%). Similarly, in response to a 1985 question about the causes of the economic crisis, 86 percent assigned "much responsibility" to corruption, as did 74 percent to "bad administration of national resources" and 50 percent to the "decline of moral values."[19]

Despite the continuing scandalmongering, only one minor character in the scandal was punished. This synthesis of the anger over the economy and the anger about corruption was more potent than either issue taken separately. It was made even more galling by the fact that now the government was asking everyone to sacrifice to help pay for these crimes. This time they directed their anger at both parties because COPEI, led by Eduardo Fernández, supported Pérez' economic policies. (Pérez pursued his policies despite muffled protests from the dominant faction of his own party, AD, but AD was blamed for his policies anyway.) In this way the Adecopeyano establishment came to be blamed for the corruption, the impunity, and the economic crisis itself.

The Search for a Viable Alternative

Initially some of this anger was turned against democracy itself. After all, it was hard to tell where the establishment ended and democracy began; they were born at the same time and grew up together, and the establishment liked to equate *itself* with democracy. This helps explain why the leaders of the coup attempt of February 1992 enjoyed such popularity: the loss of this particular "democratic" regime struck 26–32 percent of the population as a small price to pay to get rid of a hated president.[20] But the second coup attempt, in November 1992, was a turning point in the definition of an alternative to partyarchy. Its visible spokesmen were not the clean-cut, articulate, and patriotic young officers from February, but scruffy and incoherent revolutionaries. The idea of being governed by them scared away much of the support for a coup and gave new urgency to the search for a democratic alternative.

That alternative was defined in two stages over the next fifteen months. The first stage was the impeachment of Pérez in May 1993 and the selection of an interim president, Ramón J. Velásquez. As befitted a transitional figure, Velásquez was neither a party militant nor an anti-establishment figure. (He was one of Venezuela's many "independents" who never actually joined a party but were known to sympathize with one; in his case, AD, because of a close friendship with Betancourt.) Governability actually improved during the interim government, because a tax reform, a new banking law, and other urgent bills that had been put on the back burner until the impeachment vote were passed quickly with the support of AD and COPEI, knowing that the independent president would be held responsible more than either party.[21]

The second stage was the process leading up to the general elections of December 5, 1993. For their part, AD and COPEI tried to define the alternative to the establishment as a renovated AD-COPEI establishment. An electoral reform passed in 1988 had instituted direct elections for mayors and governors, and state elections in 1989 and 1992 had begun a turnover in and revitalization of the party leadership at the state and local levels.[22] A new generation of Adecos and Copeyanos, as well as MASistas and a few leaders of the Causa R, a new-unionist movement, were building a base of genuine support at these levels and challenging the dominance of the cogollos in their parties. The renovation of the parties took a startling leap forward when two members of this generation unexpectedly won the presidential nominations of AD and COPEI. In AD the nominee was Claudio Fermín, a former mayor of Caracas; and in COPEI, Governor Oswaldo Alvarez Paz of Zulia came from behind in the party's first open primary to defeat Eduardo Fernández and other prominent national leaders. Because they were officially nominees of AD and COPEI, however, and both identified with the economic policies of the Pérez administration, they were at a disadvantage against the leading candidate, Rafael Caldera.

As the founder of COPEI, a signer of the Pact of Punto Fijo, a former president, and a key participant in all of the concertación of the previous thirty-five years, Caldera would seem a most unlikely beneficiary of the anti-establishment sentiment, but he was. Two actions made his political image makeover possible. First was an electrifying speech he made in the Senate following the February 1992 coup attempt. In that speech, broadcast live throughout the nation, he stopped short of endorsing the coup attempt but expressed the popular frustration with Pérez, his policies, and unresponsive politicians so movingly that he was instantly acknowledged as the principal spokesman for the opposition. His second act was to bolt his own party in early 1993 to run for president as an independent candidate with the backing of MAS, a personalistic vehicle called Convergencia Nacional (National Convergence) and sixteen other small parties. This was the most dramatic break with the establishment possible, not simply because he abandoned (and was expelled by) the party he founded, but because such defections had become unthinkable in Venezuela. Caldera won the election with 30.45 percent of the vote, to 24 percent for Fermín,

23 percent for Alvarez Paz, and 22 percent for Causa R founder Andrés Velásquez.

The First Two Years of the Caldera Government

The beginning of the Caldera government was a critical moment for democratic governability in Venezuela: the Adecopeyano establishment had, for the first time in thirty-five years, lost power, and an anti-establishment figure was searching for a new formula for governing. His search was bound to be frustrating because of: (1) his weak base of support, (2) the potential strength of the opposition, (3) declining confidence in elections, (4) conflict with governors, (5) a wary and divided military, (6) difficult relations with organized labor, and (7) an uneasy private sector. Venezuela is far less governable during the Caldera government than it was in the 1970s. It has not, however, reached some theoretical extreme of ungovernability; it has merely lost all the advantages that used to distinguish it from its neighbors. To put the situation in perspective, Venezuela has become "Latin Americanized." Some comparisons with aspects of governance in other Latin American countries are helpful for assessing Venezuela's prospects.

Base of Support

With 30 percent of the vote in 1993, Caldera did not have much of a mandate to govern. (Indeed, after factoring in the 43.8% abstention rate, he was elected with the support of only 17% of the registered voters.) His initial governing coalition was composed of the leftist MAS plus the Convergencia Nacional and minor parties, which together controlled barely a quarter of the seats in Congress. To make matters worse, the coalition was a patchwork of sixteen tiny parties ranging from the far Left to the far Right, fleshed out by a few disaffected Adecos and Copeyanos. In his effort to distance himself from AD and COPEI and the technocratic "IESA Boys"[23] of the Pérez government, Caldera passed over both known politicians and the policy elite, leaving himself with a cabinet dominated by second-string technocrats.

While AD and COPEI were harshly punished at the polls, they still controlled a majority of the seats in Congress (see Table 1). Simple arithmetic makes it clear that Caldera could not create a legislative majority without either AD or COPEI. Conflict between the old establishment-dominated Congress and the anti-establishment president was not long in coming: in June 1994 Caldera suspended constitutional guarantees of certain civil liberties, ostensibly to deal with a banking crisis and those responsible for it. (However, the government also took advantage of the situation to crack down on street crime, suspected insurrection plotters, and annoying journalists.) When Congress balked at ratifying the emergency powers, Caldera bullied it into acquiescence

Table 1 Venezuela: Seats in Congress by Party, 1993

	Chamber of Deputies		Senate	
	N	%	N	%
AD	56	27.9	18	34.6
COPEI	54	26.9	15	28.8
Causa R	40	19.9	10	19.2
MAS and Convergencia Nacional	51	25.4	9	17.3
Total	201	100.0	52	100.0

Source: NotiSur, February 4, 1994.

by threatening to convene a constituent assembly with the authority to dissolve Congress. The president then held civil liberties hostage until July 1995, when Congress finally approved a financial emergency management law giving the president a freer hand in setting economic policy.

In the meantime, executive-legislative relations were smoothed out by an unexpected coalition. In August 1994 an "orthodox" faction led by Luis Alfaro Ucero gained control of AD and removed almost all of the younger, reformist, neoliberal leaders from the National Executive Committee. This was the most visible manifestation of a top-to-bottom purge of AD that restored party unity and left it more closely aligned with Caldera's skeptical approach to economic policy. Without formally becoming a coalition partner, AD supported most of Caldera's initiatives in Congress, making it possible for several major pieces of legislation to pass. As the December 1995 gubernatorial and mayoral elections approached, however, with growth stagnant, inflation still over 50 percent, and Caldera's approval rating dipping below 40 percent, AD ended its cooperation and the tiny parties of the coalition one by one began to distance themselves from the government, leaving it ever more isolated.

Caldera's coalition alternatives were practically nonexistent. COPEI, despite lingering rank-and-file devotion to Caldera, was led after December 1994 principally by General Secretary Donald Ramírez (an ally of former president Luis Herrera Campíns), who was an opponent of reconciliation with his party's founder. To Ramírez, Caldera betrayed the party he founded by running as an independent candidate in 1993; to Caldera, the leaders of COPEI betrayed him personally by not supporting his candidacy. The only other significant party was the Causa R, which followed an obstructionist line in Congress, routinely abstaining on and voting against government bills, and sometimes breaking quorum and boycotting sessions. There were, therefore, no other realistic coalition possibilities.

There were two ways to govern without a formal presidential coalition. First, Caldera could try to assemble ad hoc majorities for specific legislative initiatives, appealing directly to the people to pressure the Congress. This strategy did not serve him well during his first administration, when he also refused to form a coalition despite having won the presidency with 29 percent of the vote, and was stalemated by the Congress during 70 percent of his time in office.[24] This strategy could work only if he were a very popular president like Fujimori, so it ceased to be a viable option by mid-1995. If Caldera were to boost his popularity by, for example, taking some dramatic action against corruption, his relations with Congress would be easier for a while. But until that happened, the fates of less popular presidents with similarly narrow bases of support—Belaúnde (first term), Febres Cordero, Velasco Ibarra, Sarney, Collor, Illia, Allende—presaged either stalemate or a *pugna de poderes* (power struggle) with the Congress.[25] Caldera early on expressed a desire to amend the constitution to obtain the power to dissolve Congress. The Congress was hardly likely to place such a powerful weapon in his hands, and the prospect that Caldera might attempt to seize it for himself inspired speculation about a possible *Calderazo* (presidential coup led by Caldera).

The second way to govern without a presidential coalition was to form an opposition coalition in the Congress, most likely composed of the two former establishment parties. The last time AD and COPEI were both in the opposition was 1957, and they signed a pact to oppose military rule. This time a pact could lead to an opposition majority and stalemate. There are precedents for such opposition majority coalitions in both Venezuela—where the AD-led coalition legislated over Caldera's head during his first government—and Peru, where APRA (American Popular Revolutionary Alliance) and Odría's UNO (Odríist National Union) cooperated to stalemate Belaúnde from 1963 to 1968. There remained, then, two ways to avoid executive-legislative stalemate, but both carried the risk of escalating confrontation and constitutional crisis.

Confidence in Elections

Despite electoral reforms, elections lost some of their legitimacy as the sole path to power during the 1980s. Abstention was triple what it was fifteen years before, despite mandatory voting, and charges of electoral fraud were increasingly common. While the numerous upsets and the fragmentation of the vote among several parties indicated that elections were fair, many Venezuelans came to suspect that the largest parties routinely divided among themselves any votes cast for parties that were not represented at the voting station.[26] López Maya documents unsuccessful attempts by AD to steal gubernatorial elections from the Causa R.[27] Two of the gubernatorial elections of 1992 had to be held

again in 1993 to resolve questions about their fairness, and both Caldera and Andrés Velásquez claimed that AD, COPEI, and the military
conspired to deprive them of hundreds of thousands of votes in the last
presidential election.[28] Whether these claims were true or not, they
were a symptom of declining governability. Nevertheless, the issue did
not become as heated as it has been in Nicaragua, El Salvador, Honduras, Paraguay, or other less consolidated democracies. Democratic regimes such as Chile and Colombia have survived for many years
despite occasional disputes over election results, so this issue alone
would not place Venezuelan democracy in any immediate danger.

Conflict with Governors

Venezuela's twenty-two elected state governors were in a position to
make trouble for the national government because they were politicians with a base of support independent of both president and party.
Conflicts with Pérez were frequent because governors were directly
elected for the first time in 1989 and the division of powers between
federal and state governments was still murky. Procedures for resolving
disputes had to be improvised for each issue that arose. Conflicts intensified during the Caldera administration because the most effective
governors, the ones reelected in 1992, became lame ducks as the 1995
gubernatorial elections approached, with the potential to challenge
Caldera's authority by launching presidential candidacies. Their potential for disruption should not be exaggerated, however, because their
resources were quite limited, and because independent governors do
not seem to cause serious problems of governance in the other federal
presidential democracies of the hemisphere, Argentina, Brazil, and the
United States.

Relations with the Military

Caldera was perhaps the best candidate to mollify the rebellious junior
officers: on the second anniversary of the February 4, 1992, coup attempt, he promised to free the seventy rebel officers still in prison in
Venezuela and to invite back the fifty-two still in exile in Peru and Ecuador. Such acts, however, only exacerbated the tensions within the military between the junior officers and the high command, which had
already virtually severed the chain of command at bases throughout
the country. Caldera asserted his authority by dismissing the defense
minister and service chiefs ahead of schedule as soon as he took office,
but this act created further resentment toward the new president and
new divisions in the military. Some officers were also antagonized by
Caldera's accusations of military involvement in vote fraud, and were
apprehensive about his ability to govern for the next five years. Upon
resigning, outgoing defense minister Radamés Muñoz León said:

This situation has infuriated me. This cannot be the reward we receive for the democratic struggle we have waged within the Armed Forces. I am crying inside over my people because I do not know what will happen to the country with a precarious government that was elected by scarcely 8 percent of the population, or 16 percent of the potential voters, and whose first act was to strike an institution that is at the service of the fatherland and not of political parties, personalities, or economic or political interests.[29]

The divisions in the armed forces did not appear to be as deep as those typically found in the Bolivian, Argentine, or Peruvian militaries, but they were deep enough to warrant concern about future coup attempts like those of 1992 should Caldera find himself as isolated and unpopular as Pérez was.

Relations with Organized Labor

Caldera was destined to have an acrimonious relationship with Venezuela's unions. On the one hand, he promised them much, both as the candidate with the populist image and as the author of the labor law, which was reviled by the private sector for being too generous to workers. But on the other hand, Venezuela's fiscal deficit made it impossible for the state to provide workers many of the benefits to which the labor law entitled them. (A telling indicator: oil revenues, which used to cover 70% of public expenditures, covered only 40% in 1994.) And should the unions become disappointed and angry, Caldera would have no way to restrain them because he had virtually no institutional connection to the unions. Instead, most of the unions were allied with the parties in the opposition—AD, COPEI, and Causa R. (A minority sector of organized labor was affiliated with MAS and MEP [People's Electoral Movement], but it tended to follow the lead of the Venezuelan Workers Confederation [CTV], which was dominated by AD.) When AD was in the opposition in the past, it encouraged its unions to be militant, either to embarrass the government or to gain credibility for its claim to be a social democratic party.[30] There were some indications that the AD union movement was asserting its independence from the party in the 1980s and 1990s. But whether the unions were independent or not, they would have no reason to hold back their members for Caldera. Increased strike activity was therefore inevitable. Nevertheless, strike rates have always been comparatively low in Venezuela, so Venezuelan unions were unlikely to become as disruptive as their counterparts have sometimes been in Bolivia, Argentina, Chile, or Peru.

Relations with the Private Sector

The process of structural adjustment of the economy also adjusted the political relationship between the state and the private sector in Latin America. Many firms that had grown dependent on protectionism, state subsidies, and political connections found it difficult to survive in a more open market economy and lost their political influence; other firms that welcomed competition prospered and increased their influence. This Schumpeterian process of creative destruction increased conflict within the private sector in the early stages of adjustment. But where the process was allowed to proceed long enough, as in Colombia, Chile, Bolivia, and Mexico, the competitive firms became dominant and developed a more mutually satisfying, transparent relationship with the state that enhanced governability in the economic arena. In Venezuela the election of Caldera interrupted this process before the competitive firms gained dominance.

Caldera's election was an interruption because his campaign sent out mixed and vaguely worrisome signals. Some businessmen were concerned by his alliance with MAS and the communists; others were confused by the inconsistent policies advocated by his closest advisors; still others were disturbed by campaign promises to renegotiate the terms of the debt servicing agreement and to defend a fixed exchange rate when measures to fight inflation were not being discussed. After the election, Caldera's support for limited price controls, the suspension of the retail portion of the value added tax, and the lack of a clear plan to reduce the fiscal deficit added to their uneasiness. Some of the fears were alleviated by Caldera's inaugural address, but by that time a new fear had overwhelmed all the others: the fear of a financial collapse brought on by the failure of Banco Latino.

Banco Latino can be seen as a remnant of the unreformed private sector—a bank that traded on connections and corruption. It was the second largest and fastest-growing bank in Venezuela, but its success was built on political connections and lax regulation that allowed it to offer unsustainably high interest rates, and its efforts to cover its liabilities eventually degenerated into a massive Ponzi scheme. When the scheme collapsed in January 1994, U.S.$1.5 billion in deposits—20 percent of the market—was at risk, affecting not only a million small depositors but also the pension funds of Petróleos de Venezuela, the national electric company, the armed forces, and, most scandalously, nearly half of the funds available to the Venezuelan equivalent of the Federal Deposit Insurance Corporation (FDIC). This failure, when combined with the problems of other weakened banks, required a U.S.$5 billion bailout and swelled the fiscal deficit to 12 percent by 1995.[31] The overall health of the Venezuelan economy is probably better than that of some other Latin American nations, but this crisis created profound uncertainty about the country's medium-term economic future, and therefore undermined much of the progress toward governability in the economic arena that had been achieved before 1993.

In summary, the potential for governability in Venezuela was poor in the 1990s. Compared to its highly governable past, society was more polarized, the new governing coalition was fragmented and divided, and the former establishment parties, recently forced into the opposition, seemed either unable or unwilling to help the new president succeed in the long term. This does not mean that democracy is about to break down. There is little enthusiasm for a military government, and most strategic actors were willing to give Caldera a chance to prove himself. But in the meantime, Venezuela encountered increased symptoms of ungovernability: strikes and protests, disputed election results, conflict between governors and the federal government, economic uncertainty, and especially confrontation between the president and Congress.

2

Colombia: Building Democracy in the Midst of Violence and Drugs

Harvey F. Kline

Colombia has usually been considered one of the most democratic countries of Latin America by both foreign scholars and proud Colombians themselves. The basis for this familiar claim has been that civilian governments have predominated and there have been only five years of military rule in this century.

Yet there are at least three serious problems with this conventional view. First, as former president Alfonso López Michelsen has suggested, instead of a national military tyranny, the country had thousands of small tyrannies as large landowners ruled in an authoritarian fashion despite the formal democratic regime. Second, Colombian history is replete with violence and the violation of human rights, including that most basic one, the right to life. By the late 1980s both the subnational tyrannies and violence had become worse, with the latter coming from the new "small" tyrants—a combination of guerrilla groups, drug dealers, and paramilitary squads. Homicide became the most common cause of death (about 85% by "common criminals"), and Colombia with 33 million inhabitants had twice as many murders as the United States. Further, the same bands controlled a large percentage of the national territory, constituting de facto governments that were more powerful within those areas than officials of the national government.

Third, drug money has completely infiltrated Colombian politics. No one knows how many candidates have received such funds, how many did so knowingly, and what the effects have been on public policies. When the treasurer of President Ernesto Samper's 1994 campaign alleged that money from the Cali drug group had been used in electoral activities, the debate that followed in August and September 1995 led to the resignation of the minister of defense (who had been the director of Samper's campaign), as well as suggestions that either the president resign or step aside temporarily so that the influence of the drug money could be objectively studied.

As a result of the first two problems, a Constituent Assembly met during the first half of 1991 and a constitution, replacing the one of

1886, was proclaimed on July 4, 1991. One important part of the reform was the attempt to make Colombian democracy more open, so that people who were guerrillas would have no reason for violent conflict. Another part was to strengthen the justice system, so that impunity would no longer rule. This chapter, after describing the historical context of Colombian politics, considers how successful or unsuccessful this constitutional reform is likely to be in bringing democracy to that nation.

The Three Models of Governance in Colombia

Democracy has never been completely achieved during the three regimes of Colombian history. The first period of "sectarian democracy" (1849–1953) began with the founding of the Liberal and Conservative parties in midcentury and continued until its breakdown in 1953. While civilian governments were the norm during this period, fraud and violence were used to keep the respective parties in power, while the party out of power often started civil wars to oust the incumbent government, albeit seldom with success. After the frequent civil wars, the losers were given amnesty.

Despite the changes of the party in power, traumatic international events such as the loss of Panama, and dramatic social and demographic changes in the country, this basic regime persisted for more than a century because of several factors that added intensity to it. A religious context was added to politics when the Roman Catholic Church sided with the Conservative party. The civil wars were so frequent that each generation had memories of party "martyrs" from the previous one. After 1930 the government became more involved in the economy, increasing the stakes of the conflict. All this led to a culmination of the regime in a period of partisan violence so long and intense that Colombians refer to it as La Violencia. During the period between 1946 and 1965, at least two hundred thousand Colombians died in this nationwide civil war between the Liberals and Conservatives.

The second period of "consociational democracy" came when, as a way to end this violence (and the only military dictatorship of the twentieth century), Conservative and Liberal party leaders agreed on power sharing. The original duration was 1958–74, during which the National Front shared all political power equally between the two traditional parties. The presidency alternated every four years, while elective and appointive positions were divided equally. Only the Liberal and Conservative parties could hold office. Power sharing was continued after 1974 by the constitutional requirement that the president give "adequate and equitable" participation in the executive branch to the second largest political party.

The National Front was successful in ending the partisan violence, with the latter years bringing the democratic election of mayors in 1988. The consociational period seemed to have ended when President Virgilio Barco (1986–90), a Liberal, ruled with his party only. The Conservatives refused the cabinet seats offered them.

During the consociational period, however, other forms of violence replaced that between the parties. Marxist guerrilla groups appeared in the first half of the 1960s, some with direct connections to earlier liberal groups of La Violencia. Landowners formed paramilitary groups when the government failed to protect them from the guerrillas. Drug dealers began violent tactics against the government in the 1980s and, having bought agricultural land with their profits, in some cases took over the paramilitary groups.

The 1980s were so violent in Colombia (with death rates reaching higher levels than during La Violencia) that leaders of political parties, economic interest groups, and university students called for the Constituent Assembly that brought Colombia to the current period of "participatory democracy." Among the features of this newest stage, which began with the Constitution of 1991, are the following:

The president is now elected by an absolute majority, unlike the previous plurality, and can have only one term.

The Congress is given new powers (including the right to censure cabinet officials), while its members are also more controlled than before as to holding other elective positions (previously a member of the Congress could concurrently be a member of a departmental assembly and/or a municipal council), attendance, and pork barrel legislation.

No longer can a president declare an indefinite "state of siege," during which certain rights were suspended. Now the president can declare a "state of emergency" for only ninety days of a calendar year; the Congress can extend it by another ninety.

Electoral rights were changed, with election of departmental governors added. Further, the district for the national Senate was changed to a national one from departmental ones.

In addition, voters have initiative and recall rights.

The judicial system was changed from the traditional Napoleonic model to one more like that of the United States, with a national prosecutor who is to coordinate all law enforcement in the country.

A new national Congress and governors were elected under these rules in October 1991 and March 1994, and the first presidential election was held in May 1994. A popular initiative did lead to the consideration and passing of a new law on kidnapping in 1993. But there have yet to be recall elections. In late 1993 consideration for doing so in the case of the mayor of Bogotá ran into the obstacle that, although the right of recall was in the new constitution, the Congress had not yet passed enabling legislation for a recall election.

Current Status of Governance in Colombia

The current conditions in Colombia demonstrate that democratic governance is still a distant goal. Although the Constitution of 1991 is still only partially implemented, this chapter provides predictions of likely results.

Nature of the Electoral Process

The two historic political parties still dominate Colombian elections, but, at least since the National Front, they no longer effectively aggregate interests in such a way that Colombian voters can choose candidates on the basis of programmatic identity. Rather, both the Liberals and the Conservatives include a variety of ideological persuasions, including traditional conservatives with ties to the landed elite, neoliberals, populists, and welfare state liberals.

While Colombian political parties were based on the intensity of the conflict during the sectarian period, after the National Front the system became one based on personalities, images, and campaign expenditures because of the cooperation of the two parties during the consociational period, the gradual loss of inherited ascription to the parties, and the absence of distinctive party programs.

The ramifications of these changes have been seen in the current splintering of the Conservative party into at least three groups: a group still calling itself the Conservative party; the National Salvation Movement (MSN) led by Alvaro Gómez; and the New Democratic Force (NFD) led by Andrés Pastrana. Gómez supported the Pastrana presidential campaign, and Pastrana has been the most important Conservative leader since then.

Although the Liberal party has remained united, it is illuminating that its leader, octogenarian former president Alfonso López, used a "wasp swarm" strategy in the two congressional elections. Using this approach, López recruited key regional leaders to be on the party's senatorial list, leading to a majority of a disunited party.

A significant third party is the Alianza Democrática (AD, Democratic Alliance) M-19. Founded by the M-19 guerrilla group upon its demobilization in 1989, AD M-19's presidential candidate, Antonio Navarro, received 12.5 percent of the 1990 vote, by far the highest for any party of the Left in Colombian history. With nineteen seats, AD M-19 was second to the Liberals (twenty-five) in the number of seats in the Constituent Assembly, and Navarro was its co-president. Yet in the October 1991 elections, the AD M-19 won only nine of the one hundred senatorial seats and none in March 1994. As its presidential candidate for 1994, Navarro won 4 percent of the vote.

Another smaller party is the Unión Patriótica (UP, Patriotic Union), which was founded by the Fuerzas Armadas de la Revolución Colombiana (FARC, Armed Forces of the Colombian Revolution), the largest guerrilla groups in Colombia, during the democratic opening of President Belisario Betancur (1982–86). The UP's electoral success has been slight, in part because of the assassinations of its militants, including its presidential candidate in 1990.

Rates of participation in Colombian elections have been very low since the 1950s. Although there were exceptions (such as the hotly contested presidential election of 1970), most commonly participation in presidential elections has been in the 34–50 percent range. The 1986 presidential election had an abstention rate of 54 percent, while that of 1990 had 57 percent. Fifty-eight percent of the potential electors did not vote in the Constituent Assembly election in December 1990. Seventy percent did not vote in the March 1994 congressional elections, which included the Liberal "popular consultation" to choose the party's presidential candidate.

Since the particular form of proportional representation used does not punish parties with many lists, Colombian legislative campaigns are characterized by a multiplicity of slates. Most have few individuals elected from them, making the position on the list of greatest importance. Power is in the hands of departmental leaders rather than national ones. Changing the system to have a national list for the Senate was intentionally designed so that small groups, distributed widely over the country, could get some representation. Yet the chaos of congressional elections was seen in March 1994. Thirty-six political parties offered lists of candidates; there were 674 lists (with 3,355 hopefuls) for the 163 lower house positions; there were 251 lists of candidates (with 1,978 aspirants) for the 100 Senate seats, with 96 lists electing one senator and two lists winning two seats.

The traditional method that parties have used to choose presidential candidates has been a national convention controlled by regional leaders. However, in the 1980s a group of young Liberals, led by Luis Carlos Galán and calling themselves the New Liberalism movement, split from the party after the 1982 convention and chose Alfonso López to be the presidential candidate. Part of the deal to get Galán back into the Liberal party in 1990 was a kind of open primary for the selection of its presidential candidate. Under this system, individuals vote for a Liberal candidate for president at the same time that they vote in congressional elections. To guard against voters who are not Liberals from having a key say in the party's presidential candidate, the rule is that a candidate must win by at least 5 percent.

The Colombian government gives a financial supplement to candidates according to the number of votes they receive, but most campaign money is private and not controlled by the government. There is no doubt that drug money is important to many Colombian politicians. While the day has passed when someone like Pablo Escobar can be elected an alternate in the lower house of Congress from Antioquia, as he was in 1982, an unknown number of politicians are supported by drug money.

Vote counting in Colombia is done by the National Registry. Monitoring procedures include the right for all parties and candidates to have representatives at the polling places and at places where votes are counted. Charges of gross electoral fraud have been rare, although the 1970 presidential election did include them. There is a definite danger in running for public office and voting for the UP, especially in certain areas of the country.

After the intentional limitation of democratic representation during the National Front, three issues of representation became salient in Colombia. The first had to do with the bias of the traditional voting system. From 1978 until the new Constitution of 1991, various groups argued that this system kept their interests from being represented, although it was never very explicit how that was the case in a proportional representation system. The second had to do with the murder of candidates from parties of the Left, especially the Unión Patriótica; more than two thousand of its militants have been killed.

The final issue of representation had to do with the relationship of politicians to the drug trade. With the Medellín group, the problem was the danger to politicians who had opposed the illicit commerce. Along with journalists, judges, and law officers, politicians were assassinated by the Medellín group, including Luis Carlos Galán, the leading Liberal candidate in 1990, as well as two other presidential candidates in that bloody election (one each from the AD M-19 and the UP). The problem with the Cali group, on the other hand, was the degree to which *narco* money had corrupted politicians. Some analysts have even suggested that the Cali corruption of politicians became much more serious than the Medellín terrorism ever was.

While Colombia has a long way to go to take care of the problems of drug money and UP candidate assassination, the system is clearly much more open than before, perhaps too much so with the confusion for the elector. The 1994 election for the Senate shows this, with the following number of senators elected: Liberals, fifty-eight; Conservatives (including NFD and MSN), twenty-seven; Indians, two; Christians, two; and other movements, thirteen.

Executive-Legislative Relations

As a way to avoid excessive executive power, checks and balances have never worked well in Colombia. The constitutions have appeared to be much like that of the United States; however, under the Constitution of 1886, this ideal was not reached for two reasons. First, the Congress did not exercise the powers that it had, for example, waiting over a decade after the Constitutional Reform of 1968 to set up a committee to work on economic planning with the executive branch. In large part, no doubt, this had to do with the part-time nature of being a member of Congress. Second, during much of the time after 1946, Colombian presidents governed under "state of siege" provisions of the constitution. Although the Congress continued meeting, and executive decrees had to be declared constitutional by the Council of State, the president was able to rule by decree.

The Constitution of 1991 seeks to correct both of these problems. Members of Congress can no longer hold other elective positions, and no longer are there alternates to attend Congress in their stead. Missing six votes in the Congress, without excuse, leads to a member's being removed from office.

The new constitution also controls the state of siege powers. Now a president can decree a "state of exception" for only ninety days of a calendar year; the Senate can extend it for another ninety. For some, this begs the question of effective government, as the causes for states of siege (guerrilla groups, drug dealers, and paramilitary squads) are present all 365 days of the year.

The change of congressional power was far from immediate after the new constitution was approved. Perhaps because more than half of the members elected in 1991 had been in the Congress before, in its first two years the legislature showed many patterns held over from the past. Semantic sleight of hand made pork barrel legislation possible; the Liberal party was no more united than previously; and the first opportunity to use the censure power, after the escape of Pablo Escobar, was lost. The August 1995 lower house investigation of drug money in the Samper campaign does suggest, however, a gradual increase of congressional power, while executive power decreases.

The same tendency is likely to be seen in relation to the state of emergency that President Samper proclaimed during the drug investigation. While some alleged that the proclamation was a smoke screen to divert attention from the investigation, others pointed out that violence was at higher levels than usual. The key question is whether the Senate will be willing to extend the emergency after the first ninety days.

The Rule of Law and the Judiciary

With problems coming from guerrilla groups, drug dealers, paramilitary squads, in addition to "common crime," the Colombian judicial system became seriously overloaded during the 1980s. Of all the crimes reported in 1983, only 10 percent led to verdicts, according to the government, while the Inter-American Commission on Human Rights put the figure at 4 percent in 1990. Impunity became the rule rather than the exception.

One particularly serious problem of the judicial system after the 1980s came from the immense wealth of the drug leaders, who were seldom successfully adjudicated because they either bribed, threatened, or killed judges. While the guerrilla groups have had less effect on the judicial system, a notable exception to this was the M-19 seizure of the Palace of Justice in Bogotá in November 1985. The guerrilla group's stated motivation was to try President Belisario Betancur, although some would argue that it was to destroy records on drug leaders instead. Whatever the motivation, when the national military regained control of the building, more than a hundred civilians were dead, including half of the Supreme Court.

In an attempt to solve the myriad problems of the justice system, President Virgilio Barco initiated a system of "anonymous judges." To prevent retribution against the judges, the idea was that testimony would be taken in such a way that neither defendants nor witnesses would see the judge or hear his or her unaltered voice. While this had some success, the fact that some of the anonymous judges were summarily executed, apparently by drug groups, indicated that the system was not a total success.

Two other novel approaches begun in the Colombian judicial system during the Barco years were plea bargaining and rewards for informants. These policies were carried further during the government of César Gaviria (1990–94), most notably in the case of the surrender policy for drug dealers and paramilitary squad members. Under that policy, any person could receive a reduced sentence if he or she surrendered and confessed one crime. Since the maximum sentence in Colombia was thirty years at the time, the most a defendant could receive was fifteen years, even if he or she did not obtain additional reductions through studying or starting a business during the confinement.

The 1991 Constitution instituted a dramatic change for the Colombian judicial system. Rather than the traditional Napoleonic code, in which some judges do the investigation of crimes and others the adjudication, the new judicial system includes a National Prosecutor's Office (Fiscalía Nacional), with the functions of investigating and prosecuting cases as well as coordinating the activities of all military and civilian agencies gathering evidence on crimes. After the first two years, the new system was processing 50 percent more cases than the old one did, although, in a country in which impunity had become the rule, it will be at least several more years before one can definitively conclude that the legal impasse has been ended.

Civil-Military Relations

In comparative terms, civilians control the military more in Colombia than in most other Latin American countries. After all, there has been only one case in this century when a civilian was overthrown by the military (Laureano Gómez by General Gustavo Rojas Pinilla in 1953). However, the complexity of the relationship of elected presidents to the military is greater than the mere fact of having elected civilian presidents. For example, the apparent power of the military in Colombia was shown by the fact that between 1958 and 1991 the minister of war was always a ranking member of the armed forces. Further, the leadership of the military branches has largely been left up to the officers, and they have generally followed seniority in selecting leaders.

Of greater importance is the question of whether the civilian presidents are really making decisions in national security policy. During the "Security Statute" of President Julio César Turbay (1978–82), newspaper pundits alleged that many decisions were made by General Camacho Leyva rather than by the president. Likewise, members of Congress later charged that decision making was carried out by the military, although President Betancur was making the public statements, during the taking of the Palace of Justice in November 1985. The same accusations are made about the military attack on the headquarters of the Fuerzas Armadas de la Revolución Colombiana in December 1990: ranking military officers made the decision, not President Gaviria, who was not even informed of the attack beforehand. For all these declarations there are denials by both military and civilian leadership.

There have been, however, more public disagreements between the president and military officers. One major question has been about the role the military is to play: should it remain apolitical, true to Colombian tradition? Or should it speak up about the social and economic problems of the nation? On at least three occasions (the first in 1965 and the last in 1981), individual military leaders have seen it necessary to talk about the basic problems of the society. For example, in 1981 the commander of the army, General Landazábal Reyes, wrote in *Army Review*, "We are convinced that the army can militarily destroy the guerrillas, but we are also convinced that even with this, subversion will continue as long as the objective and subjective conditions in the economic, social, and political areas, which daily impair and disrupt stability, are not modified." The first two military leaders who made similar statements were relieved of their posts; Landazábal, too, was later replaced.

There was substantial military opposition to the Betancur National Dialogue. During it, military officers increasingly assisted paramilitary groups through supplies, training, and, in some cases, active participation of military personnel in the groups. Likewise, the armed forces have always felt at a disadvantage against the guerrillas, as the representatives of the Colombian state have to respect human rights (or be criticized by international groups), while the guerrillas do not have to show respect for the same rights.

The July 1992 escape of Pablo Escobar from prison near Medellín made it obvious that some members of the military have been corrupted by drug money. Although there have been instances of large groups of officers being caught taking drug money, no one has an accurate estimate of how large that group might be in the entire country.

Finally, the August–September 1995 presidential crisis led some observers to suggest that President Samper had been forced to enter a coalition with army generals and large business interests. He needed the armed forces with him in face of all the criticism from civilians, it was said. But adding the military to his coalition meant that Samper was not so reformist as before, and indeed that could be the explanation of his state of emergency to combat crime and guerrillas.

Two major conclusions seem warranted. First, the Colombian president does have real power in relation to the military. In August 1991, for example, when President Gaviria named the first civilian minister of war since 1949, there were no objections from the military. Second, it seems unlikely that the Colombian military will take over power directly. Although remarks of many political leaders, including former president Misael Pastrana, indicated their concern that a military takeover would occur during the deterioration of public order in the 1980s, the military stayed in its barracks even when the death rate surpassed that of La Violencia.

The Roles of Civic, Professional, Business, and Labor Organizations

A few economic interest groups have joined the traditional parties as the most powerful forces in Colombian politics since the beginning of the National Front. Today some even suggest that the economic groups (*gremios*) are of greater importance than the parties.

All major producer associations come from the upper sector; all seek to maintain the status quo. Although they might sometimes disagree with the policy of a government, they have supported the political regime, whether it was the National Front or the system in place since the end of the Front. The associations tend to react to governmental policy rather than initiate it. With the growth of the executive branch, in both the ministries and the decentralized institutes, the associations have developed strong ties with that branch. This does not mean, however, that they will not use connections within the Congress if that is the preferable way to block government policy.

All economic sectors of the upper- and middle-income groups are organized. The most powerful seem to be those "peak" organizations of economic activities, the National Federation of Coffee Growers (FEDECAFE) and a few other producer associations.

Probably the most politically powerful of the economic interest groups is the National Association of Industrialists (ANDI). ANDI approximates an overall peak organization of all producer associations as it includes not only the large industrialists, but also firms from the agribusiness, insurance, financial, and commercial sectors. It is the leading advocate of free enterprise in Colombia and has important roots in the industrialists of Medellín, its power coming from its wealth and social prestige, the common overlapping of membership of the group with that of the government, and the fact that industrialization has been a major goal of almost all Colombian presidents during the last half century. ANDI tends to oppose anything that might negatively affect the private sector, but historically has supported the government when there is opposition to the basic system of government.

FEDECAFE was founded in 1927 and is open to any person interested in developing the coffee industry, although it is dominated by the large coffee growers. The federation collects various taxes on coffee and has used its wealth to invest in banks and shipping. It has a close relationship with the government, given the importance of coffee to economic policy. One big difference between Colombia and other Latin American countries is the degree of "privatization" of certain key functions. Nowhere else would a legally private organization be allowed to do what FEDECAFE does; the governments would do it directly.

With the lack of differentiation of the political parties and their factions, interest articulation and aggregation increasingly have been done by the *gremios* (who have made efforts to be bipartisan) and by the church and the military. For example, in April 1981 the *gremios* stated the position of some of them when the Frente Gremial (Trade Association Front) published an analysis of Colombian problems. Composed of the presidents of ANDI, the Colombian Chamber of Construction (CAMACOL), the Colombian Federation of Metallurgical Industries (FEDEMETAL), the National Federation of Merchants (FENALCO), and the National Association of Financial Institutions (ANIF), the Frente did not limit itself to issues directly affecting the economic activities of the *gremios*. Rather, general issues such as inflation, lack of housing for the poor, and the minimum wage were considered and solutions were proposed.

The continued importance of the *gremios* was shown in 1991 when, for the first time in the history of the country and with the support of President Gaviria, the principal production *gremios* agreed to form a special entity that would have the responsibility of negotiating with the government on issues of international trade, foreign investment, and world cooperation. The National Gremial Council was supported by thirteen organizations: ANDI, SAC (Colombian Agricultural Society), FENALCO, FEDEMETAL, CAMACOL, the National Association of Exporters, the National Federation of Livestock Raisers, the Union of Insurers of Colombia, the Banking Association of Colombia, the Association of Producers and Exporters of Sugarcane, the Colombian Association of Plastic Industries, the Popular Association of Industrialists, and the Colombian Association of Automobile Parts Manufacturers. The idea of creating the council came from a suggestion of the minister of development, Ernesto Samper, who said that the business groups complained about the lack of negotiations with the government, but the latter lacked channels through which to negotiate. It was announced that the council would have a coordinating committee that would make recommendations to the government and would make statements about any step the government might take in the "economic opening."

While the activity of the Frente Gremial had not been well received by President Turbay in the early 1980s, President Gaviria had a completely different idea. Further, one should not discount the power of the *gremios* in the interim. These economic interest groups have always had considerable power in public policymaking.

Organized labor is a weaker political force in Colombia. In part this is because of the small percentage of the work force that is unionized. Divisions among labor federations, some of which are along traditional political party lines, are another cause. Several other factors also contribute to labor's weak position in Colombian politics. Labor leaders are still required to be full-time workers in their industries, a requirement that is enforced selectively. The percentage of the force that is unionized is small, only 17–19 percent in 1974, falling to 9 percent ten years later, 8 percent in 1989, and 5 percent in 1992, although the percentages were higher in industry, utilities, transportation, and communications. Further, labor legislation has promoted the development of enterprise unions and weakened the possibilities of industrywide unions.

Finally, strikes in manufacturing are limited legally to a maximum of forty days before the compulsory introduction of binding arbitration. This stipulation of the law, which has led some to conclude that Colombia has adopted many of the policies of the bureaucratic authoritarian regimes of the Southern Cone without the large-scale repression of them, weakens that key power resource of organized labor—the ability to paralyze the economy through strike actions.

The first national labor federation was the Confederation of Colombian Workers (CTC), founded in 1936 during the administration of Liberal Alfonso López Pumarejo. With the end of the Liberal hegemony in 1946, the CTC was repressed by the government of Conservative Mariano Ospina. As a rival organization, the Union of Colombian Workers (UTC) was founded by the Jesuits. The UTC was allowed to flourish during the Conservative years.

Two other labor federations emerged in the 1960s and 1970s. The Syndical Confederation of Workers of Colombia (CSTC) was formed in 1964 when numerous communist-oriented unions banded together after having been ejected from the CTC. The General Confederation of Labor (CGT), a socialist and radical-Christian labor federation, was formed in 1971. Both the CSTC and CGT existed without legal recognition until it was granted by President López in 1974. There are still other labor unions at the enterprise level, but they remain unaffiliated with any of the four federations. Estimates in 1992 gave the following breakdown of union membership: the new Central Unica de Trabajadores, 60 percent; CTC, 7 percent; CSTC, 10 percent; CGT, 18 percent; and unaffiliated, 19 percent.

Relevant Aspects of Church-State Relations

Traditionally Colombia has been one of the most Roman Catholic of Latin American nations, with the power of the church in the nineteenth century based on land and on a concordat between the Colombian state and the Vatican. As Colombians have become more urban, the power of the church has declined. Various Protestant groups, especially of the evangelical movement, have also appeared, particularly in the cities.

The church hierarchy, however, has continued to speak out when politicians raise the possibility of changes in areas considered to be church domain. When candidate López in 1982 suggested the possibility of easier divorce, the bishops' reply suggested that good Catholics should not vote for candidates with such programs. The sentiments of the church hierarchy were very similar during the Constituent Assembly in 1991. As Archbishop Pedro Rubiano Sáenz of Cali stated, "However much it is said that the Constitution approved divorce for Catholic marriage, we affirm and will always teach in accord with Catholic faith and doctrine, that valid matrimony is indissoluble and that the annulling of civil effects of sacramental marriages cannot destroy the relationship."[1]

Yet it seems that the Constitution of 1991 demonstrates what experts had already concluded: the political power of the hierarchy of the Roman Catholic Church is much less than before. This, of course, does not mean that it has disappeared. Individual Roman Catholic priests have played important roles in guerrilla demobilization, in the surrender of Pablo Escobar, and in the denunciation of human rights abuses.

The Role of the Media

Colombia has one of the strongest media in Latin America, with the notable exception to that generalization coming at those times in recent years when states of siege have included media censorship. It should also be acknowledged that the Colombian "dirty war" has affected the media. Journalists have been killed by drug dealers, by paramilitary groups, by guerrillas, and by "unknown people." In all cases the effect is censorship, as seen in the case of Gabriel Cano, the publisher of *El Espectador,* assassinated by drug groups in Bogotá on December 17, 1986. Cano's only transgression was having written articles against illicit drugs.

Media freedoms should now increase because of the state of siege limitation in the new constitution and the end of drug terrorism. Yet so long as guerrilla and paramilitary violence continue, complete media freedom is tenuous at best.

Minority Rights

Minority rights in Colombia include those of religious and racial groups. In the religious case, there has long been discrimination against non-Catholics. During La Violencia, it was assumed that all Protestants must be Liberals, hence giving Conservatives justification for killing them. Yet, with urbanization and the end of partisan violence, there is greater religious tolerance than before. One member of the 1991 Constituent Assembly was elected by an evangelical list, and the same group elected a senator in both 1991 and 1994. With the possible exception of the very isolated regions of the country, non-Catholic religions are unlikely to be the victims of violent discrimination.

Colombians are racially diverse, with large numbers of pure or nearly pure Spanish background (and a smattering of other Europeans), as well as Indians and Colombians of pure African descent. There are also combinations of the three races. The British geographer Peter Wade suggests that Colombian racial relations be visualized as a triangle whose uppermost point is white and whose bottom corners are black and Indian. The white apex is associated with power, wealth, civilization, government, and high degrees of urbanity, education, and culture. The bottom two corners are seen from above as primitive, dependent, uneducated, rural, and inferior. Blacks are stereotyped as lazy, having an abnormal family structure because of the absence of male role models, and a love for music, dancing, and celebration. Indian culture is perceived by whites as even more foreign and distinct than black culture, especially in life-style and language.[2]

It is impossible to state the exact racial categories in Colombia and to number the individuals in them, as no recent census has included a question about "race"; hence using that characteristic for statistical analysis of education, income, or anything else is simply impossible. Further, it is not a factor analyzed in public opinion polls. Nor is there enough agreement to make self-identification valid. As Wade argues, the national racial order is based on "the contradictory but interdependent coexistence of blackness, indianness, mixedness, and whiteness."

There is no legal discrimination by race. No laws have ever been passed to end such discrimination simply because laws allowing discrimination never existed. Likewise voting has never been restricted by race per se, although until literacy was removed as a requirement for voting in the 1930s, many people of color could not vote. Of course illiterate whites could not either. Many blacks and Indians still do not vote because they live in isolated areas where the Colombian government has no effective presence. The respective organizations claim that there are 3.5 million blacks and 700,000 Indians, although it is clear that most of the former do not live in such isolated areas.

This is not to say that racial prejudices do not exist. The arch-conservative President Laureano Gómez (1949–53) stated that Indians and blacks were inferior and that the "Spanish spirit" guided Colombian character. In more general terms, the system of *blanqueamiento* (whitening), while pointing out racial and cultural differences, is one that gives value to whiteness and disparages blackness and Indianness.

The Colombian Andes are different from Ecuador, Peru, and Bolivia because many people, especially in the Andean Central region, who might be racially native Colombian, are not culturally so. They are not considered *indios* because they dress in a fashion similar to other inhabitants, and they speak Spanish rather than an indigenous language. Likewise people of pure African-American heritage racially do have alternatives to escape blackness. First there is the possibility of race mixture, but there is also "social whitening" by living in the cities and integrating oneself into nonblack networks.

Government statistics indicate that there are 411,803 Indians in the country (or about 1.5 percent of the population). The National Indian Council, possibly having more reliable statistics than the government, claims to have organized 80 percent of the 700,000 Indians in the country (2.3 percent of the national population); it is of note that it was only in 1982 that the council was founded, indicating both the status as a small minority in the country and the difficulty of organizing such a dispersed group. From the perspective of the native people, there are issues that need to be addressed, most notably their traditional tribal lands. A regional indigenous organization appeared in the Cauca area in

the early 1970s, with three objectives: reestablishing Indian reserva-
tions, increasing the authority of their local governments, and reaffirming the autonomy of their regions. After the leadership of this Regional
Indigenous Council of the Cauca (CRIC) was jailed by the local authorities
or assassinated by thugs hired by large landowners, native American
members joined various guerrilla groups. In 1984 an Indian guerrilla group
was formed, the Quintín Lame Armed Movement, which for the next six
years was to average between one hundred and three hundred members.

At least in part because of these unsettled traditional demands of
indigenous groups, made more noticeable as the commemoration of
the five hundredth anniversary of the arrival of the Europeans approached, the *indígenas* were assigned two seats in the 1991 Constituent Assembly and the new constitution gives them two seats of the one
hundred in the national Senate. The constitution gave no such special
seats for blacks, perhaps reflecting the fact that solidarity for blacks is
a hard goal to achieve in Colombia. Unlike Brazil or Cuba, Colombia
has few cultural remnants of the African heritage, and, as Peter Wade
points out, the boundaries of the black category are "fuzzy and shifting"; some blacks make the most of their opportunities to "escape from
blackness."

Perhaps for these reasons, it was just before the signing of the constitution in 1991 that the participants of the Fifth Afro-American Encounter raised three issues: that Afro-Americans be recognized as a cultural
group, that Afro-American territories be given the same status as indigenous ones, and that social justice be established for the 3.5 million
Afro-Americans in Colombia. Rather than these demands being considered by the Constituent Assembly and incorporated into the new constitution, the matter was left for the consideration of the national
Congress. In 1993 it passed a law that would give two seats in the lower
house of Congress to the black communities.

Hence members of the ethnic minorities who remain in traditional
communities will be represented in the Congress. However, these communities are likely to continue disappearing simply because the quality of life in a "mixed" urban setting has the appearance of being better
to most Colombians.

Gender Discrimination

As in most of Latin America, male domination is present in Colombia,
although it might be decreasing over time. Increasingly women are economically active in the work force, making up an estimated 43 percent
of the work force in 1989 compared to 38 percent in 1980, 26 percent in
1973, and 19 percent in 1951. Studies do indicate that women are paid
less than men, even when education is the same, and that women are
more likely to be unemployed than men.

The most recent data available indicate that university education is increasingly a possibility for women. Of women holding employment, 18.7 percent had postsecondary education in 1990 compared to 15.8 percent in 1984, 14.7 percent in 1980, and 11.6 percent in 1976. The percentage of public education students who are women has increased over past decades, suggesting that even middle-income women are experiencing mobility through education.

Political rights for women came much more slowly. Postindependence leaders stressed the role of women in the family and home. During the nineteenth century, women did receive the right to vote in the province of Vélez, but attempts to make that a national right failed in 1886, 1936, 1944, and 1946. Women were granted legal capacity to administer their property in 1932, rights to access to higher education in 1933, and the right to hold nonelected public office in 1936.

Women received the vote only in 1954, not because of a feminist movement but as a gift from dictator Gustavo Rojas Pinilla. His Constituent Assembly had included two women. But women did not vote until the 1957 constitutional plebiscite, article 1 of which said "Women will have the same political rights as men." Most recent data indicate that they vote less often than men, and women seldom hold political office. Between 1958 and 1972, only 2.1 percent of the senators, 4.2 percent of the chamber members, 7.4 percent of the members of the departmental assemblies, and 6.4 percent of the municipal councils were women. In 1991 these figures were 1 percent of the Senate, 5.2 percent of the Chamber, and 2.5 percent of municipal councils. Women, however, have had more representation in cabinets of recent presidents. Both Virgilio Barco and César Gaviria appointed female foreign ministers, with Noemí Sanín during the Gaviria government becoming a "star" of the cabinet.

Most of the changes benefiting women have come from presidential initiative, responding to societal demands but not consulting with women's groups. In 1974 President Alfonso López fulfilled his campaign promises to women by abolishing *potestad marital* (the husband's marital rights over the wife and children). In 1990 President César Gaviria created the Council for Youth, Family, and Women, although he appointed a man to head it. In 1991, paid maternity benefits were extended from eight to twelve weeks for women covered by social security.

The writing of a new constitution in 1991 seemed to give women new opportunities. However, only 8 of the 119 lists were headed by women, and just 4 were elected to the Constituent Assembly of 70 members. Two notable cases were the all-feminist list headed by Rosa Turizo, prosecutor of the Superior Tribunal of Medellín, and the list presented by nongovernmental organizations and headed by Helena Páez, former minister of labor and advisor to Gaviria's Council for

Youth, Family, and Women. Neither was elected. Many women supported the AD M-19, and two of the four women elected were from that list. The other two were a Liberal and a leader of the Central Workers Union elected by the Unión Patriótica.

Feminist groups were active in letting the Constituent Assembly know its proposed changes, which can be best summarized as getting the UN statements on women's rights into the Colombian constitution. While there was some success in this effort, as with the other changes to the constitution, only time will tell if the formal stipulations will be translated into real ones. Perhaps indicative is that sexual harassment became a national issue for the first time in late 1993.

Reincorporation into Democratic Politics

In the Colombian case, the question of "reincorporation" of those who until recently employed extraconstitutional means, including violence, to secure their objectives must be divided into different discussions of the three sets of groups: the guerrilla groups, the drug dealers, and the paramilitary squads. The challenge differs for the three.

Currently, according to figures of the Colombian government, there are 7,500 guerrilla troops, two-thirds from the Fuerzas Armadas de la Revolución Colombiana and one-third from the Ejército de Liberación Nacional (ELN, National Liberation Army). This is probably about one-half of the highest level of guerrilla groups, as it has been estimated that there were fifteen thousand when Belisario Betancur became president in 1982. During the peace negotiations in Caracas, Venezuela and Tlaxcala, Mexico in 1991–92, the government was prepared to offer a reincorporation package similar to that offered to the M-19 and the Ejército de Liberación Popular (ELP, Popular Liberation Army): amnesty for political crimes and support for either education or starting a legitimate economic activity.

The first major difficulty this policy has faced in the cases of the smaller M-19 and ELP is that amnesty on the part of the government is not necessarily translated into forgiveness on the part of aggrieved Colombians. Each amnesty since the years of Belisario Betancur has been followed by the assassination of demobilized guerrilla fighters. Further, in the absence of an effective national police force, this is likely to be an even greater problem in the case of the larger FARC and ELN who, during their longer histories, have left many more Colombians with hopes of revenge.

The second problem with this policy has been the inability of the Colombian government to keep its financial promises to demobilized guerrillas. This would be an even greater problem with the FARC and ELN because they are so much larger. More important, both guerrilla groups have substantial income from the coca and poppy activities of the FARC and from various kinds of extortion from them and the ELN. In short, the comparison is between continuing as a guerrilla or demobilizing and having fewer economic resources and a probability of death that is no lower than the current one.

The case of the drug violence is far from clear. Most of the narco-terrorism connected to the drug dealers came from the Medellín group, and especially two of its leaders, Pablo Escobar and José Gonzalo Rodríguez Gacha. The violence ebbed even before Escobar's surrender in June 1991, and it did not approach its previous level during the period between July 1992 and December 1993, when Escobar was once again free. Now that he is dead, it is not clear who the new leaders of the Medellín group will be and whether or not they will use violent tactics.

The Cali drug group, now the largest in Colombia, has never used violent tactics against the government to the extent that the Medellín group did. The Gaviria policies intentionally had to do with drug *terrorism* and not drug *trade*. Although the Gaviria government used the same sort of plea bargaining it used with Escobar with the Rodríguez Orejuela group in Cali, few leaders of the latter group surrendered. Ironically most of the major Cali leaders were captured and put in jail under the presidency of the man they allegedly helped to elect.

The Gaviria plea bargaining had success with some of the paramilitary groups, notably with the surrender of Fidel Castaño in Córdoba and Ariel Otero in Puerto Boyacá. The two combined turned in more than seven hundred weapons, and 250 members of the Otero group surrendered, all of whom were investigated and are to be tried. Further, Otero was optimistic that the paramilitary group's war was over and that they would not take up arms again.

Yet one might not be quite so optimistic about the demobilization of the paramilitary groups for at least three reasons. First, the government knew that many members of the Otero and Castaño groups had not surrendered, nor had they turned in all their weapons. As stated by Commander Julio César of Puerto Boyacá, self-defense groups would be marginal only as long as the army and the police guaranteed that Puerto Boyacá remained free of guerrillas. So far the Colombian government has not established a military presence to do so.

Second, by July 1992 the Otero group was once again active, this time as they sent troops to combat guerrillas in the Casanare region. There, with recent petroleum discoveries, the ELN appeared for the first time. The paramilitary groups followed, completing the ingredients for a new dirty war in yet another part of Colombia. The third reason for pessimism came when Castaño began paramilitary activities again in 1993, in this case as a leader of the PEPES (Persecuted by Pablo Escobar), a group trying to kill the escaped drug leader. Of course the reason for this paramilitary group disappeared when Colombian army troops killed Escobar on December 2, 1993.

In short, it seems likely that individual groups in Colombia will use vigilantism as long as the Colombian government is not capable of maintaining law and order in the country. Although some progress toward that goal was made during the Gaviria years, large parts of the country (which neither governmental nor other experts have defined precisely) are still not effectively under control of the government. Vast areas of Santander are still controlled by the ELN; of the Amazon region by the FARC; of Magdalena Medio and Urabá by paramilitary groups; of Medellín and other large cities by youth gangs; and of Antioquia, Valle, the Amazon region, and the Orinoco plains by drug dealers. While the majority of the people might live in parts of cities controlled by the government, the majority of the territory is controlled by others.

The Significance for Democratic Governance of Gross Socioeconomic Inequities and Programs to Overcome Them

Colombia is in the middle range of Latin American countries in income distribution, neither as equitable as Southern Cone countries nor so inequitable as Brazil, Mexico, and Peru. While the percentage of Colombians living in poverty has decreased in recent decades (40% of the population in 1991 compared to some 70% thirty years ago), poverty is now more visible in the cities. In 1988 the lowest 50 percent of the people received only 18.9 percent of the income, while the top 10 percent had almost twice that much. What this means for many Colombians, as shown in a 1983 study, is that 54 percent of the households had incomes below U.S.$200 a month, and those in the lowest quintile spent more than their total official income for food alone.

The same maldistribution is seen in the ownership of land. In 1960, 62.5 percent of all agricultural holdings were less than 5 hectares (12.3 acres), 4.5 percent of all agricultural land. At the other extreme, 0.07 percent of the holdings were greater than 2,500 hectares (6,173 acres), making up 20.2 percent of the land. In 1970–71, after more than a decade of agrarian reform, even though there were fewer *minifundios*, there were more *latifundios* of more than 2,500 hectares. In effect, after a decade of land reform there were more large areas occupying more, in absolute terms, of the national territory.

In the past twenty years, land reform has not been a priority of Colombian governments. It appears that land might be more inequitably distributed than it was in 1971. With the new violence of leftist guerrilla groups and paramilitary bands, some landowners have fled to the cities. At the same time, drug dealers have bought more land in order to grow their coca crops, to be "gentlemen farmers," and to launder their drug profits.

To this point, these economic inequities have not been translated into political issues, in large part because the multiclass Liberal and Conservative parties have not found it necessary or useful to do so. President Virgilio Barco pledged his government to abolish "absolute poverty," an unrealistic goal in which he failed. Indeed, analysis by the independent think tank FEDESARROLLO (Foundation for Higher Education and Development) suggested in the early 1990s that the government's expenditure on social programs, including education and health, was decreasing in the 1980s, in part because of reallocation of funds to the military.

It was clear in the 1991–92 negotiations with the government that the guerrilla groups thought that the Gaviria neoliberal *apertura* (opening) would lead to an economic crisis of such magnitude that the poor could be mobilized. In 1994 one presidential candidate, Enrique Parejo, strongly criticized the *apertura,* but he lost the Liberal primary.

Conclusions: Specific Difficulties Salient in the Narcotics Trade

As the above has made clear, the drug question is paramount in Colombia. Not only has there been narcoterrorism, but guerrilla groups are difficult to negotiate with because they have coca and poppy fields. In the 1980s many paramilitary squads that had been set up by landowners were taken over by the drug lords as the new landowners, especially in Magdalena Medio. In August and September 1995, for the first time in Colombia, the question for debate became whether Colombian "democracy" had become a *narcodemocracia.*

The ways that this confrontation of the media and the drug lords distorts Colombian democracy have been discussed by María Jimena Duzán, herself a victim of it. As she has written, "Colombians, especially journalists, who deal with these themes [drugs] know that at such times our democracy itself is at stake in the form of our freedom of expression and our right to dissent." Duzán made it clear that the problem was more widespread when she added:

> Perhaps the most dramatic effect of the drug business can be seen in the decomposition and uncertainty that it has provoked on all social levels. For the nation's large middle class, including politicians, judges, soldiers, journalists, and police, drug money has inundated economic life with a flood of corruption, wiping out any semblance of a code of ethics or a value system. . . . This is a terrorized political class that has delivered itself to the designs and money of the drug dealers. Those who stand up to the bosses and challenge them have fallen victim, brave politicians such as Luis Carlos Galán, Carlos Pizarro, and Bernardo Jaramillo.[3]

The journalist concluded that if Colombia could not manage to rebuild its justice system and reopen its stagnant political system, "then the capture and extradition of individual drug bosses will mean very little indeed. We need true social reform, so that democracy—and not murder with impunity—will be universal."[4]

During the August–September 1995 debate, Duzán added: "This is the first time in Colombian history that the political establishment is being investigated. We have a restricted democracy that has been corrupted not just by drug traffickers, but by the power that the political class has held for the past 30 years. The idea was that whoever wins, everybody wins. Now, opening a Pandora's box is very difficult because everyone was involved."[5] While one might quibble with the idea that the political establishment has been in power for only thirty years, observers in the U.S. government have been concerned with the contents of this Pandora's box for a number of years.

Hence the death of Pablo Escobar was at best the beginning of the establishment of the rule of law in Colombia—and not the conclusion. At present, high officials in the Colombian government have not come up with a realistic plan of law enforcement that would allow the government to maintain that most basic human right, that of life. Vigilantism continues from the paramilitary groups, and at least 90 percent of the murders committed by them have not been punished. As long as that continues, as concluded by the Inter-American Commission on Human Rights, it "not only damages the international image of the justice system in Colombia, but also tarnishes the images of recent administrations, despite their obvious and genuine efforts to control the violence rampant in Colombia."[6]

The next Colombian governments might have a new opportunity to solve many of these problems as new revenues from petroleum become available to them. Since subsoil resources belong to the state, future governments will not have to redistribute wealth (something that Colombian governments have either not tried or failed in their efforts to do). Potentially the Cusiana petroleum earnings could be large enough to allow the governments to construct an effective national police force and to make a reality out of the promises of the 1991 Constitution of health care and education for all. However, both of those policies might have inflationary effects, and the history of Colombian politics in the 1970s and 1980s was that governments sacrificed growth to avoid inflation.

The other obvious matter that must be dealt with has to do with drug money in politics. Outsiders have long had the impression that drug money has much power in the country. Beginning in August 1995 for the first time Colombians debated that possibility. Pandora's box has been opened and cannot be closed sucessfully without a complete investigation of all Colombian politicians. That is precisely what the National Prosecutor's Office had begun in mid-1995, even before the accusations about Samper's campaign. Perhaps we will one day look back at this debate as the real beginning of more meaningful democracy in Colombia.

3

Ecuador: Democracy Standing the Test of Time?

Anita Isaacs

At first glance, democratization in Ecuador may seem irreversible. The first country in the region to complete a transition, the country has since witnessed four successive democratic presidential elections, with power alternating in almost rhythmic fashion between representatives from the political Center-Left and Right. Conflicts that have arisen between the legislature and the executive have been resolved without provoking an *autogolpe* or a military intervention, as they so often did in Ecuadorian history and, more recently, in neighboring Peru. To date, rumored and attempted coups alike have failed to materialize, suggesting that the armed forces are indeed reluctant to resume the reins of power they relinquished in 1979. Civil society has been strengthened, most notably through the emergence of the Confederación de Nacionalidades Indígenas del Ecuador (CONAIE, National Confederation of Indigenous Nationalities of Ecuador), an organization that speaks for a substantial segment of the 40 percent of the population that is Indian, with an increasingly powerful voice that the government ignores at its own peril. Finally, the recognition of the need for economic, judicial, and political reform indicates that there exists the political resolve to sustain and deepen Ecuadorian democracy.

Upon closer examination, however, these promising signs mask a system in severe crisis, plagued by a seeming inability to establish a framework for effective democratic governance. Thus, while conflicts between Congress and the president have yet to produce breakdown, the institutional reforms that accompanied the transition have also still to bear fruit. Confrontation among the political leadership continues to create gridlock, thereby preventing the enactment of critical reform. Although the growth of civil society is a welcome sign, its expression nevertheless also reveals the persistent difficulties that the country's poor and ethnic majorities face in seeking formal, regular channels of political participation. More generally, civilian disillusionment with a democratic system that has failed to deliver and to incorporate vast sectors of the population is on the rise, matched by ever louder grumblings of discontent from military quarters, whose apparent reluctance to intervene should not be equated with unwavering support for the elected civilian rule.

In this chapter I expand on these elements by exploring the state of democratic governance in Ecuador. First I examine the political, economic, and social dimensions of the current crisis and then reflect on the prospects for sustained and deepened democratic rule, emphasizing that it has become increasingly difficult for the political leadership either to shrug off or to meet the current challenges.

The Political Situation

Having promised to "arrive at democracy as a step forward," Ecuadorian transition architects dedicated three years (1976–79) to a process of concerted analysis, dialogue, and accommodation in an attempt to fulfill that pledge. Key political players, including members of the armed forces, the political leadership, representatives of the union movement, and entrepreneurial associations participated alongside members of the country's scholarly and legal communities in a prolonged process of consultation and negotiation. Political rather than social or economic reform dominated the transition agenda, with discussion centered on how to enhance the effectiveness and inclusiveness of a system in which politics was traditionally the preserve of the country's elite. Political parties and political party attachments were weak, and perennial conflicts between the executive and the legislature crippled the policymaking process. Because of the disproportionate strength of entrepreneurial groups as contrasted with that of popular sector organizations, as well as the relative health of the Ecuadorian economy at the time, participants paid scant attention to socioeconomic reform or accommodation. To the extent that economic development concerns were addressed at all, therefore, they were placed on the agenda by the military, concerned about ensuring a continued role for itself in a future democratic system.

Participants applauded the outcome, yielding as it did a set of reforms, pacts, and promises of ongoing pact making that provided the Ecuadorian transition with many of the ingredients viewed as essential stepping stones on the path toward sustained democratic rule. A new constitution approved in a referendum, and an accompanying political party law, contained political reforms designed to remedy what were perceived to be the most serious shortcomings of democratic politics as practiced historically in Ecuador. The framers of the new charter and party law (scholars and legal experts heeding the recommendations emerging from the consultative process) broadened political participation by expanding the franchise to include the illiterate population.

Participants similarly sought to strengthen the political party system. On the one hand, they hoped that the extension of suffrage would provide a natural constituency for a promising new generation of reformist political parties. But they also took direct steps, including the drafting of regulations that restricted participation in elections to legally recognized parties and to candidates who were affiliated with an official party. Finally, to guard against conflicts between the president and the Congress, as well as the ensuing policy paralysis, they introduced the concept of a second ballot. Ideally, the electoral process itself would stimulate pact making, while the election of a president with solid congressional backing would permit the passage of legislation.[1]

The political leadership and the armed forces also agreed on a set of pacts designed to ensure the military's exit without unduly limiting democracy. Having avoided the kind of repression that characterized authoritarian rule in the Southern Cone and Central America, the issue of retribution and accountability did not plague the Ecuadorian transition, as it did transitions elsewhere in the region. Rather, the Ecuadorian armed forces seemed more preoccupied with protecting the substantial economic interests they had acquired during the years of military rule and of assuring that they retained a minimal degree of political influence. This was achieved by using the relationship between security and development to justify inclusion of a clause in the new constitution recognizing the military's responsibility to "assist in the social and economic development of the country."[2]

Elected democratic governments that have come to power since 1979, however, have not lived up to the expectations generated by the transition process, as politics in the post transition era bears an uncanny resemblance to the political status quo ante. Institutions remain fragile, conflicts continue to plague executive-legislative relations, and the country's poor and indigenous communities are still effectively excluded from the political process.

The Ecuadorian experience reveals the difficulties inherent in any attempt to draft into existence a set of rules and an institutional framework that can sustain democratic governance in the absence of an ongoing commitment by the political leadership. Indeed, in the post-transition era, Ecuadorian political elites have tended to abide by the letter rather than the spirit of the well-intentioned reforms, reverting for the most part and whenever possible to traditional political practices. Thus, for instance, the vagueness of the legislation governing the participation of parties in elections has hampered its enforcement, thereby frustrating any hope of constructing a solid party system centered around a small number of political parties with a well-defined program, ideology, and constituency.

Remarkably little headway has also been made in securing the loyalty of either those who run for office under the banner of any given party or a grass-roots base, and, as much as ever, parties continue to be used as electoral vehicles by their leadership. Whereas, for example, six slates competed in the transition elections, those numbers climbed to nine by 1984, ten by 1988, and twelve in the 1992 election, in anticipation of which some sixteen parties had been granted recognition. Political attachments, moreover, often last only as long as the mandated electoral period. In a practice so common that it is referred to as a *cambio de camisetas* (shirt changing) elected deputies frequently switch parties or choose to sit as independents, enticed less by ideological conviction than by personal political calculation.

This process is well illustrated by the campaign, election, and government of Sixto Durán. Durán was elected to the presidency in July 1992 as the candidate of the Partido Unidad Republicana (PUR, United Republican Party), a conservative organization hastily put together just before the elections as a result of a split in the Partido Social Cristiano (PSC, Social Christian Party), under whose auspices Durán had unsuccessfully run in both the 1979 and 1988 elections. Only a year and a half after the elections, however, the PUR had all but disappeared. Disgruntled deputies, dissatisfied with the absence of patronage and discouraged by the declining popularity of their leader, abandoned the party. The remains of the organization have recently been absorbed into the Conservative party, in an attempt to construct a more solid base of congressional support for presidential initiatives. PUR deputies are not the only ones to have "changed shirts" in the past year and a half. Indeed, at the time of this writing, one third of those elected to Congress in 1992 have deserted the party for which they ran, many lured away by promises of government patronage.

The ephemeral nature of political parties and political party attachments has severely hindered efforts to build a mass constituency. Indeed, according to opinion polls conducted in the two major urban centers of Quito and Guayaquil, the numbers of individuals who feel strong attachments to any given political party have dwindled considerably in the past several years. Whereas an already significant 47 percent of those surveyed in Guayaquil claimed no specific party affiliation in 1989, that percentage had climbed to 67 percent by 1993. The results are even more striking for Quito, where the numbers of those without strong party loyalties has jumped from 38 percent to 88 percent of the population during that same period.[3]

Confrontation rather than cooperation also still clouds the political atmosphere, as the politics of *concertación* (governance by consensus) continue to elude Ecuador. Although the political reform process has ensured that presidents are now elected with majoritarian support, once elected, congressional support is anything but guaranteed. Congressional coalitions exist, but these rarely involve the same groupings that joined ranks in anticipation of the runoff ballot. Instead, new coalitions are forged, shaped less by a common ideological bond than by a shared crude desire to undermine the president. This is achieved either by blocking legislation or by engaging in a process of *juicio político* (political trial), in which ministers are first called to account for "abuses of authority" and, if found guilty, subsequently stripped of their authority. Occasionally, the process of *juicio político* has exposed corruption and other illegal practices. But more often than not, it has replaced debate and discussion over policies, serving merely as an oppositionist device, designed to weaken and discredit the executive.

The result is policy paralysis. For instance, for much of the Durán administration, and despite a flurry of executive activity, Congress refused to approve virtually any legislation, thus postponing the enactment of a major economic reform program. Sadly, because of the prevailing spirit of confrontation between the two branches of government, any serious discussion of revisions to legislation is impeded. Debate and compromise are precluded, for concessions are viewed as amounting to political surrender. Furthermore, because of the priority attached to economic restructuring, other key reforms of the judiciary and the political system itself can receive the attention they deserve only after the economic legislation has been dealt with.

The president also shares blame for the politics of confrontation and ensuing gridlock. Presidential responsibility for fomenting conflict was most apparent during previous administrations, in which presidents responded aggressively to initial baiting from the legislature. While more conciliatory, Durán's leadership can also be faulted for political missteps, policy incoherence, and political indecisiveness. It was, for example, Durán's commitment to radical economic restructuring that justified his selection of an economic team composed of technocrats and members of the business community rather than the political faithful who had joined his party in the hope of securing access to plum government positions. By doing so, however, he paid a heavy political price, antagonizing key members of his own party and providing an impetus for the emergence of an opposition bloc that would include former PUR deputies.

Making matters worse, Durán's ministerial appointees were not all of the same mind as to the pace and character of economic reform. This contributed to the incoherence with which economic reforms were introduced and to the eventual stalling of the reform process itself, while the political leadership floundered in the face of mounting congressional and popular opposition. Yet, despite the obvious clashes among his ministers, Durán would wait one full year before shuffling his cabinet.[4]

Persistent conflicts between the Ecuadorian executive and the Congress have done more than paralyze the legislative process. They have also had a dangerous spillover effect on the administration of justice, circumscribing the independence of the judiciary. Appointments to the Supreme Court—a right that Congress reserves—are highly politicized, mirroring the specific character of congressional alliances and the depth of congressional-executive antagonism at any given moment. The dispute triggered over the nomination of Supreme Court justices during the Febres Cordero administration (1984–88) is perhaps most illustrative.

In 1983 the Congress amended the constitution, reducing the term of sitting judges from six to four years. Two years later, in an effort to seat a court favorable to the dominant opposition alliance in the legislature, Congress claimed that the measure should apply retroactively. This produced a confrontation between the president and the opposition bloc, in which troops were actually deployed to surround the Supreme Court building in order to deny access to the newly appointed justices. Although less intense, the 1993 appointment of a new president of the Supreme Court was also caught up in party bickering, as congressional kingpins disgruntled by political losses suffered in the legislature reacted by vetoing potential candidates for the court presidency.[5]

The effectiveness of the judicial system has also been dangerously compromised. The Ecuadorian judiciary cannot rely on a constitutionally mandated portion of the budget, but rather must enter the political fray on an annual basis to lobby Congress for its share. Furthermore, it is woefully underfinanced. It consistently receives less than 1 percent of the national budget, which is very low by Latin American standards, less than even the judicial systems of Central America. Understandably, the administration of justice, already plagued by its own internal inefficiencies and hampered by the "civil law process," has suffered as a result. Salaries are insufficiently high to attract a sufficient number of well-qualified judges, there is a dearth of public defenders, and case loads are excessive.[6]

In addition, the Ecuadorian political system has yet to incorporate the country's poor majorities. Universal suffrage notwithstanding, and despite the heralded emergence of a new generation of reformist parties in recent decades, a substantial segment of the population remains marginal to the political process. Of no group is this truer perhaps than of the indigenous community. Despite their size and potential political clout, no organized party has yet to reach out to Ecuadorian Indians. Political parties of both the Right and Left instead tend to regard the indigenous community as an obstacle to modernization.[7]

The political consequences of this neglect are several and significant. First, Ecuadorian Indians have been forced to organize and to pressure largely outside the formal political system. Demonstrations and protests have thus been staged to voice indigenous demands for cultural recognition, bilingual education, and land reform—demands that might have found room on one or another political party and government agenda. Moreover, the nonviolent strategy first espoused has gradually been relinquished. Mounting frustration over the continued neglect and marginalization of the country's poor and ethnic majorities has triggered an increase in violent action on the part of indigenous organizations. As the government and landowners react in turn through repression and violent confrontation, that violence has tended to spiral dangerously.

Second, and along similar lines, in the past year a new guerrilla organization, Puka Inti (Red Sun), has also captured the headlines through acts of sabotage. At present the government appears to have gained the upper hand in battling Puka Inti. Still, one need not look too far afield to recognize that the continued economic and political marginalization of the country's Indian population could well enhance the appeal of such guerrilla organizations.

Third, the military has distinguished itself as the only organized institution to endeavor to respond to indigenous demands, suggesting that the ghost of the military pacts negotiated during the transition may have come back to haunt Ecuadorian politics after all. Faithful to its constitutionally sanctioned responsibility for social and economic development, and shocked by the depth of the rage, poverty, and neglect of the country's Indian population, the military has sought to provide development assistance. The armed forces have moved into the countryside where they have worked actively alongside the indigenous population, delivering public services and undertaking infrastructural development.[8]

The Socioeconomic Situation

Continued faith in petroleum-induced economic recovery, coupled with the election of several governments of the political Center-Left and the set of powerful political interests aligned in opposition to economic restructuring, helps explain why Ecuador for so long bucked the Latin American trend toward greater privatization and economic openness, as a means of emerging from the economic quagmire of the 1980s. Eventually, however, the pressure to restore international confidence in an economy desperately in need of renewed foreign credit and heightened investment has proved impossible to resist. Fulfilling his campaign pledge, therefore, the incumbent government of Sixto Durán presented Congress with a draft law of economic modernization in February 1993.

The proposed legislation calls for a sweeping overhaul of the Ecuadorian economy. According to the law, the public bureaucracy would be drastically reduced, strategic sectors of the economy, previously reserved for the state, would be opened to private competition, and a massive program of privatization of state enterprises would be undertaken under presidential regulation and supervision. Sectors of the petroleum industry and a set of enterprises controlled by the country's armed forces figure among the areas targeted for privatization. The modernization law has been accompanied by complementary legislation, including the passage of a revised foreign investment code and new hydrocarbons legislation, both intended to enhance foreign investor interest in the Ecuadorian economy.[9]

While there is an acutely felt sense that the political leadership must take immediate steps to resolve the economic crisis, the character and the course of the proposed legislation have generated considerable opposition among large segments of the population. To begin with, there is a genuine concern that the process of privatization will merely open the gateway to further corruption. Most Ecuadorians are already persuaded that corruption among the political leadership is pervasive. In a recent survey, for instance, almost 90 percent of those polled noted that the principal accomplishment of the process of *juicio político* was to expose rather than to check against corruption. Understandably, many fear that the dismantling of the state will involve even more bribes and illicit payoffs as potential investors seek to buy up public firms. Arguably, those fears have already been realized, although not entirely in the manner envisioned. Indeed, during the summer of 1995, Vice-President Dahik, who was the inspiration behind the economic reform initiative conceded to having been blackmailed into granting money and special favors in exchange for congressional support in securing the passage of the economic legislation.

Popular sectors vehemently object to further economic adjustment and reform of the sort envisioned in the law. To be sure, the Ecuadorian poor have suffered a substantial swelling of their ranks in recent years, with roughly 50–60 percent of the population now deemed to live below the poverty line. Furthermore, the already precarious existence of the country's poor has deteriorated considerably in recent years. According to some estimates, the passage of the initial structural adjustment program in September 1992 triggered as much as a 50 percent decline in living standards and a 15 percent rise in official unemployment during the first year of the Durán administration alone.

Current estimates suggest that only 28 percent of the economically active population of 3.6 million earn a minimum wage which, at U.S.$30 a month, is far from sufficient to buy a basic basket of goods for an average family, which costs approximately U.S.$250 a month.[10] In labor's view, poverty would only be exacerbated further by the passage of the modernization law, not least by the massive layoffs resulting from bureaucratic downsizing and privatization, which could affect as many as 120,000 workers in a public sector labor force that currently employs 400,000. Having already witnessed the effects of Durán's austerity programs, therefore, labor representatives have brushed off government promises to cushion the blow through the enactment of a variety of social programs. Rather, they have insisted that Ecuadorian workers simply cannot afford either continued austerity or the loss of jobs that would be occasioned through reform of the state sector.[11]

The rural poor have equally good reason to oppose the reform package. The existence of the rural poor, estimated to comprise two-thirds of the rural population in a country where some 45 percent of the population still lives in the countryside, is as precarious as that of the urban poor. Indeed, despite the passage of two agrarian reforms during the military regimes of the 1960s and 1970s, the pattern of land ownership in Ecuador remains highly skewed. Eighty-three percent of the land is held by the wealthiest 20 percent of the population, while the poorest 40 percent controls a mere 3 percent. *Minifundia* and landlessness also abound. The average holding of 58 percent of the population is a meager 0.4 hectares, and one of every four rural Ecuadorians is landless.[12] To complete the picture, the problems of the rural poor, most notably those indigenous communities located in the Ecuadorian Amazon (Oriente), are compounded by the insecurity of their land titles and by the environmental destruction resulting from unregulated oil exploration. The pollution of lakes, lagoons, and rivers has threatened the health and livelihood of those Indian communities who live near these waterways.

The rural poor thus fear the impact that reforms will have on their living standards. Subsistence will be jeopardized further, as austerity takes its toll and the modernization push attracts private investors anxious to strike it rich in the Oriente. Renewed challenges to indigenous land tenure and environmental destruction are likely to result from the rush to exploit the full economic potential of the region.

So often at odds with each other, labor and indigenous organizations have spoken in remarkable unison in opposing the reforms. Not only have both groups focused on the intolerable economic impact of the reforms, but they have denounced the undemocratic character of the reforms. They have criticized both the concentration of economic decision-making power in the hands of the executive as well as the absence of popular input into the economic development process, a long-standing demand of indigenous groups. They have also urged the government to subject the law to a popular referendum before its enactment.

Popular discontent has not been limited to public appeals but has also given rise to widespread social unrest. Here again, labor and Indian groups have on occasion managed to collaborate in staging strikes and demonstrations. Worthy of note in this regard is the general strike of June 1993, launched jointly by the Federación Unitario de Trabajadores (FUT, United Federation of Workers) and CONAIE, with the additional support of students and white collar workers. Although the FUT's decision to call off the protest prematurely angered fellow strikers, the action nevertheless broke with a pattern of heretofore uncoordinated labor and Indian protests. Moreover, that action also set a precedent that would be repeated several months later when CONAIE also endorsed a bitter teachers strike.[13]

The Durán government's response, moreover, has served to exacerbate social and political tensions. Strikes have occasionally been settled, with the government acceding to some of the requests of striking workers. But more often than not, whenever negotiations occur, they usually do so only after a period of confrontation provoked by the government labeling the strike a national security threat, thereby justifying the dispatch of troops and subsequent arrest and dismissal of striking workers. This was the case, for instance, during both strikes mentioned above: the general strike of June 1993 and the prolonged teachers strike, which dragged on through the fall and winter of 1993. Along similar lines, the imposition of a state of emergency following the outbreak of a border war with Peru in January 1995, and that would remain in place long after the hostilities ceased, had the effect of justifying the government's hard line toward strike and protest activity.

Furthermore, the strikes reveal a conditioned response to popular grievances that has characterized the past several Ecuadorian administrations. When questioned, for instance, about the objectives of the general strike, Durán's labor minister responded by noting that the action was designed to bring about "anarchic internal commotion." The description was surprisingly reminiscent of that attached to labor unrest by ministers in both the Borja (1988–92) and Febres Cordero governments, who also deployed troops to quell strikes launched to protest the effects of economic crisis. Under conditions such as these, therefore, where strikes and demonstrations tend not to be viewed as legitimate democratic mechanisms for voicing popular discontent, but rather as subversive forms of political activity, the preferred response has favored repression over negotiation, with attendant social and political costs.[14]

The tensions generated may also have been aggravated by the business community's attitude toward economic reform and the relationship between business, labor, and government. For the most part, Ecuadorian entrepreneurial groups welcomed the proposed reform package, which they viewed as long overdue and which several of their representatives helped craft from positions in the administration. But while private sector support for the program remains high, the popular opposition that it has triggered and the slow-moving, uncertain process of legislative approval have proved disheartening to many. Fear of antagonizing the country's economic elites will certainly heighten pressures for a probusiness government to continue to pursue economic restructuring in a swift and steadfast manner, albeit at the risk of further alienating popular sector organizations. It is at times such as these, moreover, that the absence of a tradition of socioeconomic pacts is most sorely felt. Pacts might have served to temper the conflict produced by the conjuncture of severe crisis, reform, and difference of opinion between strengthened popular sector organizations and ever influential entrepreneurial groups.

Complicating matters even more, the government feels disquieting pressures from another politically powerful source, pressures that are undoubtedly linked to the tenacity with which Ecuador confronted Peru during the border clashes of 1995. For a variety of reasons, the Ecuadorian military has joined the chorus of voices objecting to the proposed reforms. In a process that began during the era of military rule (1972–79), the Ecuadorian armed forces have amassed a vast and diverse economic empire, the holdings of which range from textile manufacturing, agricultural exports, munitions plants, a merchant fleet, and oil tankers to banks, airlines, travel agencies, and hotels. As the current government has already made it quite clear that many of those enterprises are slated for immediate privatization, the military has sprung into action, mobilizing to defend its economic interests against attack.

In addition to the very real material interests that are at stake, the armed forces also have opposed the reforms on more ideological grounds. After all, it was in the name of nationalism and reform that the military leadership of the 1970s expanded dramatically the economic responsibilities of the state while curtailing those of foreign investors. Consequently, it should come as no surprise to hear the current defense minister warn that "there are enterprises of strategic value that cannot be handed over to monopolistic foreign hands and capitalists." For the armed forces, therefore, it is more than their economic interests that are at stake: so, too, is the legacy of the Rodríguez Lara dictatorship. Finally, much as they did during the period of military rule and transition, the Ecuadorian military continues to draw a connection between security and development, still insisting today that security is threatened by excessive poverty and injustice. The heightened poverty and aggravated social discontent that has been a hallmark of the years of civilian rule is not lost on the armed forces, who fear a dangerous escalation of both as a result of the selected course of economic reform.[15]

The armed forces have been straightforward, in both voicing their opposition to the modernization law and discussing the range of actions they could pursue to block the effort. To date they have chosen to engage government officials and the public in dialogue about the direction of the proposed reforms. After years of silence, and indicative of the legitimacy they still command as both individuals and leaders of a military regime, retired officers who served in the military regime have been drafted into political action. With the apparent blessing of their colleagues in active service, several of this group's members—including the nationalist minister of natural resources, Admiral Jarrín Ampudia, and General Rodríguez Lara himself—have wandered the halls of Congress lobbying its members and have appeared on television to explain their objections to the reforms. In these and other fora, they have highlighted the social and economic threat posed by the modernization law. But they have also mused about the possibility of more concerted military action, justified in their view by the fact that the proposed dismantling of the economic apparatus of the state violates the constitution and by their constitutionally mandated responsibility for national security and development.[16]

Brinkmanship and the Possibilities for Reform

Efforts at political reform have thus far been frustrated in Ecuador, as the political leadership remains wedded to traditional patterns of political behavior. Despite attempts to use the transition to establish a framework for a more representative and effective democratic system, institutions remain weak and the politics of exclusion and conflict have prevailed. Fragile political parties lack a strong internal organization, rank and file, or mass constituency. The vast majority of Ecuadorians continue to stand outside the formal political system, and the process of governance has again been crippled by a seemingly endless series of personal conflicts between the executive and the legislature.

Nevertheless, and despite the attendant social and economic consequences, elected civilian rule has survived for a decade and a half. Somehow the political class has muddled through, pulling back as democratic governance veered perilously close to provoking breakdown. Ultimately, political conflicts have been resolved, permitting constitutional alliances to be forged, albeit at the last moment. Rumors of military intervention have also come to naught, and attempted coups have been aborted. Poor and ethnic majorities have found alternative means to organize and to pressure the system. Given the proliferation of political parties, there has been no dearth of new political organizations willing and able to take the place of a governing party that tends to exit in disgrace at election time.

Another critical political juncture appears to have been reached today. The imperative of economic and political reform, coupled with intense disagreements over how to proceed, has produced renewed confrontation between old adversaries: the Congress and the president. As it has on so many previous occasions, the policymaking process has been paralyzed, impeding the enactment of necessary economic reform as well as the serious consideration of other critical legislation.

Just as important, the discussion of economic reform has done more than fan the flames of congressional-executive conflict. It has also brought other influential political actors into the fray, whose opposition could prove potentially explosive. The increasingly shrill voices of the strengthened labor and indigenous organizations have still not found effective formal means of expression, with the result that greatly exacerbated sociopolitical conflict is not easily contained. Complicating matters further, they have found an ally in the armed forces, who are equally vociferous in resisting the enactment of the proposed economic legislation and who have refused to rule out direct forms of intervention.

Time, therefore, once more appears gradually to be running out on democratic governance. As we have seen, popular frustrations have mounted, giving rise to an almost constant pattern of strikes and protests. The business community has grown increasingly disenchanted with a political class that does not lead. And the armed forces have become impatient, preoccupied by the likely impact of economic crisis and reform on both the armed forces as an institution and on national security for which they feel responsible. Popular confidence in the capacities of the elected political leadership and of the democratic system is at a particularly low ebb. Recent opinion polls reveal that more than 80 percent of the population feel that political parties do not serve the public interest; some 64 percent believe that democracy is not the best form of government for Ecuador; the majority argue that some form of dictatorship is necessary to halt corruption; and the armed forces, along with the Catholic Church, are listed as the institutions most respected by Ecuadorians.[17]

As it has so many times before, the political leadership has again responded to crisis by recognizing the need for reform. Several members of Congress concede the need to move forward on economic reform and to begin to consider other key political reforms. Their public declarations reveal an understanding of the gravity of the political, social, and economic situation and an awareness of the importance of demonstrating the political leadership's capacity to enact effective and meaningful reforms. There is thus growing pressure to revise the economic legislation to take into account popular grievances and to begin to review pending legislation that would address the inefficiencies of the judicial system.

Discussions have also begun in earnest over a set of proposed constitutional reforms passed in a popular consultation held in late August 1994. The Ecuadorian electorate approved several politically significant measures, including a proposal that would permit the reelection of deputies to consecutive terms, another that would allow independents to compete for political office, and a third that would transfer responsibility over the budget from Congress to the executive. Although congressional passage of these reforms is by no means guaranteed, their approval and subsequent enactment would represent an effort to attack some of the central problems plaguing Ecuadorian politics. Measures such as the election of independents and the reelection of members of Congress are thus seen as necessary to tackle the corruption and political opportunism that seem to drive Ecuadorian politics as much as ever today, as evidenced in phenomena such as the *cambio de cami-*

setas. In addition, the reelection of deputies is viewed as contributing to the creation of an experienced and professional political class, able to view the policymaking process in longer terms than permitted by the current two-year congressional cycle.

These advantages notwithstanding, the reforms currently under consideration are unlikely either to tackle or to resolve other (arguably the key) critical problems afflicting Ecuadorian politics today. First, the proposed reforms do little, and indeed may well exacerbate, the conflicts between the executive and the Congress that produce the logjams that cripple the policymaking procèss and that understandably serve to discredit democratic governance. As things stand at present, Congress has relatively little responsibility for the formulation of policy. Its power resides essentially in its capacity to veto legislation passed on to it for approval by the executive branch. It is thus not entirely surprising that congressional coalitions seem to form for little other than the express purpose of preventing the enactment of legislation, a process that is only likely to intensify should the executive also gain full control over the budget.

Seen from this perspective, moreover, it could be argued that constitutional reforms that transfer greater powers to the legislature would contribute more to the enhancement of democratic rule than those that seek to heighten the role of the executive. If awarded greater policymaking responsibilities rather than even fewer, members of Congress might be encouraged to engage in coalition building with a view to formulating acceptable and sound policies rather than merely to vetoing legislation. Politically constructive pacts that at present appear only to accompany electoral campaigns might thus either survive the election itself or be extended to include additional players during the period of democratic governance.

Second, the proposed reforms ignore the acute problem of political marginalization of the majority of Ecuadorians. Transition architects were very much concerned with introducing reforms that would render Ecuadorian politics more inclusive. As we have seen, the failure of those efforts has taken a toll on the system, contributing to the intensification of violence and repression that accompanies persistent protest today. The key to greater inclusiveness is not self-evident. Nevertheless, it is worth noting that, despite the emerging concern over how to reform the state so as to preserve, or indeed buttress, certain critical social and economic capacities, little similar concern has been articulated surrounding the political capacities of the state. In an era in which the concept of civil society has been reified, however, the stability of democratic governance surely demands that commensurate attention be paid to enhancing the political effectiveness of governments in the region, if only to ensure their ability to respond to demands placed upon them by civic organizations.

In emphasizing as it does the absence of a strong commitment both to democratic governance among the country's political leadership and, increasingly, to sustained democratic rule among a majority of Ecuadorians, the above discussion underscores the importance of undertaking creative and more precisely targeted domestic political reforms. It also thereby highlights the secondary nature of international democracy assistance efforts, including those pursued by governmental, nongovernmental, and multilateral institutions.

Bearing those limitations in mind, there are nevertheless several targets of opportunity for members of the international community concerned with assisting Ecuadorians to overcome some of the most immediately apparent obstacles to sustained and deepened democratic rule. Targeted poverty alleviation programs, similar to those undertaken in recent years in neighboring Bolivia, could cushion some of the worst effects of prolonged austerity for the neediest Ecuadorians. Other measures could strengthen the hand and the capacities of those elements in the political leadership most genuinely committed to enhancing democratic governance through institutional reform. First, financial and technical assistance for judicial reform is both timely and essential. Second, legislative exchange programs and other forms of assistance to parliamentarians could encourage serious thinking about creative and effective political mechanisms that might address the more structural obstacles to effective democratic governance.

There may also be opportunities in the Ecuadorian case to provide international assistance in ways that serve multiple purposes: attenuating some of the deep-seated resentment that has been a cause of the heightened sociopolitical tensions of the past several years; enhancing popular participation in and, by extension, popular commitment to the democratic political process; and in the process also reducing inequalities over the longer term. For instance, an innovative legislative assistance program focusing on indigenous political organization could address the problem of continued marginalization of indigenous communities by all major political groupings as well as capitalize on the emerging interest of indigenous leaders in organizing themselves into a political party.

International efforts might also explore ways of drawing Ecuadorian nongovernmental organizations into discussions of economic and political reform. This could be achieved by rendering academic and educational research and study opportunities, as well as opportunities for internships with counterpart organizations abroad, more readily accessible to Ecuadorian nongovernmental organizations. Arguably, this would have the effect of bolstering the analytical and organizational capacities of these organizations and, by extension, their ability to have a demonstrable impact on the policymaking process. Along similar lines, the international community might also continue to encourage and indeed sponsor dialogue among representatives from nongovernmental organizations and the Ecuadorian government as well as, where relevant, members of international organizations.

Although to be effective such efforts must occur in tandem with domestic initiatives, taken as a package they could together have the combined effect of addressing the strongly articulated popular demand for inclusion in the decision-making process and contributing to making necessary reform more widely acceptable. In the process, democratic governance in Ecuador might stand the test of time and find itself both sustained and deepened.

4

Peru: The Rupture of Democratic Rule

Susan Stokes

Peru is the only Latin American country since the most recent wave of democratic transitions where a consolidated democratic regime was destroyed by a coup d'état, only to be revived after the April 1995 presidential and legislative elections and the installation of the elected government in July 1995.[1] The hiatus in democratic rule and the re-emergence, however brief, of de facto government make Peru unique in South America. But the forces that destroyed democracy in Peru are not unique to that country. The reasons for the breakdown of democracy in Peru, the nature of the de facto regime, and the processes and pressures pressing it back onto a course of democratization will therefore all be of considerable comparative interest.

Democracy in Peru, 1980–1992

The Democratizing Legacy of Populist Military Rule

The election of a civilian leadership in 1980 made Peru the second Latin American country to return to civilian rule in the most recent wave of democratization. Economic crisis and internal divisions within the military lay behind this transition. At a deeper level, populist military rule under General Juan Velasco Alvarado (1968–75) sparked political mobilization of industrial workers, shantytown residents, and peasant communities, and unintentionally breathed life into political parties of the Center and Left that sought to lead this mobilization. Populist military rule, then, had a certain contradictory quality: it left in its wake a level of from-the-bottom participation and a broadened party system that were inconsistent with continued military control.

These features of the military period carried over into the period of renewed civilian rule. A Constitutional Assembly was elected in 1978 in which the Center-populist APRA (American Popular Revolutionary Alliance) was the largest party and in which socialist and Marxist parties controlled a powerful bloc. This distribution foreshadowed a three-party (or three-force) system that crystallized in the 1980s: the Right (AP, Popular Action; PPC, Popular Christian Party) won presidential elections in 1980, was a majority of the legislature in 1980–85, and won many local elections; the Center (APRA) won the presidency in 1985, controlled the legislature in 1985–90, and controlled many local governments; and the Left was the second force in the legislature in 1985–90 and won many local elections, including the mayorship of Lima (1983–86). This party system, though eventually unstable, was broader and more socially representative than Peruvian party systems of earlier periods. The Peruvian military, moreover, proved more tolerant of traditionally antagonistic parties than it ever had before. Finally, Peruvian civil society emerged, ironically, enriched by the period of military rule: the peak business associations were joined by an enlivened labor movement and other organized expressions of Peruvian society. Since the founding of the republic, never had Peruvian civil society been as rich or as broad.

Fragilities in the Democratic System

But Peruvian politics faced serious challenges. First among them were guerrilla movements. The largest was Sendero Luminoso (Shining Path), itself a by-product of the mobilization and radicalization of the Velasco years, but a by-product that parted ways with most of the Left when the latter adopted an electoral strategy. Successive governments failed to win over Sendero's support bases, and halfhearted peace initiatives foundered on its intransigence. In the apt words of an Americas Watch report, the response to Sendero of Peru's first elected administration (Belaúnde, 1980–85) was to "abdicate democratic authority" and turn over not just the implementation but the conceptualization of the counterinsurgency to the armed forces. The García government initially tried to assert civilian direction over counterinsurgency but returned to a militarized approach after a prison massacre in June 1986.

By 1990 the Peruvian military, after a decade of internal warfare, had succeeded only in driving the guerrillas out of parts of its native territory. But Sendero dug in in new areas, such as the coca- and cash-rich Upper Huallaga Valley, and made inroads in poor communities in Lima. The human costs of the insurgency were twenty-five thousand dead at the hands of both Sendero and the military; five thousand "disappeared," and more than one hundred extrajudicial executions; a string of massacres by military and paramilitary groups that tarnished the government's image; the enduring involvement of the military in shoring up the civilian government's power and authority; and a gnawing sense of insecurity of which no Peruvian was free.

Peru was unique among Latin America's new democracies in facing a serious guerrilla threat. But other fragilities in the democratic system were common to many South American countries. One was the concentration of significant power in the hands of the president. This concentration rested on some constitutional supports. The Constitution of

1979 gave more power to the executive than did the Constitution of 1933, such as in allowing presidents to make laws by decree when the legislature was out of session. The 1979 drafters enhanced presidential power because they perceived that impasses between a minority president and the legislature were a cause of the military coup of 1968. But in the 1980s even presidents from parties commanding majorities in the legislature (Belaúnde, García) relied on decree powers to make law. It is not clear why this was so, although the perception of the legislature's ineffectiveness probably played a role.

Excessive executive power exacerbated another frailty of Peruvian democracy, weaknesses of political parties. Seats in the upper and lower chambers were apportioned by the D'Hondt formula of proportional representation, with Chamber of Deputies seats apportioned by votes in departments and Senate seats by votes in the nation as a whole. This system broadened the representation of parties in the legislature but weakened the representational link between constituents and legislators. The ranking of candidates within party lists was established by popularity with the voters, giving individual candidates an incentive to campaign as personalities rather than as party members.

Thus, although the party system was broader and more accurately reflective of the electorate's preferences, with weak mechanisms of accountability, these signals were far from guarantees of the course of policy once candidates were elected. At worst, then, party affiliation was a superficial label that politicians adopted and sloughed off at will. And parties were organizations without discipline, as activists could not control leaders (evidenced by the erratic behavior of Alan García as president) and party leaderships could not impose order in the ranks (evidenced by the rupture of the fractious United Left coalition in 1989).

With these preexisting weaknesses in the party system, and with a grave economic crisis and other factors discrediting governing parties in 1980–85 (AP) and 1985–90 (APRA), it took little additional tinkering with the electoral system for Alberto Fujimori to render Peru a country virtually without real political parties (see below). Ironically, the party-less society, the ideal of Latin American military rulers of the previous period, was nearly achieved in Peru with little repression.

Guerrilla movements enhancing the role of the military and eroding the sense of civilian authority, presidents facing few institutional checks, a deteriorating party system—all of these were political precursors to the breakdown of democratic rule in Peru. Our picture would be incomplete without mentioning the dire economic conditions that Peru suffered for most of the recent period of civilian government. Crossnational research shows that the likelihood of coups d'état is a function of both level of income and rate of growth: coups are more likely among poor countries and those with slow growth.[2] Given the

Table 2 Peru: Some Economic Indicators, 1980–1990

	1980–84[a]	1985	1986	1987	1988	1989	1990
GDP[b]	22.8	22.3	24.7	27.1	25.1	22.0	21.5
GDP growth	0.4	1.7	10.8	9.7	−7.4	−12.4	−2.4
Per capita GDP growth	−1.9	−0.5	8.5	7.4	−9.3	−14.1	−4.3
Consumption growth	1.4	0.8	14.3	9.2	−8.8	−16.6	−2.2
Inflation	84.5	169.8	78.9	81.5	580	2,821	7,417
Foreign debt[c]	11.2	13.7	14.5	15.4	16.5	16.8	17.4
Real wage in Lima[d]	95	148	185	194	134	110	57
% change demand for labor	27%	12%	3%	−45%	−21%		

Source: Richard Webb and Graciela Fernández Baca de Valdez, *Perú en Números 1991*.
[a]Average.
[b]In billions of 1986 U.S.$.
[c]In billions of U.S.$.
[d]Average monthly real wage in millions of 1990 intis

economic decline reflected in Table 2, perhaps we should be surprised that Peru experienced only one successful coup and one serious coup attempt (November 1992, see below) in recent years.

Alberto Fujimori: From Election to Coup

The Peruvian electorate's choice of Alberto Fujimori in 1990 represented a mandate to resolve the country's economic crisis without the harsh measures proposed by the Right. Mario Vargas Llosa, the leading candidate and the only one backed by traditional parties with a chance of winning the election,[3] campaigned for a neoliberal revolution: immediate price adjustments and removal of subsidies, withdrawal of the state from the economy, an early and substantial reduction in the number of public employees, privatization and trade liberalization. Campaigning against Vargas Llosa, Alberto Fujimori charged that an orthodox price shock would exacerbate inertial causes of inflation. Fujimori called instead for concerted wage and price agreements to fight inflation, a downsized but activist state, and an economic model emphasizing labor-intensive "microindustries." What little organized support Fujimori had came from socially progressive evangelicals, representatives of the informal sector, and the Japanese-Peruvian community.

Fujimori placed a strong second in the first round of the elections, forcing the dispirited Vargas Llosa into a second round. Fujimori won the runoff, 57 percent to 35 percent. Immediately the president-elect came under intense pressure from domestic and international sources to abandon the neo-Keynesian model he had outlined in the election campaign. New advisors who gained access to the president-elect, some of them erstwhile associates of Vargas Llosa, pressed for an orthodox stabilization policy. In late June 1990 Fujimori, a new figure in Peruvian public life and decidedly without international stature, made a visit to the United States and Japan. At meetings with officials at the highest level of the international financial institutions in the United States and with the Japanese prime minister, the president-elect was repeatedly pressed to reach an agreement with the International Monetary Fund (IMF).

The Fujimori government's economic policies in the end were closer to those of his former opponent than to those outlined in his own campaign. If the 1990 election had represented a mandate to stabilize while eschewing economic orthodoxy, that mandate was violated. On August 8 the price adjustments were announced: the price of 84 octane gasoline rose by 3,140 percent; the price of kerosene, widely used by the lower classes for cooking, rose by 6,964 percent. Subsidies for many basic foodstuffs were removed, and the prices of these soared: bread by 1,567 percent, cooking oil by 639 percent, sugar by 552 percent, and rice by 533 percent. Medicine prices rose on average by 1,385 percent. During the first eighteen months, the following structural reforms were implemented: exchange rate unification and liberalization, reduction and simplification of tariffs on imports, elimination of tariffs on exports, capital market liberalization, reduction of employees in government ministries and state-owned enterprises, elimination of job security laws, elimination of wage indexation, and liberalization of labor relations. Gone was any sense of policy implementation through *concertación* or negotiations with the representatives of labor and business; in fact, Fujimori frequently bypassed even the legislature, using decree powers to make laws.

This episode is important not only because it points to the weakness of mechanisms of accountability in Peru but also because it is likely that at this point Fujimori began to adopt a style of leadership uncontrolled by any constraints from other branches of government or political parties. He began to sense that public opinion could be mobilized in support of actions that violated the commonly understood rules of the game.

The constitutional period of Fujimori's rule (July 1990–April 1992) was also one of growing reliance of the president on military officials, and officials in his newly created National Intelligence Service (SIN), for information, protection, and support. This reliance grew in part because Fujimori's own pre-election institutional sources of support, thin though they were, were lost to the president as a result of his economic policy shift. Thus the evangelicals broke with Fujimori in the wake of his orthodox price shock in mid-1990. And his initial multiparty cabinet, reflecting the support of APRA and the Left in the second round of the presidential election, gave way fairly quickly to a succession of cabinets of independents of rightist orientation.

Thus Fujimori increasingly turned to the military to fill the void of organized support for his presidency. After the June 1990 election, Fujimori took up residence in a military residential zone in a suburb of Lima. He spent considerable time cultivating military personnel and made numerous public appearances at military events, from commemorations of battles to cadet graduation ceremonies. By the second year of his term, Fujimori's closest advisor was Vladimiro Montesinos, a shadowy former army captain, lawyer, and now head of the National Intelligence Service. Fujimori's reliance on the military and its intelligence service left him increasingly insensitive to foreign and domestic pressures to curb and investigate human rights abuses.

The immediate backdrop to the coup d'état of April 5, 1992, was a conflict between the president and the Congress over executive powers and counterinsurgency and economic policy. In November 1991 Fujimori issued a package of 126 decree laws, including measures limiting press freedoms, extending military powers over civilian authorities in emergency zones, and a "national mobilization law" declaring that any person residing in Peru was obliged to collaborate in the fight against terrorism and drug trafficking. The military was given free access to the universities, and a "national defense system" was established, allowing the military to intervene in the production, marketing, and consumption of goods. Critics of the measures limiting press freedoms noted that a recent massacre by paramilitary groups could not have been reported had the law been in place. Critics from across the political spectrum decried the militarization of the Peruvian state.

At the same time the measures strengthened the president's control over the military, provoking dissent among constitutionalists in the armed forces. The measures provided that the president would nominate the chiefs of the armed forces and retain them in office past their age of retirement. Retired General Luis Cisneros Vizquerra complained that the package of measures "militarizes the population while politicizing the armed forces."[4]

A retrospective look at the record leaves the impression that (as was later reported) Fujimori and a close group of advisors planned the April coup for months in advance. In early 1992 Fujimori embarked on an apparent campaign to poison the public's opinion of the Congress. He suggested that Congress was beholden to drug traffickers and money launderers, he virtually ignored the constitution by refusing to accept the resignation of a minister whom the Chamber of Deputies had censured, and he reminded Congress of his constitutional right to dissolve that body and hold new elections under certain circumstances.[5] For its part, congressional leaders reminded the president of their right to declare him morally incapacitated and call for new presidential elections, and they attempted to block some antiterrorist and fiscal reform measures.

The struggle between Congress and the president was also over aspects of economic policy. Congress was balking at a proposed fiscal reform and objected to the government's agricultural policy, leading to the censure of Enrique Rossl Link, the agriculture minister. Carlos Boloña, Fujimori's economic minister, who had served as a World Bank official and had close ties with the international financial community, complained that congressional interference threatened the stabilization and economic reform programs and violated agreements the government had reached with multilateral lending institutions. (In fact, as noted above, a long list of structural reforms had already been put in place without significant congressional resistance.) Just as the conflict of powers intensified, the World Bank issued a statement endorsing Fujimori's economic program, noting the government's achievements in trade liberalization and claiming that the policy was yielding results faster than those of Chile and Mexico. The international financial institutions further signaled support of Fujimori when the IMF's Michel Camdessus scheduled a visit to Lima in February 1992.[6]

This conflict of powers culminated in the April 5, 1992, coup d'état. With the support of the military, public opinion still favorable, and the prospect of a mild international response, Fujimori orchestrated a self-coup: he dissolved Congress, placed congressional and party leaders and some journalists under house arrest, jailed some members of the former García administration, interrupted judicial functions, and censored major newspapers. Fujimori declared that he would head an "emergency government of national reconstruction." In the weeks following the coup, the regime dismissed 135 judges and prosecutors, threatened opposition politicians with long prison terms if they continued to exercise "public functions" (a threat extended to his own previous vice-presidents), and launched an attack on terrorist suspects at the Canto Grande prison outside Lima that left thirty-six prisoners dead.

The Interlude of De Facto Rule and the Trend toward Redemocratization

Between April 1992 and July 1995, Peru has been ruled by a civilian-military government, one that begrudgingly succumbed to pressures to liberalize and to return to a formal state of constitutional rule.[7] The gradual shift toward reconstitutionalization and liberalization was the result of international pressure (comforted by high public opinion ratings, Fujimori was immune to domestic pressures). In the week following the coup, the OAS (Organization of American States) held an emergency session to consider the Peruvian crisis, issuing strong statements of condemnation and suspending Peru from the Rio Group. But it could not muster support for economic sanctions. U.S. Secretary of State James Baker noted the fallacy of destroying democracy to save it, and U.S. Assistant Secretary of State for Inter-American Affairs Bernard Aronson worked actively to reverse Fujimori's actions. The Peru Support Group, a group of eleven industrialized countries that were to help Peru secure loans to pay off arrears to the IMF, suspended these loans.

The international financial institutions (IFIs), in contrast, sent ambiguous signals after the coup. There can be little doubt that they were dismayed by the coup and saw it as threatening the reinsertion of Peru into the international financial community. Still, these institutions gave signals that Peruvian leaders could well have interpreted as meaning that, if forced to choose between the two, the IFIs valued economic reform over democracy. Indeed, the data shows that the coup slowed the disbursement of funds for several months, but by the end of 1992, the Inter-American Development Bank (IDB) had disbursed U.S.$390 million, the amount independent analysts had predicted before the coup would be forthcoming from that institution.[8] The IDB representative announced in Lima in September 1992 that full resumption of loans was not conditional on a return to democracy.

The IMF and the World Bank also sent mixed signals. The World Bank proceeded with several missions to Peru in the months following the coup. Soon after the coup the IMF let it be known that a standby agreement could still be reached if economic targets were met by the end of the year. In September the IMF found that Peru had achieved goals laid out in a 1991 Letter of Intent, giving Peru access to loans.[9]

Toward Reconstitutionalization (April 1992–November 1993)

Between mid-April 1992 and November 1993 the new authoritarian regime, pressed by the OAS and foreign governments, entered into a process of limited reconstitutionalization. This period encompassed three sets of elections: in November 1992 delegates were elected to a Democratic Constitutional Congress (CCD), in January 1993 voters elected municipal governments nationwide, and in November 1993 they voted in a referendum on the new constitution.

Two facts about these elections should be noted. First, they were carried out under rules modified by the de facto regime, rules that were designed to augment the power of the regime and about which there was no negotiation with political parties or other political actors. Thus the government announced that delegates to the CCD would be barred from holding office for two subsequent terms; this and a sense of the illegitimacy of the process led most of the major political parties to abstain.[10] In the January 1993 municipal elections, the regime considerably lowered the number of signatures required on petitions allowing candidates to appear on the ballot. The intended effect was to drown the traditional political parties in a flood of novice candidacies. Thirty-eight candidates appeared on the ballot for mayor of Lima, and seventy-seven for the provincial city of Huaura, with an electorate of about twenty-five thousand.

But the regime's efforts to eliminate parties and to aggrandize official party power were not entirely successful, which brings us to the second fact about post-coup elections worthy of note: never did the regime register sweeping electoral successes. In elections for the CCD the two pro-regime lists received only 40 percent of the vote. In January 1993 municipal elections the Cambio '90 candidate for mayor of Lima was so low in public opinion polls that he withdrew from competition two weeks before the election, and the incumbent mayor, who later became openly hostile to Fujimori, was elected in a landslide. Candidates tied to traditional parties, although not necessarily representing those parties, were elected in Arequipa, Cuzco, Callao, Trujillo, Chiclayo, and many smaller cities and towns. Finally, in the November 1993 referendum on the constitution, the "yes" vote barely beat the "no" vote by a margin of 52 percent to 48 percent. Only Fujimori himself managed to mobilize large margins of victory, as in the 1995 presidential elections.

Although pro-Fujimori forces failed to win an absolute majority of votes in elections for the CCD, they controlled forty-three of eighty seats in the constitutional body. Thus, although the CCD was a forum where opposition views were voiced, the constitution that was produced and eventually ratified was a faithful reflection of the regime's desires. The 1993 Constitution is considerably more politically authoritarian and socially conservative than the 1979 Constitution. It expands the president's powers to dissolve Congress (article 134) and to declare states of exception (article 137), and places promotion of military personnel in the hands of the president, without requiring congressional ratification (article 118). The 1993 Constitution introduces presidential reelection (article 112),[11] and the death penalty (article 140), which Fujimori showed interest in applying retroactively. It removes state commitment to free elementary education and job security, and places new barriers in the way of labor organization (article 28).

Constitutional Rule (November 1993–April 1995)

This period was one in which the regime's commitment to constitutional rule, now under a constitution of its own design, was tested. Although ultimately the regime did permit national elections in April 1995, events in 1994 gave rise to questions regarding the regime's independence from the military and its commitment to the rule of law.

A February 1994 political crisis occurred when the CCD majority and the president intervened to move the prosecution of military officers accused of extrajudicial executions from a civilian to a military court.[12] A Supreme Court justice had earlier ruled that the case of officers implicated in the massacre of nine students and a professor from La Cantuta national teachers university should be heard in civilian court.[13] The CCD majority hurriedly wrote a law allowing a simple majority of the Supreme Court to decide cases of jurisdiction, and the law (dubbed "Ley Cantuta" by critics) was quickly signed by the president. A majority on the Supreme Court then voted to turn the case over to a military court (recall that Fujimori had drastically altered the composition of the Supreme Court after the coup). The action appeared to violate separation of powers, as laid out in the 1993 Constitution. The upshot was international condemnation, the resignation of the prime minister, and declining support for the president in public opinion polls.

A second incident in 1994 raised further questions in Peru and abroad about the government's capacity to respect the rule of law and human rights. In April, as part of a counterinsurgency campaign in the Upper Huallaga Valley known as Operation Aries, the military carried out aerial attacks against civilian targets, resulting in widespread casualties. Military officials in the region barred access by journalists and by the International Committee of the Red Cross. The number killed in the attacks may never be known.[14]

The significance of these events was to suggest that the Fujimori government, despite the return to constitutional rule, was heavily bound by its allies in the military. The events throw into relief the cross-pressures Fujimori faced. On one side he was pressed by foreign governments, domestic political leaders, the opposition press, and public opinion to return to democracy. But at the same time he was involved in a delicate and potentially destructive operation of courting and controlling the military. The sense of Fujimori's enduring obligations to the military at the expense of democratic procedures was reinforced again when, soon after his reinauguration in July 1995, he announced an amnesty for all military officials accused of human rights abuses.

Earlier I noted that Fujimori had turned to the Peruvian military as his primary, in a real sense his only, institutional source of support. Fujimori's late 1991 efforts to militarize the state and exert direct control over the armed forces strained his relations with the military; these relations were further complicated by the April 1992 coup. Although the military establishment on the whole has remained loyal to the president, in fact Fujimori relies on a small group of high-ranking officers. Fujimori relied on General Nicolas de Bari Hermoza, the army commander and chief of the Joint Command of the Armed Forces, retaining him in that position after his scheduled 1992 retirement. This caused discontent among other officers. Also controversial among the military establishment was Fujimori's close association with Vladimiro Montesinos, the former army captain and lawyer who has been accused of disloyalty and ties to drug traffickers.

Military discontent twice erupted into open revolt. On November 13, 1992, a high-level group of active and retired officers attempted a coup to return the country to constitutional rule. Later from their jail cells the would-be coup-makers complained that Fujimori "demoted or retired professionals, while promoting a clique of corrupt officers and shadowy security advisors."[15] Then, in early 1993, members of the military provided opposition members of the CCD with evidence leading to the discovery of graves of nine students and a professor "disappeared" from La Cantuta in September 1992. The officers' apparent motive was to undermine General Hermoza by linking him with human rights violations.

In April 1993 Army General Rodolfo Robles, a constitutionalist suspected of being the source of the incriminating information, was removed from his position as chief of army instruction. Robles later went into exile in Argentina, issuing a statement condemning military officials for human rights violations. In late April and early May, tanks appeared on the streets of Lima in support of Hermoza, who had made controversial statements accusing CCD members investigating the La Cantuta case of being apologists for terrorism.

Economic Performance, Public Opinion, and International Response

International opposition to the Peruvian coup d'état was harsher than the coup-makers anticipated and amounted to effective pressure for a return to some sort of constitutional rule. But international opposition was more muted than it might have been because of some common misperceptions about the Peruvian situation. Before moving to the policy implications of my analysis, I address three "facts" that have softened international criticism of Peru's departure from a democratic course.

No Democracy to Interrupt

"Democracy has not been destroyed in Peru for the simple reason that, in any meaningful sense, it never existed." The reasoning in this case of Caleb Rossiter appeared in several influential newspapers in the United States.[16] Many accounts enumerated Peru's problems—"economic ruin, cocaine traffickers, disease, starvation and a civil war with Shining Path terrorists"[17]—and concluded that (1) a country with such problems could not be a democracy, and (2) a drastic change in the political system was justified as a way of resolving those problems.

The fallacy is to confuse "democracy" with a just society. Moreover, although some critics were correct in their Aristotelian observation of the degrading effect of deep poverty and inequality on democracy, it does not follow that poverty and inequality are likely to be eliminated if democracy is eliminated. Here Jorge Castañeda's formulation is apt: "Democracy without reducing inequality can only endure under great stress and given exceptional conditions; but only democracy can reduce the disparities that make it untenable."[18] Caleb Rossiter went so far as to suggest that poor "Indians and mestizos" inhabiting Lima's shanty-towns are "disenfranchised." In fact, about 85 percent of the adults in those shantytowns voted in eight separate elections between 1978 and 1990, and many voted for candidates for president, Congress, and mayorships whose party programs called for the redistribution of wealth.

Fuzzy analyses abounded in the days following the coup. In a news analysis, Thomas Friedman wrote "does it make sense to tell an impoverished country whose courts are widely believed to have been corrupted by drug traffickers, and whose capital is under attack from vicious Maoist guerrillas that the only way out of its problems is to restore the democracy that existed before the Government crack-down?"[19] The difficulty is that Fujimori did not carry out the coup to resolve these problems. His actions are better understood as arising from an intolerance for checks on executive power by Congress and the judiciary. Mistaken accounts of the motives behind the coup led U.S. analysts to "hope . . . that with a little time" to "get his country back under control . . . public pressure will ensure that whatever [Fujimori] does he does quickly and then restores democracy."[20] The scenario lacked credibility.

Fujimori's Resolution of Peru's Security and Economic Crises

One of the disputes between the president and Congress leading up to the coup was Fujimori's controversial antiterrorist laws. These laws were not proposed as a serious effort to reorient a failing counterinsurgency campaign; indeed, they represented a hardening of a policy that had already been in place for a decade, with paltry results. All serious analyses noted that the proposals were intended to solidify Fujimori's support among the military. Later successes in counterinsurgency since the coup (the capture of Abimael Guzmán and Sendero's top leadership) were the result of good police work by a special police investigative unit that had been at work for many years before the coup. Furthermore, politicians from across the political spectrum, lawyers' associations, the press, and all democratic forces found Fujimori's proposed antiterrorist laws anathema.

Those who justify the move away from democracy because of Peru's recent economic successes have their chronology wrong. Most of Fujimori's economic reforms were put in place during the first year after his election: these included price liberalization, deficit reduction, and trade liberalization. Still on the agenda at the time of the coup were fiscal reform and privatization. By the time of the coup, structural adjustment was a fait accompli; although congressional opponents might have tinkered with economic policy, they would not have fundamentally undermined it or altered its course.

Public Opinion in Peru in Support of Fujimori

Nothing has inhibited international critics more than Fujimori's much-touted popularity and that of his coup. According to public opinion polls, Fujimori's approval ratings have varied between about 30 percent and about 80 percent. The high point in his approval ratings came after the coup. But polls immediately after the coup showed that large majorities wanted a quick return to democracy. So Peruvians supported the coup and democracy at the same time. What does this mean? It is likely to mean that they felt deep frustration and insecurity because of Sendero Luminoso and because of the economic recession (note that recession, and the perception of economic crisis, persisted well into the Fujimori administration). This frustration and insecurity left many open to the claim that Congress lay at the root of all problems; they were reassured by a decisive show of authority by the chief executive. But there is little indication in public opinion polling that Peruvians favored an authoritarian form of government over a democratic one. Indeed, when faced with the brutal and arbitrary side of authoritarian systems, as in the La Cantuta massacre and cover-up, Fujimori's support ebbed.[21]

Those who wished to moderate international criticism after the coup noted Peruvians' disdain for political parties, implying that Fujimori was the country's only available popular leader. But the decline of political parties has been overstated. First, as noted earlier, for a full decade after the return to civilian rule, Peru enjoyed a broad and relatively stable party system. The 1990 elections, rather than indicating a collapse of the party system, reflected the fact that one of the traditional parties (APRA) was the discredited incumbent and a second force (the IU, United Left) had divided. The third traditional force backed a candidate whose policy positions failed to win him majority support. The decline of Peru's political parties in the 1990s is not only a result of disaffection among voters but also of intentional manipulation (lowering barriers to entry for candidacies, lowering incentives to participation for legislators, post-coup exile, and arrest for political leaders).

Likely Future Developments and Policy Implications

In a formal sense, democracy was restored in Peru after the April 1995 elections (elections, however, that were not free of irregularities). One hopes for a certain liberalization of the political system during Fujimori's second term (1995–2000).[22] Liberalization would require a reduced role of military tribunals in what are properly civilian cases; a return to regularized processes of promotion within the military; election rules that promote a stable party system, and hence a strengthened legislature; and the vigorous protection of human rights.

The reelected Fujimori government is unlikely to initiate such liberalization, however, of its own accord, and the government's military allies press it in the opposite direction, as the postelection amnesty for those accused of human rights abuses indicates. International policymakers must give very clear signals of their unwillingness to accept curtailments of democratic rights, even though they might be tempted to think of these curtailments as the price of policies they approve. Precisely the opposite signals were transmitted in the past. Policymakers and international institutions with strong preferences for the Fujimori government's economic reform program must be steadfast in support of true political liberalization. Similarly, international actors must realize that true political liberalization does not threaten to breathe new life into Peru's now nearly vanquished guerrilla movements, just as the turn toward authoritarian rule did not produce victory over those movements.

Signals emanating from the international community must be strong and unambiguous. What U.S. officials and representatives of international financial institutions say today enters into the Peruvian leadership's calculations of what it can and cannot do tomorrow. Past actions have been tainted by ambiguities. That international financial institutions eschew formal political conditionality should not lead them to believe that they play no role in politics. The IMF, World Bank, IDB, and other institutions have strong policy preferences; when they support politicians who advocate the policies they prefer, they can alter the domestic balance of power in developing countries. When such favored politicians destroy democratic institutions and justify their actions as necessary to sustain reforms, the IFIs are dragged, whether they like it or not, to the center of the arena of political conflict. In short, international actors cannot simultaneously hold policy preferences and remove themselves from any political role. The responsible alternative is to combine policy preferences with some general criteria for acceptable modes of governance.

5

Bolivia: Managing Democracy in the 1990s

Eduardo A. Gamarra

For the first time since the transition to democracy began in 1978, on June 6, 1993, Bolivians voted and elected a president on the same day. With almost 35 percent of the vote, the Movimiento Nacionalista Revolucionario's (MNR, National Revolutionary Movement) Gonzalo Sánchez de Lozada and his Aymara running partner, Victor Hugo Cárdenas scored a fourteen-point victory over the ruling Acuerdo Patriótico (AP, Patriotic Accord). Under the terms of a constitutional provision (article 90), however, when no candidate achieves an absolute majority, the national Congress must elect a president from the top three contenders. On August 6 Sánchez de Lozada won the congressional round and was sworn into office.

Things did not go as well for Sánchez de Lozada in 1989. Despite winning the elections, he was denied the presidency after a congressional coalition of the second and third place parties, Acción Democrática y Nacionalista (ADN, Democratic and Nationalist Action) and the Movimiento de Izquierda Revolucionaria (MIR, Revolutionary Movement of the Left) respectively, elected the latter's chief, Jaime Paz Zamora. That election, in turn, was a replay of 1985 when the ADN's General Hugo Banzer Suárez lost the presidency to the MNR's Víctor Paz Estenssoro despite winning the elections. This sequence highlights the complexity of the democratization process in Bolivia.

Transition, Governance, and Economic Reform

In a country where turbulent political change had been the norm, the 1993 electoral context may appear anomalous. In fact, democratization has not been easy. The transition to democracy came only after three decades of profound turmoil sparked mainly by the dynamics unleashed by the 1952 revolution. Between 1952 and 1964, the MNR nationalized the mining industry, declared universal suffrage, and approved an agrarian reform law. Moreover, the MNR initiated a state-led development strategy that, despite its overthrow by a military junta in 1964, lasted until the mid-1980s.

Throughout most of the 1960s and 1970s, a period that coincided with the most extreme days of the U.S.-directed national security doctrine, Bolivia was ruled by a variety of military rulers. While these military governments generally followed the contours of the state development strategy introduced by the MNR, they were distinct from one another mainly in terms of ideological and generational differences. Between 1978 and 1982, seven military and two weak civilian governments ruled the country. Coups and countercoups characterized one of the darkest and most unstable periods in Bolivian history. The unsolved dilemmas of the MNR-led revolution, worsened by decades of military dictatorships, accounted for Bolivia's convoluted transition to democracy.

Not surprisingly, the transition to democracy came during Bolivia's worst-ever economic crisis. Hernán Siles Suazo, the first civilian elected president to assume office, could do little to control hyperinflation, respond to pent-up social demands, overcome an opposition-controlled Congress, put down military coup attempts, and satisfy a hostile private sector. Even his own ruling coalition, the Unidad Democrática y Popular (Popular and Democratic Union), turned on the president. Among the many conspirators against the government was then vice-president Jaime Paz Zamora, who entertained the opposition's offers to topple Siles in a so-called congressionally sanctioned constitutional coup. The hapless Siles government was also trapped by demands from the international financial community for greater economic austerity and from the United States to carry out a controversial interdiction-based counternarcotics strategy.

Considering the magnitude of the crisis facing Bolivia, in the mid-1980s the challenge for any government was first and foremost to control the spiraling economic crisis. But the political challenges were equally pressing. Institutions, such as legislatures and parties, were undisciplined and constantly conspired to end prematurely Siles Suazo's mandate. Whoever came to power faced the impossible task of producing a government with both an executive and legislative force.

Between 1985 and 1993 Bolivia had two governments whose style of rule set in motion significant trends, which may not have solved the country's deep structural problems but fundamentally transformed the pattern of governance. The elections of 1985 brought back to the presidency for the fourth time Víctor Paz Estenssoro, one of the major leaders of the revolution of 1952 and arguably the most important statesman of twentieth-century Bolivia. Paz Estenssoro's government successfully introduced the Nueva Política Económica (NPE, New Economic Policy), until then, one of the most profound stabilization programs in Latin America. After sustaining his NPE for four years and ending the country's record-setting hyperinflation, in August 1989 Paz Estenssoro handed power to Jaime Paz Zamora. The NPE was judged so successful that with a few nuances, such as calls for social spending, all of the major contenders in subsequent elections in 1989 and 1993 pledged to uphold the program.

The key to the NPE's success was largely rooted in the deal president Paz Estenssoro struck with General Hugo Banzer Suárez to form the Pacto por la Democracia (Pact for democracy) between the MNR and the ADN. The pact was not a program of cogovernment but a legislative pact to support the Paz Estenssoro government and the imposition of the NPE. Behind the rhetoric about patriotism and newfound commitment to democratic values, the pact was an agreement through which ADN would share in state patronage by assuming control of a number of state corporations. A secret addendum (signed in May 1988) provided for the MNR to support Banzer's candidacy in the next election. In short, the pact provided the Paz Estenssoro government with an important device to end the gridlock between executive and legislative authority in Bolivia.

The pact institutionalized an important decision-making style that was arguably antidemocratic. In the national Congress, the members of the pact rubber stamped most executive initiatives, legitimating a policymaking process that gave no room for an open debate about economic policy. The pact also enabled the Paz Estenssoro government to control any challenges to the counternarcotics agreements signed with the United States. In many ways, this pattern of policymaking was reminiscent of the exclusionary processes of previous authoritarian experiences. The governing style introduced by the MNR called for an executive-centered system to "manage" the economy in much the same way in which a chief executive officer (CEO) manages a large corporation.

The decision-making style that resurfaced in 1985 was built upon a long tradition of recruiting "apolitical" technocratic advisors to bolster and lend credibility to the actions of a strong executive. In the 1970s, for example, military rulers surrounded themselves with civilian technocrats to implement an exclusionary decision-making process. As Malloy notes, Bolivian policymakers in 1985 reproduced the decision-making style of the authoritarian rulers they replaced by recruiting civilian technocrats to deal with the crisis and imposing a closed policymaking process.[1] Bypassing Congress, utilizing the military to impose states of siege, and neglecting or postponing the demands of social groups, the style of governance of these leaders clearly restricted access to the decision-making process. Because of its success, however, this decision-making style was perceived as the only way to implement Bolivia's highly touted NPE successfully.

In the 1980s the policymaking process allowed a number of business groups and other social actors greater access to the policymaking process. The common factor is that both authoritarian and democratic rulers determined the degree and the nature of access to the decision-making process. Defined narrowly, the key to governing Bolivia rests with how rulers frame access to the policy process.[2]

Not surprisingly, the most prominent person to emerge from this governing style was Gonzalo Sánchez de Lozada, a wealthy mining industrialist, who is owner and manager of the Compañía Minera del Sur (COMSUR, Mineral Company of the South), one of Bolivia's largest private mining enterprises. Sánchez de Lozada was not only one of the principal intellectual architects of Bolivia's NPE, but as the MNR's minister of planning between 1986 and 1989, he was the man charged with implementing neoliberalism. "Goni," as he is popularly known, became Bolivia's corporate-style CEO who slashed public spending, called for decentralization, deregulation, and privatization, and carried out most of the neoliberal reforms of the 1980s. His success as minister catapulted him to prominence and thrust him into the limelight as the MNR's presidential candidate in 1989.

The elections of 1989—basically a three-way race between Sánchez de Lozada (MNR), Banzer (ADN), and Jaime Paz Zamora (MIR)—produced no clear winner with Sánchez de Lozada winning a slight plurality of 23.07 percent, followed by Banzer with 22.70 percent, and Paz Zamora with 19.64 percent. For a number of reasons neither Banzer nor Paz Zamora would deal with Sánchez de Lozada, and hence they were left with each other. In a bizarre arrangement dubbed the Acuerdo Patriótico, which was either an act of statesmanship or of opportunism, Banzer and the ADN struck a deal with Paz Zamora and the MIR. This time it was a two-step arrangement first to elect Paz Zamora to the presidency and then to form a government in which Banzer would play a major role as head of a so-called Consejo Político del Acuerdo Patriótico (COPAP, Political Council of the Patriotic Accord), a bipartisan policy board that would oversee both political and governmental affairs.

Between 1989 and 1993 Bolivia was governed by the Acuerdo Patriótico. In contrast to the Pacto por la Democracia, this formal alliance lacked any real economic plan of its own and was largely perceived as the caretaker of the NPE policies introduced by Sánchez de Lozada and the MNR. The new pact emulated many of the dimensions of the MNR-ADN pact. First and foremost, it pushed through Congress legislation designed to deepen NPE economic reforms. Moreover, throughout its four-year period in office, the performance of the Acuerdo Patriótico, especially the MIR, was clouded by widespread accusations of corruption. As in most of Latin America, corruption associated with political parties had a tremendous impact on the fortunes of incumbents. The lack of any innovation in economic policy combined with corruption were key factors in the dramatic ascendance of Sánchez de Lozada in 1993 and also in the emergence of two key outsiders.

The Emergence of New *Caudillos*

Public perception regarding the nature of the three principal parties led to the emergence of two leader-dominated and populist-style parties, Conciencia de Patria (CONDEPA, Conscience of the Fatherland) led by Carlos Palenque and Unidad Cívica Solidaridad (UCS, Solidarity Civic Union) headed by Max Fernández. As in other Latin American countries, these neopopulist parties emerged outside of the political mainstream and delivered mainly an antipolitics message. Because they are led by strong men, both are reminiscent of old-style Bolivian *caudillismo*. It is probably a mistake, however, to explain their emergence solely as a result of the inability of the traditional parties to channel the interests of marginal sectors of Bolivia's population. The reasons are more complex and varied.[3]

One possible explanation is suggested by Guillermo O'Donnell's notion of "delegative democracy." Owing to the state's incapacity to enforce the law, the popular classes become disenchanted with the ineffectiveness of democratic institutions in resolving their problems. This disenchantment translates into political withdrawal and mass apathy. As these groups become more marginal, they "delegate" their grievances to these new leaders whose commitment to representative democracy is largely suspect. Through traditional mechanisms, such as clientelism and appeals to populism, these new leaders convey to the citizenry that participation within the framework of representative democracy is obsolete and undesirable. Moreover, they offer a more direct and unmediated channel of representation. In a direct way, these leaders offer some hope for the displaced sectors.

CONDEPA was successful because of the appeal of its founder, Carlos Palenque, a popular radio and television announcer revered by the Aymara-speaking working classes of La Paz. Palenque's nickname, "el Compadre," revealed that the basic logic of Bolivia's party system was still patrimonial. CONDEPA made huge inroads in the lower-class sectors of Bolivia's capital city. Through his Radio y Televisión Popular (RTP, Popular Radio and Television), for example, Palenque offered a unique alternative to Bolivia's often discriminatory administration of justice. Palenque's RTP programs, especially one called "La Tribuna del Pueblo," provided a quick "resolution" to the myriad social problems afflicting recent non-Spanish-speaking arrivals to the capital city, domestic servants, and the vast population of the informal sector that encircles La Paz. "Palenquismo," as Lazarte called it, provides the only linkage these groups have to the system.[4]

Since the 1989 elections, Palenque has attempted to develop a broader crossregional, crossclass, and interethnic base of support. After demonstrating his party's ability to win municipal elections (in 1989, for example, CONDEPA defeated all three major parties in La Paz and also won the race for mayor again in December 1991), Palenque moved decisively on several fronts. First, he expanded his base of local La Paz support by recruiting prominent defectors of the agonizing Left. He also attracted many members of the old nationalist Right. The most significant pillar of support was drummed up through the airwaves of RTP. Finally, to contest the national elections he courted prominent members of the Santa Cruz business sector.

The other threat to the traditional parties came from Max Fernández and his UCS. Beginning in 1989, Fernández converted the UCS into a mechanism to deliver promises and prebends to vast and remote sectors of Bolivia. The slogan "Max obras" (Max[imum] [public]works) became more than a simple political statement. Throughout the country, Fernández built hospitals and schools, paved roads, and handed out sporting equipment and generators.[5]

Fernández first made his appearance in 1986 when he purchased enough stock to control the Cervecería Boliviana Nacional (CBN, Bolivian National Brewery), Bolivia's largest brewery. Fernández, a Cochabamba native of humble background, claimed that his business skills enabled him to establish a monopoly over the commercialization and distribution of beer in Santa Cruz, which he then used to control the entire company.[6] It is worth noting that control over the commercialization and distribution of beer in Bolivia of the mid-1980s was indeed a very profitable venture. During the hyperinflationary period of 1984–85, for example, rumor had it that the government could pay its salaries only when the CBN paid its taxes.

Much speculation has surrounded the origins of Fernández' fortune. Until recently the U.S. embassy was obsessed with indicting him for alleged ties to the narcotics industry. Little evidence to indict Fernández was ever produced. In 1993 U.S. embassy officials considered it imprudent to go after Fernández primarily because of the increase in his popular support.[7] This contrasts with the obstacles placed in his path during the 1989 elections, when U.S. embassy pressure forced the National Electoral Court to prohibit him from running for office.

Because Fernández' UCS was not allowed to run in the 1989 elections, it held no seats in the National Congress. The Acuerdo Patriótico government and the opposition parties used this as an excuse to exclude him and his party from all major and minor negotiations. This exclusion ended abruptly during the December 1991 municipal elections when the UCS showed its strength on a national scale. Since then the UCS has been a part of every attempt to negotiate reforms to the electoral law reform, and Fernández has played a prominent role in all political party agreements to reform the constitution signed since 1989.

Fernández runs the UCS in an authoritarian manner, and, in classic populist style, control over his political party is determined by his capacity to deliver prebends. His wealth has enabled him to establish a wide network based on old-style vertical and hierarchical patron-clientelism. Fernández names the party leadership; no assemblies or elections are held to elect the governing body of the UCS. Most striking, however, is Fernández' rather unappealing personality. He lacks charisma, speaks Spanish poorly, and is unable to articulate any party platform coherently. To overcome these shortcomings, Fernández has hired prominent members of the political class, who generally present UCS campaign promises. As Lazarte argues, however, Fernández resembles Gonzalo Sánchez de Lozada in many ways. Both are entrepreneurs, CEOs, and pragmatic men of action rather than words.[8] Although both appeal to the same social sectors—the lower middle classes and the urban proletariat—Fernández' humble social origins may give him an electoral advantage.

Most appealing to the working classes was Fernández' innovative employer-worker relations at his brewery. Workers in the CBN enjoy high wages and other benefits not available to blue collar employees elsewhere in the private or public sector. Reportedly, on one occasion when the Acuerdo Patriótico government decreed a wage increase, Fernández doubled the salaries of his workers. Periodically newspapers carry declarations from grateful workers who defend him from his political opponents.[9]

In short, Fernández and Palenque resorted to patrimonial methods to mobilize support during elections. Like all other parties in the system, however, the central objective of CONDEPA and UCS is to penetrate the party system and obtain access to state patronage through the formation of alliances with the three principal parties.[10] The irony of these neopopulist parties is that, while they have emerged partially in response to the patrimonial practices of the traditional parties, Fernández and Palenque use the same methods.

Palenquismo and Maxismo shared the same constituency, and the electoral battle demonstrated that this was, in fact, a most important political battle. Palenque, and not the traditional parties, for example, often raised charges of Fernández' alleged links to the drug industry. In 1993 Fernández slapped a libel suit against Palenque and, true to form, announced that if he were to win the suit he would donate the U.S.$10 million to homeless children and to senior citizens.

In any event, both Palenquismo and Maxismo may have been born out of public disdain for the three principal political parties resulting from their inability to aggregate the demands of the popular sectors. They became key national political options that are unlikely to disappear, although their support will ebb. Yet their actions, rhetoric, and personal histories demonstrate only a vague commitment to democratic values. Moreover, as Lazarte notes, the social sectors that support both parties are only superficially committed to democracy because no other option is available.[11] Of course, the same could be said

about nearly every social sector and political group in the country. Palen-
quistas and Maxistas have organized neither in favor nor against representative democracy, but outside of the democratic process. Hence,
although Fernández and Palenque can play a positive role by attempting to integrate these excluded sectors into the institutions of the democratic process, they could also tilt the balance against democracy.

In sum, the popular sectors attracted to Palenquismo and Maxismo
may be reluctant to accept the logic of representative democracy and
may also be swayed by the promises of a more direct form of democracy. Uncomfortable with the mediation of parties, these sectors in
Bolivia have historically displayed an affinity for a direct relationship
with the leader. It is important to note, however, that Palenquismo and
Maxismo may have played a crucial role in the stability of Bolivian democracy and may have become the only mitigating force that has prevented the emergence of radical groups among the marginal sectors of
Bolivia.

Sánchez de Lozada and the Agenda for the Mid-1990s

Gonzalo Sánchez de Lozada's campaign in 1993 raised a great deal of
expectations across the social spectrum mainly because of the image he
had developed over the previous eight years. To vast sectors of the electorate, "Goni" was a man of action who would deliver all of the promises
made during the campaign. To the working class, the MNR platform
offered the best hope that, in some measure, demands for higher wages
and the alleviation of the levels of critical poverty brought about by the
economic crisis of the 1980s would be met. Sánchez de Lozada's campaign platform, dubbed "el Plan de Todos," promised to reduce the impact of market-oriented reforms introduced in 1985 that stabilized the
economy but brought only low growth rates.[12] Most of the electorate,
but especially the middle class, believed his promises that corruption
in government would be eliminated.

The election of Víctor Hugo Cárdenas of the Movimiento Revolucionario Tupac Katari (MRTK, Tupac Katari Revolutionary Movement) as
vice-president constituted a significant watershed. The symbolism associated with the MNR's ticket is worth noting. In the MNR's campaign, Sánchez de Lozada and Cárdenas were portrayed as "children of
the revolution" in a calculated attempt to tap into those social sectors
that were once strongly identified with the MNR, such as the peasantry, but that had long abandoned the party. As the first Aymara to
achieve such high office, Cárdenas brought with him a great deal of
expectations of the indigenous sectors of Bolivia. Cárdenas delivered a
huge voting bloc of mainly rural Aymara *campesinos* to the MNR.
Moreover, to prevent the growth of guerrilla-type movements that used
ethnic symbols to mobilize support, Cárdenas represented the most

important hope for bridging ethnic and linguistic cleavages and extending Bolivia's young democracy to the indigenous masses.[13]

Despite its obvious margin of defeat, the ruling AP did not immediately concede the victory to Sánchez de Lozada and Cárdenas. General Hugo Banzer Suárez, the AP's candidate and former de facto president, refused to recognize the MNR's victory, correctly claiming that the constitution still gave them the option of contesting the presidency as no candidate had achieved 50 percent of the vote. As the results filtered in, confirming an embarrassing defeat, the old general's grip over ADN, his own party, faltered.

One sector of Banzer's ADN initiated negotiations with CONDEPA to give the presidency to the populist Carlos Palenque, who had won only 14 percent of the vote. Another reportedly entered into talks with Sánchez de Lozada. By mid-June, internal disputes between members of ADN became public and in some cases vicious. A similar situation developed inside the MIR, as factions positioned themselves for the next four years. About the only clear trend was the dissolution of the AP and the almost certain fragmentation of ADN and the MIR, its component parties.

The first confirmation of the MNR victory came when Antonio Araníbar of the Movimiento Bolivia Libre (MBL, Free Bolivia Movement) announced his unconditional support for Sánchez de Lozada. With only 5 percent of the vote, the MBL lent its support, expecting some role in the future government. The MBL's announcement had an immediate impact. On June 8, Banzer took the face-saving but belated decision to congratulate Sánchez de Lozada and promised that the AP would vote for the MNR in Congress in August. Paz Zamora, in turn, delivered an impassioned speech stressing the need for a peaceful transition and the development of a stable ruling coalition to ensure the governability of Bolivian democracy and the continuity of economic reforms.[14]

Sánchez de Lozada's search for a governing partner culminated in yet another surprise. On July 2 the MNR struck a deal (dubbing it the "Pacto de la gobernabilidad," Governability Pact) with Max Fernández, Bolivia's controversial beer baron and chief of the UCS. As in all previous pacts, the distribution of key government posts in exchange for the UCS's twenty-one seats in Congress sealed the agreement.[15] Moreover, Sánchez de Lozada was able to broker the first visit by Fernández with the U.S. ambassador since accusations had surfaced of his alleged ties to narcotics trafficking. The MNR's deal making did not end there. On July 7 Sánchez de Lozada signed a Pacto por el Cambio (Pact for Change) with the MBL doling out yet another set of government posts.[16] With his election in Congress assured, Sánchez de Lozada departed for Washington to sell his new government to the State Department and other U.S. government agencies that closely followed the deal making in Bolivia.

Implementing El Plan de Todos

On August 6, 1993, Gonzalo Sánchez de Lozada became the fourth democratically elected president of Bolivia since the transition from military rule to be sworn into office. At issue was how the Sánchez de Lozada government and the new ruling alliance would deliver their campaign promises and press ahead with market-oriented reforms. Despite having had two months to prepare an orderly transition and hit the ground running, the new government stumbled and staggered in its first few months in office. On his first day in office, Sánchez de Lozada named only ten ministers as part of an ambitious project to reduce the size of the executive branch. The actual plan as such did not go into effect until September 17; the opposition promptly accused the government of creating a tremendous power vacuum. Of the ten ministries, three areas—finance, services, and production—became "super" ministries and were turned over to prominent members of the private sector.[17] Filling the nearly one hundred other posts in the ten ministries, however, took a long time mainly because the government failed to secure the congressional approval of the decree regulating the reorganization of the ministries. Fernando Illanes, one of the "super" ministers, made a stir when he claimed that the delay in filling posts was a result of the lack of honest and capable candidates in Bolivia.[18]

The MNR's ambitious Plan de Todos, which promised a social-market economy alternative to the rigid continuity of the New Economic Policy, must be evaluated with a degree of caution. The plan included seven "pillars": attracting investment; job creation; ensuring economic stability; improving health and education; popular participation; changing the role of government; and combating corruption. The key to the MNR's investment proposal rested on the "capitalization and democratization" of public enterprises, a significant departure from the dogma of privatization. Contrary to privatization advocates, the MNR proposed to "increase the capital of the principal state enterprises [YPFB, National Hydrocarbons Enterprises of Bolivia; ENAF, National Smelting Company; ENDE, National Electricity Company; ENTEL, National Telecom Enterprises; LAB, Bolivian National Airways; and ENFE, National Railroad Enterprises] through foreign investment, but maintaining a majority participation of Bolivian citizens in said enterprises to convert them into the effective owners. . . . At least 51 percent of stock holdings in these enterprises will remain in Bolivian hands, while foreign partners will own up to 49 percent of stock."[19]

In February 1994 the Bolivian Congress approved a capitalization law that essentially authorizes a joint venture association in which a state enterprise contributes its assets and a private investor contributes an equivalent amount in capital. In theory, this would double the original value of the enterprise. Once an enterprise is capitalized, the investor would receive 50 percent of the company's stock and sole management control. The remaining stock would be distributed evenly among the 3.2 million Bolivians over the age of eighteen.[20] The government also claimed that this program would result in the creation of half a million new jobs. According to government consultants, besides capitalizing six state enterprises, the government would also privatize the state retirement system by partially funding the establishment of private pension funds.[21]

The government also promised that revenue from the sale of state enterprises (expected to reach about U.S.$8 billion) would be employed in a pension fund for all Bolivians over the age of eighteen. Government economists argued that the capitalization of state enterprises would be equivalent to investing approximately 35 percent of Bolivia's GDP (gross domestic product). In 1993 foreign investment dropped relative to 1992, and public investment more than doubled overall private investment.

While turning over the ownership of state assets to Bolivian citizens and workers and the establishment of a pension fund were an important shift from pure privatization, its feasibility was questionable. Nevertheless, the very notion of workers becoming shareholders of former state companies was a unique innovation in the current Latin American neoliberal era. Whether this arrangement will serve to attract foreign and national investors is still doubtful. Nearly two years after the law's enactment, even the promise of granting national and foreign capital the administration of former state monopolies has yielded few takers.

In his first two years in office, Sánchez de Lozada discovered that it was quite difficult to govern efficiently and simultaneously deliver the promises made during the electoral campaign. In fact, the new president has not modified the general thrust of austerity policies. One of the government's first acts was to "relocate" nine thousand middle-class workers. Almost immediately the government faced major confrontations with the Central Obrera Boliviana (COB, Bolivian Worker Central), which regained some of the strength it lost in its battles against the two previous administrations. Opposing Sánchez de Lozada's relocation of workers plans and his efforts to "capitalize" state enterprises, the COB staged general strikes and stoppages and forced the new government into church-mediated negotiations. To quell labor unrest, the government announced a so-called Relief Plan (Plan Alivio). Additionally, the government opened a "Bolsa de Trabajo," where workers who made less than Bs.1,000 monthly would receive a stipend of Bs.500. The only problem has been that most workers make less than Bs.1,000 and the Bolsa de Trabajo never found a steady funding source. The government produced several innovative programs aimed at reducing the state's payroll. In late 1993 the government offered a U.S.$1,000 bonus per year of service to workers who chose to retire voluntarily from the mining sector. At closing time on February 28, 1994, the deadline established by the government, about one thousand workers had taken the government's offer. These measures, however, were not enough to satisfy labor's demands. As will be seen later, the recurring plot of the conflict with the COB—threatened and actual general strikes, failed negotiations, and church mediation—eventually forced the government's hand.

The health of the economy was probably the most pressing aspect of governance facing the Sánchez de Lozada government. Years of austerity under the NPE and falling social indicators led to deteriorating conditions throughout Bolivia. In the rural areas, for example, 90 percent of the population lives in poverty compared to about 40 percent in the urban centers. Basic services such as potable water are not available to 65 percent of the population in rural areas. To revert these trends in Bolivia, it is clear that more than just "good governance" will be required.

Basic economic indicators, however, point out that at least in terms of growth rates, inflation, interest rates, exchange rates, and international reserves, the situation is at least stable. In 1993 inflation reached only 9.31 percent, the lowest in South America, and the economy grew a moderate 3.18 percent. Open unemployment continued to drop, reaching only 5.4 percent in 1993. The government has had a very difficult time keeping its electoral promise of creating 250,000 new jobs and improving the working conditions of another 250,000. But Bolivia's basic problem is the concentration of wealth in a very reduced sector of the population. With a poverty rate exceeding 70 percent of the population, social tensions are likely to explode if the trend is not reverted. Events in April 1995 revealed that ten years of economic stability and GDP growth had not alleviated the social situation and led instead to great unrest.

Legislative Successes

During the first twelve months of the Sánchez de Lozada government, five significant laws were passed by Congress including the cabinet restructuring law, the capitalization law, the popular participation law, the education reform law, and the constitutional amendments law. As far as government officials were concerned, this body of legislation provided a reform agenda as far-reaching as Bolivia's 1952 National Revolution.

The most innovative of these laws was the popular participation law (discussed in the following section). As mentioned above, the cabinet restructuring law reduced the number of cabinet ministries from seventeen to twelve. The new cabinet included a politically correct Ministry of Human Sustainable and Economic Development that served to launch Bolivia's successful bid to host the 1996 Presidential Summit of

the Americas on Sustainable Development. The approval of the capitalization law signified the beginning of a unique new plan to dismantle
state enterprises. As of this writing, the National Electricity Company
(ENDE, Empresa Nacional de Electricidad) has been capitalized, and
government officials were optimistic that the remaining five enterprises would be capitalized in the future. The proposed pension plan,
however, was another story, as the concept has been developed but not
fully implemented.

The education reform law was aimed at strengthening Bolivia's public school system, which has been in a severe crisis for the better part
of the last two decades. In some measure the reform intended to decentralize school management by turning over these responsibilities to
elected municipal governments and other legally recognized community groups. The law also links municipal, provincial, departmental,
and national citizens' groups with the national education secretary.
The new law established mechanisms to monitor teacher qualifica-
tions and academic standards, and promised to increase teacher compensation. Government officials noted, however, that the intent of the
new law is to establish an educational system that reflects local "cultural, linguistic, and ethnic identities, stressing primary education, the
education of young girls, and early education in the native language of
pupils." This, of course, is an opinion not shared by most of the unionized teachers around the country, who oppose the new law. In March—
and, as will be seen, in April 1995—the Teachers Union held the
government at bay and prevented the implementation of the law by
literally taking over the streets of La Paz.

President Sánchez de Lozada's intention during his second year in
office was to dedicate time to "govern in detail," to enact and implement his "revolutionary" set of five laws. Sánchez claimed that while
his first year was filled with legislative successes, he had not been able to
govern effectively. Sensitive about these shortcomings, Sánchez intended
to "govern" for the rest of his term. His record in 1994–95 was not remarkable, and his leadership came increasingly under heavy scrutiny.

The Popular Participation Law

The popular participation law, promulgated on April 21, 1994, may radically change the territorial, economic, and democratic conditions of
local government in Bolivia. The government claims that the transfer
of political and economic power to municipal governments, along with
increased social participation, is a revolutionary process equivalent to
the 1952 transformation of the country.[22] Territorially, the new law de-
fines the municipality as a section of a province and places every rural
and urban square inch of the nation under the political-administrative

jurisdiction of one of about three hundred municipal governments. It also provides a relatively large amount of financial resources to municipal governments on a per capita basis. In short, the popular participation law may eventually ensure that central government resources that have been accumulating in the central bank since early July 1994 will be disbursed to the newly constituted municipalities. Moreover, it grants legal status to traditional citizens' groups at the grass-roots level, arguing that it will facilitate their participation in and oversight of municipal government.

According to the government, during the law's first year more than three hundred municipal governments were established. With the resources they receive from the state, these have initiated the construction of more than one thousand schools, sanitary posts, roads, public bathrooms, and the like nationwide. The government expected nearly eight thousand such projects to be completed in 1995. As of April 1995, approximately three thousand communities and neighborhood associations had been recognized with an additional seven thousand pending.

The popular participation law proved to be quite popular internationally, as extensive media coverage of its implementation painted a very positive picture of a law intended to empower local government and allow citizens to decide how revenues would be spent. Domestically, however, the law was a much more difficult sell. The principal accusation was that the so-called territorial base communities and the vigilance committees were less instruments of "accountability" and more MNR mechanisms to control local government. The truth probably lies somewhere in between; however, the opposition used this as a rallying cry against the government. Moreover, the popular participation law appeared to go against the grain of previous administrative decentralization initiatives. In addition, the law bypassed the powerful civic committees in each city and department, who considered the new law a potential threat to their vision of decentralization. Civic committees called for an elected prefect in each department and a weaker municipal council. In April 1995 this debate came to a head with a severe confrontation, with regional civic committees from Tarija, Santa Cruz, and elsewhere demanding the implementation of a decentralization law.

Sánchez de Lozada and the Armed Forces

Sánchez de Lozada's relations with the military have also been problematic. His difficulties with the armed forces should not have been surprising given that the commanders of the armed forces did not welcome the MNR's victory in the June 1993 elections for at least two reasons. First, the commanders feared a full-blown investigation into charges of corruption by members of the armed forces and their allies in the outgoing Paz Zamora administration. Second, the armed forces were wary of both Sánchez de Lozada's lack of expertise in civil-military relations and the MNR's historic favoritism toward the police. Sectors within the institution believed the MNR would attempt to politicize it.

For the Bolivian armed forces, the process of adapting to democracy has been quite difficult as it faced a tremendous reduction in its prerogatives and waged a battle with the police over the scarce foreign economic resources provided by the counternarcotics campaign. In contrast, the national police adapted quickly to the new democratic process and regained prerogatives it had lost during the military period and, in fact, appropriated several additional prerogatives normally reserved for the armed forces. With Sánchez de Lozada and the MNR in office, the armed forces feared a continuation of this trend.

In October 1993 Sánchez de Lozada sacked the entire armed forces command, bypassed the next *tanda* (graduating class) in line for command, sent thirteen generals into early retirement, and named a new command comprised of officers deemed to be free of corruption. Older officers publicly expressed their outrage and voluntarily retired. General Carlos Casso Michael, for example, noted that while a "soldier must obey the orders of the captain general of the armed forces, as a person I cannot allow myself to be under the command of a promotion that was younger than mine."[23] The response from both the sacked officers and those sent into retirement sent a clear message that the Bolivian armed forces are still a major power contender. General Moisés Shirique, who was in line for commander of the army, retreated into the Estado Mayor and refused to follow the president's directive. In the tense days that followed, Shirique was rumored to be preparing a coup attempt. Although Shirique eventually desisted and accepted a new position as chief of staff, the confrontation was severe enough to warrant concern over the course of civil-military relations in Bolivia.

The changing of the guard may have come at a particularly problematic moment for the armed forces, especially the army. Within the institution several groups—such as Vivo Rojo of Trotskyist leanings, Tres Estrellas, a self-described institutionalist movement, and Movimiento Boliviariano (Bolivian Movement) of nationalist tendencies—have made their demands known publicly. Pamphlets and other items have circulated widely, revealing a great deal of internal turmoil. At least three issues appear to be generating internal dissent. First is the increasing reliance on U.S. military assistance tied exclusively to the counternarcotics effort. At issue more specifically is the increasing presence of U.S. military personnel in civic action exercises. Second is a general sense that democracy has not been generous to the institution. Officers argue that there is an inverse relationship between the military's support for democracy and the benefits it has derived. In other words, instead of being rewarded for defending democracy, the institution has been severely penalized through budgetary restrictions and attempts to privatize its enterprises.

Related to this issue is what many military officers consider another inverse relationship between their support for democracy and improvements in the conditions of the police forces. In the past decade, the police institution has increased in size, its budget has expanded, it has had virtually unlimited access to U.S. funds, and, at least according to disgruntled military officers, the MNR government has covered up corruption within the police force. Moreover, some officers are convinced that the time is ripe in Bolivia for the emergence of subversive groups and that the military is now unprepared to respond.

Despite these problems, the naming of the new military command in October 1993 averted a major investigation into charges of corruption and may have indeed prevented an even more serious confrontation with the armed forces. In the following months the armed forces appeared satisfied with the deal worked out with Sánchez de Lozada. But tensions with civilians resurfaced in January 1994 when the *Bolivian Times*, an English-language newspaper owned by foreign journalists based in Bolivia, revealed that military lodges (*logias*) tied to Colonel Luis Arce Gómez, the former minister of interior under García Meza who is currently serving a thirty-year sentence in a U.S. prison, had placed a bomb in an airplane that crashed in 1969 and carried out the murder of two prominent journalists who were about to uncover an alleged arms trafficking network.[24] A few days later, however, the story took a bizarre turn when it became clear that the reporters from the *Bolivian Times* had been sold a fictitious story by none other than Antonio Arguedas, the man who, after a stint on the CIA's payroll, sold Che Guevara's diary to Fidel Castro. The incident was dismissed as an attempt to discredit the armed forces; the commanders, in turn, reiterated their commitment to protecting the constitution. No perceivable danger of a military coup is visible in the near future, but it is clear that civil-military relations require constant nurturing.

The unraveling social situation in early 1995 forced the Sánchez de Lozada government to rely on the armed forces for a great number of missions. As was already the case under previous governments, the MNR has increased its reliance on the armed forces for maintaining order in the Chapare, Bolivia's largest coca growing area. And, as was also the case under the two previous governments, the military was charged with enforcing a state of siege imposed on April 18, 1995. The armed forces were given added public security roles that included the right to arrest and detain hundreds of striking labor leaders.

A Fragile Ruling Coalition

Few would dispute that Bolivia's institutional and legal matrix made governing the country difficult, and it is no wonder that president Sánchez de Lozada made institutional reform the centerpiece of his government. To understand the institutional dilemmas, it is important to review some of the principal features of the process of transition to democracy and the place of institutional dynamics in the democratization process that followed.

The difficulties faced by Bolivia during the transition to democracy highlight the current debate about constitutional reform and gave ample ammunition to those who advocated replacing presidentialism with a parliamentary system. Yet the continuity of the Bolivian experience demonstrates that ways out (or *salidas*) of severe crises were not the product of an abstract debate among political scientists but the result of the creativity of political leaders responding to a specific set of circumstances. In other words, Bolivian political leaders produced hybrids between old-fashioned tools of governing and the "modern" thrust of neoliberalism and democratization.

To reiterate a point made earlier, to govern Bolivia in the context of a severe political and economic crisis and demands from the international community to carry out counternarcotics programs, decision makers had to deal with several issues simultaneously. Perhaps most significant was the necessity of dealing with pressing institutional questions ranging from electoral laws to constitutional reform. A recurring issue involved relations between the branches of government: every president since 1982 has had to face and attempt to resolve executive-legislative impasses.

This task translated into a crucial need to build coalitions not only of groups in civil society but also among the political parties that had fought intense and bitter electoral battles. Coalition building in Bolivia has required three aspects: electoral coalitions, required to compete for formal power; congressional coalitions to achieve control of the executive branch following the vote in Congress; and ruling or sustaining coalitions to support governments and specific policy lines. The important characteristic of this process has been the ability of some leaders to craft coalitions both to get elected and to govern.[25]

Political coalitions, such as the Pacto por la Democracia (1985–89) and the Acuerdo Patriótico (1989–93) and the current Pacto por el Cambio (Pact for Change) (with the Movimiento Bolivia Libre, MBL [Free Bolivia Movement]) and the Pacto por la Gobernabilidad (Governability Pact) (with the UCS), played several key roles. They linked the domestic arena with international themes, such as market-oriented reforms, provided support for governments, and enabled these to carry out specific policy initiatives. Since the mid-1980s the dynamics of coalition formation and competition have driven the process of democratization.

The recurrent need for political coalitions institutionalized a quasi-parliamentary feature, which has essentially convérted Bolivia's political system into a hybrid form of presidentialism. This has been the key to governance in Bolivia. The hybrid nature of the country's presidential system facilitated the implementation of stabilization measures and contributed to the continuity of the democratization process.

As of this writing, most relevant political actors perceived that they had a stake in the system and pursued strategies aimed at coalition formation. Some analysts point to the recurrent practice of coalition formation as a sign of the maturing of the Bolivian political party system.[26] As discussed elsewhere, political parties are still primarily vehicles to capture and circulate state patronage among the dependent middle classes. Political parties are driven more by issues of access to patronage than in constituting programmatically focused governments. Nevertheless, parties are an essential part of governing Bolivia not only because they are the principal source for the recruitment of future leaders but because they are responsible for bringing democratic governments into and out of office. The paradox is that political parties are both the principal source of the difficulties of governing and the only real source of a potential solution.

Given this immediate legacy, Sánchez de Lozada faced the critical task in 1993 of forging an alliance that could resist any challenges from the opposition. Unlike 1985, however, the governing pacts the MNR entered into with the MBL and UCS were extremely fragile. Despite this fragility, Sánchez managed to carry out a great deal of his agenda, albeit at a snail's pace. Most of the government's problems rested with the nature of the ruling coalition, which had difficulty controlling its ranks as both interparty and intraparty disputes proved destabilizing. A recurring conflict between the president's party and the cabinet was problematic, leading to at least three major cabinet shifts in two years. Sánchez de Lozada's first cabinet was comprised of technocrats and businessmen, while Congress was left in the hands of the MNR's old guard. A joke circulating among the opposition in the early months illustrates the problem. According to this version, Sánchez de Lozada forgot that to govern Bolivia one must always make a pact with the MNR. These tensions eventually produced a cabinet crisis in March 1994 forcing Sánchez de Lozada to replace the private sector members with members of the MNR. Predictably, as problems occurred with its private sector allies and with the political parties in the coalition, the government charged ahead with the *movimientización* (the movement to staff the cabinet with MNR members). In 1995, with only one notable exception—foreign minister Antonio Araníbar—the entire cabinet was made up of MNR personnel.

The ruling coalition proved extremely unstable. On any given week, unsubstantiated rumors abounded about a split or defection. Fernández, who felt excluded from the decisions taken by the government, lashed out often against the MBL and the MNR. He was finally ushered out of the coalition in late 1994, and his party showed serious internal splits. More important, however, the defection showed serious problems of stability in the ruling coalition.

By the same token, the MBL found itself in the difficult position of having to defend policies it had opposed over the previous eight years, such as U.S.-designed counternarcotics programs and deepening "neoliberal" economic reforms. A "national summit" held in January 1994 with Sánchez de Lozada cemented the MNR-MBL relationship, and the coalition is still together as of this writing (February 1996). Antonio Araníbar, the MBL foreign minister, performed extremely well and, at least according to opinion polls, was the most popular member of the cabinet. A more accurate picture would reveal that the MNR has engulfed the MBL and that its fate may be entirely in the hands of Sánchez de Lozada and the MNR. Despite attempts by members of the MBL to retain their identity independently of the MNR, the fact remains that the future of this small band of well-intentioned former leftists is tied intimately with the fortunes of this government.

In the early phases of the Sánchez de Lozada period, it appeared that if these alliances held, the MNR could garner enough power to make all other parties irrelevant and achieve single-party status to close out the twentieth century. This statement can be understood, however, only by explaining the crisis of the opposition political parties. The origins of the crisis are rooted deeply within the confines of a vast web of political corruption that unraveled in early 1994.

Corruption and Political Parties: Toward a Hegemonic Party?

President Sánchez de Lozada faced an all-out battle with opposition political parties from the very day he took office. In November 1993, for example, a few members of the two former ruling parties (ADN and MIR) called for his impeachment and/or the convocation of early elections. Then in December, when the MNR-controlled Congress amended the electoral law, the opposition parties charged Sánchez with attempting to rig the rules of the game to favor his party. Despite the absence of a constitutional mechanism to shorten his term, the opposition repeatedly called for a revocation of the president's mandate.

But these moves were not significant as these parties faced internal crises that could force their disappearance. The unraveling of the opposition warrants more concern because it is intrinsically linked to the explosion of political corruption that has plagued Bolivian democracy and that has serious repercussions for the governability of the country.

After it left office in August 1993, ADN became engulfed in a tremendous internal political battle as a result of General Banzer's retirement from politics in November of that year. Banzer's retirement confirmed the institutional weaknesses of ADN, especially the inability of the party to name a viable successor. No single individual appeared capable of bringing the party together in time for the 1997 elections. ADN's internal crisis was fueled by speculation of widespread corruption during the 1989–93 period. In late 1994, to avert the complete collapse of ADN, General Banzer returned to politics and will apparently run for office in 1997.

Concern for corruption in office became the single most significant factor in the total collapse of the MIR. Since August 1993 former president Paz Zamora attempted to distance himself from his party and attempted to pursue lofty international objectives that included possible stints at the Wilson Center in Washington, D.C., and serving on the International Peace Commission in Chiapas, Mexico. These goals, however, were dramatically altered with the March 1994 accusations by the Special Counternarcotics Force (FELCN, Fuerza Especial de Lucha Contra el Narcotráfico) that widespread linkages between the MIR and narcotraffickers have existed since at least 1987.[27] These accusations extended to the entire leadership structure of the MIR and put a serious damper on the party's quest for a return to political office at mid-decade. In a dramatic sequence of events, drug traffickers described in painful detail before congressional committees the manner in which Paz Zamora and the MIR had allegedly come to rely on the cocaine industry to finance their electoral campaigns. The impact of these accusations was great. On March 25, 1994, Paz Zamora resigned from politics claiming that "errors were made during his administration but no crimes occurred."

Paz Zamora's own appearance before the congressional committee added an important dimension to the process. In a four-hour-long testimony, the former president accused the United States of conspiring to unravel the MIR because Paz Zamora had dared to invite Cuban president Fidel Castro to the August 1993 inaugural ceremonies. Whatever the merits of the MIR's defense, the alleged linkages between the MIR and traffickers appeared to confirm previous charges of widespread corruption when that party was in office.

In December 1994 the FELCN indicted, arrested, and imprisoned Oscar Eid Franco, the MIR's second in command, for charges related to the party's linkages to the drug industry. In early 1995, despite the accusations against him, Paz Zamora surprisingly reemerged as the only person capable of saving the MIR and, along with Banzer, the only one capable of unifying the opposition. While polls did not favor him—he barely received a 5 percent rating in most polls—the average person in Bolivia in early 1995 believed that Paz Zamora would run for office in 1997.

With the demise of the Acuerdo Patriótico and the troubled future of ADN and MIR, the only real opposition force was CONDEPA, the populist party headed by Carlos Palenque, which in the December 1993 municipal election expanded its support outside of the department of La Paz and again won the mayor's office in the capital city. In 1995 CONDEPA appeared to be the only party capable of posing a serious challenge to the MNR. During Sánchez de Lozada's first year in office, all signs were that the MNR could achieve hegemonic party status. But impressions in Bolivia do not last long. By April 1995 the MNR was well on its way to its own unraveling, and the Sánchez de Lozada government appeared headed for a very rough final two years.

Constitutional Reform

The principal challenge in Bolivia in the 1990s was to determine whether the ad hoc arrangements of the 1980s and early 1990s, which were dependent on specific personalities and conjunctures, could be transformed into stable institutional changes. Both the Paz Estenssoro and Paz Zamora governments generated central authority by reducing the power and influence of other institutions such as legislatures, parties, labor unions, and the judiciary. This appeared to be the trend in the Sánchez de Lozada government as well. In his first two years in office, Sánchez de Lozada relied mainly on his cabinet to design and implement policies and used Congress merely as a rubber stamp mechanism. Paradoxically, these exclusionary practices resulted in high support for democracy among the Bolivian masses but overwhelming rejection of parties, legislatures, and judiciaries, the principal institutions of representative democracy.

It became increasingly clear, however, that the Bolivian government would have to consult with the very same institutions that were so denigrated in the previous years. It was also clear, however, that substantial reforms would have to be considered and effected by political institutions in the next few years. These could enhance the process of democratization; they could also serve to create more trouble for whomever sits in the Palacio Quemado.

Two reforms are illustrative of this dilemma. The first involves yet another reform to the electoral law. Aimed at resolving both the difficulties in electing a president and garnering a majority in Congress, the new electoral law proposed a German-style system whereby 50 percent of the lower house will be elected by single-member district norms and the rest will be allotted by the current proportional representation system.[28] The single-member pattern may indeed ensure a majority in the Chamber of Deputies, which would in turn facilitate the election of a president. At the same time, however, the new law may limit the access to the system of smaller parties and erode the faith in the system of larger parties that lose in single-member districts, leading to an unwillingness to enter into pacts. Critics note, for example, that the single-member district would facilitate the election of a majority in the lower house reinforcing the rubber stamping role of the Congress.

A second debate over constitutional reforms is illustrative of the pattern of confrontation faced by the Sánchez de Lozada government. In April 1993 the three principal parties signed a law "on the necessity to reform the constitution." Signed into law by then vice-president Luis Ossio, the law paved the way for proposals such as a five-year presidential term, the eighteen-year-old vote, the congressional election of a president from only the top two vote-getters, and the establishment of a constitutional tribunal that would perform a judicial review function.

In January 1994 this law became a great source of controversy as two conflicting interpretations emerged. On one side, members of the opposition parties argued that a constitutional convention must be elected to reform the constitution. The government argued that the April 1993 law passed with the deliberate intention of avoiding a constitutional convention that could throw out the entire constitution instead of focusing on only a few articles.[29] In any event, this debate was resolved in the government's favor in the early part of 1994 as it took its case before the national Congress it controls. Sánchez de Lozada achieved the reforms he had long sought; however, the outstanding question was whether these would make governing Bolivia any easier.

The answer to the previous question does not lie in the judiciary, which became engulfed in the worst crisis of the century. Owing largely to allegations of corruption at every level, the judiciary was one of the least respected institutions in Bolivia. Notwithstanding the prevalence of corruption, the most serious problem facing the judicial system was still Bolivia's multiethnic population and the lack of access most of the population has to the country's courts. By law, all proceedings must be conducted in Spanish, even though this is not the primary language for a substantial percentage of the population. It is not surprising, therefore, that a large proportion of the population bypasses the judicial system and seeks an alternative form of justice. Until now, the principal alternative has been the emergence of Carlos Palenque, the populist presidential candidate and radio and TV talk show host.

Proposals to reform the judiciary abounded, but the government's aim to adopt a constitutional tribunal prevailed. Such a tribunal would presumably become an "apolitical" chamber for judicial review handling all constitutional claims and thus averting the type of debilitating interbranch confrontations that have characterized Bolivia's political system in the past several years. The constitutional tribunal would simultaneously serve as a constitutional complaint council where individual citizens would bring charges of human rights violations and the like.[30] Opponents of the tribunal argued that it would establish a fourth branch of government that would essentially undermine the judiciary. Whether this new institution will resolve the kinds of problems of access and unfairness that have characterized the system remains to be seen.

In August 1994 thirty-five articles of the constitution were amended through the constitutional amendments law including: direct election of half of the members of the lower house of Congress from single-member districts; an increase in the terms for presidents, members of parliament, mayors, and municipal council members to five years, with general and municipal elections alternating every two and a half years; clear procedures favoring the direct election of the president and all mayors; voting age lowered to eighteen; increased powers to departmental prefects; departmental assemblies composed of national representatives doing double duty as the only assembly members of the department from which they were chosen by the single-member district procedure; the establishment of an independent human rights ombudsman; and the establishment of a constitutional tribunal. These reforms are significant and warrant an extended discussion beyond the scope of this chapter. Suffice it to say that the most significant in the medium to long term may have to do with the way in which members of the lower house of Congress will be elected. If the reform is successful, legislators may indeed become more like the districts they ostensibly represent. Opposition to these reforms is also evident. Charges abound that two types of legislators have been created: those elected through single-member districts who will see themselves as true representatives and the rest who will be seen as pure party hacks. Moreover, there is no guarantee that this reform will foster coalition building, the only strength of the Bolivian system.

Coca and Cocaine: The Principal Foreign Policy Issue

Despite promises to the contrary, the Sánchez de Lozada government pursued the same U.S.-designed counternarcotics strategy of its predecessors. Given the fact that the government had to implement outstanding agreements with the United States, this was no surprise. Between August 1993 and January 1994, Bolivia was one of the principal recipients of civic action missions related to drug control missions; moreover, U.S. presence in the country increased. Initially, things appeared to go well on the bilateral front. The Bolivian government unveiled a new so-called Option Zero that called for industrial projects and mass training programs for coca growers in exchange for the complete eradication of illegal coca leaf crops. These efforts and programs received extensive praise from Lee Brown, the U.S. government's drug czar. But all was not well on the counternarcotics front.

In 1993 and again in 1994, the cultivation of coca crops expanded, and the government again failed to meet established eradication goals.

As a result, for two consecutive years the White House recommended to the U.S. Congress that Bolivia be granted only a "national interest certification," a probationary type of certification. Future noncertification could result in a complete cut-off of U.S. economic assistance and a negative U.S. vote on multilateral agency support for Bolivia.

Sánchez de Lozada faced an all too familiar dilemma: comply with agreements with the United States and, at the same time, prevent any civil unrest in the coca-growing regions. The government's initial response was forceful; for the first time since the coca-cocaine theme came to dominate U.S.-Bolivian bilateral relations, a Bolivian government recognized that the coca crops in the Chapare region were grown exclusively to provide raw material for the cocaine industry. Predictably this fueled a major confrontation with the peasant unions of the Chapare. The government's policy to eradicate coca forcefully headed toward an all-out confrontation with peasant coca growers. In early March 1994, for example, eradication workers clashed violently with peasants in the Chapare. For the Bolivian government, things did not appear to work out at any level.

Then in early September 1994, confrontations with peasants in the Chapare increased as the government arrested prominent union leaders. Coca growers unions staged a march on La Paz demanding an end to eradication policies, police and military actions in the coca-growing regions, and a broader set of issues including greater funding for alternative development programs. The coca growers march stirred a national debate that in some measure prompted a reexamination of bilateral agreements with the United States. This strategy, however, did not pay off as Washington simply tightened the noose.

The U.S. national interest certification of Bolivia in 1995 stirred numerous other conflicts with coca growers and in some measure contributed to the launching of a state of siege in April. The United States issued an ultimatum that in no uncertain terms stated that the government must reach a specific eradication goal by July 1, 1995, and approve an extradition treaty or face a withdrawal of economic assistance. In its haste to satisfy U.S. demands, the Bolivian government agreed to the eradication terms and negotiated an extradition treaty. The Chapare coca growers, however, were not pleased with the U.S. ultimatum. In short, the confrontation between the government and coca growers could escalate considerably in 1995 and lead to unpredictable outcomes.

The Future of Democratic Governance in Bolivia

In April 1995 Bolivia faced a general strike by the COB, a teachers strike demanding an end to educational reform, an incipient separatist movement from the southernmost department of Tarija, and a potential insurrection by coca-growing peasants in the Chapare Valley. Responding to these pressures, president Sánchez de Lozada declared a state of siege on April 18 for a ninety-day period. Shortly before midnight on April 18, the military and police arrested hundreds of union leaders and confined them to remote jungle towns in northern Bolivia.

The problems confronting the Sánchez de Lozada government had dragged on for six weeks. Demanding that the government rescind the educational reform law that would ostensibly leave them unemployed, striking teachers erected roadblocks, threw dynamite sticks at police, and, in general, paralyzed life in the capital city. In the Chapare, coca growers unions organized a movement, presumably to resist the government's attempts to enforce a voluntary and involuntary coca eradication program.[31] The COB, in turn, was in its thirteenth day of a general strike to protest low salaries and the government's refusal to give in to demands for higher levels of social spending. Finally, after staging a march with twenty thousand or so supporters, civic leaders in the city of Tarija threatened to secede from Bolivia if the central government refused to implement a decentralization law that would establish stronger local governments.

Throughout most of Bolivia, public opinion had little or no sympathy for the striking workers and teachers. Most Bolivians wondered when and if the government would take decisive action to end the strikes that prevented them from going to work or walking the streets without dodging tear gas, rubber bullets, and rocks. President Sánchez de Lozada's attempts at establishing dialogue with the strikers, with the mediation of the Catholic Church, were seen mainly as a reflection of the weakness and indecisiveness of the government.

On April 19, 1995, the day after the state of siege was declared, public opinion in general favored President Sánchez de Lozada's decision to mobilize the armed forces and arrest labor leaders. Television "man on the street" interviews reflected a sense of relief and support for the reestablishment of order in the streets. Most did not question why the rules of exception had been implemented; instead, they wondered why the government had taken so long to react. A taxi driver quoted in the *Miami Herald* captured this generalized sentiment and highlighted an all too common reaction throughout Latin America: "What we need here is a Fujimori who, as in Peru, will enforce the principle of respect for authority, will put things in their place, and will resolve the country's problems without cutting any political deals."[32]

It is still too early to make any assessment of the impact of the state of siege under way in Bolivia. If the past will be repeated, then labor unions will be weakened considerably and will resurface in a few years to contest the process of neoliberalism that the government has promised to sustain for the rest of the century. The likelihood of greater unrest is high, however, as this is the first time that any government—military or civilian—has targeted coca growers, unions, and civic committees simultaneously. All three sectors have legitimate claims that will not go away.

If President Sánchez de Lozada's statement to the military academy a day after launching the measures of exception, that in modern democracy the role of the armed forces is to sustain the legally constituted regime, is a sign of things to come, then Bolivia can expect an even greater reliance on the military to carry out public security matters.

What can be learned from the recent Bolivian experience? First, we now know that imposing and sustaining market-oriented reforms in a small and poor country is a very difficult task indeed. A decade after the imposition of Decree 21060, Bolivia has reached a critical juncture. Although the country's economy has grown steadily, averaging 2.5 percent per year, this has not been enough to deal with declining socioeconomic conditions in the country. Three democratically elected governments since 1985 have imposed states of exception to deal with labor and other social unrest. In the process, they have relied on the armed forces to engage in public security missions.

Second, the Bolivian experience suggests that decision making must be largely executive-centered, with legislatures playing little or no legislative role other than approving executive initiatives. To achieve this, stable ruling coalitions are essential to avoid executive-legislative impasses. In some sense, however, this style of rule has resulted in a profound crisis of all major political institutions. Political parties are perhaps more disconnected from society in 1995 than at any time since the transition to democracy in 1982. The legislature and the judicial branch rank at the bottom of citizen confidence. Third, the Bolivian case suggests that profound constitutional reforms are difficult to enact but even more difficult to implement. The Sánchez de Lozada administration's promise to resolve age-old problems of representation and administration of justice will take time to take hold and have an impact. Few in Bolivia, however, are willing to give the reforms a chance to succeed, as the only term that is of significance there is the short term.

Fourth, it is clear that successive Bolivian governments have done quite a bit over the course of the past decade to fit into the neoliberal wave that has engulfed the Americas. Yet the relative insignificance of the country in regional affairs has resulted in little international interest or investment. Innovative ideas, such as the capitalization initiative of the current government, have received extensive praise from international financial institutions, but the program cannot survive on praise alone.

Finally, the Bolivian experience reiterates what Central American countries learned in the 1980s. Countries that are the target of U.S. security concerns will have an even more difficult time with governance. Every government in Bolivia will continue to be trapped by numerous domestic and international ramifications of the counter-narcotics issue. In 1995, confrontations with coca growers reached their highest level ever, and given current trends there appears no short-term solution. This trend is likely to aggravate if U.S. insistence on eradication persists. The state of siege measures that were imposed in April 1995 were but the beginning of what is likely to escalate into a full-blown confrontation between the government and coca growers. All proposals to solve the problem, ranging from the Bolivian government's zero option to Washington's renewed focus on targeting the supplying countries, are infeasible and will invariably translate into a major problem of governance for any Bolivian president.

6

Chile: The Political Underpinnings of Economic Liberalization

Timothy R. Scully, C.S.C.

In terms of the two axes of economic and political liberalization, Chile differs in a number of important ways from other contemporary cases in Latin America. First, more than a "transition" to democracy, Chile (along with Uruguay) should be considered a case of "redemocratization," of reviving previously well-established democratic practices and political institutions. Institutional legacies from Chile's democratic past continue to shape contemporary politics in decisive ways. Second, though comparatively tardy in returning to democratic rule, Chile's move toward economic liberalization was by far the earliest and probably the most far-reaching in Latin America. Moreover, with respect to sequencing, Chile constitutes the region's only unambiguous example of a regime transition *following* substantial economic liberalization.

This distinctive path serves notice that lessons from Chile may be difficult to draw in a way that travels comfortably from one context to another. Rather than drawing lessons from the Chilean case, this chapter explores the political underpinnings of Chile's rather comprehensive economic liberalization. More precisely, I seek to analyze the relationship between Chile's democratic political heritage, its authoritarian interlude and continuing authoritarian *amarres* (ties), and the exemplary economic policies and performance of contemporary Chile.

In many ways, Chile has been extraordinarily fortunate. I argue that the contemporary consensus over economic policymaking, and the government's capacity to implement these policies effectively, rest not only upon Chile's democratic heritage, nor entirely upon certain legacies of the authoritarian period, but rather precisely upon the combination of these experiences. Strong political institutions arising from the democratic past, made in part more conducive to consensus policymaking by authoritarian holdovers built into the 1980 Constitution, have endowed Chile's democratic government with a remarkable capacity to implement and sustain coherent economic policy.

After a brief review of the results of economic policies in today's Chile, this chapter explores key elements of the political context that have facilitated its success. I argue that Chile is able to sustain a profound process of economic liberalization better under democratic conditions than would have been possible under dictatorship, in part because of the reappearance of Chile's well-institutionalized party system, and in part because of a crucial shift in the ideological center of gravity toward moderation. Ironically, certain nondemocratic limits built into the democratic game by the dictatorship of Augusto Pinochet, for the time being at least, have also contributed to making democracy and economic reform both possible and compatible in Chile.

Beyond Liberalization: Growth with Equity

By now the turbulent story of economic restructuring designed and carried out from the mid-1970s through the 1980s by the most repressive regime in Chile's history is familiar enough. The fruits of the relatively orthodox shock therapy applied to Chile's economy were first visible mostly in terms of the deep economic and social dislocations it produced. After almost a decade of rather freewheeling neoliberal experiments in the 1970s and early 1980s, brief cycles of economic boom and bust had resulted in virtually no growth in per capita income. However, by the mid-1980s a more pragmatic set of economic policies had restored overall macroeconomic balance to the economy, resulting in steady growth from 1985 onward.

Though almost certainly more disruptive than it needed to be,[1] the overall program of economic liberalization carried out by the Pinochet government nonetheless endowed the country with a relatively solid foundation for economic growth. The expansion and diversification of the export sector, and the emergence of a more dynamic and competitive business class—largely legacies from the Pinochet era—contributed decisively to the country's newfound status as the region's showcase economy.[2] In 1992 the Chilean economy outperformed even optimistic government predictions, growing at the brisk annual rate of 10.3 percent, with unemployment at a remarkably low 4.9 percent of the work force and inflation at a reasonable level (12.7%). During 1993 growth remained high at 6 percent, yielding an average growth rate for the Aylwin period (1989–93) of more than 6 percent. By the end of the Aylwin period, practically every macroeconomic indicator, including inflation (11.5%), unemployment (4.6%), investment in fixed capital (27.2% of GDP [gross domestic product]), domestic savings (21% of GDP), productivity and wage rates (both growing more than 4.5% annually), all pointed to the same phenomenon: Chile is booming.[3] The first years of the Frei government have been marked by the same success: inflation in single digits and falling, foreign reserves at U.S.$14.8

billion and rising, a booming export sector (growing more than 25 percent in 1994), and foreign investment continuing to pour in. Though Chile surely experienced a painful and disruptive economic adjustment, in 1995 Chile had an economy that it was difficult to find fault with. Indeed, the Pinochet experience has raised larger comparative questions about the relationship between authoritarianism, democracy, and the possibilities for successful economic restructuring.

While there is little argument that the opening of the economy and the deliberate drive to pursue export-led growth have positively affected growth, there is likewise no room for doubt about the effects of these changes on distribution under Pinochet. As many authors have shown, there was a seamy side to Chile's "economic miracle."[4] By the end of the Pinochet period, income distribution had worsened considerably: the poorest 40 percent of households in Santiago saw their share of consumption fall from 19.4 percent in 1969 to 12.6 percent in 1988, while the share of the richest 20 percent rose from 44.5 percent to 54.9 percent. By all measurements, the proportion of families defined as living in poverty and extreme poverty had risen dramatically during the years of authoritarianism. For example, in 1987, 44.7 percent of all Chileans lived in poverty; 16.8 percent were classified as indigent.[5] From 1970 to 1988, total social expenditures per capita fell 8.8 percent; health expenditures alone fell by nearly 30 percent.[6] As Eugenio Tironi put it, by the end of the military regime, Chile had become in some respects a "dual society" wherein a large portion of the population was left without the benefits of the miracle.[7]

Observers have emphasized the many ways in which post-Pinochet economic policy simply mimics that initiated by the Chicago Boys. However, these assertions are unfair. A central component of the Aylwin administration's economic strategy sought to demonstrate that growth need not necessarily come at the expense of equity. The first major piece of legislation enacted by the new democratic government in 1990 was tax reform, which collected an additional 2 percent of GNP (gross national product) and boosted tax revenues by approximately 15 percent, making it possible to increase government spending on social programs from 9.9 percent to 11.7 percent of GDP.[8] Between 1989 and 1995, government social spending rose by 50 percent in real terms.[9] Chile's government was spending unprecedented resources on social programs, including training and vocational programs for youth, an expanded public health program, and an ambitious public housing initiative. Perhaps most strikingly, at the same time that Aylwin's government sought to address the more urgent social demands inherited from the Pinochet regime, the public sector experienced growing budget surpluses every year he was in office. Income distribution improved during the Aylwin administration, with the income share of the wealthiest one-fifth of the population falling from 59.9 percent in 1989 to 54.7 percent in 1991.[10] The numbers of Chileans living in poverty fell between 1990 and 1995 by more than one million people, from 40.1 percent of the population to 28 percent.[11] Though far from eliminating the enormous social debt incurred during the military dictatorship, the Aylwin and Frei administrations have made important progress in bringing about a more equitable distribution of the fruits of economic growth.

Chile's born-again conversion to private initiative and the market has been remarkably complete, but it would be misleading to suggest that privatization has removed the state entirely from the market scene. The conversion to private initiative and markets requires a strong state with ample initiative and regulatory capacity, and Chile is endowed with a relatively coherent state apparatus with a long-standing developmentalist tradition. The Chilean state continues to play a key role in coordinating economic activity, but it is undergoing its own transition from the predominantly entrepreneurial state dating from the years of import-substituting industrialization to the contemporary regulatory state.[12] In fact, several fundamental aspects of the precise role the state will play in Chile's future development, such as the nature of state involvement in the giant (as yet still nationalized) Chilean copper industry, have yet to be resolved and still haunt the political landscape like ghosts from another era.

The Reemergence of Strong Democratic Political Institutions

I argue that the restoration of what was previously a long-standing democratic regime endowed the Aylwin administration with unusual leverage to craft coherent economic policy. And, perhaps more than any other feature of this transition, the recovery of strong, viable, and relatively well-institutionalized political parties provided the Aylwin government both the legitimacy and the initiative capacity to do so.[13] Despite the vast social debt left by the Pinochet regime and earlier blistering critiques of neoliberalism by those who now comprise the leadership of the Concertation Alliance, the Aylwin government has not deviated from the authoritarian regime's fundamental free market orientation.[14]

With the return of competitive politics after 1988, parties resumed their role as the backbone of the Chilean political system.[15] The reappearance of Chile's institutionalized party system facilitated the possibility for coherent policymaking in the post-Pinochet era because it allowed for political participation and conflict in ways that did not overwhelm the political system.[16] Faced with seventeen years of pent-up popular demands, Chile's institutionalized party system has been key, together with organized labor, in helping government policymakers express and channel social conflict, directing it toward recognized institutions. Where party systems are less well institutionalized, such as is the case in Brazil, Ecuador, and Peru, presidents may enjoy widespread backing in congress—and therefore broad executive initiative capacity—at moments of peak popularity. Yet such backing often evanesces in the legislature with signs of diminishing public approval. Chile's institutionalized party system by no means assures congressional support for government initiatives, especially given its problematic multiparty presidential character, but it increases the likelihood.[17]

The degree to which a party system is institutionalized provides an important key for understanding success or failure of efforts at economic restructuring in many Latin American countries. It is no accident, for example, that the leadership of Chile's Concertation government (as well as the political leaderships of Costa Rica and Uruguay) have eschewed rule by executive decree (*decretismo*) for carrying out economic policy. Where parties and other political institutions, such as congress and the judiciary, are well established, presidents must deal with them and negotiate major policy directions. These political institutions help orient economic actors by laying down clear and legitimate rules of the game, and for this reason they help ensure a framework of predictability for economic decision making. With well-established political institutions such as coherent and well-organized parties, actors are more likely to know the rules of the game and generally have some sense of how to pursue their interests, even when surprises occasionally confront them. Institutionalized parties are certainly not a sufficient condition for explaining successful economic policymaking in new democracies, but they may be necessary. However, in addition to the degree of institutionalization present within a party system, it is also important to explore the kinds of parties and the ways they interact.

The reappearance of a highly institutionalized party system is a key legacy from Chile's democratic past, but the dynamics that characterize the contemporary party system differ in significant ways from its pre-coup predecessor.[18] Several of these differences greatly affect the capacity of the democratic government to formulate and pursue coherent policy. First, current party leaders, with the exception of the communists and a minority of socialist leaders on the Left, and to some extent the Unión Democrática Independiente (UDI, Independent Democratic Union) on the Right, now try to emphasize the centrist nature of their positions and programs. Renovación Nacional (RN, National Renovation) insists repeatedly that it is a "Center-Right" party, and the Unión del Centro Centro (UCC, Center-Center Union) puts this notion into its very label. This reorientation toward the center is especially striking among a majority of the socialists. Whereas in the late 1960s and early 1970s the predominant group in the party was influenced by the Cuban Revolution and espoused positions generally considered to be to the left of the communists, most—and in the case of the socialist-inspired Party for Democracy (PPD), virtually all—are now close to the current, more liberal outlook and policies of the Spanish socialists.[19] As a result of these changes, the Chilean party system—at least during the years of the democratic transition (from 1988 to the present)—is no longer characterized by the same sharp ideological cleavages between the main parties as was the case before the 1973 breakdown, and therefore is not currently subject to the centrifugal pulls of polarized pluralism.[20]

Crucially, today there is a rough consensus over fundamental issues pertaining to the nation's socioeconomic institutions, and voters are not asked to choose between radically different models of development. This general ideological convergence toward the Center and, in terms of economic policy, toward export-led growth and free markets, has sharply reduced conflict, thereby making it far easier to formulate and implement coherent policies. This is not to suggest that dissenting voices, such as that of the (now greatly diminished) Communist Party (MIDA), are completely absent. Notwithstanding, there is perhaps as much or more ideological consensus on the appropriateness of the current economic model in Chile today as there was correspondingly widespread agreement in the 1940s on the correctness of import-substituting industrialization led by a strong developmentalist state.[21]

Second, and equally consequential for the Aylwin government's capacity to shape successful economic policy, the pattern of party alliances during the Aylwin years is very different from what it was in the late 1960s and early 1970s. Whereas in the earlier period the Christian Democrats were at loggerheads with the parties of the Left and the Radicals, and in the early 1970s the Christian Democrats struck an alliance with the Right to oppose the Popular Unity government of Salvador Allende, the Concertation government is comprised principally of Christian Democrats and parties that were formerly part of the Popular Unity government, except for the communists. Two decades ago the coalitional patterns were determined mainly by support or opposition to the left-wing government of President Allende, while more recently they have been determined by party acceptance or rejection of the military regime.

This change in the pattern of political coalitions is of the utmost importance. By introducing a new dimension of party division along the lines of support or rejection of the military government, it has submerged—at least for the time being—traditional sources of conflict between the parties, contributing to the decrease in ideological distance between them.[22] The current Chilean party system has been recreated in a manner reminiscent of the Popular Front governments in the late 1930s to late 1940s, when there was also a Center to Left alliance, but an alliance in support of a very different socioeconomic model (that of import-substituting industrialization). The principal differences in terms of political support between the Concertation and the Popular

Front coalitions are that the Christian Democrats, and not the Radicals, now act as the fulcrum of the party system at the Center, and that the Communist Party, whose vote is a fraction of what it was then, does not belong to the present coalition. The differences separating the two periods in terms of economic policy are far greater, replacing a state-directed development model with Latin America's most liberal, market-oriented economy.

These changes in Chile's political landscape have powerfully reinforced the capacity of the democratic government to pursue a strategy of pacts and *acuerdos* (agreements) leading to successful economic policies. The symbolic importance of Finance Minister Alejandro Foxley, a Christian Democrat, and Economics Minister Carlos Ominami, a socialist, both early and intractable opponents of the Chicago Boys, reinforced the first Concertation government's efforts to strengthen Chile's export-led growth strategy. Their leadership lent to the current economic model legitimacy that it never enjoyed under the military regime. Since both the Christian Democratic and socialist parties have traditionally identified themselves as opponents of unbridled capitalism, the fact that they now find themselves leading the efforts to sustain inherited liberal economic policies places them in some respects in an even stronger position vis-à-vis economic liberalization than the Chicago Boys![23] At home their economic policies commanded the support of practically the entire spectrum of political opinion, and abroad they became a model for developing countries undergoing economic and political liberalization.

Recovering Democracy within the Framework of the 1980 Constitution

Democratic governance returned to Chile with the inauguration of Patricio Aylwin in March 1990, yet the battle toward full recovery of a consolidated democratic political regime has been a difficult and, to date, unfinished one. The institutional framework inherited by the Aylwin government is loaded with features built into the 1980 Constitution that constrain and potentially undermine the authority of the democratically elected government.[24] Though much of the 1980 Constitution restores familiar republican elements to Chile's democratic institutional order, it also includes institutional privileges for the military and its political allies that are inimical to the democratic process.

Within the framework of the 1980 Constitution, Pinochet and his supporters ostensibly sought to craft a "protected" capitalist democracy and to resolve once and for all the most fundamental conflicts that had rocked twentieth-century democratic politics in Chile. While economic managers Sergio de Castro and Miguel Kast were busy designing and implementing dramatic policies aimed at liberalizing the economy, the regime's chief ideologist, Jaime Guzmán, and others were drawing up the legal framework to support them.

Perhaps more crucial than any other feature, the inviolability of private property enshrined in the 1980 Constitution resolved, at least for the time being, a central axis of decades of social and political conflict in Chile and a key source of uncertainty in the economic arena. Ever since the new constitution took effect, the Supreme Court has consistently given a narrow interpretation to the constitutional provision that "protects the right to private property of all persons" (article 19). In contrast to the 1925 Constitution, expropriation is now possible only by legislation specifically "authorizing expropriation by virtue of public utility or national interest." "In all cases," the constitution continues, "the owner will have the right to indemnification for any alienated property," the total compensation being fixed by common agreement or adjudicated by a decision of the appropriate court. Given the interpretation of these clauses by the Supreme Court, any expropriation must be compensated at market value and with full cash payment in advance.

The sacrosanct status of private property enshrined in the 1980 Constitution, combined with constitutional provisions placing strict limits on the role of the state as entrepreneur, in a country where laws traditionally carry a great deal of weight, has contributed mightily to resolving the problem of economic credibility and has contributed to a positive climate for domestic and foreign investment. This provision, together with the creation within the constitution of an independent central bank and important changes in the ideological climate referred to above, reinforced confidence among entrepreneurs that the parameters of economic policy will not fluctuate unexpectedly. That none of the major political actors in post-Pinochet Chile has challenged either the fundamental inviolability of private property or the limited role of the state is a telling indicator of just how much the nature of the political agenda has changed. As a consequence, compared to the days of factory takeovers and land seizures that preceded the 1973 coup, the stakes involved in politics have been dramatically reduced, resulting in a shrinkage of the political arena itself.

Additional features of the 1980 Constitution granted institutional privileges to the military and its allies. For example, it grants the Chilean armed forces tutelary powers within Chile's political arena.[25] Whereas the only reference made to the armed forces in the previous constitution stated that "The armed forces are obedient and nondeliberative" (article 22 of the 1925 Constitution), the 1980 document states that "The armed forces . . . exist in order to defend the nation, and are essential in order to procure national security and to guarantee the institutional order of the republic" (article 90 of the 1980 Constitution). Though the constitution stipulates that the heads of the respective branches of the armed forces are subordinate to the president, the most critical element of that subordination, the power of appointment and removal, is absent for a period of eight years, thereby virtually tenuring the entire command structure of the military until 1997. As a result, the same military leaders who commanded the armed forces during the dictatorship—including Pinochet himself at the head of the army—have continued to do so since March 1990.

To assist the armed forces in carrying out their new tutelary role, the 1980 Constitution (as amended by plebiscite on July 30, 1989) created a National Security Council whose purpose includes, in addition to ensuring national security, examining all matters that may "gravely undermine the bases of the institutional system" (articles 95 and 96). Of the eight positions on the National Security Council, four are to be occupied by the heads of the army, navy, air force, and national police. Two other members were named, indirectly, by General Pinochet before leaving office. General Pinochet's control over this body was enhanced by the creation of a Strategic Advisory Committee, an agency comprised of approximately fifty full-time staff persons designed to keep watch over every aspect of national policy and to give political advice to Pinochet. In addition to its other responsibilities, the National Security Council is charged with designating two of the seven members of the Constitutional Court.

The institutional autonomy of the armed forces enshrined in the 1980 Constitution is further enhanced by a number of policy domains reserved for the privileged action of the military. As J. Samuel Valenzuela notes, in contrast to the diffuse and generally ambiguous character of tutelary powers, reserved domains "remove specific areas of governmental authority and substantive policy making from the purview of elected officials."[26] For instance, the 1980 Constitution prescribes that the defense budget may never fall below the amount spent in real terms by the military government in its last year. Lest there be some misunderstanding, the law also states that funds to ensure these levels of military spending must be provided automatically from 10 percent of all copper sales by the state-owned National Copper Corporation (CODELCO). Elected government officials cannot interfere in the preparation of military budgets or the acquisition of armaments, and thereby are barred from making changes in military doctrine or from altering the curriculum of studies in the military academies. Perhaps most important, military intelligence, which was deeply involved in human rights violations during the seventeen-year dictatorship, is also left entirely in the hands of the armed forces.

The continuing presence of General Pinochet at the head of the army has been a considerable source of concern for both the Aylwin and Frei governments. Though, at the outset of his presidential term in 1989, Aylwin asked Pinochet to resign his command "for the good of the country," Pinochet openly refused to do so. While the other military branches, the navy, air force, and national police, have adjusted their rhetoric and even much of their behavior to the reality of civilian rule, the army and its top leadership have at different times been openly critical of both the Aylwin and Frei governments. The army's hard-line stance has been especially visible in its continuing and vehement objections to investigations of abuses committed by the military during the authoritarian period. In December 1990, while top military leaders, including Pinochet's son, were undergoing judicial and congressional review for misuse of government funds, the army garrisoned its troops, precipitating rumors of an impending coup. Again in May 1993, unhappy with the Aylwin administration's insistence that the constitution be amended to curtail the autonomy of the armed forces, and indignant at a new court interpretation of the 1978 amnesty law that allowed courts to investigate human rights violations, Pinochet called army units to general quarters and surrounded public buildings in downtown Santiago with soldiers dressed menacingly in battle fatigues. The drama of this event occasioned a firm public rebuke to Pinochet by President Aylwin, who insisted that "no demonstration of force from state institutions, individuals, or private groups will lead to solutions."

Aylwin later reflected sullenly that he may have been "overly optimistic" in 1991 when he had affirmed that the transition to democracy was complete in Chile. "Events have clearly shown that key institutional aspects have yet to be resolved in the Chilean transition."[27] Deep unhappiness within the ranks of the army became perhaps most evident during June and July 1995 when, after the arrest of the former head of Chile's dreaded secret police, General Manuel Contreras, public demonstrations of "off-duty" army personnel critical of the Supreme Court's decision to put Contreras and his army accomplice behind bars for the Washington, D.C., murder of Orlando Letelier once again placed in high relief the army's ambivalence toward the institutions of democracy. In sum, an important obstacle still blocking Chile's path to full democratic consolidation is the institutional autonomy granted to the military in the 1980 Constitution.

The sharply increased role of the military within the state set forth in the 1980 Constitution might well have been substantially mitigated if the electoral majorities won by the Concertation for Democracy in 1989 had translated into a proportional number of congressional seats. In such case, key elements of this "perverse institutionalization" might have been removed by way of congressional reform.[28] However, two mechanisms—a heavily biased electoral formula and the presence of Pinochet-designated members of the Senate—have prevented the preferences of the electorate from being fully represented in the composition of the membership in Congress.

Electoral systems in most democracies are biased in the sense of un-derrepresenting minority parties and candidates. However, the elec-toral formula adopted by the Pinochet regime departs from this practice. The electoral law provides that, for the elections of both dep-uties and senators, each congressional voting district (or region in the case of senators) elect two candidates. Parties are allowed to form elec-toral alliances, or "lists," in order to maximize the vote obtained by a given political tendency. For a single list to obtain both seats in a given voting unit, the list achieving the majority is required to double the combined total of their nearest competitors, thereby allowing (at least theoretically) a list obtaining minority support (33.4% or more in the case of only two lists; the percent decreases the more lists there are) to win one-half of the seats. This system was designed to provide maxi-mum representation of the second-highest lists, which in this case are partisans of Pinochet.

In addition to systematically favoring the candidacies of the minor-ity rightist candidates, the boundaries of electoral districts erected by the military regime made extensive use of gerrymandering. For example, since opposition to Pinochet in the plebiscite of 1988 tended to be much more concentrated in urban areas, urban electoral districts were given far less representation proportionally than rural areas.[29] While Santiago accounts for 40 percent of Chile's population, it is represented by only 26 percent of the nation's deputies. Whereas twenty small rural districts containing one and a half million people elected forty deputies in 1989, the six most densely populated urban districts, also accounting for one and a half million people, elected fourteen deputies. The same dis-tortion occurred in the design of senatorial regions. In practically every case, the lines of districts and regions were drawn in such a way as to overrepresent areas that voted for Pinochet in the 1988 plebiscite.[30]

The results of the 1989 elections demonstrated the effectiveness of the military regime's electoral formula for rewarding the Right and punishing the Left. The law's most egregious effects were reflected in the allocation of seats in the Senate. In the 1989 elections, whereas the Right (National Renovation, the Independent Democratic Union, and various independent candidates) obtained 42.2 percent of the Senate seats with 33.9 percent of the vote, the Left won only 12.5 percent of the Senate with 20.6 percent of the vote. The country's largest party, the centrist Christian Democrats, were left largely unaffected, winning 34.2 percent of the upper house with 32.3 percent of the vote.[31]

It would be misleading, however, to focus the analysis of the impact of the electoral formula exclusively on election results. In some ways a far more important consequence of the regime's electoral formula is the almost inexorable bipolar logic the new electoral rules impose on all the major political actors. Since the rules are designed to reward the two largest political alliances and at the same time punish small or nonallied parties, parties are left with practically no choice but to join together to form large coalitions and alliances. This imposed bipolar logic has resulted in several unintended consequences for the major political parties. First, intense pre-electoral negotiations between party leaders within the same alliance play a decisive role in selecting candidates for office in each district. These often result in arcane intra- and interparty deals, wherein popular candidates are sometimes sacrificed by their own party leadership and prevented from running in the interests of the larger alliance ticket. In some cases, these practices have led to revolts among local party rank and file who view these as opportunistic electoral calculations of national party leadership and an attempt to thwart popular choice.

While this practice has had its costs for the various partners within the Concertation Alliance, it has been especially divisive among the parties of the fractious Right. Tension within the Right has been further heightened by two additional factors. First, a nettlesome populist leader, Francisco Javier Errazuríz, and his Center-Center Party joined forces with the rightist alliance to compete in the 1993 elections, thereby further complicating the already acrimonious relationship between the two major parties of the Right, National Renovation and the Independent Democratic Union. Second, whereas the logic of competition permits the Concertation to aim for both seats in any given electoral unit, the (expanded) Center-Right alliance, termed the Union for the Progress of Chile, could realistically hope for only one seat in each district. The larger number of actors within the alliance, combined with the reduced stakes, have made pre-electoral negotiations and intra-alliance electoral competition among the parties of the Right intensely competitive.

The legislative "fail-safe mechanism" of the Pinochet-inspired 1980 Constitution is its provision for nine designated members to be added to the thirty-eight elected members of the Senate.[32] According to article 45 of the constitution, four of these "institutional" senators are chosen by the National Security Council from among retired commanders in chief of the army, navy, air force, or national police; two are chosen by justices of the Supreme Court from among retired justices, and a third must be chosen by the justices from among retired attorneys general of the republic; one is to be chosen by the president of the republic from among ex-rectors of an officially recognized university; and finally, the president selects one from among former cabinet ministers. Fifteen days after Pinochet lost his bid to stay in power in October 1988, the names of those designated to hold positions were announced to the public. Not surprisingly, all of those chosen were unwavering supporters of General Pinochet.

Repeated efforts by the Aylwin and Frei administrations to remove nonelected members of the Senate failed to gain the support of the

Right. In effect, the former allies of the Pinochet regime have used the presence of their elected colleagues to veto legislation they consider incompatible with the institutional legacy of the military regime. The Concertation Alliance has found itself in a very difficult position: its capacity to respond effectively to antidemocratic features of the institutional framework left behind by the military regime has been severely constrained by the strength of the Right in the Senate. Even with an electoral formula that overrepresented more conservative rural areas, if the Senate had been free of designated members, parties loyal to Aylwin would have controlled 60 percent of the seats in the lower house and 58 percent of the Senate. This would have permitted the government much broader freedom in enacting its legislative agenda. Ironically, however, this feature of the 1980 Constitution and other constraints left behind by Pinochet have forced the new democratic government to govern by seeking to gain the consent of its opponents, thereby strengthening the political system's newfound culture of consensus.

By the early 1990s, Chile had reaffirmed its commitment to a liberal economic regime, but important tutelary powers, electoral discriminations, and reserved domains stood in the path of a consolidated democracy. Returning to the two dimensions that form the focus of this chapter's concerns, economic and political liberalization, we are left in post-Pinochet Chile with considerable asymmetry in terms of the government's capacity to pursue policies in these two areas. Whereas the Aylwin government was almost singularly empowered to pursue liberal economic policies, its capacity to consolidate a democratic political regime was quite constrained.

The 1980 Constitution: Blessing in Disguise?

Perhaps not surprisingly, many of the same features of the 1980 Constitution that have made it difficult to consolidate fully the democratic political regime in Chile have reinforced the choice to continue liberal economic policies. In fact, some have argued that once the opposition to Pinochet accepted the overall institutional framework set forth in the 1980 Constitution, it was left little choice but to follow the conservative bias of the new institutional order.[33] Though this latter claim may be an exaggeration, the provisions within the constitution that overrepresent supporters of the Pinochet regime within the Congress, combined with other reserved domains discussed above, have had the effect of requiring the Center-Left government to seek consensus among an even wider array of political forces, pushing the government to go beyond the parties that comprise the Concertation Alliance.

The Right holds considerable power in the Senate owing to the presence of designated senators, so that the Aylwin and Frei administrations often have had to satisfy the minimal demands of the representatives of

Chile's business and landholding groups in order to pass legislation. While clearly a nondemocratic feature of the new institutional order, this bias has provided important guarantees to capitalists during the transition to democracy. The presence of constitutional restrictions unfriendly to the Center-Left alliance may have given economic policymakers within the Concertation government a necessary weapon to defend themselves from the pressures of populist demands from the Left upon the return to democracy.[34]

Also contributing to this climate of consensus, the 1980 Constitution resolved Chile's perennial problem of what Genaro Arriagada has called the "double minority system" established by the 1925 Constitution. First, whereas the earlier constitution allowed the president of the republic to gain election to office without the support of a majority of the electorate, the 1980 Constitution requires election by a majority of the votes cast (either in the first round or in a runoff election). Even though the 1925 Constitution called for elections (in the case of a no-majority winner) to be decided upon by a majority vote of a joint session of Congress between the two leading candidates, it became a political impossibility to elect anyone other than the candidate with the first plurality. Second, the earlier constitution enabled the president to pass legislation with the support of a simple majority in either house and only one-third plus one in the other. This attribute, combined with other extraordinary executive powers, reinforced a dangerous proclivity of presidents (in many cases elected by a bare plurality) to govern without sufficient popular support, and helped precipitate a deep crisis of legitimacy during the government of Salvador Allende. However, though the current constitution eliminates the possibility of a president elected with minority popular support (with a second-round election), it by no means ensures parliamentary support for the sitting president. Indeed, the president is forced to seek broad alliances with multiple parties in order to enact legislation.

The 1980 Constitution requires the president, who must be elected by at least a majority, to pass legislation with a majority in both houses—and depending on the policy area, substantially more than a majority—thereby requiring broad agreement on policy before legislation is enacted. Though, as we have seen, the requirement of achieving such levels of support has prevented the Aylwin and Frei administrations from removing most elements of perverse institutionalization from the constitution, at the same time it has powerfully reinforced the political logic behind the Concertation Alliance. And this newfound Center-Left alliance, in turn, has provided for, in the words of socialist cabinet minister Enrique Correa, "a more solid political majority for social change than was possible under the government of Salvador Allende."[35] Rather than adopting an openly and completely hostile posture toward the initiatives of the democratic government, the rightist opposition has generally manifested a pragmatic attitude, often engaging in intense parliamentary negotiations to blunt legislation aimed at the interests of capital. Conscious perhaps of the often high levels of popular support enjoyed by both presidents Aylwin and Frei throughout their tenure in office,[36] important elements of the Right have lent their support to government-sponsored reforms ranging from key changes in the tax and industrial relations codes to wide-reaching reforms of local and municipal government.

In sum, while the 1980 Constitution is characterized by multiple elements of perverse institutionalization, at least in the short term, some provisions of the new constitution may have provided a legal and institutional framework to reinforce the policies of economic liberalization. The legal guarantees given to private property and the creation of an independent central bank, as well as other constitutional provisions, enhance the potential for government credibility and consistency. The constitution also sought to resolve several destabilizing propensities inherent in the earlier institutional order, removing the chronic problem of an executive elected with only minority support. These factors, combined with the requirement of parliamentary majorities (and sometimes a supermajority) to pass legislation, reinforce centripetal drives within the political system and contribute to building consensus.

Consensus: A Key Facilitating Condition

Many of the ideological and institutional changes in Chilean politics discussed above suggest that collective learning can occur, making major political actors more tolerant and disposed to compromise.[37] Reflecting on this political sea change, Aylwin's finance minister, Alejandro Foxley, noted that, "the long authoritarian recess created, almost imperceptibly, a new political culture which made possible agreements, accords, and consensus that had simply been unthinkable earlier."[38] The experience of seventeen years of dictatorship profoundly altered belief systems and strategies among politicians in Chile and the capacity of political leaders to engineer compromise. The greater degree of consensus among political forces in Chile, and the enhanced propensity for broad coalitions and alliances, have provided a propitious context for the continuation of the dual processes of economic and political liberalization.

The notion of "consensus" can be a slippery one. Giovanni Sartori proposed a general definition of consensus to be "a sharing that somehow binds." He then usefully identified three levels where such a sharing may hold relevance for the existence of democracy: first, the level of "ultimate values (such as liberty and equality) which structure the belief system"; second, that of "rules of the game, or procedures"; and finally, of "specific governments and governmental policies." He calls the first level of consensus a "facilitating" condition for the existence of democracy, whereas the second level he argues is a fundamental prerequisite. The third level, that of specific governments and government policy, is an area where consensus would be both unnecessary and in some ways undesirable for democracy: the existence of dissenting views over specific policy lies at the heart of democratic government.[39]

In terms of the first level, that of ultimate values that structure the belief system, there is abundant evidence that the transition in Chile has coincided with a substantial narrowing in ideological distance between major social and political actors. Belief systems, especially among opponents to the dictatorship, have reemerged from the experience of authoritarianism substantially transformed. Chastened by the defeat of the Allende regime, and sobered by the global collapse of international Leninism, the Left in Chile is barely recognizable as the heir to its more ideological pre-coup predecessor. The policy agenda of the Left has taken a sharp turn in the direction of liberalism, based on a rethinking of both the value of political democracy and the usefulness of the market.

In this new environment, the centrist Christian Democrats no longer advocate "communitarian socialism" but have resorted to the language of their European cousins proclaiming support for a "socially responsible" market. Comparatively, the Right has traveled the least ideological distance from its pre-authoritarian counterpart, mainly because their goals in economic policy have largely been realized. The near-convergence of these formerly irreconcilable political actors has introduced a moderating dynamic into the political system that has undoubtedly served as a facilitating condition for the return of democracy. The newfound capacity and willingness of political leaders to bridge long-standing animosities and to forge coalitions and alliances among key parties of the Center and Left (within the Concertation), and those of the Center and the Right (within the Union for the Progress of Chile), has supplied a useful lubricant within the political system.

Sartori's second and most fundamental level of consensus, that of basic agreement upon rules and procedures, has been more problematic in the Chilean case. As we have seen, the legal framework established by the 1980 Constitution, though formally acknowledged as the "rules of the game" by major political and social actors, retains authoritarian holdovers that are unacceptable to the parties of the Concertation Alliance. Disagreement over the institutional framework of Chile's democracy will doubtless intensify during the six-year presidential period of Eduardo Frei R. Since the forces of the Concertation failed to gain the seats necessary to remove the legacies of authoritarianism in the December 1993 elections, parties of the Concertation, especially those most disadvantaged by the provisions of the 1980 Constitution, such as the socialists and the PPD, may lose patience with what appears to be an endless waiting game. This in turn could contribute in the not-so-distant future to political instability.

Finally, with regard to the level of policy, the Aylwin and Frei governments succeeded in crafting delicate political understandings and skillfully engineered policies in three critical areas: the economy, the gradual consolidation of political democracy, and human rights. Though sometimes a battleground, in general the terrain of economic policy has been one of broad agreement between Chile's major social and political actors. Pursuing a strategy of "growth with equity," the Concertation government has demonstrated to believers and skeptics alike that responsible and highly successful management of the economy is possible in a democratic context.

In the area of reform of political institutions, success has been more limited. The democratic government has pursued a strategy of incremental reform of the legacies of authoritarianism. Though the Concertation governments gained the support of the Right in securing some progress in this area (such as municipal reform), the more fundamental problems of civil-military relations, nonelected senators, and the reform of the electoral law have not been solved as of mid-1995. It seems likely that these reforms can only be made in piecemeal fashion. In perhaps the most painful policy area for the Concertation government, the area of human rights, Aylwin consistently resisted pressures from the Right and the military to enact legislation putting an end to the investigation of past rights abuses (the so-called *punto final*, or "end point" legislation). Instead, Aylwin insisted on a policy he called *justicia posible*, or "justice of the possible," a measure that required the clarification of the circumstances of the crime, moral rehabilitation of the victim, and material compensation to the victim's family. Under this policy, most of the perpetrators of human rights abuses have not been subject to either trial or punishment. Just as in the area of full democratization, in this third policy area, agreement between the parties of the Concertation and the opposition has been elusive.

Conclusion

I have argued that the democratic government led by Patricio Aylwin, and his successors in the Concertation Alliance under President Eduardo Frei R., have been uniquely positioned to consolidate a free market, outward-oriented political economy. Since 1990 Chile's democratic government has successfully formulated and implemented a set of coherent economic policies that have respected the general market orientation pursued under Pinochet. However, it has been much less successful in removing the legacies of authoritarianism that block the full consolidation of democracy. In some ways, perverse institutional legacies built into the 1980 Constitution have strengthened the new democratic regime's hand in economic policymaking.

The institutional framework set forth in the 1980 Constitution has contributed powerfully, though not always democratically, to the Aylwin government's capacity to pursue coherent policy. The decisive resolution of the status of private property within the constitution helped provide the requisite guarantees without which capitalist investment at current levels would be unthinkable. The systematic over-representation of Pinochet's allies in the Congress, especially the presence of nonelected members in the Senate, introduced into the system the requirement of a new level of consensus in order to pass legislation. This latter feature, though again nondemocratic, has reinforced centripetal ideological dynamics already present within the political system and, somewhat ironically, contributed to the overall continuity and effectiveness of the government's ability to pursue coherent economic policies.

Democratic transition in Chile should be understood in terms of a recovery of well-established democratic practices and institutions. Several factors have influenced the government's capacity to formulate and implement coherent policy. The reappearance of strong parties capable of channeling and expressing diverse social and political interests has provided a powerful institutional buffer, at least in part protecting policymakers from populist temptations. However, the presence of strong parties is not enough. The dynamics that characterize the contemporary party system in Chile differ in multiple and salutary ways from the pre-coup period. The ideological distance separating the major contenders within the party system has narrowed markedly, and the newfound capacity among the parties to join alliances and coalitions has greatly enhanced democratic governability. Not surprisingly, coherent economic policymaking is more feasible where political polarization is absent.

The trauma and dislocation caused by the experience of authoritarianism in Chile, combined with other global ideological changes, have contributed to a new political culture in which political compromise and agreement are more likely. This new consensus, at the level of ultimate values that structure the belief system among elites, has enabled policymakers to seek common ground among opposing social and political actors, and has served as a key facilitating condition for economic liberalization in a democratic context.

What of the future of this slightly heterodox, Center-Left Concertation Alliance and its warm embrace of economic liberalization? A fundamental question for the post-Aylwin period is whether the parties of the Concertation can continue to recreate in the mid-1990s the sense of excitement and urgency that characterized the transition to a democratic government at the end of the 1980s. Once the novelty of this historic agreement wears off and the fabric of the implicit social pact upon which it rests becomes thin, will the major parties of the Center and the Left be willing and able to forge new agreements over programs and political leaders that go beyond those created for the transition? As the dominant issue for which the Concertation was created recedes— that is, the goal of defeating Pinochet in the 1988 plebiscite and winning the presidency for the forces pressing for full democratization—the cleavage between supporters and opponents of the authoritarian regime may increase as enthusiasm for maintaining current party alignments diminishes. In this new situation, the political leadership within the various parties of the Concertation will be tempted to try to strengthen their own parties and political identities around issues other than a rejection of the dictatorship, and may, for this reason, welcome more open, unstructured electoral competition.

With the December 1993 election of Eduardo Frei R. to succeed Patricio Aylwin at the head of Chile's second Concertation government, the question arises how the dual reality of relatively unencumbered markets combined with a political regime still harnessed by the constitutional constraints left in place by Pinochet will evolve. Has the political arena undergone a fundamental change, or has the consensus of the Aylwin period been more a necessary truce to see parties through the transition? Will renewed party competition revolve around such specific policy-related issues that the fundamental consensus over basic questions can be retained, thereby avoiding the reemergence of centripetal tendencies in the party system and permitting the recreation of the Concertation during the entire term under Eduardo Frei R.? Most probably, the pressure will mount during the Frei period to strip away, one way or another, these constraints. Despite these pressures, lessons from the relatively recent past may be powerful enough to ensure that party divisions remain moderate, allowing the formation of new alliances between forces around the Center of the ideological spectrum and winning the time needed to consolidate democracy in Chile.

7

Paraguay: Transition from Caudillo *Rule*

Diego Abente Brun

The process of transition to democracy in Paraguay, which began on February 3, 1989, with the overthrow of the dictatorship of General Alfredo Stroessner, has yet to be completed. It was expected to end with the general elections of May 9, 1993, the subordination of the military to civilian rule, and the reorganization of the judiciary and the electoral system. However, as a typical transition from above, its pace and course were dictated more by the willingness or need of the ruling elite to make concessions than by the ability of the opposition to extract them. With no significant elements of pressure, the opposition consented to recognize the hastily arranged postcoup election of May 1, 1989, which assured the ruling party a two-thirds majority in the 1989–93 legislature and the total control of the judiciary, the state apparatus, and the military, and thus went to the 1993 elections at a significant disadvantage.

As a result, the 1993 elections were marred by countless irregularities, from a ruling-party controlled electoral system without the effective control of the opposition, to last-minute changes in the rules of the game and a campaign of public intimidation of voters. Furthermore, the active participation of military officers in the electoral campaign and a judiciary subjected to the political influence of the government demonstrated that polyarchy is still in effect.

Thus in Paraguay the issues of strengthening democratic governance are not yet relevant. Instead, the imperative is that of completing the transition begun in 1989 and successfully addressing its challenges. Before exploring them, however, a brief overview of the 1993 elections is needed.

The Electoral Process and the Emergence of the Wasmosy Government

The elections of May 1993 were to be the first freely contested elections in some seven decades. They were characterized by two cleavages: that of dividing the ruling party's candidate from those of the opposition and the fierce competition within the ruling party for such a candidacy.

On the opposition front, two candidates soon captured the lead: Domingo Laíno, the populist leader of the Liberal Radical Authentic Party (PLRA), and Guillermo Caballero Vargas, a prominent businessman with old ties to the political opposition and a message of change, modernization, and social justice. Laíno won the candidacy of the PLRA, one of Paraguay's two traditional parties, while Caballero Vargas led the formation of a new party, the Encuentro Nacional (EN, National Encounter).

Two major candidates fought the Colorado Party (ANR) primary, Luis María Argaña and Juan Carlos Wasmosy. Argaña had been a principal civil figure in the coup against Stroessner but fell from grace because of constant confrontations with the president, General Rodríguez. A right-wing populist, he was able to appeal to the core membership of the party with a message that in many ways echoed the absolute hegemony enjoyed by the party under Stroessner. On the other hand, Wasmosy, a wealthy businessman who made his fortune in activities connected with the construction of the Itaipú dam in the 1970s, presented himself as the candidate of change representing the idea of a new party ready to adjust successfully to more competitive conditions.

The bitter Colorado campaign confronted an Argaña portrayed by his opponent as nothing but the return of Stroessner and a Wasmosy portrayed by his opponent as a former liberal who had infiltrated the party and was seeking to capture it through his money and close relationship to the military elite. These extreme characterizations represented, if in an exaggerated way, some distinct elements of reality. Argaña's discourse had traditionally been aggressive, and he managed to get the support of a majority of the Colorado faction that followed Stroessner to the end. Wasmosy was clearly the candidate of the government establishment, the business elite connected to it, and especially the powerful First Army corps commander, General Lino C. Oviedo.

By most accounts, the outcome of the primary election produced an Argaña victory. However, by forcing the resignation of several members of the party's Electoral Tribunal and replacing them with others that excluded representatives of Argaña from the vote counting, Wasmosy managed to be declared the winner with a narrow-margin victory over Argaña. The stage was thus set for a three-way race with Wasmosy, Laíno, and Caballero Vargas as the main contenders.

The electoral campaign was full of uncertainties—including a Colorado attempt at cancelling the polls via a judiciary injunction that was dismissed only two weeks before the election—and was marred by several last-minute changes in the electoral code designed to weaken opposition control, by lack of access to and control of the electoral rolls and the electoral apparatus, and by overt military intervention including General Oviedo's proclamation that no matter what, the Colorado Party was to rule *per seculae seculorum.* The outcome of the May 9, 1993, election is shown in Table 3.

Table 3 **Paraguay: Results of the 1993 National Elections**

	Presidential		Senatorial	
	Votes	%	Votes	%
Wasmosy/ANR	473,176	40.09	498,586	42.3
Laíno/PLRA	378,353	32.06	409,728	34.76
Caballero Vargas/EN	271,905	23.04	203,213	17.24
Others[a]	8,198	0.66	20,411	1.73

[a]Includes six candidates of small parties from the Right and Left.

Wasmosy assumed the presidency on August 15 in questionable circumstances: many Colorados questioned his very candidacy, and the opposition questioned the elections of May 9. Yet, for the sake of political stability and social peace, the opposition decided to accept the outcome of the election, hoping to complete the tasks of democratization in the 1993–98 period. Weighing heavily in the opposition's decision was the fact that, in this democratization game, the democratic opposition had gained a distinct advantage. In fact, for the first time in Paraguayan history, the elections of May 9, 1993, produced a divided government. The distribution of congressional seats was as shown in Table 3.

As Table 4 shows, the opposition enjoys a 25–20 majority in the Senate and a 42–38 advantage in the lower house. Besides, as a result of the internal split in the Colorado Party, the product of the primary elections of December 1992, some eight Colorado senators and some six Colorado deputies, Argaña supporters, have been voting with the opposition, thus reducing even further the strength of the government party's representation in Congress.[1] This distinct advantage in Congress, it was hoped, would put the opposition in a strong position to negotiate the later steps of the transition.

The Challenges of the Transition

The Paraguayan process of transition to democracy confronts three main challenges. The first has to do with the resolution of political

Table 4 **Paraguay: Seats in Congress after the 1993 Elections**

	ANR[a]	PLRA	EN	Total
Senate	20 (12)	17	8	45
Deputies	38 (32)	33	9	80
Total	58 (44)	50	17	125

[a]Numbers between parentheses represent the number of Colorado congressmen that support the government; the rest are dissidents.

conflicts between the ruling elite and the democratic opposition. The issue involves the basic question of power: on the one hand, a politico-military-economic elite that does not want to lose power and, in its attempt to retain it, is prepared to tamper with democratic procedures, and, on the other, a political opposition that wants to preserve those democratic procedures as a means of acceding to power in the future. The issue is whether or not Paraguay will have a truly competitive political system in which all actors will have equal opportunity to attain power. This involves the restructuring of the judiciary, the adoption of a new electoral system, and removing partisanship from the state apparatus. Only the first of these has been tackled so far. The second challenge is that of civic-military relations, which implies the consolidation of a system of full military subordination to civilian rule. The third challenge is that of responding to rising social demands to build support for the process and to guarantee the long-term sustainability of the democratic system.

Furthermore, all these challenges must be met in an orderly, or evolutionary, fashion. Paraguay is a conservative country characterized by a history of shifts between periods of order associated with authoritarian rule (1820–70 and 1954–89) and of instability associated with democratic freedoms (1870–1936 and 1946–54). Thus the imperative of completing the transition and facing the challenges associated with it has been made more complex and difficult by the need to maintain what has been known in Paraguay as "governability."

Governability, or the ability of the government to govern and maintain stability and institutional continuity, has a different meaning and strategic value for the government and for the opposition. For the government, of course, governability is an end in itself. The transition need not be completed. Perpetuating a *democradura,* emptying democratic institutions of any substantive content while maintaining their form, is a far more attractive political formula.

For the democratic opposition, though, governability is a means to an end. Governability is important insofar as it leads to a successful completion of the transition. The democratic opposition seeks a climate of governability as insurance against any possible institutional retrogression. Social chaos, continuing economic hardships, or a political power vacuum may well be the pretext for return to an authoritarian regime. At the same time, the opposition must be careful not to allow such an attitude to lead to the freezing of present conditions which, while much better than those of the dictatorship, are still far from the standards of democracy for which Paraguayans are striving.

In short, the democratic opposition in this period needs to achieve acceptable levels of democratization, successfully addressing the challenges it confronts while maintaining acceptable levels of governability—the former in order to avoid a return to authoritarian government and the latter in order to overcome a simple *democradura*. Paraphrasing Robert Dahl, the Paraguayan dilemma may well be summarized as follows: for the ruling coalition, it is a question of finding the cost of a *fujimorazo* higher than that of toleration; while for the democratic opposition it is a matter of lowering the cost of toleration below that, of regression, or, put differently, raising the cost of regression beyond that of toleration.

Its comfortable congressional majority enables the opposition to deal with the government from a position of strength. In fact, even before convening on July 1, 1993, the congressmen elected by the PLRA, the EN, and the Colorado dissidents forged a parliamentary alliance bent on exercising a strong congressional control over the newly elected president. The first test was the election of the leaders of both houses: president, first vice-president, and second vice-president. At that opportunity, the opposition alliance took over all three positions in both houses. In the Senate the presidency went to a member of the PLRA, the first vice-presidency to one of the Colorado dissidents, and the second vice-presidency to a representative of the EN. In the Chamber, the presidency was also given to the PLRA, but the order of the two vice-presidencies was switched: the EN took the first and the Colorado dissidents the second. Committee memberships were decided on a proportional basis, but their chairmanships were also elected only from the opposition alliance.

Yet, just as the opposition enjoyed a comfortable margin, it also inherited the vices of the petty politics of the past. No sooner had the parliamentary alliance begun to bear fruit than the former presidential candidate, Domingo Laíno, began a campaign to sign a so-called Governability Pact between the government and the opposition, which took place on October 14, 1993. Ill-defined and confusing, the pact was first presented as a compromise to defend public liberties and democracy, as if no constitution existed. It was later redefined as a simple dialogue agreement. But by unilaterally engaging in a dialogue with the government, adopting an "appeasement" strategy, and offering it parliamentary support, the pact severely weakened the chances of the opposition to extract quick concessions from the government on the key issues of the reform of the judiciary and the reorganization of the armed forces.

The Struggle for an Independent Judiciary

Soon after the new Congress was inaugurated, the opposition alliance approved legislation rescinding a highly controversial law passed by the Colorado-controlled previous legislature, which had established the functioning of the Consejo de la Magistratura (Council of Magistrates). According to the 1992 Constitution, the judiciary is to be completely restructured, from the highest court to the lowest justice of the peace. The council is the body charged with selecting and proposing candidates for all judiciary appointments, especially members of the Supreme Court and the Supreme Electoral Tribunal, which will serve until age seventy-five unless impeached by Congress. According to the constitution, the latter are designated by the Senate from three names (*ternas*) proposed by the council and with the *acuerdo* (agreement) of the executive. The law approved by the previous legislature, which had not yet been enacted, provided for a system of election of members of the council highly likely to produce a Colorado majority, and at the same time vested in the executive an absolute veto power over the Senate's Supreme Court and Supreme Electoral Tribunal designations. Such a law provided no guarantee of a real change in the judiciary. Therefore, even though in the short term rescinding that law increased the tension between both branches of government, it was indispensable to do so in order to ensure the long-term viability of a democratic system that would be impossible without an independent judiciary.

Upon rescinding that law, and in a climate of division within the opposition, the Congress passed a new law that provided for a fairer system of electing members of the council and for a procedure that equated the *acuerdo* of the executive for the nomination of Supreme Court and Supreme Electoral Tribunal justices with a presidential veto, thus allowing the Congress to override it.

As expected, the executive threatened to veto it in its entirety and to resort to the Colorado-controlled Supreme Court to obtain a ruling of unconstitutionality if the veto was overridden. This triggered a negotiation that led to an agreement known as the Democratic Compromise between the executive and a majority of congressmen, which was signed on January 13, 1994. The compromise called for both branches to find a consensus concerning the members of the new Supreme Court and Supreme Electoral Tribunal.

The success of the Democratic Compromise created a new atmosphere of cooperation between Congress and the executive. But this climate lasted only a short time: in a surprise move, the government delayed the promulgation of the law as much as was legally possible and immediately thereafter issued a decree with a massive number of changes in the judiciary, sending judges considered honorable to unimportant posts and promoting those of questionable integrity to high positions, especially to appellate courts. Appellate courts are very important in the Paraguayan judiciary system because Supreme Court justices are subject to recusation by plaintiffs, in which cases the vacancies are filled by judges from appellate courts. Through this kind of maneuver one can easily manipulate the process in order to ensure a subservient court.

As if all this was not enough, a group of Colorado lawyers with close ties to governmental sectors and to the party sought a ruling of unconstitutionality against the law of the council of Magistrates, questioning the proportional system adopted to allocate the two seats that are to be filled by lawyers.[2] After a long delay, the Supreme Court ruled 3–2 in favor of the Colorado lawyers. The outcry over the Supreme Court ruling led to the calling of elections on October 22 according to the proportional system the court had earlier declared unconstitutional.[3] Immediately the Colorado lawyers threatened to resort to an *amparo*, a judicial measure designed to protect the rights of persons that "consider themselves gravely injured or in danger of being injured by an act or an omission, obviously illegitimate, of an authority or person."[4]

If anything, this situation led to a unification of opposition forces that had before been separated on the issue of the governability pact. The results were encouraging. Not only were elections held on schedule, but also a united opposition slate won a resounding victory. There is no question that the strategy of complacency and weakness previously supported by those supporting the governability pact failed to produce results and that a new strategy, such as the one chosen in the case of the judiciary, needs to be adopted. It remains to be seen if what has been accomplished is going to last.

The Military Question: Will Institutionalism Prevail?

Another early challenge confronted by the Congress was the institutional status of the armed forces. Before finishing its term, the Colorado-controlled Congress had approved a law of organization of the armed forces that provided for the creation of the post of a Pinochet-like commander of the military forces, to be filled by an active duty military officer. The law also gave this military commander the powers of the commander in chief, which, according to the new constitution, belong exclusively to the civilian president and cannot be delegated. Beyond the discussion of the issue.itself is the question of why the government was seeking to create such a position. The opposition believed that the post of commander of the military forces was tailor-made for General Oviedo and that the government intention was to give him even more power over the armed forces.

To prevent this, the opposition-controlled Congress rescinded the law and reinstated the earlier one. The executive vetoed the military law bill, the Congress overrode the veto, and the executive then resorted to the Supreme Court alleging that the bill was unconstitutional because Congress could not simultaneously rescind a law, reinstate an old one, and modify it. The Colorado-controlled Supreme Court ruled in favor of the executive.

This allowed Vice-Admiral Eduardo González Petit to retain the post of commander of the military forces to which he was named by former president Rodríguez and confirmed by President Wasmosy. It also opened a yet unfinished debate on a new law of the armed forces which is still being discussed in the lower house.

In a way, the Paraguayan military has demonstrated a remarkable ability to adjust to the new situation and play by the rules of democracy. The institution has accepted a certain degree of subordination to civilian rule, a civilian commander in chief, and the concept of military subordination to civilian rule. Also, confronted with some budget cuts and drastic changes in the chain of food supplies, the military, although grudgingly, has accepted congressional decisions. The military has also accepted congressional rejection of a major salary increase for 1995.

Yet, in other areas, military prerogatives are quite significant. On the one hand, purely institutional concerns, such as the budget, prestige, respect, and so on, are voiced by authorized spokespersons. But, when high-level military officers up for promotion were invited by the Senate Defense Committee to appear before it, the president and commander in chief—in reaction to pressures from the military—denied them permission to appear, on the pretext that the officers were not to "parade" before the Senate. According to the constitution, however, promotions to the rank of colonel and higher need Senate approval.

The military question in Paraguay does not have only an institutional dimension. There is also the constant intervention of the powerful General Lino C. Oviedo, the German-trained cavalry officer who played a key role in the 1989 coup, personally arresting General Stroessner, and who rose through the ranks from colonel to major general in four years. He is now commander of the army and is considered the main architect of the Wasmosy triumph. It is a well-known secret that General Oviedo harbors presidential ambitions, and his meddling in party politics is as evident as it is pervasive. General Oviedo is surely acting in a personal capacity, but if the institution is not strong enough to stop him from getting involved in party politics now, how is the officer corps going to react if and when confronted with a conflict between respect for the constitution and the military institution and loyalty to their commander and his personal leadership? In this climate of uncertain loyalties, Oviedo continues to expand his influence in the armed forces, promoting his loyalists to high positions and demoting his adversaries.

Until recently, it was clear that Oviedo and Wasmosy maintained a close relationship. Yet recent developments suggest that Wasmosy's 1998 plans might not include Oviedo's candidacy, and therefore the question becomes how far General Oviedo can go in his attempt to control political developments in the Colorado Party so as to ensure his candidacy for 1998. Some observers suggest that Oviedo supporters are behind the wave of social unrest discussed in the next section, and that their main objective is to destabilize the Wasmosy government and create the conditions for his impeachment.

At the end of 1994, tensions within the military and between General Oviedo and President Wasmosy rose to unprecedented levels, threatening the rupture of the process. The crisis erupted over the transfer of General Carlos Ayala, commander of the First Infantry Division, a key garrison located in the outskirts of Asunción, to a remote outpost in the Chaco. President Wasmosy canceled General Oviedo's order for the transfer, which led to a virtual insubordination of Oviedo, who placed his loyal troops on high alert and deployed a force of tanks to neutralize the main air force base located in Asunción. Wasmosy received the support of the navy, the police, and the air force, which managed to arm and disperse a significant number of its T-33, Xavante, and Tucano war planes in preparation for combat. The crisis was settled on still unclear terms, though General Ayala was retained as commander of the First Infantry Division.

Less than two weeks later, another crisis developed when once again General Oviedo placed his troops on high alert. It was unclear whether he was preparing to launch a coup or whether he was preparing to resist what he thought was an incoming presidential decision to retire him. The proportions of this move led Brazilian President Fernando Henrique Cardoso to issue a statement warning that a coup was unacceptable and would throw Paraguay into regional isolation including its exclusion from the MERCOSUR (Southern Cone Common Market). This is the first time that a Brazilian government issued such a strong statement in defense of democracy in Paraguay and played a significant role in deterring its interruption. The crisis was overcome when General Oviedo apparently received assurances that his retirement was not being considered.

Although it seems that General Oviedo's base of power suffered a considerable erosion as a result of the latest events, the issue remains his still unprecedented influence and the lack of control over him. Although the number of officers opposing his ambitions seems to be considerable, the strength of the troops he commands, his popularity in a segment of the armed forces, and the wealth at his disposal give him a powerful position. Will Wasmosy be able to send him into retirement? Will he accept it without a major military confrontation? As we enter a period of unstable equilibrium between Wasmosy and Oviedo, this remains perhaps the major cloud hanging over the political process in Paraguay.

The Social Question: Rising Popular Demands

If the political climate evolved from confrontation to some sort of cohabitation to a new climate of confrontation, the social climate followed a different path. The Wasmosy government began its term without major social pressures. However, as time went on, social demands began to increase. First, the discussion of a new labor code produced a high-intensity confrontation between labor and business. The Senate passed a compromise bill that lowered tensions significantly, but the issue is still pending as the bill is up for consideration in the lower house.

Immediately thereafter the discussion of the 1994 budget produced another series of confrontations. Teachers demanded a 40 percent salary increase, and so did doctors and nurses employed in public hospitals, and later all public employees. The issue was resolved successfully through salary increases ranging from 3.5 percent to 15.5 percent.

But the most serious episode of social unrest was yet to come. It began in mid-February 1994 and was connected with the problem of landless peasants and low prices for agricultural products. At that point, and as the harvest approached, the traditional demand for land was coupled with the cyclical issue of the price of cotton. Cotton is grown by a large majority of Paraguayan peasants, some 250,000 to 260,000 families, and is their main cash crop. After three consecutive years of bad prices, adverse climate, and a diversity of pests, the peasantry is looking for a way to recoup previous losses. Even though prices are comparatively good, peasants are asking for higher ones.

Unhappy with the situation, peasants began to occupy roads, interrupting the normal flow of traffic in demand for higher cotton prices. On a number of occasions there were confrontations with police, and, although the level of police repression was not unusually high, the risk of fatalities has been significant. The peasants' demands faced a government that insisted it could do nothing about it and cotton exporters that demanded a more competitive exchange rate.

As the pressure kept mounting, peasants organized a large rally in the capital city of Asunción for March 15. Despite an all-out government campaign aimed at hindering its organization and the transportation of people to Asunción, the march was a great success, and some fifteen thousand peasants gathered before parliament. Students and labor leaders supported the march and closed public roads in solidarity with the peasants. Throughout the streets of Asunción, the outpouring of popular support for the marchers was evident.

At the same time, the major labor confederations called a general strike for May 2, demanding an across-the-board 40 percent salary increase. It was the first general strike in thirty-six years.

In short, Paraguay is witnessing a wave of unprecedented social unrest, the product of long-repressed social demands that are exploding in the climate of political freedoms that characterizes democratic systems. The number of land occupations, road closings, strikes, marches, and other such measures has increased dramatically. The perception among the wealthy is that the situation may be getting out of control. What makes all this even more significant is that it goes along with a generalized sense of frustration with the current economic and social situation. In fact, at the end of January, a well-respected public opinion poll showed that for 75.4 percent of the population the economic situation was worse than it was under Stroessner. Only 33 percent of the people thought that, overall, things had improved after the coup; 34 percent considered that the general situation had deteriorated, and 33 percent felt that the situation remained the same.

In responding to this situation the government has two options: either it resorts to old-fashioned repressive tactics or it seeks reasonable solutions via effective policymaking. The temptation, perhaps even the dream, is to do away with "populist" pressures and pursue an iron-fist Cavallo or Büchi-style policy. Yet currently the government lacks the political support to do so, but it also lacks the political will to do something else. In such a situation, unless the government makes up its mind and does something, the growing disenchantment with the current situation will continue to encourage adventurers and social problems will become increasingly harder to solve.

Conclusions

The problems of governance in transitional Paraguay have three dimensions. One dimension is that of the extent to which the ruling coalition is willing to accept truly democratic procedures when those procedures are likely to throw them out of power. This is an issue of cost and benefits: in Dahlian terms, a question of the cost of toleration and the cost of repression. But it is also an issue of realigning the ruling coalition, as the meaning of "being out of power" varies from case to case. The working hypothesis is, then, that there are some sectors that are prepared to "survive" outside the bubble of state power in contrast to those that are so inextricably linked to a structure of power and graft that they are likely to resort to extreme measures to retain it.

The relationship between the government and the political opposition has revolved around such a dynamic. Until now the opposition's level of flexibility has been remarkable. By and large, the opposition supports the government insofar as it is the expression of the process of democratic transition. It supports it, as well, in an attempt to strengthen and enlarge the group of the ruling coalition that sees itself as able to survive and even do well when out of power. The opposition does not want any interruption of the process, and thus Wasmosy has strong supporters in that group. The opposition's main challenge is to entice government into cooperating in the democratization of the state, basically in the restructuring of the judiciary, the reform of the electoral system, and the reform of the state. Electoral legislation will also have to undergo changes and, most important, the electoral apparatus will have to be reorganized.

The second question revolves around the role of messianic military leaders who distort normal civic-military relations. The Oviedo case is reminiscent of the Aldo Rico or Mohamed Ali Seineldin cases in Argentina. But in Argentina the level of institutionalization of the military acted as a deterrent, while in Paraguay the level is much lower, and Oviedo is not a colonel but a major general and the commander of the army. To help in the removal of this threat the Congress is clearly separating the Oviedo case from all other civil-military issues and furthering an aggressive program of multilevel contacts with military officers. The lower house has invited a number of high-ranking officers to discuss the new military legislation. At the same time, the Senate Appropriations Committee is making a significant effort to improve salary allocation, redoubling investment efforts, and equalizing allocations so as to strengthen the more democratic sectors of the armed forces. The primary responsibility, though, falls on the executive and the armed forces themselves. Will the government do something? Will the armed forces as an institution be able to control this phenomenon? How long will the current unstable equilibrium last?

Complicating an already complex military scenario is the growing influence of drug trafficking, a significant risk factor. Paraguay has long been considered a drug route but not a major one. Lately, though, friction between the U.S. and Paraguayan governments has developed over the effectiveness of Paraguayan efforts at combating that scourge. The late 1994 assassination of retired General Ramón R. Rodríguez, the chief of Paraguay's Drug Enforcement Agency, by some of his own people raised questions about the extent to which the local police and armed forces could be infiltrated by drug traffickers. Well-respected observers believe that some in the military are still involved in illegal trade rings which, while not intended for drug purposes, are prime cover schemes used by drug traffickers. If this threat is not dealt with effectively, a further and formidable obstacle for the successful completion of the transition to democracy is likely to develop.

Finally, there is the question of managing the rising social demands. In and of themselves, social demands could be manageable. But, when mixed with the political elements discussed above, the possibility of their being manipulated for nondemocratic goals is high. Yet, as manipulators cannot be wished away, the government must begin to do away with the underlying problems. As the government continues to ignore the social question, labor organizations keep growing and the business sector becomes increasingly fearful of labor instability, which leads to delaying badly needed investment decisions. Deactivating conflicts by meeting grievances with effective solutions should be the answer, but the government seems not to understand this.

Overall, the prospects for the medium term, although not good, are not necessarily bad. A great deal depends on the intelligence, flexibility, patience, and firmness of three actors: the presidential entourage, the parliamentary opposition, and the highest echelons of the military establishment. The decisions that they must make need to strike a balance between the absolute necessity to establish democratic rules for a democratic game—which means equal opportunity for all parties to accede to power through elections—and the guarantee that the strategic interests of all parties will be duly contemplated.

Therefore, both positive and negative inducements are needed. It is essential to strengthen within the ruling coalition a sector willing to risk democratization, even if that means they lose "power." It is also necessary to raise the cost of any possible authoritarian adventure. International organizations and great powers must send unmistakable signals that any coup will throw the country into total isolation, as the Brazilian government did so effectively and in such a timely fashion at the end of 1994. Cooperation to strengthen democratic institutions is also critical. Finally, there is also necessary a great deal of "thoughtful wishing," that happy expression coined by Abraham F. Lowenthal, for the issue of democratic governance in Paraguay is a complex one and ought to be the subject of a deeper reflection that transcends the day-to-day pressure of politics.

Epilogue: A Civilian President without Civilian Rule

Only a year after writing this chapter, the overall prospects for the transition process look significantly more somber. The Wasmosy government was greatly discredited as a result of its inability to steer the country into a process of economic growth, and as a consequence its authority is constantly challenged by General Lino Oviedo's state of virtual insubordination. Even more than a year ago, the Paraguayan transition continued to be characterized by having a civilian president but no civilian rule, a democratic constitution but not the full rule of law, a powerful ruler but a weak president, and a strong opposition that cannot use its majority to the full extent lest it lead to the further weakening of the president and the interruption of the process.

Only one important development can be counted on the positive side: after much give and take, the new nine-member Supreme Court was sworn in. Made up of four members identified with the opposition, four with the government, and one Colorado of independent background accepted by the opposition, the new court must now proceed to restructure the entire judiciary, a long and complex task. The new three-member Supreme Electoral Tribunal was also set up in a similar fashion, with one Colorado, one liberal, and one independent.

On the negative side, however, the list of developments is long. Social and economic problems continued to increase, and no progress was made in solving the agrarian question. Furthermore, the combination of corrupt and inept financial management led first to the "robbery" of some U.S.$4 million from the central bank vault (only one employee has so far been charged) and then to the collapse of four banks, which thus far has cost U.S.$300 million of taxpayers' money to honor public debts. As the inability of the government to attain a minimum degree of policy coherence became increasingly evident, the government engaged in a systematic campaign to blame the Congress for all the country's ills. A weak and isolated executive resorted to the cheap tactic of portraying everything, from the lack of a clear economic policy to the ineptitude of the public sector, as the failure of the Congress. The hard-liners within the ruling coalition, as if in a well-orchestrated campaign, jumped to the "logical" conclusion that the country would be better off without a Congress, that is, without democracy. As a result, dissatisfaction with the government is at risk of growing into a full-blown alienation from the democratic system.

In a way, Wasmosy's difficulty in coming to terms with an opposition almost eagerly willing to help him out of the critical situation he created is a function of the deep division within his party's ranks between the followers of his vice-president, Angel Seifart, the more democratic wing of the party, and those betting on the 1998 presidential candidacy of General Lino Oviedo. The Seifaristas are more willing to engage in a cooperative relationship with the opposition, while the Oviedistas adopt two-thirds of Wasmosy's already small group of supporters in the Senate and retain little, if any, political support in the party. With such a small power base, Wasmosy lacks the ability to engage in any substantive agreement with the opposition short of a straightforward coalition government, anathema in Colorado circles.

On the other hand, General Oviedo continues to meddle in politics, in defiance of constitutional and legal provisions. He once again challenged President Wasmosy in early September, placing his troops and tanks on high alert when a judge charged him with violating the law prohibiting the military from engaging in party politics and word spread that Wasmosy would retire him. Wasmosy backed down, and Oviedo's lawyers resorted to legal chicanery to impugn the judge and force the case to be moved to another judge who, within hours, dismissed the case.

Wasmosy's political-military problems are a reflection of the internal power struggle within the Colorado Party not only among his would-be supporters (Seifaristas and Oviedistas) but also between these two groups and the rest of the party apparatus. In fact, the upcoming elections for party leaders will confront the official sector with the challenge of winning over Argaña's supporters, the only way to support the claim that the government is the legitimate representative of the party. Yet all existing evidence points to a distinct Argaña lead. In short, Wasmosy, with his supporters divided and in the minority, must confront a solid and united Argañista front that is in the majority.

As this situation unfolds, the challenges become greater and more complex. The opposition must:

1. Support an unpopular and weak president in order to guarantee the completion of the process;

2. Figure out how to deal with President Wasmosy who does not rule, General Oviedo who should not rule, and Vice-President Seifart who cannot rule;

3. Struggle to achieve true civilian rule and the definitive severance of the incestuous relationship between some military leaders and a sector of the Colorado Party without alienating the rest of the armed forces, when the president himself is unwilling to reassert his prerogatives as commander in chief;

4. Withstand the legitimate pressure of the popular sectors that demand clearer policies toward social problems and justify postponing their solution for the sake of stability;

5. Persuade the economic elites that democracy is a workable system for achieving economic reform, while living with governmental excuses to do little to move the country away from statism in order to retain what little support it has among public employees;

6. Be able to go on and on, from no. 1 to no. 5, for the next three years; and

7. Develop a strategy to ensure an opposition alliance capable of achieving a clear-cut victory in the forthcoming elections over the forces of a party that—whether led by Argaña, Oviedo, or Seifart—offers no alternative for real change.

The successful completion of the transition depends on this last item. The EN proposed a united front with the PLRA based on using a method similar to Argentina's FREPASO (National Solidarity Front) or Chile's Concertación Democrática to select candidates. If accepted, this would imply holding primary elections with open rolls in which candidates for a united state would be selected from PLRA and EN lists. Both parties would support the candidates thus elected and present lists based on the proportion of the votes won by each of them.

There has been no peaceful transfer of power from one party to another in Paraguay's 185 years of independent history. For such a transfer to occur, there would need to be both an overwhelming electoral victory and as wide-based and strong a political front as possible. Whether or not that is to be achieved remains to be seen.

8

Uruguay: From Restoration to the Crisis of Governability

Juan Rial

The stability of Uruguayan democracy was historically rooted in an anticipatory style of government that preempted social demands by dealing with them before they had a chance to manifest themselves.[1] The role of the state was preeminent: state intervention was used to "correct" social inequalities and to deflect sociopolitical unrest. This was coupled with a strict separation of church and state, which officially took place in 1919 with the reform of the constitution, but which had gradually been incorporated into the political culture of the country and the mores of its inhabitants since the end of the nineteenth century. Despite the recent efforts of organizations such as Opus Dei on the one hand and movements such as *basismo* (grass-roots Catholic movements) and liberation theory on the other, the Catholic Church could not permeate social habits and political action. An imperfect welfare state[2] buffered tensions and social conflict, while, at the political level, institutional and political engineering created a model based on power sharing between the two major political parties, the Colorado Party and the National Party.

The principle of coparticipation (minority party representation in all paths of institutional life, from the boards of directors of public enterprises to the state bureaucracy) gave the opposition a share in the system but also colonized the state apparatus and impeded the formation of a neutral civil service.[3] The party apparatus is thus hidden inside the state bureaucracy. To maintain this equilibrium born of consensus, interparty pacts were complemented by formulas of political engineering destined to deal with intraparty conflicts and factionalism.[4] Thus, since 1924 Uruguayan electoral laws do not allow ticket splitting, forcing voters to choose all candidates—for local government and for the legislative and executive branches—from the same party (*lema*). The so-called double simultaneous vote (*doble voto simultáneo*) effectively hinders the potential multiplication of parties, making it more convenient for political actors to make alliances within the existing parties than to create new political organizations.[5]

This political system was based on the riches generated by an agrarian economy. The Uruguayan welfare state was financed by economic profits from very favorable external conditions, especially the two world wars and the Korean conflict.[6] When the Uruguayan economy proved unable to adapt to adverse international economic conditions, the politics of extreme consensus that guaranteed democratic stability proved a hindrance and was at the very heart of the country's social and political stagnation. In the 1960s, Uruguayans began to realize that there were limits to equitable social welfare in an underdeveloped economy. The country entered an era of radicalism and ideological polarization as different groups fought to maintain what they perceived as their entitlement to happiness, upward social mobility, and well-being. Organized political violence erupted with the National Liberation Movement (Tupamaros) and other lesser groups.[7]

In 1973, after a long coup that lasted from February to June, the armed forces took control of the country. After 1976 a collegial military-technocratic group attempted to rule the country.[8] The armed forces, however, proved unable to produce an alternative political model and maintained only a very harsh, twelve-year-long "commissarial" dictatorship.[9] Repression alone is never enough. The military was very effective in creating a culture of fear,[10] which served only to paralyze the citizenry; it could not provide the necessary foundation for a new political system. It was therefore relatively easy to restore democracy during the transition process as, despite appearances, many of the country's basic political structures had remained unscathed.[11]

Negotiations between the military and members of the political class resulted in a restoration. As with the nineteenth-century political situation, widely used at the time as a metaphor of current events, the idea was to go back to that point in history where the fracture had taken place and consider the period of military rule as a mere interruption in the normal course of events. Although the main goal of political leaders was to return to a well-known—and safe—political path, they were forced to admit that important changes had taken place during twelve years of authoritarian rule.

The process of negotiation concluded with an election. However, two of the main leaders of the opposition were forced to choose candidates to represent them, as they were forced out of the electoral contest by regulations of the military government still in power. This very special election was won by Dr. Julio María Sanguinetti, who had been the main political negotiator of the transition.[12]

During the first term of Sanguinetti's presidency (1985–90), many tasks of restoration were undertaken. The country returned to the practice of political consensus, while, little by little, the citizenry, recuperating from the strain of the previously pervasive culture of fear, regained confidence in the guarantees of the *état de droit*. In April 1989 this process was completed when the issue of human rights abuses during the military era was put to rest with the passage of the Law-Bill of Amnesty for the Military.[13]

Most of the work of President Sanguinetti centered on managing civil-military relations. Dealing with the legacy of the past consumed four of the five years of his term. As a result, politicians were extremely prudent in their management of the state and in public policymaking. There were no great innovations in economic or social policy. Nonetheless, the reform measures recommended by the so-called Consensus of Washington were cautiously carried out.[14] Governability was guaranteed by the factions of the Colorado Party that followed President Sanguinetti and by a temporary alliance over key issues with Por la Patria, the main sector of the National Party, which was led until his death by Wilson Ferreira Aldunate.

Thanks to this basic agreement, Sanguinetti was able to pass some essential laws that enabled him to govern and begin anew, especially the budgetary law and the law of Amnesty. Other attempts at reform had to be postponed. The president used his veto power to control parliamentary initiatives to increase public expenditures. To forestall pressures from the different political groups that supported him, Sanguinetti was also forced to shoulder much of the burden of administration personally. His tenure in office was characterized by a strong executive that retained control over all important decisions in the hands of the president. Although the constitution states that in certain cases—for example, when discussing and approving budgetary laws—the executive must assume a quasi-parliamentary form by convening the full Council of Ministers, Sanguinetti never implemented these constitutional precepts.[15]

On November 26, 1989, Dr. Luis Alberto Lacalle, a candidate of the National Party, was democratically elected president.[16] Even more important, Dr. Tabaré Vázquez, a Broad Front candidate, was elected mayor of Montevideo, the capital city, where half the country's population lives. With the uneventful alternation of parties in power, the transition process ended. In the same election, the constitution was amended in a measure commonly known as the Plebiscito de los Jubilados (plebiscite on retirees). In a sense, it synthesized and presaged many of the problems and challenges that Uruguayan democracy would have to face during the next period. This addendum to the constitution specifies two conditions for increasing retirement pensions: they must be increased when public sector wages are raised and the index to be used for the increase is the average wage index, which includes private sector salaries. The second condition means that retirees are to receive higher increases than public employees. Moreover, 2 percent of the GNP (gross national product) must be allocated to pay for this reform. The plebiscite on retirees passed with 81 percent of the vote.

The New Challenges Faced by Uruguayan Democracy

Perhaps one of the greatest challenges the country has to face stems from its very demographics. With a total population of almost 3 million, the active economic population is only 1.2 million. While nearly a million persons contribute to an unreformed Social Security system, there are 600,000 pensioners and retirees and nearly 300,000 public servants.[17] The average voter age in the 1994 general election was forty-two. Middle-aged and overeducated, Uruguayans fear and resist change, even though they have experienced many transformations in their everyday life over the last few years.

Thus President Lacalle's government undertook a program of economic adjustments based on fiscal reform. This course of action included an increase in the value added tax (VAT)[18] to finance the deficit-ridden Social Security system, modernization and enhancement of tax collection and tax control procedures, steady reduction of public expenditures, and a monetary policy aimed at reducing the amount of money in circulation in order to control inflation. These policies have achieved some important goals. Compared to 1992, economic growth decreased in 1993 but again increased in 1994.[19] Inflation continues to show a slow decrease,[20] even if the country has not reached the lower levels of inflation of most Latin American countries.

The Economic Commission for Latin America (CEPAL) has therefore placed Uruguay among the countries in a state of "controlled instability." The government deficit in 1995 was only 1.3 percent of GNP.[21] In 1993, real wages of public employees increased 7 percent and those of workers in the private sector 3.3 percent. In 1994, private sector salaries increased 1.1 percent and public sector salaries 0.6 percent. In 1995, real wages decreased 2.2 percent for the private sector and 2 percent for public employees. However, the imbalance of exports and imports (–6 percent and +8 percent respectively for 1993) preoccupies economic groups of exporters and industrialists as the commercial deficit was U.S.$680 million in 1993, U.S.$613 million in 1994, and nearly U.S.$847 million in 1995. Meanwhile, groups of entrepreneurs such as importers and financiers are flourishing.

The economic policies of the Lacalle administration have contributed to the decline of the traditional agrarian sector. On the other hand, as both an effect of Uruguay's participation in Mercado Común del sur (MERCOSUR, Southern Cone Common Market) and the weakness of the U.S. dollar in the region, the internal market has been flooded by imports that have accelerated the country's deindustrialization. As a result of both these factors, Uruguay has increasingly evolved into a service economy.

Thus many of the hopes that had been placed on the process of economic integration have been disappointed. Many entrepreneurs, especially small business owners, and whole groups of workers facing potential layoffs are afraid of the effects this process might have on their interests. This fear has led to a short-term alliance of entrepreneurs and workers in opposing what they perceive as the harsher aspects of the economic policy of the Lacalle government. They also demand some measure of protection against the undesired effects of free trade.

Social inequality has slightly increased over the past few years as there has been a tendency toward income concentration at the top.[22] Sectors below the line of extreme poverty are still minor compared to other countries of the region. However, the vulnerability of previously well-off middle-class sectors has become an urgent problem that must be tackled before it evolves from a social issue into a political problem. The government has launched a series of programs—basically administered through organizations outside and parallel to the state structure—to deal with questions related to extreme poverty: basic health care, education, and housing. But no such programs exist to help and support the sinking middle class, and this is a potential source of political unrest.[23]

The Lacalle administration's original program included reform of the state as one of its main components, but the government was unable to form the political alliances that would have enabled it to implement the proposed changes. Although the administration negotiated a temporary alliance with key sectors of the Colorado Party to pass the law of public enterprises that established the legal framework for privatizing some public enterprises, this coalition could not be sustained after a popular initiative to hold a referendum on the law succeeded in overthrowing some of its articles. In 1992 the Foro Batllista, led by former President Sanguinetti, formed a limited partnership with the Broad Front to oppose the law of public enterprises. The referendum was won by those that opposed privatization by a nearly two-thirds vote.[24]

The Lacalle administration was thus forced to use a dual strategy to achieve its ends. On the one hand, it reduced the size of the state by using a "default" option, banning the hiring of new employees and cutting the salaries of existing ones to make public employment less desirable. On the other hand, it created a structure that ran parallel to that of the state and was not hindered by the constraints and privileges of the public sector. This new structure was put under the administration's direct control and acts in those areas where quick and efficient state intervention is necessary.

Nevertheless, the main problem of the size and cost of the state remains untouched: Uruguay has three hundred thousand public employees, and the average monthly salary per employee is U.S.$240. Although public employment is an underpaid and low-prestige activity, the security it offers makes it a very sought-after occupation in a country where the measurable unemployment rate in 1993 was 8.3 percent and as high as 18 percent when informal activities are included. The squeezing of

Table 5 Uruguay: Economic Performance, 1985–1994

Year	GNP (millions of current U.S.$)	GNP Per Capita (current U.S.$)	Commercial Balance Index (millions of current U.S.$)	Payments Balance (millions of current U.S.$)	Wages Index	Unemployment (%)	Inflation Rate (%)
1985	4.719	1.569	145.8	–64.8	100	12.0	74
1986	5.859	1.937	217.8	256.4	81	10.1	70
1987	7.330	2.409	40.4	44.5	71	9.1	62
1988	7.583	2.478	227.7	73.1	64	8.6	71
1989	7.992	2.598	396.0	94.6	80	8.0	101
1990	8.355	2.700	350.0	80.9	95	8.5	106
1991	10.041	3.226	–31.8	–237.0	111	8.9	85
1992	11.849	3.785	–342.6	120.0	72	9.0	61
1993	13.453	4.272	–680.4	182.8	61	8.3	56
1994	15.543	4.908	–859.1	238.0	46	9.2	45

Source: Central Bank of Uruguay and Instituto Nacional de Estadísticas.

salaries in the public sector has bred discontent among workers: the Lacalle administration has had to deal with increased labor conflicts and strikes of state employees.

There have been several important labor conflicts during the Lacalle administration.[25] However, the most significant challenge in this area stems from major changes within the trade union movement itself. In fact, the labor movement, formerly dominated by the Left and highly centralized in the PIT-CNT (Interunion Workers Council–Workers National Caucus), has suffered three major transformations. First, it has lost the power to raise active and favorable support for its positions and directives among workers and the general public. Second, some trade unions belonging to the federation of organized labor are acting autonomously, disregarding the centralized levels of decision making within the movement and favoring those issues more directly related to the concerns of the sector or enterprise to which they belong. Finally, within the trade union movement, the tendency toward a polarization of the positions that divide moderates from radicals has increased. The PIT-CNT is also facing a financial crisis that clearly reflects the weakening of the power it held over salaried workers: plagued with huge debts, it cannot obtain more money from its affiliates because many federated trade unions have inflated membership lists that do not correspond to the scant levels of support they can raise.[26]

In the future the present structure of the organized labor movement will probably lose most of its current elements. The empty shell will then fall under the control of the more radical factions, further alienating the old organizational structures from newer worker groups. Perhaps new structures will emerge to promote the interests of these workers: the new trade unions may be much more directly linked to the problems and concerns of the workplace itself. Thus the association between trade union and enterprise may be stronger than it is now,[27] while the traditional links between unions and leftist parties or movements may be weakened.

The armed forces are another institution that has endured profound transformations during the last few years. After a series of crises that included military unrest, isolated acts of armed propaganda, the Berríos scandal,[28] the dismissal of the commander in chief of the army, the transfer of two generals to other posts, and the freeze on several promotions of senior and junior officers, the military has entered a phase of internal reorganization. The attempts at professional reform necessarily meet a certain degree of resistance within an institution that still has difficulty in coming to terms with its recent past. However, another source of tension comes from the budgetary constraints the armed forces have to face. These restrictions entangle the issue for military reformers because structural innovations cannot be accompanied by changes in obsolete equipment. The military is carrying on an internal discussion on this matter; it has thus become a conflict of interest among the generals rather than a civil-military issue.

Lieutenant General Daniel García, the commander in chief of the army in the last years of Lacalle's administration, reformed the institution by suppressing the mounted cavalry regiments and transforming them into modern combat units. García was one of the promoters of Uruguayan participation in United Nations peacekeeping forces.[29] This issue has divided the generals while winning acceptance among junior and middle-rank officers, who perceive it as a source of extra income and professional practice. García has also said that the army should be managed as a modern enterprise, and he intends to sell some of its valuable property in order to help pay the cost of internal restructuring. However, these funds will not be sufficient to implement his entire reform program. In 1995, the new army commander, Lieutenant General Juan C. Curuchet, slowed down the process of reform.

The navy has also been undergoing a deep process of transformation. This branch of the military was the first to sign an agreement with the civilian university to modify its own curricula and make them equivalent to those of the university, and was also the first to incorporate women into its ranks. Open to outside influences, the navy has tried to obtain equipment through agreements with countries such as Germany, France, and the United States. Internally less divided than the army, the naval high command wants to accelerate the navy's modernization, thus diminishing the traditional gap between its forces and those of the army.

The air force is no challenge for either of them. It suffers from a chronic shortage of equipment, has no external clout among politicians, and has an unfavorable position vis-à-vis the other two services. Traditionally, the air force has sought to play second fiddle to the army.

Last but not least, the former leftist guerrillas that took arms against institutional order in the 1960s and 1970s are now fully, if negatively, integrated into the system. The National Liberation Movement (Tupamaros) forms the axis of the radical pole within both the Broad Front coalition and the organized labor movement. The bearer of a high-voltage discourse that defends the main tenets of the ideology of the extreme Left, the Tupamaros have nonetheless renounced violence as a convenient political means. The movement has also polarized positions within the leftist coalition, increasing tensions among more moderate groups that want to adopt a more realistic attitude toward the exercise of political power.

The Political Scenario

The framework of electoral rules that regulate Uruguayan political life has only slightly changed since 1925 when the first electoral laws gave guarantees to voters by creating the Electoral Court and the Permanent Civic Register. These laws also implemented the system of "accumulation" designed in 1910 that shaped political parties that are in fact federations of factions covering a wide ideological spectrum and including significant intraparty rivalries among leaders.

Since the constitutional reform of 1967, elections are held every five years for political offices at all levels of government (executive, legislative, and local).[30] Except for the *juntas departamentales* (local councils), proportional representation is used to assign seats in Congress, while executive office, at both the local and national levels, is won by simple majority. The electoral system allows the accumulation of votes among factions (*sub-lemas*) of the same party (officially called *lema* in the electoral jargon of the country) in order to win the presidency (*doble voto simultáneo*, or double simultaneous vote). By this procedure, after counting the ballots in an election, electoral officials must first determine which party has won the election. The candidate of the majority faction of the winning party is then elected to the presidency. The same procedure is used to determine the seats in Congress. Here the first step (called *primer escrutinio*) is to ascertain how many seats have been won by each party through proportional representation. Once this information is known, seats are allocated to each faction using first a quotient and then a modified D'Hondt formula.

Voters cannot choose freely among candidates from different parties for offices at different levels of government. Thus, in the Uruguayan system, parties are seen as self-contained and separate entities: voters must elect one among the different candidates within the same *lema* but cannot trespass the boundaries of the party to select a mayor or a list for Congress from another party. No ticket splitting is allowed under any circumstances.[31] Due to the simultaneity of the different electoral processes, there is a bandwagon effect as the national election influences the local election. This system also gives preeminence to the party leaders, as the first real election is held at the moment of drawing up the list of candidates.

The rules have not changed since 1925, so there is no regulation of political campaigns with regard to the length of the campaign, financing of political parties, or use of the media. The law forbids electoral propaganda forty-eight hours before election day; polls are not regulated except for forbidding electoral propaganda; and only one provision regulates party fund raising. While the government pays each political party U.S.$7 per vote received,[32] there are no limits on political contributions from private citizens, businesses, or interest groups.

Nor is there any provision for monitoring elections using international observers or delegations, as this was not a common practice in the 1920s and 1930s. The normal practice in Uruguay since 1925 has been to have party representatives monitoring the whole process on election day. Until 1980, polling station workers were also designated by political parties. Since then they have been recruited among public employees—usually clerks, teachers, and professors—to speed up the process and make it more efficient. Vote counting is public: any citizen can watch the procedure. After the first counting of the ballots, they can be recounted by the electoral authorities if there are challenges. Exit polls and quick counts, by both parties and the media, are a normal practice. Voting is mandatory, and heavy sanctions for those not participating are strictly enforced.[33] Therefore, voting rates are normally 80 percent or higher.[34]

Uruguay has a presidential system based on two key premises. First, continuous negotiation among all political actors is needed for the system to function; and, second, since the constitutional reform of 1967, the preeminence of the executive branch has increased. Only the executive branch has the right to introduce legislation in the areas of finance and the budget. As in any presidential system, the president has the right to veto acts passed by Congress. However, Congress can override a presidential veto by a two-thirds majority (86 out of 130 votes). This special majority is difficult to achieve in a fragmented party system.

Since 1934 some provisions have been made in the constitution aimed at altering the presidential system. These semiparliamentary mechanisms have not been able to function as intended. According to the constitution, Congress has the power to vote to censure one or more cabinet ministers, who must then leave the government. However, if the vote of censure carries by more than 51 percent but less than

66 percent in the General Assembly, and if the current administration is not in its first or last year of government, the president can retain his minister. If the president chooses this path, he or she must call for a parliamentary election within sixty days. Then the new Congress must confirm or reject the previous vote of censure. The presidential office itself is never jeopardized by this mechanism.

This institutional trend corresponds to the personalization of politics, which has come to be associated not with programs or identities closely linked to political parties but with particular personalities. While this tendency is universal, its impact on more traditional political life in Uruguay cannot easily be dismissed. On the one hand, it has increased the power of the real party leaders and diminished the importance of party structures, as presidential candidates do not depend on these structures to win the election. They rely more on the media to further their interests than on the old party bosses and branches. On the other hand, it creates tension with Congress, as legislators often try to encroach on the role of the executive by invading those areas reserved for the president's initiative in order to obtain some measure of visibility for themselves. The tensions between these two branches of government do not recur in their relationship to the judiciary. Uruguay follows the continental school on this matter: it is an *état de droit*, and the judiciary cannot create laws. Even jurisprudence has only an advisory role, and following its pronouncements is not mandatory.

This tendency toward a concentration of power in the executive branch is tempered by a trend toward direct democracy using the constitutional mechanism of referendum. The original idea of the political elite when writing the constitutional provision on referendums had been to enable the president to bypass Congress and appeal directly to voters when there was an institutional deadlock. However, since the referendum on the amnesty law for the military, the philosophy behind it has changed. Voters began to use this means as a way of colegislating when they did not agree with the actions of the politicians. While this trend has provided an important check on the possibility of an unbalanced exercise of power by the executive, it has also impeded many initiatives that need to be implemented if Uruguay is to outgrow its present stagnation. It has also increased the role and power of the media in the political arena. While this trend has not attained the dimensions it has in Argentina, politics is evolving into media politics in Uruguay. Meanwhile there are important shifts among the interest groups that control the media. Cable TV is being installed in Montevideo and its metropolitan areas, and important groups are fighting to be included in this new way of influencing public life.

After the election of 1994, political and electoral reform became the main priority. It is necessary to address the key issues of governability in the country: (1) In a context of party fragmentation, can the executive branch carry through a program without harmful interference on the part of Congress made only for the sake of publicity or to gain privileges for a political or corporate sector? (2) Can the executive branch have real, as opposed to formal, control of government policies? These issues must be addressed especially in order to prevent a process of "Fujimorization," as the next administration must face some problems that the Lacalle administration could not resolve. Among these are: (1) government reform, which includes trimming down the state bureaucracy and making it more efficient in its central administration as well as transforming many state enterprises into mixed-management operations; (2) reform of the Social Security system, which might entail some form of privatization of retirement funds and a curtailment of existing rights and privileges; (3) designing educational policies that conceive education as an investment and a competitive advantage for the country; (4) designing social policies that alleviate the worst effects of economic reform programs on the lower strata of society; and (5) the challenge of economic integration, even if at a slower pace, through agreements like MERCOSUR.

These and other issues will need governments that can govern. As the challenges the country must face increase, so also does the tendency toward a fearful conservatism on the part of the citizens. The results of the national election in 1994 were very significant: three parties obtained a similar number of votes and seats in the Congress.[35]

The newly elected president, Julio María Sanguinetti, faces a serious dilemma. Strong leadership will be needed to conduct the country through these turbulent times. The institutional setting does not enable politicians to exert this leadership without violating or at least bending constitutional precepts.

Existing institutional arrangements were designed to favor the interaction and mutual accommodation of two political parties. Reality shows that the citizenry today is divided into thirds. In addition to winning a solid one-third of the votes in the last election, the Left won, for the second time, the municipal election in Montevideo with 45 percent of the votes.

Given the new political scenario, Sanguinetti has inaugurated a new style of political action, betting that this new strategy will ensure the governability of the country. Instead of being the omnipresent decision maker in day-to-day matters—a style of government all too frequent in Latin American presidents—he is highlighting his position as head of state while reducing his public appearances as head of the government. In this, the style of his present administration varies significantly from the one he developed between 1985 and 1989.

In this new phase, Sanguinetti apparently allows greater autonomy to his ministers. However, this greater autonomy is curtailed by four factors. First there is the president himself. In certain cases, he directly indicates the boundaries of freedom he concedes to a given minister. In others, he merely suggests what these limits might be or uses one of his political operators—the unofficial "voices" of the president—to do so. The second element of control is provided by the existence of an unofficial head of government who acts on behalf of the president. Usually, this role is fulfilled by the minister of planning or the economic minister. Sometimes the secretary of state assumes the role of an unofficial prime minister. All these members of the executive have one trait in common: they lack independent political backing. They all fulfill roles that help preserve the political capital of the head of state. The third constraint to the autonomy of the ministers is internal: their portfolios lack both human and material resources. Therefore, it is very difficult for any official to introduce major innovations during his or her administration. Attempts at innovation are also reduced by the features of the political scenario: the division of the political arena into thirds forces politicians to act with extreme caution to obtain the necessary support of their peers.

The current situation dictates a coalition government. Sanguinetti has as his chief partner Dr. Alberto Volonté, the candidate of the National Party who received the most votes. Volonté is in fact paying the political cost of providing vital support to the Sanguinetti government while expecting to reap the benefits of such an alliance in the 1999 election.

This political mechanism—a coalition government, the separation of the functions of head of state from the day-to-day management of the state, and the strategic use of areas of autonomy for his ministers—provides Sanguinetti with the space necessary to dissociate himself from his party while preserving his own political capital. He knows he will use it in the coming years to help pass essential reforms and avert a crisis brought on by the unavoidable erosion of the coalition.

The plan of President Sanguinetti is to obtain a series of essential adjustments: reform of the state-controlled retirement system to open it partially to private initiative; reduction of the number of state employees; reform of the educational system to adapt it to new challenges; undertaking some needed public works, such as the bridge between Buenos Aires, the capital city of Argentina, and Colonia, a small Uruguayan city. Sanguinetti's main concern is to manage the administration of the country in an orderly way. This plan, which might seem unambitious, is fraught with difficulties because of the lack of institutional arrangements that could provide him with a majority in parliament and because of resistance from a Uruguayan society condemned to conservatism by its very demographics.

The new style of government of the Sanguinetti administration does not favor his own group, the Colorado Party. Although the internal life of the party is almost nonexistent between elections, it is still the only cohesive political organization that presents a united front on key issues. The oligarchy of power, in Robert Michels' terms, still works.[36] Some Colorado political groups have pointed out that their party has been losing twenty-five votes per day since 1984. Using the words of a well-known Uruguayan political scientist,[37] they say that the Colorado votes "go to heaven," as traditional Colorado supporters die of old age while the party is unable to attract younger voters. Those same groups warn that the Colorado Party may suffer an important defeat in the 1999 election if it does not take the steps necessary to attract these younger citizens with a stronger commitment to change.

The Left has inherited those votes lost by the Colorados. After the breakup of the Soviet Union, the Uruguayan Left went through a series of internal disputes involving its moderate and radical sectors. The internal structure of the Left changed between 1989 and 1994 because of the end of the cold war. The Uruguayan Communist Party ceased playing its traditional pivotal role. However, the Left did not disappear mainly because the existing traditional parties could not and would not incorporate into their own platforms political programs that called for maintaining a strong state that would provide social justice and equality. Therefore, the Left remained in the Broad Front.

Two competing strategies have been devised inside the organization to adapt and grow in the frame of changed circumstances. Tabaré Vázquez, the "new *caudillo*,"[38] the mayor of Montevideo (1989–94) who lost the presidency by sixty thousand votes, sees the possibility of invading a part of the political spectrum normally occupied by the traditional parties. This would be done by creating a new alliance, the Encuentro Progresista (Progressive Encounter), with dissident members of the traditional political organizations. His plan did not work well in 1994. The failure of the Encuentro Progresista to increase significantly the number of votes the Broad Front received on its own opened the door to a new grouping inside the leftist coalition, the Asamblea Uruguay (Uruguay Assembly). This somewhat amorphous group is an electoral movement of citizens more than a group of activists. Their leader, Danilo Astori, a technocrat lacking the popular appeal of Tabaré Vázquez, incarnates a discourse of moderation—a leftist sensibility turned toward social justice in the framework of "politics as the art of the possible" more than an ideological platform. His strategy to invade the space previously occupied by the traditional parties relies precisely on this moderation. He aims at co-opting voters, more than political leaders or structures, from the traditional organizations. His strategy is very effective in a conservative society that cringes at the rhetoric of the extremes after the trauma of the military era.

The rise of Astori has forced Vázquez to lean toward the more radical sectors of the Broad Front. Eventually this move might compromise his chances of winning the internal contest, as any radicalization of discourse makes him lose the support of moderate voters oriented toward an option at the center of the political spectrum. Curiously enough, under very changed sociopolitical circumstances, the conflict that opposes Vázquez and Astori is almost a replica of the confrontation between socialists and communists in the 1960s. Socialists always tried to invade the space of the traditional parties by co-opting dissident members of the establishment and the structures of the traditional organizations. Their efforts were always condemned to failure, as they forgot to include the voters in their political calculations. The failed experience of Unión Popular (Popular Union) in 1962, an alliance of the socialists with the dissident leader of the National Party, Enrique Erro, is perhaps the best example of this type of strategy. On the other hand, the communists, led by their secretary general, Congressman Rodney Arismendi,[39] tried to win the battle for the "hearts and minds" of sectors of the population discontent with politics as practiced by the traditional parties. The transfer of voters from the traditional parties to the Communist Party was permanent.

As for the National Party, it is torn by internal strife. There is an open conflict for party leadership that opposes former president Luis Alberto Lacalle—who wants to win a second presidential term in 1999—and Alberto Volonté, the "new *caudillo*" who emerged as a politician after a successful term as chief executive officer of UTE, the public utility that provides electricity for the country. Volonté has chosen to become the main partner of Sanguinetti in his coalition government. Lacalle also participates in the coalition but has publicly expressed his aversion to it. Political observers consider that he will try to leave the coalition when it is feasible.

This brief description of the situation of the political parties shows that there is urgent need to reform the prevailing institutional design. Contacts are being made to promote constitutional reform, but the outcome of this issue is uncertain.

Many things are still uncertain in Uruguay, a society torn by its desire to keep the achievements of the past while adapting the new circumstances. Uruguay ranks among the highly developed countries in terms of quality of life in the human development index created by the United Nations Development Program (UNDP), with an index of 0.881 in 1994.[40] One of the main goals of Uruguayan society is to preserve that quality of life by defending the social welfare mechanisms created in the past. This goal is extremely ambitious at a time when small countries such as Uruguay cannot make decisions without considering the pressures and conditions imposed by their larger neighbors, the international financial system, and multilateral agencies. Consequently, there is still room for the growth of an old leftist alternative such as the Broad Front. The challenge the political class should meet is how to effect the necessary changes in the state, the institutional arrangements, and the parties without generating social upheavals.

9

Argentina: Democracy in Turmoil

Liliana De Riz

A la memoria de esa experiencia debe su fuerza el orden socioeconómico y político que hoy vemos perfilarse; es el recuerdo aleccionador el que le da a la mayoría la fortaleza necesaria para soportar la ostentosa indiferencia de los sectores privilegiados por las penurias que siguen sufriendo los que no lo son, y ofrecer su acquiescencia a la progresiva degradación de las instituciones cuya restauración celebraron con tan vivas esperanzas hace diez años. Gracias a él, en suma la Argentina que ha logrado finalmente evadirse de su callejón se resigna a vivir en la más dura intemperie.

[The strength of today's socioeconomic and political order is due to the memory of that experience; it is the instructive memory which gives the majority the necessary strength to cope with the ostentatious indifference of the privileged sectors to the hardships suffered by those who are not privileged, and offer their acquiescence to the progressive degradation of the institutions whose restoration they celebrated with great expectations ten years ago. Thanks to it, the Argentina that was finally able to avoid its deadlock is now accepting to live in the most harsh conditions.]
—Tulio Halperín Donghi, *La agonía de la Argentina peronista*

For the third time in twelve years, Argentina has a democratically elected president. This is a remarkable achievement in a country in which political instability was the dominant feature for the main part of its contemporary history. For more than a decade, Argentina has moved away from economic decline and political authoritarianism.

While the principal task for the Radical Party was to restore the rule of law, it rested with the Peronists to straighten out the economy. In the May 1995 elections, Peronist president Carlos Menem was rewarded with a second term in office. Menem's success in controlling the hyperinflation that led the country to the brink of ungovernability in 1989 was the source of his renewed strength.

The economic reforms and their social cost under Menem's first administration have already been well analyzed.[1] So have some of the main features of the Argentine "hybrid" democracy that it brought about.[2] This chapter focuses on the political dynamics underlying Argentina's economic reforms under Menem, the uniqueness of Menem's leadership, the transformations of the country's party system, and the impact of constitutional reforms. All these features are essential to understanding the evolution of democratic governance in the near future.

At present, President Menem must confront the outbreak of financial crises in the provinces in the context of an unprecedentedly high unemployment rate, and he must do so in a drastically changed scenario that lacks the peace and confidence he enjoyed throughout his first term in office and that is now reshaped by the new constitutional rules.

Menem's second term raises some crucial questions regarding the condition of democratic governance in the near future: will he be able to lead a nation with growing social costs resulting from economic reforms? Will he be able to control the political conflict that, far from declining, has exploded inside Peronism? To put it differently: will it be possible for Menem to manage a second presidential term in which the discretionary exercise of power must be replaced by constant negotiations both within and outside party ranks? Will new constitutional rules contribute to reshaping presidential powers? What lessons did the parties learn from twelve years of democracy and economic reforms?

This chapter explores the factors that underlie the answers to these questions. It is necessary to recognize, however, that political reflection, at a time when a society is experiencing a succession of critical episodes, needs to adopt a double and simultaneous reflection: in order to see the present, it is imperative to look back at the past and try to capture those elements that the present reactivates. Nevertheless, current circumstances make tentative assessments prone to be disproven by coming events.

The Politics of Economic Crisis

The Construction of Presidential Authority

President Menem, who emerged from the first primary elections to win the presidency democratically, came to power with the extraordinary resources bestowed on him by the situation of hyperinflation and by having been elected by a political movement that defined itself as the interpreter of national and popular tradition. With this political capital, he crafted a coalition strategy toward the Right of the political spectrum. The uniqueness of his governing style, which was based on a powerful coalition that encompassed the large unions (initially in charge of the Ministry of Labor) and the sectors that emerged as the most representative of economic power, conferred on him inordinate autonomy vis-à-vis his party. This allowed him to create and recreate his cabinet and to react to the situation with strong pragmatism.[3] The members of his administration professed to be free of any conditioning that did not properly stem from the will of the president. Quickly the concentration of political power in the hands of the president reached an extraordinary dimension.

During the first two years of his administration and as a consequence of the absence of cooperation strategies to moderate the distributive struggle, economic stability could not be achieved. The arrival of Domingo Cavallo at the Ministry of the Economy, toward the beginning of 1991, should be seen more as a response to the institutional crisis that had been unleashed by the so-called Swiftgate than as a response to inflationary turmoil. Corruption proceeded to occupy center stage, fueled by a shadowy process of privatizations, which were carried out by government officials who were protected by the great autonomy of action accorded to them by the economic emergency and by an architecture of power that was exclusively accountable to its own vertex, the president.[4] The resulting erosion of the supervisory capacity of the state contributed to weaken the already precarious autonomy of these powers. This situation resulted in lack of accountability and in horizontal control of executive decisions.[5]

The climate that surrounded the departure of the third minister of the economy, Erman González, was not favorable: the sudden increase in strength of the dollar and widespread skepticism, which was a combined product of the recessionary effects of the economic policy that was in place and of almost a decade of failed adjustment attempts, caused the disappearance of the "initial magic" of the government. The Cavallo plan to fix the exchange rate was approved by the Congress. This strategy bolstered confidence in the irreversible nature of the decision made regarding the exchange rate and the free convertibility of the currency.[6] Productivity was established as the defining criterion of wage levels with an eye toward delinking salaries from inflation, as much in the public as in the private sector.

The program was as successful in the economic arena, with an abrupt decline of inflation, as it was in the political one. The government won the congressional elections for the renewal of one-half of the Chamber of Deputies and the gubernatorial elections during the second half of 1991. The results of the elections, interpreted by the administration as an undeniable success, exhibited a decline in the electoral strength of Peronism compared to 1989, the loss of provinces like Salta, Chaco, and Santa Cruz, and the retention of political predominance in others, thanks to the *ley de lemas* (law of the *lemas*), which was implemented in eleven provinces (this electoral system was making its debut in the majority of these elections).[7]

Tax measures, which were approved by the Congress (unlike in the previous administration), together with deregulation of markets, liberalization of imports, and privatizations, created a closed economy with strong state intervention. The state achieved greater autonomy from social and economic actors (the convertibility law assures its own self-disciplining), but at the cost of an extreme personalization of political power. The direction undertaken remained tied to the ability of the executive to maintain its coalition of support and to stay in office.[8] Decisiveness, secrecy, and surprise—the three qualities that define a skillful politician, according to a saying attributed to the deceased Peronist *caudillo* from Catamarca, Vicente Saadi, whom Menem likes to recall—are the hallmark of the style with which this government exercises political power.

The June 1992 elections for senator of the federal capital were won by the Radical candidate. Fernando de la Rúa won 52 percent of the vote by picking up the support of Peronist voters as well as those from the Right and the Left.[9] President Menem's candidate did not manage to gain support from the Center (the bulk of the electorate in the capital). In light of these results, the hypothesis of the alternation in power took shape both inside and outside of Peronism. Economic stability remained at the margin of political competition: it was a common banner of the Radicals and the Peronists. What the elections seemed to show was a change in the social significance of state reform: the demand for a reduced and efficient state was transformed into a demand for the recreation of the state and the reining in of corruption. The resulting privatizations showed the need to create a state that would regulate private monopolies of public service providers and act as a guarantor of essential goods such as health and education. Demonstrations of support for the protests of teachers and pensioners, and for resistance to the practices of the private monopolies (for example, the marches against highway tolls) revealed the widespread uneasiness brought about by the reduced role of the state.

The management of the state itself was in the eye of the storm. An administration whose record included the Yoma case, the appointment of family members to government positions, disastrous municipal administration of the capital, disturbing personal biographies of its civil officials, and a false quorum in the Senate to get a vote on an important law (the *diputrucho*, or false deputy) was punished in the elections in the capital.[10] Presidential reelection, an aspiration of Menem's supporters that was announced early on, became an even harder-to-achieve objective. The results of the senatorial elections in the capital compelled the government to redefine its political agenda. It is in this context that the proposal for political reform was presented as a complement to the economic reform implemented by the government. The sudden injection of political reform into the public debate demonstrated the president's skill in putting the opposition on the defensive: participation, transparency, and representativeness became his banners. Institutional reforms and the means to carry them out—among them, the president's reelection—were portrayed as the instruments to guarantee continued economic stability.

Constitutional Reform

The year 1993 began with the government's announcing a new agenda that had political reform as its core. The first half of the year was marked by the debate over the official proposal in a rarefied climate as a result of certain Supreme Court rulings and the resignation of the minister of justice, Ricardo Arslanian, in open disagreement with the makeup of the Chamber of Annulment, a tribunal that was created by the new Code of Procedures in legal matters.[11]

The political reform bill presented by the minister of the interior, Gustavo Béliz, combined elements contained in a plethora of bills of the ruling party and the opposition.[12] The resignation of Minister Béliz in August, in the midst of a climate of aggression and threats to journalists, highlighted the shady side of the initiative. The text of his resignation reveals the use of corrupt procedures to achieve certain objectives, especially constitutional reform, and the actions of those operating at the periphery of the president's will, who were eager to pay any price in order to continue in power.

The elections of October 3, the second elections for the partial renewal of the national Chamber of Deputies, were preceded by the privatization of Yacimientos Petrolíferos Fiscales (Argentine Petroleum Company), which was carried out with the stated objective of improving the situation of pensioners just at the point of voting (there are approximately 4 million pensioners). The elections took place in a unique political context whose most outstanding aspects were the initiative to reform the constitution and secure the right of the president to be reelected, the scandal in the days prior to the elections involving the Supreme Court over the revoking of a court ruling in favor of a suit against the central bank, and the accusations of corrupt activities that affected those who headed the ruling party ballots in the capital and in the province of Buenos Aires.

The Peronists (PJ, Partido Justicialista) won the 1993 elections with 42.3 percent of the vote, over the 30 percent obtained by the Radicals (UCR, Radical Civic Union). The clear triumph of the PJ came as a rejection of any mechanical link between the severity of the economic adjustment implemented by Minister Cavallo and social discontent. Economic stability was collectively perceived as an achievement capable of neutralizing the impact of excluding growing sectors of the population from the rights of social citizenship, the accusations of corruption, and the scandals that shook the Supreme Court on the eve of the elections. From the perspective of the evolution of the national electoral map, these figures do not substantially alter the tendencies that were recorded up to 1991. However, a more disaggregated analysis of the results shows discontinuities with the pattern recorded since 1983, which is not readily evident from an overall perspective. Peronism managed to win in the capital, where Radicalism has traditionally predominated, with 32.5 percent of the vote compared to the 29.9 percent obtained by the UCR.[13]

In the strategic province of Buenos Aires, which comprises one-third of the electorate, the PJ won with 48.1 percent of the vote over the 25.9 percent obtained by the UCR. The UCR grew with respect to 1991, but its distance from Peronism grew as well. The overall registered tendencies confirm the emergence of a new process: Peronism conquered areas previously reserved for Radicalism, and Radicalism advanced in traditionally Peronist zones.[14] The results of the 1993 elections reveal the presence of a restructuring process of the representational system. This raises some issues: the consolidation of a conservative-popular coalition with a strong electoral predominance in the face of an array of dispersed opposition forces; a greater weight for the third forces to the Right and Left of the political spectrum (now that the parties of the Right are free from the influence exercised by the currently disintegrated UCEDE (Union of the Democratic Center), could they act with greater autonomy with respect to Peronism?); and the formation of a Center-Left coalition.

Interpreted from the perspective of the objective of constitutional reform, the results of the October elections indicated that the reform could be achieved only through negotiations among the main parties. However, the reaction of the government was to rush its reform bill through the Senate, achieving approval by means of a shady process of negotiations within Peronism and thanks to the decisive vote of the senator from the province of San Juan, Leopoldo Bravo. In exchange for this vote, the government abandoned premises that were fundamental to its original bill, such as the direct election of the president, and laid bare the fact that reelection was its only goal. In the Chamber of Deputies, on the other hand, Peronism fell short of rallying the two-thirds vote needed for passage.[15] The centerpiece of the institutional offensive launched by the government was to call for a plebiscite, in which the citizenry could declare itself in favor of or against constitutional reform.

Radicalism appeared before the public on the horns of a dilemma: either reaffirm its refusal to ratify the reform and thus face another electoral defeat in the plebiscite, or agree to negotiate (thereby avoiding an electoral contest) and resign itself to bestowing legitimacy on the reform, knowing as they did that the government was willing to approve a new constitution even without the endorsement of the opposition.[16]

The institutional offensive of Peronism settled into the void created by a party that was in crisis and dismayed by its electoral defeat. The faction led by Raúl Alfonsín decided to negotiate with the government. The negotiations, which took the public by surprise, did not occur in a vacuum: a good part of the Radical leadership began to lean toward a negotiated solution. However, the followers of Fernando de la Rúa in the capital and those of Federico Storani and Juan M. Casella in the province of Buenos Aires, as well as other recognized leaders at the national level, were opposed. Recognized once again as party leader, Alfonsín conducted the negotiations and crafted an agreement with Menem over the contents of the partial reform of the constitution. The immediate corollary of the so-called Olivos Pact was the suspension of the plebiscite. In early December, with 70 percent of the votes in favor, the national convention of the UCR approved the decision to negotiate the reform. The new bill saw the light of day shortly thereafter. The resignation of Supreme Court justices and negotiations over the appointment of new justices, both of which were opposition demands, were the framework of the accord. Once consensus was reached, the text was approved by the Chamber of Deputies and then by the Senate.

However, in the Senate, Peronists and Radicals rejected the modification of the length of a senator's term (from nine to four years), which formed part of the original basic points of agreement. This rejection fueled uncertainty about the binding nature of the accord. The debate began to revolve around the constitutionality of the procedure used to obtain the approval of the law and the powers that the future Constituent Assembly should have. Could the Assembly declare itself sovereign? Are the delegates obligated to respect the basic points of agreement of the Olivos Pact?[17] In a society in which political pacts were always labeled pejoratively as *contubernios* (concubinage, cohabitation), the agreement became the target of criticism that never wavered in reducing the significance of the agreement to the mere political ambition of its signatories. One of the principal arguments used by the critics of the Olivos Pact was that it meant the disappearance of political opposition.

The political pact once again posed an old dilemma in new terms: what is the role of the opposition in a political system that faces the challenge of redefining its constitution? Does an opposition that consents to presidential reelection necessarily give up its role as the opposition? If so, one might conclude that presidential reelection is the only watershed: once it is conceded, the opposition is condemned to disappear from the scene. On the other hand, to forgo the opportunity to negotiate institutional changes entails the danger of being reduced to voices of protest and eventually becoming spectators who lack the necessary power resources to alter the course of reform.[18]

The political pact, which emerged from the presidential ambition to remain in power and the impotence of the opposition, meant, first and foremost, an end to the situation of confrontation between a government that was obsessed with obtaining reelection and an opposition that lacked any goal other than to block it. In effect, the UCR, devoid of leaders capable of giving direction to the party and of convincing the public that they had any vocation for statesmanship, failed to contain the authoritarian concentration of power. Its criticism of the Menem administration never successfully translated into an alternative program of government. The road of negotiating with Menem, which Alfonsín defined as "a response to a confining situation of the party" and as "a return to politics," opened the door to a dialogue with the government.[19]

Menem's decision to negotiate the reform of the constitution with his principal adversary in order to legitimize his ambitions constituted a novelty in the history of Peronism. Negotiations with the main opposition became indispensable for embarking on the transition toward a new presidential term and preempting the possibility that the Constituent Assembly would be transformed into a platform for satisfying, on a symbolic level, a wide variety of social demands.

The willingness of Menem and Alfonsín to come to an agreement created the space for a political convergence: in the executive, by means of the creation of the office of chief of the cabinet; in the election of the presidential ticket, with the ballotage; in the elections of the magistrates, with the incorporation of their representatives; in the control of the exercise of power, with the General Accounting Office of the Nation in the hands of the opposition. Its protagonists became the organizing core of a fragmented society in which the political parties do not function as channels of conflict mediation.

The difficulties that are taking shape on the horizon, forecast by the outbreak of violence in the province of Santiago del Estero, leave no doubts about the precariousness of decisions based on secrecy and surprise.[20] The need to open new topics for discussion, previously blocked by the debate about the pros and cons of presidential reelection, and to legitimize the policies of transformation of the Argentine economy and society were present in the strategy unfolded by the government.

The votes cast by the citizens in the elections for constitutional convention delegates were the only guarantees that the agreements would be respected. In the April 10, 1994, elections, Peronism and Radicalism jointly obtained 57 percent of the vote. The results demonstrated the strong growth of third political forces in tandem with the crisis of the captive vote. In effect, the PJ lost 6 points and the UCR, 11 points, compared to the results of the October 1993 legislative elections.[21] The perception that personal motives acted as the engine of institutional redesign, be it explicitly, as exemplified by presidential reelection, or covertly, as suggested by the renewed protagonism of former president Alfonsín, is at the root of the massive desertion of the Radical vote and the decline of support for the ruling party. This perception also accounts for the apathy of the public toward the constituent debates before and during the sessions of the Assembly.

From the perspective of the novelties that surrounded these elections, the most significant facts are the electoral debacle of the UCR, the erosion of the electoral base of the ruling party (its lowest figure since its 1983 electoral defeat) and the strong growth of the Center-Left represented by the Frente Grande (FG, Broad Front) led by Chacho Alvarez and of the MODIN (Movement for National Dignity and Independence), although to a lesser extent but with a more even distribution across districts. These facts affect the ability to predict the traditional picture of majoritarian alignments.

From the perspective of the constituent process, the results obtained by the ruling party reduced its eventual margin of maneuver to impose rules that would not respect the basic points of agreement with the UCR or that would not achieve sufficient consensus from outside the party in order to be included in the agenda of the Constituent Assembly.[22] Undoubtedly this was one of the factors that encouraged the ruling party to adhere to a pluralistic style of decision making.

The election of convention delegates leveled a strong blow at bipartisanship. At the same time, the geography of the April 1994 vote shows the salience of local issues in determining the vote of each province and precludes drawing hasty conclusions about voting tendencies at the national level.

The process of reconstruction of the system of representation is the context that gives meaning to the reforms introduced into the historic constitution. These reforms can induce innovative political strategies with respect to a past of Peronist-Radical predominance, mutual blocking of initiatives, and congressional gridlock.

The Constituent Process

Each of the points included in the core of the basic points of agreement was a target of criticism. Although not entirely devoid of persuasive arguments, these criticisms were characterized by an analysis that failed to take an overall view of a new institutional architecture that managed to surface in a context of restrictions stemming from the structure and dynamics of party competition. The limitation of reelection to only one consecutive term and the reduction of the presidential mandate to four years were seen as granting ten uninterrupted years to the government of Carlos Menem. By permitting indefinite reelections with a four-year interval, reelection in the medium and short term was conceived as a mechanism of authoritarian concentration of power. The taming of hyperpresidentialism that is sought in the division of the functions between the head of state and the head of government on the one hand and parliamentary controls on the other lost significance.

Distrust concerning the eventual efficacy of parliamentary mechanisms (the chief of the cabinet can be removed by the vote of an absolute majority of the members of each house) and about the powers of the chief of the cabinet stripped these innovations of their original importance. The election of a third senator for the minority was considered a concession to the Radical party owing to the fact that the UCR was the second major political force at the provincial level. By specifying percentages, the ballotage in the presidential election appeared invalidated: it would be applied only when the ticket receiving the most votes did not exceed 45 percent of the vote, or, in the event that it obtained 40 percent of the vote, when its distance from the second force was less than 10 percent. Some argued that this variant of ballotage suited Menem's desire for reelection. The regulation of presidential Decrees of Necessity and Urgency was considered as a legitimation of the authoritarian exercise of presidential power. The Council of Magistrates for the selection of judges appeared as a straightforward politicization of justice.

Topics such as the constitutionalization of political parties, the General Accounting Office of the Nation in the hands of the opposition, the limitation of federal intervention in the provinces, the autonomy of the city of Buenos Aires, and the direct election of the intendant were underestimated in a debate that was obsessed with the issue of presidential reelection. Topics that the pact left open to constituent debate remained unaddressed: the strengthening of the federal regime, municipal autonomy, mechanisms of semidirect democracy, the Office of Public Defender, the public ministry as an outside-of-power agency,[23] and the incorporation of new legal, civic, economic, and environmental rights. Although many of these topics had been raised by the opposition, they remained eclipsed by the prevailing notion of conspiracy, which stripped them of meaning.

Unlike the context in which the constitutional reform was set forth during the Alfonsín administration, the reform during the Menem administration took place in the context of a profoundly modified state. The hasty process of privatizations carried out by the new administration replaced state ownership of public services with unregulated private ownership or, in some cases, with regulatory entities whose boards included representatives of the privatized firms. The institutional deficit for sanctioning the monopolistic behavior of the privatized companies and corruption, made even more serious by the process of privatization of key sectors of production and public service provision, speaks openly of the need for the institutional reform of the state. However, during the six months that preceded the inauguration of the Constituent Assembly, the new reality of the state and the resulting need to endow it with adequate institutional control mechanisms did not form part of the debate, which remained centered around the anti/pro dichotomy on reelection.

The beginning of the deliberations at the Constituent Assembly on May 25, 1994, did not surprise a public that had already interpreted this process as a simple ratification of an agreement between bosses. However, the Constituent Assembly set in motion an unprecedented party dynamic. As a reflection of the new electoral map, the political composition of the Constituent Assembly superimposed on the traditional cleavage of Peronists, Radicals, and minor parties of the political spectrum new criteria of political aggregation: between the "Pro-Pact" and the "Anti-Pact" groups (the latter, comprised of the opposition that fought to eliminate the so-called dead bolt clause and to submit to a separate vote each of the points of the core of the agreement); and between the Menemists and the anti-Menemists, thereby creating an unprecedented situation of great fluidity, especially because the debate on certain topics led to a rise of anti-Menemists within the ruling party and Menemists in the opposition.

A novelty of the Constituent Assembly was the circumstantial alliances formed by different forces, including those situated at the extremes of the ideological-partisan spectrum, regarding issues that were open for debate. Seen from the perspective of the traditional rigidity of Argentine political parties for finding negotiated solutions, the Constituent Assembly served to disentangle the political game by creating multiple spaces of negotiation of institutional issues, around which the parties gradually positioned themselves.

It is in this sense that one can affirm that the Assembly, conditioned by the pact between Menem and Alfonsín, provided a scenario for mutual recognition, the learning of tolerance, and the encouragement of old and new forces of the partisan spectrum to negotiate their differences. The provincial parties found in the Constituent Assembly the space to begin to weave an electoral coalition around a unique presidential candidacy for the first electoral round of 1995.[24] The moderated and moderating tone of Chacho Alvarez on behalf of the Frente Grande and the explicit acceptance of democratic rules on the part of Aldo Rico, head of the MODIN, in spite of the professed antisystem vocation of his party, demonstrate the new political dynamic that surfaced in the constituent process.

The origin of the new constitution was a secret pact between the president and the former president that took the political parties and the public by surprise. Regardless of its merits and defects, this constitution is the first to enjoy a broad consensus of the entire partisan spectrum. Could its origin discredit the reformed constitution? One could interpret the Olivos Pact as the possible agreement in a society whose parties function as electoral machines, lacking the capacity to operate as channels of aggregation of diverse social demands.

President Menem might have emerged euphoric from a reform that authorized his reelection, but the celebration was not exclusively his. The Constituent Assembly brought an array of positive factors. This is its principal novelty: all parties had something to gain from the constituent experience. This is the principal significance of the unanimous endorsement of the new constitutional text.

The Reformed Constitution

The great themes of the constituent process were the structure and functions of the state, the balance of powers, the powers of the executive, territorial representation, the reform of justice, the electoral system, and the relations between the national government and the provinces.

The Reformed Constitution transfers to the legislative power the right to enact special laws that should discipline a series of agencies and regulate the functioning of the new state structure. These rights deal with determining who will comprise the Council of Magistrates (the entity responsible for overseeing judicial power) and the Trial Council, which can remove, without any appeals whatever, lower court federal judges; making decisions about the Decrees of Necessity and Urgency remitted to Congress, based on the opinion of a permanent bicameral commission created ad hoc; defining the scope of the public defender's office; and enacting the rules for electing the attorney general of the nation, a decisive point for assessing whether the Public Ministry will be independent of the other powers.

Constitutional reform opens a unique opportunity to transform the role of Congress in its effective capacity to legislate and control. That opportunity is at the same time a challenge for the political parties, especially for opposition parties. The debates in Congress will serve as a test to discern whether the strength of the protest vis-à-vis the authoritarian concentration of power is transformed into institutional innovation and a subsequent capacity on the part of the new institutional mechanisms to carry out balance-of-power functions vis-à-vis the executive within the framework of a presidential system. The performance of the new institutional architecture will depend on the special legislative regulation that may arise from Congress and on the capacity to resolve, through a wise combination of doctrine and jurisprudence, the problems that might arise in the functioning of the newly created structures.

The institutional reforms have redefined key rules of the political game. The constitutionalization of the Decrees of Necessity and Urgency, prohibiting their application to cases of penal, tax, and electoral legislation, and making them subject to ratification by Congress without time limits, can be interpreted as a moderation of the exceptional powers of the executive. The electoral system adopted in the Reformed Constitution establishes that a candidate be elected in the first round if he or she obtains: (1) more than 45 percent of the validly cast affirmative votes or (2) when the most-voted ticket in the first round obtains at least 40 percent of the validly cast affirmative votes and, in addition, there exists a difference of 10 percent with respect to the validly cast affirmative votes over the ticket that obtains the second highest number of votes.

This is a hybrid form of ballotage (in classic ballotage, the candidate who obtains an absolute majority of the valid popular vote—more than 50 percent in the first round—is president). The two rounds in the presidential election are designed to guarantee the head of state a legitimate mandate based on a majority of votes. In the first round, the voter is guided by sincere vote and opts for the preferred party, while in the second round the voter faces a strategic option and might opt for the candidate who departs the least from his or her expectations. In the variation adopted by the convention delegates, the two objectives mentioned might not be met. Provided that the presidential candidate faces a fragmented opposition, he or she could arrive at the presidency with 40 percent of the votes obtained in the first round, very much below the majority demanded in the classic form of ballotage. In these conditions, the sincere vote of the first round could be neutralized by the useful vote, thereby restricting pluralism. This negotiated formula encourages polarization in the first round, which is, in turn, an incentive for the formation of an opposing electoral coalition.

If the forces of the opposition compete among themselves, they run the risk of not making it to the second round. Without a doubt, this variation of ballotage, which emerged from the negotiation between the UCR and the PJ, encourages electoral coalitions in a society that lacks a tradition of this sort. The institutional reforms do not necessarily generate the intended effects: the decisive variables are the skill with which the political actors define their strategies in relation to the new rules of the electoral game and the interpretation of those rules that the voters make. One can interpret the fragmentation of the party system that is evidenced by the growth of third forces, and the ideological-programmatic depolarization that is reflected in the moderate nature of the forces that place themselves toward the Left of the opposition camp as a symptom of profound changes in the Argentine party system. At the same time, the reforms introduced into the constitution can push in the direction of a Chilean-style electoral convergence as an alternative form of government.

The reformed constitution reveals a society that has escaped institutional impasse and tries to respond to the will of the majority to check the authoritarian exercise of power, to create an honest and independent system of justice, and to render the political leadership accountable to the citizenry. As such, it implies a decisive step in the consolidation of democracy, while simultaneously reflecting a political leadership that seems to have learned from the past. How much of this learning will translate into an improvement in the quality of government remains to be seen. What is certain is that an indispensable step has been taken to put an end to Caesarist temptations and the irresponsible behavior of some legislators.

The May 1995 Presidential Elections

The 1995 elections took place in a climate of electoral anxiety brought about by the prospect of an eventual second round of voting. Menem was faced with a rival in the figure of Peronist senator José Octavio Bordón, presidential candidate for the FREPASO (National Solidarity Front).[25] Bordón has portrayed himself as a modern intellectual modeled in the image of the Brazilian president, Fernando Henrique Cardoso. Representative of the liberal democratic components of Peronism, Bordón tried to capture the vote of the anti-Menemists from both Peronism and Radicalism. His motto, "Por un cambio seguro" (For a certain change), appeared to be far more moderate than Radical candidate Horacio Massaccesi's call to defeat Menem.

Despite the incentives to form coalitions that the ballotage created, the FREPASO and the Radical Party stood alone as independent actors with their own electoral agendas. Their campaigns challenged the present government's policies but failed to produce reliable alternatives. Menem's presidential campaign, on the other hand, was based on the economic performance achieved during his previous government. Menem toured the cities and the countryside, opening schools, hospitals, and roads as if he himself were competing for the office of mayor. He refused to debate with the candidates of the opposition. The media meanwhile focused on the shifting figures yielded by polls while just skimming over the parties' platforms.

It was in this context, on May 14, that the electorate voted for Menem. In the first round, Menem received 48 percent of the vote, surpassing the 46 percent he had obtained in the 1989 elections.[26] In 1995 the Peronist party won, as it had in the previous five national elections that took place since 1985. The Peronists' loyalty to the party has remained unchanged over the last decade, despite Menem's drastic parting from the traditional public policies that Perón had sponsored. This confirms the fact that the Peronists' political identity is not based on programs and policies but rather on a mixture of memories of values such as social justice and a unique leadership style, a combination of charisma and pragmatism, which Perón instituted and Menem copied.[27] The modification in Menem's support is greatly due to non-Peronist voters.

The two-party system that emerged in 1983 was replaced by another composed of three main parties plus other minor ones. In this new arrangement, Peronism continues to be the dominant party.[28] The Radical Party, the second major party since 1987, dropped to third place with 17 percent of the vote.[29] FREPASO, with 28 percent of the vote, swept away the UCR's aspirations to become the second political force in the country. Menem's ticket was 20 points ahead of Bordón's. The minor parties, which represented 15 percent of the total in the 1989 elections, virtually disappeared from the struggle for the presidency.[30] These figures suggest the formation of a broad Menemist electoral coalition that goes beyond the conservative-popular one that supported Perón in 1946. Both the heterogeneity inside the FREPASO—more like a coalition against Menem than a programmatic alliance—and the UCR's lack of national leadership prevented these two parties from organizing a solid front.

The contrast between the results of the presidential elections and the elections for deputies reveals that the Radicals retained broader support in the latter (the difference is about 5 points in favor of the deputies' list of candidates), while the FREPASO was able to impose a national leadership but did not obtain similar support for its deputies (the presidential ticket totaled 8 points more than the deputies' list). In the PJ, there was a difference of 7 points in favor of Menem's presidential candidacy.[31]

The minority parties decreased: from 27 percent in 1993 to only 14 percent in 1995, a figure that is closer to 13 percent of the votes obtained in 1983. The MODIN, which had received 6 percent of the vote in 1993, obtained only 1.66 percent in 1995. The UCEDE continued to decline and obtained barely 3 percent of the vote in 1995.

The distribution of institutional power resulting from the elections gave Menem a clear majority in the lower house: 132 seats out of 257. The Senate is under full control of Peronism, as is the greater majority of the provincial governments.[32] Opposition parties are too weak to benefit from their accrued power under the new constitution to alter the course of government policies. Given these circumstances, will the Peronist Party become a hegemonic party as it was under Perón?

As long as the other parties and coalitions remain weak and disjointed, the traditional Peronista tendency to behave as if no other political force in government counted will continue to strengthen. As a consequence, the internal disputes and the urge to transform them into state issues will persist. The present conflicts between the government and its internal opposition may prove to be more crucial to the evolution of democratic governance than the misadventures of the opposition parties.[33]

The Postelectoral Scenario (Mid-May to Mid-September)

On July 18 Menem began his second term in a climate of general indifference, despite the magnitude of his electoral success. Menem's second term in office was not received with the widespread relief and hope that surrounded his first one. The new government was clouded by two political facts. Eduardo Angeloz, three times Radical governor of the province of Córdoba, resigned as the only means of solving the crisis in his province, and General Antonio Bussi was elected governor of the province of Tucumán, where the Peronist Party had come in first in every election since 1983. The contrast between the magnitude of Menem's electoral triumph and the general atmosphere of crisis that surrounded it characterizes the present situation.

It was not until mid-July that the Argentines learned that the unemployment rate had reached 18.6 percent. As Argentina is a country with a tradition of full employment, open recognition of this figure shook the foundations of society.[34] Opinion polls showed the consistent drop in Menem's popularity: by the end of July it had sunk to 30 percent. The initial confidence in the country's future shifted toward uncertainty. Menem's "magic" lay with the government's macroeconomic performance. At present, past economic achievements are less important than the solutions to new problems, but these new problems cannot be solved by imposing emergency plans on the citizenry. The generalized quest for participation in decision making and establishing control over the exercise of power is narrowing the government's room for maneuver. This is not only because of the Peronists' growing demands for participation but also because the new constitutional framework gives the parties more room to maneuver.

Menem's magic is eroding. This situation has aggravated the latent conflict between the political sector of government and the technocratic staff led by Minister Domingo Cavallo, the guarantor of the economic reforms. The tactical alliance between them was based on economic and electoral success. With electoral success obtained and the opposition "pulverized," the economic problems have caused internal disputes.[35] Cavallo's enemies inside Peronism are openly forcing him to leave, but their strident rhetoric reveals that they have not yet produced a credible alternative program to meet the crisis. President Menem keeps governing in his way, that is, standing apart from Peronism's internal disputes. Everybody knows, on the other hand, that these disputes are the corollary of the present fight for Menem's succession in 1999. Will Menem be able to impose his decisions on a party in turmoil?[36]

The chief of the cabinet created under the new constitution limits Cavallo's action to imposing a decision without negotiating with multiple fronts. For the first time, Cavallo will have to negotiate the 1996 national budget with the chief of the cabinet, Eduardo Bauzá.[37] Neither Menem nor Cavallo can rely on the resources that allowed them to act swiftly in the past. To restore lost fiscal austerity will not be an easy task. Nor will it be easy to form policies to decrease unemployment. The Menem-Cavallo duo's political power is deteriorating in the context of a generalized weakening of the parties. In effect, as a consequence of the extreme personalization of power, the leaders rather than the parties are the winners of each election, and as long as the government is pervaded with corruption, the discredit of the politicians will continue to grow.

In early 1995 the collateral effects of Mexico's financial cɪ. closed the Achilles' heel of the economic program: Argentines ι save enough, and the economy relies on the capital available in thᴇ ternational markets. Latent economic crisis was brought into ι. open.[38]

Cavallo's dangerous assumption that strong economic growth would be uninterrupted, and its obvious corollary—the lack of anticyclical measures to prevent a crisis in the economy—confront the government with unexpected problems whose solutions can in no way rely on the unanimous consensus that stabilization policies had hitherto enjoyed. Cavallo's recent measures devoted to overcoming the present crisis face resistance from various social sectors and the provincial govern-ments.[39] The conflict inside Peronism, far from ceasing, has peaked.

In mid-August, Cavallo publicly denounced the existence of mafia organizations that exercised an influence on decision making and the amendment of laws. This revelation cast a blanket of doubt on the three powers: neither the executive, nor the legislative, nor the judicial were left unscathed. The minister confronted his moment of greatest political weakness with a direct attack on the corruption that pervades the government. Although he targeted postal services magnate Alfredo Yabrán in particular, his declarations gave voice to the generalized and acknowledged need to put an end to widespread corruption. Since then, the corruption issue has proceeded to take center stage as it had in early 1991 when Cavallo first arrived at the Ministry of the Economy. Bribes, overpriced services for the state, and tax evasion by means of bogus receipts were exposed as mafia operations.

The political crisis unleashed by Cavallo's accusations went to the core of the country's present problems: the weakness of its political institutions.[40] The Argentines leaned out over the abyss, and Cavallo providentially became the one to remove the specter of ungovernabil-ity, in both the domestic and the international scenario.[41] President Menem was forced to renew his confidence in Cavallo, who was gener-ally recognized as the man for the job. Nevertheless, this way out of the institutional crisis seems to be more a respite than a solution to the problems it brought into the open. Argentina has to make a transition from a "Menem-Cavallo" government to the government of institu-tions, a task for which Peronism is particularly ill prepared. It should also be apparent that this transition requires a search for formulas of cooperation that replace decisionism-based strategies, such as those that proved successful during Menem's first term.

Problems and Prospects

It should be evident from the preceding discussion that the success of Menem's economic adjustment policy appeared to be associated in its initial phase with the concentration of power in the executive and its technical cabinet. This has been so not only in Argentina but in most of Latin America, as the studies by Stephan Haggard and Robert Kaufman point out.[42] Great presidential autonomy and an authoritarian concentration of power in the person of the president, at the expense of the systematic violation of the principle of separation of powers, and not just the policy measures adopted, are at the root of the success achieved in controlling inflation. This autonomy stems from the crucial role played by the style of presidential leadership.

An astute and pragmatic politician, recognized for his skill in putting his adversaries on the defensive and his speed in reacting—the manner in which he controlled the December 1990 military uprising consolidated his image of political efficacy and authority—Menem showed an ability to interpret the collective moods of the country.[43] His stabilization policy benefited from the consensus of a public for which nothing could be worse than hyperinflation, the acquiescence of unionism,[44] the discipline of his party, and an opposition that was in crisis and incapable of providing a credible alternative program of government. *Fortuna* and *virtu* are united in the figure of the president, allowing him to set in motion the process of transforming the Argentine economy and society.

During the latter half of President Menem's first term in office the country was midway toward a new economic and political order. Throughout the period after 1989, economic reform was accompanied by important changes in both political and economic debates. The political opposition was keen to point out convergences and not just their differences with the ruling party. The issues of stability, fiscal equilibrium, and trade liberalization were excluded from partisan competition. In the economic debate, the discussion of alternative strategies from a common point of departure was also a novelty, as the work of Pablo Gerchunoff and José Machinea reveals.[45]

President Menem's second term has commenced in a very different political and economic situation in which neither peace prevails nor the will for consensus that is indispensable for consolidating democracy and sustaining economic reforms. As the recent institutional crisis has revealed, in order to ensure the durability of the stabilization policy and the structural reforms, more is required than the president's skill in concentrating power and exercising it at his discretion.

Argentina is now in the process of reconstructing its system of representation. This process is taking place in the context of economic recession, rampant unemployment, and social unrest and with the country being led by a government riddled with corruption and internally split on strategies to overcome the crises.[46]

Argentina's restoration of democracy followed years of terror and fear. Economic reforms have been forced by the severity of the economic crises, above all by the need to put an end to runaway inflation. Will the current political crisis impel the political leadership to "clean house" and undertake the reconstruction of the institutions that are crucial to their own survival? If the answer to this question is no, the ghost of ungovernability will stalk the country once again. The recent political crisis in the province of Santa Fé sowed doubts about the transparency of the country's recent and future electoral processes. This crisis reveals the absence of an independent control of the electoral process, a fact that had already been highlighted in Deborah Hauger's report for the United Nations Development Program in 1992. No electoral judge has yet been nominated in any of the twenty-four electoral districts as was established in the Electoral Code. The minister of internal affairs has practically total control over the electoral process. What is more, this crisis also indicates that the current struggle for the presidential candidacy in 1999 has destroyed republican institutions.[47]

The remainder of Menem's second term remains uncertain. Is the commitment to democratic consolidation and economic renewal strong enough to prevent the country from returning to its past?

Apparently the clock of reform cannot be turned back, not only because there is a general recognition that the political and economic order that emerged in 1946 can in no way be restored, but also because there is a pluralistic civil society calling for dialogue and policies of consensus. Nevertheless, it must not be forgotten that Peronism has always converted its internal conflicts into state crises. What is more, Peronism never left office peacefully. This does not presage a future with the necessary peace and willingness to build the broader consensus that the country's democratic governance requires.

In mid-September 1995, Argentina was still undergoing a political crisis best described as a crisis of confidence in political leadership. A return to the past is highly unlikely. One probable scenario in the near future might be that characterized by isolated and spontaneous outbreaks of violence that open the way to power for such men as retired General Bussi in Tucumán Province. A second scenario might be that of a ruling party willing to negotiate the transformation to democracy with political and social leaders in order to reach a balance between stability and growth, and in this way rebuild a more egalitarian society. In such a scenario, alternation in power would no longer be perceived as a relapse into disorder. Once again this challenge falls on Peronism. The coming months will show which scenario is to prevail.

10

Brazil: The Hyperactive Paralysis Syndrome

Bolívar Lamounier

No more than a jeep with four soldiers would be needed, if the military really wanted to shut down the national Congress. This is how a senator with experience in such matters summed up the situation in October 1993 at the beginning of the public uproar caused by revelations of widespread corruption made against members of Congress by a former advisor to the Budget Committee, himself involved in serious crimes including his wife's murder. The senator's remark was partly a joke, but it was also his own peculiar way of raising that ancient question: what, after all, is the matter with democracy in Brazil?

Perhaps one should begin by saying what it is *not*. Brazil does have regional and ethnic problems, even a little separatist rumbling in the south, but very few analysts would say that these cleavages are capable of threatening either democracy or the country's territorial integrity. There is drug trafficking, but it is not as powerful and organized as in Colombia. There is political antagonism, but it is not as confrontational and violent as it used to be in Argentina or Venezuela. There is no guerrilla movement, let alone anything like Peru's Sendero Luminoso (Shining Path). Why, then, was the first post-transition decade so difficult, and why did apprehensions about democracy continue to surface with disturbing regularity?[1]

Apprehensions with regard to Brazilian democracy have been largely defused, in Brazil and abroad, since Fernando Henrique Cardoso's appointment to the Finance Ministry in May 1993, his election to the presidency in 1994, and the marked improvement in executive-legislative relations during the first part of 1995. All's well that ends well? Not quite. A better understanding of what was going wrong before Cardoso's rise may shed light not only on the Brazilian case but also on unstable or poor-quality democracies in general. One must also ask whether this giant step toward democratic consolidation was not too dependent on a single individual, on the appearance of the right leader at the right time. If Brazilian democracy was faltering because of underlying economic dilemmas and income inequalities, it is clearly too soon to celebrate; if the country's flawed formal political structure was responsible for it, again, nothing has changed. Recognition of the major changes that have taken place since Cardoso took center stage should not, therefore, cause one to forget the larger question of the threats that ineffective policies may pose to Brazilian democracy, or, more generally, of whether poor-quality democracy is not the same thing as unstable democracy.

My argument is that Brazil is an impressive deviant case, so deviant that much can be learned by taking a closer look at it. Some fundamental traits of its economic, social, and institutional makeup are clearly unfavorable to democratic consolidation and high-quality democracy. Worse still, the last stage of the transition from military to civilian rule, in the early 1980s, planted the seeds of a serious, prolonged crisis that I call the hyperactive paralysis syndrome. During this period, most political leaders seemed either unable to understand the syndrome or unwilling to change some features of the underlying institutional context and of their own behavior in order to overcome it more quickly. As a result, economic stagnation, yearly inflation rates in excess of 200 percent a year from 1982 to 1994, ineffective policies, the aggravation of already dismal conditions of poverty and income inequality, increasing ideological polarization even in the late 1980s when the cold war was coming to a close, and the increased salience of corruption to the public agenda combined to keep the country in a situation of continuing doubt about the sustainability of democracy. But democracy did not break down: elections became tremendously competitive, civil society became undoubtedly stronger and more complex, and public debate was intense and rich during this whole period. The question, then, is how it all happened.

Arguments about democratic prospects in Brazil (and generally in Latin America) move back and forth between holistic views (a political culture "inherently" inimical to or a socioeconomic structure "incompatible" with democracy) and the equally untenable opposite extreme: the neorationalist assumption that democracy can live with any political culture and withstand virtually any amount of social inequality and hardship, provided that politicians play the "right game." This chapter steers a middle course and demonstrates that, from the 1980s to the early 1990s, a downward spiral of serious economic dilemmas, deteriorating social conditions, government ineffectiveness, and discredit of representative institutions represented (and perhaps still does) a serious threat to Brazilian democracy.

I will not dwell on the methodological underpinnings of the argument, but three brief remarks are useful. First, the economic difficulties that Brazil has been facing since the late 1970s partially precede and hence cannot be fully explained by the political factors analyzed here. However, I do assume that the hyperactive paralysis of the 1980s entered the picture as a major additional hindrance to monetary stabilization and growth resumption, thus making the loop more complex and dangerous. Second, the reason I dwell at length on the early 1980s is that I regard some features of the democratic transition itself as the factors that triggered the hyperactive process of crisis formation and hence as an important point to be taken into account in the comparative analysis of transitions. Third, because I contend that Brazil experienced a prolonged crisis-formation process that seems to have been broken by Cardoso's rise to the presidency, the question is: why was that process not interrupted at some earlier point? My answer is that the factors just referred to intertwine with the institutional and cultural factors studied below.

Historical Background

What, in short, is wrong with democracy in Brazil?[2] It is worth pointing out that the need to pose this question already indicates some progress toward democratic consolidation. In the 1920s and 1930s it was common for prominent writers and political leaders to peg their disbelief in democratic development directly on a holistic view of the country's cultural formation. In a formerly colonial, slaveholding society, so the argument went, liberal democracy is merely a superstructure, a facade too thin to hide the "hard facts": sharp levels of stratification, bossism from above and deference from below, and a complete lack of public awareness among economic and political elites.

Simplistic as it is, this view sounded persuasive until the 1950s and then began to lose ground, mainly for three reasons. First, a competitive democratic system began to function in 1946 after the downfall of Getúlio Vargas' Estado Novo dictatorship (1937–45) and the Allied victory in World War II. Second, industrialization and urbanization progressively eroded the underpinnings of the colonial heritage argument and even gave rise to a naive "developmentalist" belief that all good things (democracy included) would henceforth go together. Third, and most important, threats to democracy began to appear in a single and definite shape. Throughout Latin America, the threat came to be perceived as a by-product of the cold war context, always involving a combination of external pressure and domestic response to (actual or alleged) revolutionary insurrection. In 1964 democracy did in fact break down, leading to twenty-one years of military rule.

Unlike ideal or typical Latin American dictators, the Brazilian military maintained a substantial part of the previous constitutional framework. Military presidents were formally elected by Congress and were subject to the usual fixed term of office. Likewise, state governors were elected by the respective assemblies. Popular elections continued to be held at regular intervals for the legislature at all three levels—all of this, needless to say, under severe legal and paralegal constraints. The pre-1964 multiparty system was replaced by a compulsory two-party system in 1965, with the Aliança Renovadora Nacional (ARENA, National Renovating Alliance) providing support and the Movimento Democrático Brasileiro (MDB, Brazilian Democratic Movement) harboring the many shades of opposition to the military regime. Military rule in Brazil was thus a peculiar dyarchy: an authoritarian macrostructure that nonetheless allowed considerable space for the reaccommodation of the existing civilian political forces.[3] To describe this system simply in terms of noncompetitive elections is misleading because the electoral arena as such was quite competitive. The distinctive trait was that electoral competition was designed to fill offices largely deprived of their traditional prerogatives and power resources, and constantly subject to a Damocles sword: the so-called institutional acts, a legal reserve of supraconstitutional or emergency powers to which the president and the National Security Council could resort at any time.

This dyarchical pattern, more perhaps than the weakness of the pre-1964 party system, explains why the Brazilian military, unlike their Southern Cone counterparts, were completely successful in their attempt to extinguish all preexisting party organizations. Politicians willing to participate in the electoral game had no option but to join one of the two parties permitted by the new regime. The highly artificial two-party system imposed by the military authorities began to produce unintended effects in the mid-1970s as the so-called economic miracle of the late 1960s waned, resistance to human rights violations grew, and public opinion began to question military rule as such. The MDB quickly became a plebiscitarian symbol of the resistance to military rule: a broad opposition front instead of the narrow and tame parliamentary party that the military probably had in mind when they decreed it into existence. The turning point was the 1974 election when the MDB won sixteen of the twenty-two senatorial seats then being contested. From this point on, the redemocratization process gained momentum and followed what I have elsewhere described as an "opening through elections" logic. By this time, the new (and fourth) military president, General Ernesto Geisel, had already proclaimed his intention to conduct a "gradual and secure" decompression ("abertura gradual e segura").[4]

A major step in the decompression process would take place in 1979 when the government agreed to surrender the dictatorial powers embodied in Institutional Act number 5, negotiated an amnesty law with the Brazilian Bar Association (OAB) and other civil organizations, and suspended the existing legal restrictions on party formation, thus paving the way for the return to a multiparty system. Direct elections for state executives were held in 1982, with five parties already competing and the opposition winning ten of the twenty-two governorships, including those of the three largest states, São Paulo, Rio de Janeiro, and Minas

Gerais. In 1984 massive nationwide demonstrations (the "Diretas-Já," or "Direct Elections Now" campaign) were not sufficient to convince the military to accept the direct election of General Figueiredo's successor in the presidency. The "gradual and secure" process envisaged by General Geisel ten years earlier was thus concluded within the framework of the military regime with the election of Tancredo Neves, a leader of the moderate opposition, by the same Electoral College that used to ratify military nominations.

The Brazilian transition from military to civilian rule was thus an eleven-year-long, partially, and sometimes implicitly, negotiated process. Institutional reform initiatives have proliferated since 1985, and this, as we shall see, is another Brazilian sphinx posing a number of questions: have they been fruitful? Were they inevitable? From a procedural point of view, it is not farfetched to argue that the Brazilian experience since the mid-1980s has been an embarrassment of riches, a wellspring of democratic initiatives. A Congress with full constitution-making powers was elected in November 1986, and a democratic constitution was adopted on October 5, 1988, after almost two years of highly decentralized work. Free and highly competitive elections have been held on schedule since 1985: for the mayoral offices of the capital cities in 1985, for the governorships and federal and state legislatures in 1986 and 1990, and for all (nearly five thousand) mayoral offices throughout the country in 1988 and 1992.

A direct presidential election (the first since 1960) was held in 1989, with full ideological polarization between left-of-center Lula and right-of-center Collor in the runoff balloting. Collor's momentous but orderly impeachment made the headlines throughout the world in 1992. Ideological conflict began to wane, as in most of the world, after the election of 1989, reflecting the collapse of socialism in Eastern Europe and the end of the cold war. The Brazilian military did retain in the 1988 Constitution roughly the same institutionalized political role they have had since the 1930s, but they have asserted it in a moderate way since 1985. Still, a widespread feeling persisted, at least until the election of 1994, that democratic institutions were vulnerable—but vulnerable to what?

From the 1980s to the 1990s: Declining Governability

From the mid-1980s to the early 1990s, Brazil was under the spell of what may be rightly called a hyperactive paralysis. Instead of striving to consolidate interests and issues and negotiate a broad settlement, the political elite was busy doing the opposite, working on a very disaggregated basis, heightening expectations, then finding itself engulfed by the ensuing sea of disappointment.

By hyperactive paralysis I mean a syndrome of declining governability rooted in a pervasive feeling, among the country's elites, of insecurity regarding their cohesion and legitimacy and aggravated by a mistaken attempt on their part to meet the problem by constantly overloading the formal political agenda.[5] From the transition in 1985 up to 1993, the elites, in the midst of increasingly adverse economic and social conditions, continuously tried to regain legitimacy by multiplying the number of issues subject to public debate and decision. In the constitution-making process of 1987–88, for example, they worked literally without programmatic party directives; they also flatly rejected presidential leadership from the very beginning, leadership the Sarney administration was clearly too insecure to provide anyway. The consequence was a waste of time and effort on secondary issues: too many trees and no forest. Worse still, by the end of the decade, Brazil had not only failed to undertake needed economic reforms, but had in fact entrenched a bewildering variety of old-fashioned statist economic concepts as well as corporate interests into the extremely detailed and rigid 1988 Constitution.

The positive side of this story should not go unnoticed: what from one point of view looks like paralysis, from another was an impressive series of redemocratizing and democratic institution-building initiatives: organizing peaceful mass demonstrations for direct presidential elections in 1984 (the Diretas-Já campaign), recapturing that energy and transforming it into the broad coalition that elected Tancredo Neves indirectly in 1985, calling a full-fledged and highly decentralized constitution-making Congress in 1987–88, managing a highly polarized (Collor against Lula) presidential election in 1989, impeaching a president by orderly means in 1992, submitting a change toward parliamentary government (and the restoration of the monarchy!) to a popular plebiscite in 1993, and trying a full revision of the constitution as determined by the 1988 text itself, that is, by simple majority and unicameral vote, instead of the normal three-fifths majority, in two rounds and separately in the Senate and the Chamber of Deputies. Lower-level examples would include direct elections for university chancellors and attempts to involve the local community in the elaboration and approval of municipal budgets.

This ambitious series of democratic experiments has no parallel in Brazil or in other contemporary cases of transition from military to civilian rule. The question is whether Brazilian politicians and other leaders were not biting off more than they could chew: engaging in too much proposing and too much reforming, all of it through lengthy and cumbersome procedures—a questionable course for a country known for the weakness of its political parties, where the final stages of the transition coincided with a violent recession and a jump to three-digit yearly inflation rates, and whose most respected political leader, President-elect Tancredo Neves, through whom civilian rule was being reinstated, fell ill on the day of his inauguration in 1985 and died without taking office.

The net balance of this decade-long experiment does not seem especially brilliant. An inquiry into the roots and consequences of such a manifest instance of hyperactivism should therefore be seen, not as a digression, but as an essential step in this attempt to evaluate democratic prospects in Brazil.

Hyperactive Paralysis in the Making

From about 1984 to early 1993, in a clearly adverse economic environment, it became increasingly clear that there was no party, no coalition, not even an informal group of leaders capable of authoritatively identifying the key issues and stratifying them into a viable agenda. The hyperactive paralysis thus became a self-sustained, progressively autonomous loop. The deeper roots of this phenomenon, as noted below, are to be found in the weakness of the Brazilian party system, in the country's fragile institutional architecture, and even in some remarkably utopian traits of the changing elite political culture. But one must first examine when and how the problem began, that is, the situation Brazil faced in the early 1980s.

The immediate causes of the hyperactive paralysis are to be found in dilemmas arising from the protracted character of the transition itself. The origins of the Brazilian transition date to General Ernesto Geisel's gradual decompression blueprint. That process would unfold over eleven years, from 1974 to 1985, when Tancredo Neves' indirect election to the presidency marked the formal return to civilian rule. Positive insofar as it prevented traumatic confrontations, that slow and implicitly negotiated decompression led to a substantial depletion of political capital on both sides, a simultaneous erosion in public confidence vis-à-vis both the declining military and the ascending civilian authorities. More so than in the Argentine or even the Spanish transition, in Brazil would-be civilian leaders began to lose standing before they were allowed by the military to take over and, needless to say, before they could undertake any serious measure of economic adjustment.[6]

The extent of the damage done to the Brazilian economy by the debt crisis of the early 1980s, a critical juncture in the redemocratization process, must also be taken into account. A key step in the Brazilian transition, as we have seen, was the direct gubernatorial election of 1982, when the opposition parties won ten out of twenty-two governorships, including those of the three largest states, São Paulo, Rio de Janeiro, and Minas Gerais. The proximity in time between this event and the deterioration of the country's economic environment in the wake of the debt crisis is essential to understand the roots of the hyperactive paralysis syndrome. As stated in Lamounier and Bacha:

> The external shocks of the late 1970s and early 1980s hit the Brazilian economy very hard indeed. These shocks included the doubling of the dollar oil prices and the tripling of dollar interest rates in 1979–80, added to a sharp decline in export commodity prices beginning in 1980, and led to the col-

lapse of foreign lending in 1982. Taken together, these shocks meant that real net transfers from abroad fell from plus two percent of Brazil's GDP [gross domestic product] in 1980 to minus seven percent in 1985. This violent reduction imposed a drop of nine percent in the domestic spending ratio to GDP between 1980 and 1985. The transition to democracy thus became much more difficult than anticipated in early 1979, when General Figueiredo promised in his inauguration speech that a civilian would replace him in the presidency in 1985.[7]

The extent of this damage was reflected in the sharp deterioration of the social services provided by the government, in the intensification of redistributive conflicts, and hence in an anxiety for quick results, which would in turn make utopian shock therapies against inflation increasingly attractive to economic policymakers. The first attempt along this line, the Cruzado Plan (February 1986), elicited an overwhelmingly positive popular response, but its failure and each subsequent one led to the public's deeper disappointment in and distrust of the authorities.

A third important factor was the exhaustion of the state-led growth model inherited from the 1930s. Unlike the armed forces in Chile, the Brazilian military did not spare its civilian successors the political costs of public sector reform. On the contrary, twenty-one years of military rule reinforced the pattern of state interventionism inherited from the Vargas era in both practice and ideology. Though disastrous from a redistributive point of view, the state-led industrialization model inherited from that era was a remarkable success as an engine of growth until the late 1970s. This past success story made the political effects of that legacy more powerful in Brazil than elsewhere in the Southern Cone.

Arguably, the vicious circle whose emergence is sketched here could have been broken from the economic side, as in Argentina with the Cavallo Plan. But one must not forget that Raul Alfonsín failed before Carlos Menem succeeded, that the legitimacy of José Sarney's presidency was undoubtedly weaker than Alfonsín's, and that the Brazilian political agenda was already heavily loaded when the Cruzado Plan was launched in February 1986. Though Sarney's popularity and leadership potential did initially soar, the plan's collapse in late 1986 brought back and aggravated the full range of political difficulties the country was facing. Suffice it to recall that the Constitutional Congress, beginning its work in early 1987, had the legal authority to and did in fact try to reduce Sarney's powers and term of office.

The Brazilian situation from that point on is best described as one with two parallel, open, and mutually reinforcing crises—a political and an economic one. Substantially weakening the first civilian government, the Cruzado Plan fiasco of 1986 caused another abrupt fall in the aggregate supply of leadership because Sarney had been able to secure a five-year mandate, due to expire only in March 1990, and also because by this time neither the conservative opposition associated with the *ancien régime,* nor that emerging from the Left under the aegis of the Workers' Party (PT), could seriously challenge Sarney's governing Democratic Alliance (PMDB+PFL).

Like Argentina, Brazil entered the 1990s with a strong-willed president committed to stop inflation and implement market-oriented reforms: Sarney's successor, Fernando Collor de Mello. Unlike Menem, however, Collor was not lucky enough to have his liberal reform package endorsed by a powerful and historically "statist" party, not to mention that, more than a party, he would have needed a miracle to complete his term of office after the charges of corruption made against him by his own brother, Pedro Collor, in May 1992. Collor's failed attempt to curb inflation and implement public sector reform pushed the pendulum at least halfway back to the old Brazilian statist, high-growth-cum-high-inflation economic ideology.

Another useful contrast can be made with developments in the former socialist countries. In most of Eastern Europe and in the Soviet Union, the former "statist" (communist) parties came out of the transition almost totally demoralized. In Brazil, though ideologically declining among average citizens, statism was given a new lease on life by Collor's fall and, more generally, by the marked presence of the leftist and economically antiliberal civil organizations in the process of agenda building and by the growing "ethics in politics" demand. Thus, unlike Eastern Europe, where the statist flag was borne only by apparently moribund communist parties, in Brazil it was also shouldered by some political groups whose legitimacy was on the rise, for example, the Workers' Party, arguably the strongest left-wing party Brazil has ever known.[8]

A further understanding of the progressive autonomy of the hyperactive loop can be gained by comparing the variants of economic ideology and the political resources for economic policymaking actually available in different moments of the transition process.

Implementing a serious economic adjustment was still probably easier in terms of sheer power, and despite the erosion in public confidence referred to above, under the last military administration (Figueiredo) and during the initial four years of the first civilian administration (Sarney). Though increasingly questioned as illegitimate on the political side, the framework provided by the 1967–69 military constitution was more favorable to that objective on the economic and fiscal side. To mention but one example, a massive transfer of tax receipts to states and municipalities would be entrenched in the constitution only after October 1988. The problem was that, at that time, the economic policymaking community was still largely faithful to the Brazilian high-growth-cum-high-inflation ideological tradition. Like Figueiredo and

Sarney themselves, the country's business community and economists were generally not yet convinced that enduring stabilization could not be achieved without serious public sector reforms and fiscal balance. A decade later, having gone through Sarney's Cruzado Plan fiasco, the 1987–88 clumsy attempt to alleviate poverty (and even fix the maximum real yearly interest rate!) by constitutional fiat, Collor's blocking of 75 percent of all financial assets to implement his "single shot" anti-inflation strategy, and perplexity over President Itamar Franco's firing of three finance ministers in seven months, the country's economic imagination had undoubtedly become more sober. The need for major change seems to have dawned even on Franco, a politician bred in the interventionist-nationalist tradition. His decision to appoint Fernando Henrique Cardoso as finance minister (and de facto prime minister) in May 1993 was widely applauded as finding the right combination of intelligent reformism and political experience.

A Fragile Institutional Identity

The essence of the crisis of the 1980s and early 1990s, according to the view set forth here, is the closed loop of hyperactive paralysis: a feeling of illegitimacy begetting ineffectiveness, disaggregated strategies, and utopian reform proposals with a high chance of failure, each failure in turn reducing the chances of effective leadership for a broad negotiated settlement. Nine years after the transition, there could be no question that this vicious circle had seriously discredited most politicians and institutions. As usual, the brunt of public criticism was borne by the legislature, but the executive branch had been affected as well. The underlying terrain was—and in the institutional sense still is—moving sand.

Most analysts agree that the Brazilian political system suffers from some sort of congenital weakness, but too often they look only at the party system or, even more narrowly, at the number of parties, failing to point out the difficulties associated with virtually every cogwheel of the institutional machinery. However, a full understanding of Brazilian political functioning must take into account the inherent shortcomings of the institutional architecture inherited from the 1930s, and whose worst features have been pushed to their ultimate consequences by the above-mentioned dilemmas of the transition, as well as by some emerging political traits.

The institutional model to which I refer is a contradictory combination of highly plebiscitarian and extremely consociational procedures, practices, and symbols. Plebiscitarianism applies to the popular legitimation of the presidential and other executive offices. Consociationalism prevails in the spheres of party, legislative, and federate representation. The overall mechanism is thus based on a multiplicity of mutual vetoes and counterweights that end up providing powerful incentives toward fragmentation, on the clearly illusory expectation that the resulting deadlocks can be neutralized or overcome by the president insofar as the president is the direct incarnation of the "people."[9]

The dangers inherent in the institutional model described above began to be perceived by a number of analysts and practitioners in the 1950s. Irrelevant as public issues during the twenty-one years of military rule, they reemerged during the post-transition Constitutional Congress (1987–88) and continued as a subject of heated debate until the April 21, 1993, plebiscite on presidential versus parliamentary government.

The presidentialist victory settled that issue for the time being but did not resolve the larger problem of the country's insecure institutional "identity," the persistent inability to translate democracy as an abstract aspiration into a consistent and workable set of institutional mechanisms.

The identity crisis to which I refer is partially a consequence of large-scale demographic changes that took place during the twenty-one years of military rule. Less even than Chile, Uruguay, or Argentina, Brazil did not simply "return" to a preexisting format of political competition in 1985 when civilian rule was reinstated. In Brazil the controlled decompression initiated in 1974, and even the limited competition permitted by the military before that year's watershed election, hid an enormous expansion of the electorate and thus an acceleration in the underlying transition from a narrow to a broad-based, mass democracy. Only 13 percent of the Brazilian population voted in the 1945 presidential election; in 1960, in the last presidential election before the military coup of 1964, this figure was still only 22 percent; but in the 1989 election, the first held after the end of the military regime, it had jumped to 55 percent. In absolute figures, it is now an electorate heading toward 100 million, a sixfold increase since 1960.

One is tempted to paraphrase Kant on inequality and say that such a portentous change is "a rich source of much that is evil, but also of all that is good."[10] Massive urbanization and a large electorate mean that demands will exceed any reasonable governmental response and that electoral volatility will increase. But pressure and volatility also mean that individuals are becoming autonomous and demanding citizens, that bossism and deference are probably gone forever, and that the average voter has more information at his disposal and is somehow becoming more involved in the political process. This optimistic note is undoubtedly worth sustaining, but it is easier to sustain when one is confident that the formidable energies released by structural change are being transformed into democratic capital and that the semblance of order formerly ensured by oligarchs and bosses of every description is not simply vanishing but being replaced by institutions suitable to a large-scale society and democracy.

This, indeed, is where the Brazilian shoe pinches. Already in the 1950s when the political system was still quite oligarchical, some right-of-center analysts and politicians were alarmed by rapid party fragmentation and the emergence of antiparty "populist" leaders. In substance, they did not differ much from those Marxists who were then struggling to understand the same signs of instability as a "hegemony crisis." If this was the case four decades ago, one may easily gauge the impact that this huge new electorate would begin to exert in the 1980s.

The problem with the Brazilian institutional framework, as stated above, is its precarious balance between the exacerbated plebiscitarian legitimation of the executive and the extreme consociationalism applying to the format of congressional and federal representation. Clearly, a plebiscitarian element exists in the U.S. presidential model and even in parliamentary governments, personified in the latter case by the leader of the victorious party who becomes a natural candidate for prime minister. The problem in Brazil, and in much of Latin America, is that the plebiscitarian symbols and doctrines about executive offices are a lot more radical, and the institutional environment (judicial and legislative branches, political parties, federation, "civil society") is much too weak to exert effective counterweights. The dangers of executive plebiscitarianism can be serious not only when incumbents are politically too strong but also when they are too weak. If the party system is bipolar, as it used to be in Argentina, Uruguay, or Venezuela, the danger is that the country may be divided into irreconcilable "camps." If it is a mobile plurality in which parties proliferate and subdivide easily, as in Brazil, the president will often find himself in a distinctly minority position, which will tempt him into resorting to dictatorial practices to obtain what he regards as needed legislation. Such practices, in turn, may induce strong antagonism or at least irresponsible behavior on the part of legislators.

Unlike advanced democracies, underdeveloped nations do not as a rule have effective mechanisms to reabsorb the enhancement of personalities that takes place during electoral campaigns. The institutional environment is usually too weak to accomplish this task. Thus, whether the party system is bipolar or a multiparty one, the excessive personalization of political appeals tends to leave serious scars. Since Max Weber, much has been written on the positive functions of "charismatic" leadership, but much less has been said about the negative side of this phenomenon. In Weber's description, charisma rises or declines ("routinizes") as a function of the intensity of belief among the leader's followers: the biblical context of his examples leads him virtually to ignore what happens among those who disliked the leader from the very beginning. But the Latin American and Brazilian experience with such figures suggests that charismatic leadership can easily elicit formidable amounts of positive and negative feelings, love and hate, at the same time and while the leader is still rising. Personal devotion to him or her among parts of the electorate seldom fails to elicit an equally personalized and rancorous rejection among other parts. This phenomenon is perhaps inevitable, but the threat it poses to democracy seems much greater in an institutional framework based on exacerbated plebiscitarianism and consociationalism. In this connection, it is worth recalling that only two of the five presidents of the 1945–64 democratic period—Eurico Gaspar Dutra and Juscelino Kubitscheck—succeeded in completing their terms of office. The landslide that brought Getúlio Vargas back into power in 1950 seemed to indicate that the dictator deposed in 1945 had been forgiven by the "people." Four years later, threatened with a second deposition, he chose to kill himself, but his death did not bridge the deep gap between Getulistas and anti-Getulistas into which the country had been divided.

These well-known dilemmas of the Brazilian presidential system have been seriously complicated by two new phenomena in today's highly urban, inflation-ridden, poll-addicted, and media-intensive society. First, confidence in the incumbent may rise or fall abruptly, sometimes seriously straining the entire institutional framework. Second, the combination of TV campaigning and extreme party fragmentation makes it much easier for candidates without serious party backing to win the presidency, even where a runoff election is required. Sarney's trajectory provides a good example of the first danger. Sarney was chosen by Tancredo Neves as a running mate in a typical ticket-balancing maneuver. Hoisted to the presidency by Neves' death, he was destined to be a weak, faceless president, but his popularity suddenly soared in the wake of the wage and price freeze known as the Cruzado Plan (February 1986). Four years and several heterodox plans later, on the eve of the 1989 presidential election, his performance was rated good by 8 percent of a national sample and by 4 percent among the subset made up of highly schooled respondents.[11]

If Sarney's last three years were disastrous enough, the "real thing" would come with Collor. Capitalizing initially on wildly moralistic appeals and later on the anti-Left, anti-Workers' Party sentiment, Collor climbed from his insignificant Alagoas governorship to the top of the polls and rode on substantial popularity throughout the campaign. With 28 percent of the vote (against Lula's 16 percent and way ahead of the other twenty candidates) in the first round, he was finally crowned by the infallible arithmetic of the runoff election: with only two candidates, one is bound to score an absolute majority. There remained two small problems, however. The party that nominally backed his candidacy (the PRN, Party of National Renovation) had only 3 percent of the seats in the Chamber of Deputies in 1989. Furthermore, the 53 percent of citizens who voted for him in the runoff election, and the much greater majority who told pollsters he was doing an excellent job as president when he decreed the expected "single-shot" package against inflation on his first day in office, began to crumble four months later when the megashock proved ineffectual. The "people" were no longer there to applaud; now the stage was occupied by a diversity of organized groups united by an invisible thread: a profound dislike for Collor.

The "people" had vanished, but the Congress was there. A survey of congressional opinion conducted by IDESP (Institute of Social Economic and Political Research) in August 1991 found that only 6 percent of the deputies and senators were willing to rate Collor's administration as "good" or "excellent," meaning that support for his administration was dwindling even among his ghastly PRN. Not by chance, the president's "political isolation" and the "danger of institutional breakdown" had by then become the daily bread of the Brazilian press, eight months before his brother Pedro's interview in the newsweekly *Veja* set the impeachment machinery into motion. Although Collor's impeachment in 1992 was due to charges of corruption, his steep fall in popular confidence was evident since the second half of 1990 (his first year in office). In mid-1991, 48 percent of a sample of São Paulo and Rio de Janeiro voters interviewed by IDESP said they had more confidence in the legislature than in the president, with 28 percent expressing the opposite sentiment. Coming from a country imbedded in a wildly plebiscitarian presidential tradition, these figures should perhaps be collected by the *Guinness Book of World Records!*[12]

The instability of popular support for presidents and the virtual certainty that he or she will be in a minority in Congress have been stressed above in connection with the weaknesses of the Brazilian system. But do these shortcomings really matter? Do they hinder executive initiatives? In a country known for chronic inflation and unwilling to reduce the existing battery of incentives to party fragmentation, the trend seems to be toward reinforcing rather than attenuating plebiscitarian presidentialism. At the electoral level, it has been reinforced by the highly polarizing procedure of the runoff election. At the legislative level, the constitution not only maintained the old legal figure of the decree law, duly rebaptized, but in fact enlarged its scope, thus making it more arbitrary. The constitution now authorizes the president, in cases of "relevance and urgency," to issue "provisional measures," which become immediately (and remain) effective unless rejected by a legislative majority within thirty days.

This, as the experience since 1988 has amply shown, is the inevitable Caesaristic counterpoint to the idealistically consociational but in fact spineless system of party and legislative representation. Exactly 1,075 such "relevant and urgent" measures have been issued during the seven years since the adoption of the constitution in 1988. The answer to the questions raised above is therefore simple. In a country where consociational democracy and rampant fragmentation have become virtually coterminous, executive initiative and predominance must be somehow ensured. Because changing the underlying institutional architecture is a formidable task, most of the elite chose to believe that arbitrary legislative initiative is compatible with democracy or simply a fact of life.

Brazilian parties are notoriously weak, individually and as a system. Three features stand out as we look at the Brazilian party system. First, the parties lack continuity. Except for the communist parties, both of which claim to be the true descendants of the original organization created in the early 1920s, none of today's parties can claim to descend in direct line from those of the pre-1964 era.

Rapid social change does not explain this instability, which derives from dictatorial interventions and hyperpermissive legislation. Contrary to the other authoritarian rulers of the Southern Cone, the Brazilian military was successful in its attempt to extinguish the pre-1964 party system. Their success in this regard can be compared to a disastrous ecological intervention, as they succeeded in eliminating organizations already advanced toward fragmentation, failed in their attempt to replace them by two artificial ones, and in so doing stimulated a large number of political entrepreneurs to start all over again, this time in a complex and highly mobilized society.

Second, the struggle against the military regime, which in Brazil had a decisive electoral component and coincided with an immense expansion of the electorate, was waged by a "plebiscitarian fraternity"—a broad opposition front bound to collapse after victory, not by a coalition of preexisting parties, each capable of reaffirming its identity and taking responsibility for government programs in the post-transition context. The insecurity brought about by Tancredo Neves' death in 1985 and the disastrous lack of coordination that crippled the Sarney administration (1985–90) and the constitution-making Congress (1987–88) can be largely ascribed to the plebiscitarian and hence amorphous nature of the redemocratizing coalition. Third, as already stressed, the parties are extremely fragmented. Party fragmentation in the Chamber of Deputies, as measured by the Laakso-Taagepera index, has been about 8.5 since 1986—twice the score of the pre-1964 era—leaving aside the question of whether this sort of measurement has any meaning when "real" parties are a large multiple of the "nominal" ones, when internal party cohesion falls below an acceptable level, as is manifestly the case in Brazil.[13]

The belief in the unifying and stabilizing force of the plebiscitarian presidency may not be entirely farfetched in consolidated democracies or in presidential regimes that drastically reduce the consociational component of the overall system, to enable the president to count on the support of a majority or a substantial minority in the legislature. In Venezuela the party system was bipolar for a long time, and congressional elections, held simultaneously with that of the president, are based on hierarchical party lists, excluding the voter's personal choice among individual candidates. In Argentina the provincial multiparty system was subordinated to the antagonism between Peronistas and Radicals, and still contrasts with the three-way division now shaping up at the national level. This degree of coordination from above, which certainly has its own shortcomings, never existed in the Brazilian presidential system. Brazil went from the backward and highly decentralized bossism of the First Republic (1889–1930) to a certainly more modern and democratic, but equally decentralized (and consociational), framework.

The occurrence of two major dictatorial interludes (1937–45 and 1964–85) has misled most analysts into depicting this century-long history as a homogeneously archaic, authoritarian—one could even say proto-institutional—pattern. The fact, however, is that the contemporary framework is an extension of deliberate institution-building efforts undertaken after the 1930 Revolution. It contains strong consociational elements, even though the ethnic, linguistic, or religious cleavages normally associated with consociationalism elsewhere in the world are virtually absent in Brazilian political life. A look at some key features of the Brazilian political system will show its excellent fit with the consociational model as set forth by Arend Lijphart:[14] a preference for proportional, instead of majoritarian, single-member district voting; a multiparty system practically without deterrents against fragmentation; a three-layered federation with autonomous states and local governments; a bicameral national legislature with both houses retaining substantial prerogatives; and a rigid and detailed constitution that can be amended only by broad coalitions and in which a bewildering variety of regional and corporate interests are entrenched.

These mechanisms were constructed to protect specific minorities and facilitate their access to substantial power resources. Brazil's multiparty system, for example, is based on extremely low barriers against party formation and is sustained by substantial power grants, such as free access to prime time, nationwide radio and TV networks twice a year for parties having at least one representative in the national Congress. The proportional electoral system, initially established by the Electoral Code of 1932 and technically improved in 1950, stands out among most proportional representation systems worldwide in that it does not require the voter to endorse a blocked party list. In this sense, it combines the worst of all worlds: it ends up being as "individualistic" as the Anglo-Saxon single-member district system but without the latter's incentives for accountability of the representative vis-à-vis a geographically bounded constituency.

Even a quick listing like this must include a few words on the rules that govern the representation of the member states in the lower house, the Chamber of Deputies. A federation is inherently a consociational mechanism in the sense that a political force unable to make its presence felt at one level may elect representatives at another. It is also consociational in the sense that it guarantees the governing autonomy of and ensures representation for each of its territorial divisions (states and municipalities). But the Brazilian federation is probably unique in the world in the extent to which it overrepresents sparsely populated states (those of the northern and central-western regions) and sharply underrepresents the country's most industrial and densely populated state, São Paulo. Though framed in the heat of the democratic transition, the 1988 Constitution completely disregarded the democratic principle "one person, one vote" and sustained the traditional "federative balancing" principle: large power grants to the small states (now entitled to a minimum of eight deputies each) and a highly restrictive ceiling of seventy for São Paulo, which by sheer arithmetic should be entitled to about one hundred fifteen federal deputies.[15]

The institutional framework described above began to be built in the 1930s, but its worst features were exacerbated in the course of the democratic transition. If the president resigns, dies, or is impeached, he or she is replaced by the vice-president, who is not voted for individually but elected with the president as a running mate on the same ticket. As long as he or she is the legal incumbent and benefits from diffuse plebiscitarian popularity, the president wields an enormous amount of power—best exemplified by the president's authority to issue provisional measures. This is the plebiscitarian half, the upper part of the institutional iceberg. The lower part is the sphere of political parties, legislatures, electoral procedures, the federation. Here the consociational principle, which in practice means powerful incentives toward fragmentation, reigns supreme.[16]

A Changing Political Culture

Brazilian political culture is often depicted as an unchanging authoritarian propensity rooted in Brazil's distant Iberian origins. Elitist at heart, centered on "organic" notions of hierarchy and obedience, founded on a deep-seated denial of individual autonomy, the implication is clearly that such a value system cannot sustain genuine democratic institutions. If this extreme description fit the facts, one would be hard pressed to explain why, despite the imminence of economic catastrophe, the country's elites consistently shun the idea of making "pacts," seem unable to build strong political organizations, and have brought the country to the verge of ungovernability during most of the post-transition decade.

If any simplification made sense, I would rather argue that Brazil is a highly utilitarian, fragmented, individualistic, and in many respects quite anarchical society. If the interpretation of the last decade set forth here is plausible, there can be no question that the Iberian-origins argument vastly underestimates the strength of other factors—such as urban living, the spread of mass communications, and paradoxically even chronic hyperinflation—that tend to erode ancient patterns of stratification. In my view, major changes have already taken place: (1) a wish to preserve democracy has emerged among key elite and middle-class sectors; (2) the rigid segmentation that prevented reasoned public debate across institutional (notably between civilian and military) sectors is gone; (3) among the mass public, allegiance to explicit democratic values seems weaker than in the Southern Cone, but there is a growing subjective feeling of citizenship, in line with the actual expansion of the electorate; (4) there has been an enormous increase in the supply of political information, which means a significant potential for political involvement; (5) the country is no longer divided by rigid symbolic cleavages, as it was around figures like Getúlio Vargas until the late 1950s.

Students of political culture often forget that this concept refers to patterns of orientations toward political objects. The overall patterns of political organization that a society deems viable or desirable—its institutional utopias—are thus the kernel of that concept. The problem with Brazilian political culture is, in my view, that the same emerging democratic ethos seems inclined to lend support to contradictory institutional "utopias." As the recent plebiscite on presidential versus parliamentary government has shown, it is not uncommon for an individual or group simultaneously to combine strongly plebiscitarian views of executive authority with sympathy for parliamentary government and both with *participacionismo*, or wildly utopian dreams of direct democracy. As long as this coexistence among incompatible blueprints prevails, the attempt to translate broad democratic aspirations into workable democratic institutions will probably involve the risk of the sterile hyperactivism described in this chapter.[17]

Democratic sentiment is undoubtedly stronger today than in the pre-1964 era. To understand how democratic values reemerged after twenty-one years of military rule, it is useful to approach them as having a positive and a negative side, as two sides of the same coin.

The positive side is democratic-aspirational: it is a strong wish to consolidate but also to go beyond and somehow enrich the democratic experience. In a country with grim indicators of poverty and inequality, there is a permanent tension between the concepts of democracy as an institutional framework for political competition and democracy as a high likelihood of "just" outcomes, and this is why democracy does not appear in social consciousness as a state of affairs already good and worth "conserving."[18] Elite opinion surveys conducted by IDESP since 1989 show that faith in democratic consolidation is very high among high-status Brazilians; this is especially remarkable if one considers that the respondents have been consistently pessimistic about economic stabilization, growth resumption, and poverty alleviation during the remainder of this decade. In a survey taken in 1989–90, 64 percent of the 450 elite respondents expressed a strong belief that democracy would be consolidated in the course of the 1990s, but 63 percent of them thought it was "very likely" or "almost certain" that the country would undergo "a chronic state of social convulsion" if it failed to reduce poverty and income inequality substantially over that same period. These figures suggest that elite political culture has become strongly democratic, or democratic-aspirational, in the course of the last generation.[19]

The negative side of the coin is what Amaury de Souza and I have elsewhere described as a wholesale rejection of the past.[20] Most Brazilians today seem inclined to take a very negative view of the country's past, interpreting today's evils as the result of five centuries of consistently tyrannical rule. Sharp discontinuities in historical memory due to rapid population growth are compounded by the fact that millions do not know and do not want to learn much about a political past they tend to reject as homogeneously evil. On this point, there is a startling similarity between diffuse mass sentiment and elaborate elite arguments: a dominant or virtually unanimous conviction that the country (meaning past elites) failed utterly in its attempt to reconcile economic growth with social justice.

Needless to say, this negative attitude is also rooted in the marked deterioration of urban living conditions. The perceived association among poverty, crime, mob outbursts, and police brutality reinforces that expectation of imminent "social convulsion," a fear not limited to elite groups. In every social stratum, citizens increasingly ask themselves why so much misfortune has befallen the society, and the answer they find, simplistic as it may be, is that all past generations were monstrously insensitive, greedy, and incompetent. Though comparative data on this point are hard to come by, I am inclined to assert that few countries reject the past so thoroughly (and naively) as Brazilians do.

The impact of this "rejection of the past" attitude on the political sphere is clearly perverse. If the past was elitist and authoritarian, any attempt to simplify or regulate political competition must be an elitist plot against the worthy majority. As the 1993 plebiscite on presidentialism has shown, radical plebiscitarian or populist discourses stand a better chance of gaining the public ear as they convey the notion that the humblest citizen will be "directly" heard. Proposals to reduce extreme consociationalism are too complex to reach the mass electorate but find staunch resistance among part of the elite, especially among left-wing intellectuals, who also tend to see them as an elitist plot.

Carried to its ultimate conclusion, this wholesale rejection of the past makes democracy virtually coterminous with unbridled fragmentation. It feeds on the dubious historical assumption that a rich diversity of parties, associations, and currents of opinion would have emerged had they not been consistently repressed and denied representation by tyrannical elites. Democratic institution building thus comes to be equated with the blooming of these more "authentic" political flowers whose latent existence is assumed and with institutional arrangements designed to maximize their emergence and protect and grant special privileges to the weaker among them. The consequence is an extraordinary paradox: consociational mechanisms originally established to pacify and accommodate regional oligarchies within a patrimonial state (obviously socializing the costs of their peace) come to be acclaimed as the very essence of the struggle for justice within the framework of a modern, mass democracy.

Conclusion

As argued above, the 1994 election seems to have been a turning point toward economic recovery and better governance, but it also has the potential to worsen things considerably. No matter how much Cardoso achieves as president, the crisis of the 1980s and early 1990s was aggravated by serious flaws in the underlying institutional machinery. The succession of failures that Brazil collected over the last decade—the hyperactive paralysis syndrome—resulted from the confluence of an exaggerated reform zeal with a dangerous combination of plebiscitarianism and consociationalism, the latter leading to a highly disaggregated modus operandi. A democracy capable of functioning effectively under average presidential leadership can hardly be expected to emerge in Brazil within the existing institutional framework. An effort must therefore be made to improve democratic governance, and a few strategic reforms will probably be necessary to accomplish this goal.

First and foremost, there is a need to reverse the trend toward exacerbated consociationalism. No one seriously proposes engineering a complete reversal, which would include, for example, the adoption of a two-party system. The military experiment failed in this regard, and there is no reason to assume that such a model, if deemed desirable, could be successfully introduced under democratic conditions. But moderate and effective pluralism will not emerge "naturally" from the present state of exacerbated consociationalism, with its unparalleled battery of incentives to fragmentation. Electoral reform, with the adoption of the German "mixed" or even the Anglo-Saxon majoritarian, single-member district model, should be seriously considered. A threshold equivalent to 5 percent of the national vote for a party to have access to the Chamber of Deputies and to free radio and TV time would seem more realistic than the present highly permissive rules. A somewhat smaller Chamber is also desirable, as well as apportionment of seats in conformity with the "one person, one vote" formula, if the democratic principle embodied in article 14 of the constitution is to be taken seriously.

The second set of problems concerns the excessively plebiscitarian aura surrounding executive offices. The presidentialist victory in the plebiscite of April 1993 limited the range of alternative remedies but did not eliminate the need to find one. Strengthening the party system, an imperative in itself, is also necessary as a means of gradually reducing diffuse plebiscitarianism. Without a stable party system and predictable decision-making procedures within the main parties, the legislature cannot be expected to vote consistently and to make prudent use of its prerogatives. Without stronger parties and more consistent behavior in the Congress, there will be no consensus to do away with the highly arbitrary and potentially Caesaristic right of the president to issue provisional measures. Conflict among the three branches of government is always possible in a democracy, but it seems especially dangerous when the constitution allows the executive branch to exert so much legislative initiative.

A third set of problems concerns public sector reform. The economic difficulties that Brazil has been facing since the early 1980s are largely due to the exhaustion of the state-led growth model, that is, to the overextension to which the government has been led by the immense scope of its regulatory, welfare, and entrepreneurial roles. A substantial part of the corruption unveiled by recent investigations is clearly related to this fact. Market-oriented reforms have been proposed, as in much of the world, but they are usually defended only on economic (or economic-doctrinal) grounds. In the Brazilian case, the weakness of the political system under democratic conditions would seem to be an additional argument for reducing economic interventionism. Doctrines aside, effective state intervention presupposes a true "state" with a substantial degree of cohesion in the government machinery. Cohesion is a variable, not a constant: it does not follow automatically from the definition of the state or from some mystical view of it. Cohesion increases or decreases over time, depending on the country's political process. In Brazil, state cohesion, and hence governability, has declined dramatically over the last decade because of the exhaustion of the state-led growth model and because of the manifest weakness of its underlying political substratum.

There is also a diffuse but nonetheless important set of problems arising from the cultural sphere. Some disturbing new features of Brazilian political culture have been described above. I disagree with the well-known "Iberian-legacy" hypothesis in view of its exaggerated stress on the continuity of a political tradition that is viewed solely as one of hierarchy and rigidity. Brazil has gone a long way toward developing a democratic political culture and has already overcome some of the crucial obstacles in the process of democratic institution building. The franchise has been broadened to a remarkable extent, without the bitter conflicts that marked this process in the United States and in some European countries. Yet I would prefer not to regard the development of a realistic democratic ethos simply as a by-product of political competition. A deliberate effort must be made to increase familiarity with the complexities of the democratic mechanism among key groups. Frequent and preferably informal interaction among various sectors—academic, political, military, the press—should be stimulated. Essential as it obviously is to democratic vitality, press criticism may on occasion give rise to perverse effects, which can be minimized by reasoned and continuous dialogue concerning media approaches.

Last but not least, a strong democratic ethos depends on a firm defense of politics as such. In Brazil, and generally in Latin America, part of the elite and the majority of the mass electorate alternate between wild idealism and rancorous rejection, both rooted in the same lack of even a rudimentary understanding of political behavior and institutional mechanisms. Experiments could be devised to extend the reach of genuine political reflection throughout the body politic. As long as the cold war continued, citizenship training was regarded with suspicion, and rightly so, in view of the Left's frequent attempts to manipulate educational institutions and of the military's wish to impose its own authoritarian brand. Now that the cold war is over, it is time to recall that the 1988 Brazilian Constitution extended the right to vote to sixteen-year-olds (without the mandatory character it has for those over eighteen). The spontaneous effort made by numerous high schools during the 1993 plebiscite campaign should be taken as an indication that training in citizenship ought to begin at the high-school level and include a firm defense of politics. In all of these aspects—mechanisms of representation, the party system, the role of the state, political culture, citizenship training—the consolidation of democracy will not be a "natural" consequence of political competition but more a matter of deliberate effort and crafting, "the state as a work of art."

Notes

Chapter 1 Venezuela: The Rise and Fall of Partyarchy (Coppedge)

This chapter was originally prepared for the Inter-American Dialogue Project on "Democratic Governance in the Americas" and was later published, with permission, in the *Journal of Inter-American Studies and World Affairs* 36, no. 2 (1994): 39–64.

1. For an elaboration of this approach to governance, see Michael Coppedge, "Institutions and Democratic Governance in Latin America," paper presented at the conference on "Rethinking Development Theories in Latin America," University of North Carolina, Chapel Hill, March 1993.

2. This concept is fully developed and contrasted with Robert Dahl's concept of polyarchy in my book *Strong Parties and Lame Ducks: Presidential Partyarchy and Factionalism in Venezuela* (Stanford: Stanford University Press, 1994). This section summarizes arguments developed at length in chap. 2.

3. Daniel H. Levine, *Conflict and Political Change in Venezuela* (Princeton: Princeton University Press, 1973).

4. Franklin Tugwell, *The Politics of Oil in Venezuela* (Stanford: Stanford University Press, 1975); Michael Coppedge, "Venezuela: Democratic despite Presidentialism," in Juan J. Linz and Arturo Valenzuela, eds., *The Crisis of Presidential Democracy* (Baltimore: Johns Hopkins University Press, 1994), 322–47.

5. The church, which has always been comparatively weak in Venezuela, ceased to intervene actively in politics in the early 1960s; see Levine, *Conflict and Political Change in Venezuela*. On relations with the private sector, see Terry Lynn Karl, "The Political Economy of Petrodollars: Oil and Democracy in Venezuela" (Ph.D. diss., Stanford University, 1982). For a different point of view, see José Antonio Gil Yepes, *The Challenge of Venezuelan Democracy* (New Brunswick, N.J.: Transaction Books, 1981).

6. John D. Martz, *Acción Democrática: The Evolution of a Modern Political Party* (Princeton: Princeton University Press, 1966).

7. Daniel H. Levine, "Venezuela since 1958: The Consolidation of Democratic Politics," in Juan J. Linz and Alfred Stepan, eds., *The Breakdown of Democratic Regimes: Latin America* (Baltimore: Johns Hopkins University Press, 1978), 82–109.

8. Terry Lynn Karl, "Petroleum and Political Pacts: The Transition to Democracy in Venezuela," in Guillermo O'Donnell, Philippe C. Schmitter, and Laurence Whitehead, eds., *Transitions from Authoritarian Rule: Latin America* (Baltimore: Johns Hopkins University Press, 1986), 196–219.

9. Robert J. Alexander, *The Venezuelan Democratic Revolution* (New Brunswick, N.J.: Rutgers University Press, 1964).

10. Martz, *Acción Democrática*, 174–92.

11. Donald L. Herman, "The Christian Democratic Party," in Howard Penniman, ed., *Venezuela at the Polls* (Washington, D.C.: American Enterprise Institute, 1980), 133–53.

12. Karl, "The Political Economy of Petrodollars," 17.

13. Mina Silberberg, "Change and Continuity in 'Extra-Clientelist' Politics: Alternative Organizations of the Venezuelan Poor," paper presented at the In-

ternational Congress of the Latin American Studies Association, Los Angeles, 1991.

14. Alfredo Castro Escudero, "Venezuela: La encrucijada de la democracia," *Comercio Exterior* 42, no. 3 (1992): 244–51.

15. There is some evidence that the provision of water and electricity actually improved in 1981–89, which implies that concern about deteriorating "public services" was mostly focused on rising violent crime and shortages of essential goods and services. Andrew Templeton, "The Evolution of Popular Opinion," draft paper presented at the conference on "Lessons of the Venezuelan Experience," Woodrow Wilson International Center for Scholars, Washington, D.C., October 1992.

16. David J. Myers, "Perceptions of a Stressed Democracy: Inevitable Decay or Foundation for Rebirth," paper presented at the conference on "Democracy under Stress," sponsored by the North-South Center of the University of Miami and INVESP (Venezuelan Institute of Social and Political Studies), Caracas, November 1992, 4–5.

17. Ibid.

18. Elías Santana, remarks at the forum on "Venezuela: Recent Events and Future Prospects," sponsored by the Center for Strategic and International Studies and CAUSA, Washington, D.C., May 1992.

19. Templeton, "The Evolution of Popular Opinion."

20. Ibid.

21. Julián Villalba, "Venezuela's Future: Outlook for Investment and Privatization," talk given at the Council of the Americas, Washington, D.C., September 16, 1993.

22. Allan R. Brewer-Carías, "La descentralización política en Venezuela: 1990, el inicio de la reforma," in Dieter Nohlen, ed., *Descentralización política y consolidación democrática* (Madrid: Editorial Síntesis; Caracas: Nueva Sociedad, 1991), 131–60; Miriam Kornblith and Daniel H. Levine, "Venezuela: The Life and Times of the Party System," in Scott Mainwaring and Timothy J. Scully, eds., *Building Democratic Institutions* (Stanford: Stanford University Press, 1995), 33 note.

23. Technocrats recruited from the elite Institute of Higher Administration Studies (IESA), who were pro-market like the "Chicago Boys" of Pinochet's Chile, but less dogmatic.

24. Coppedge, "Venezuela: Democratic despite Presidentialism," 338–40.

25. Juan J. Linz, "The Perils of Presidentialism," *Journal of Democracy* 1, no. 1 (1990): 51–69; and Scott Mainwaring, "Presidentialism, Multiparty Systems, and Democracy: The Difficult Combination," *Comparative Political Studies* 26, no. 2 (1993): 198–228.

26. Personal communication from Luis Gómez Calcaño, February 1994.

27. Margarita López Maya, "El ascenso en Venezuela de la Causa R," paper presented in March at the XVIII International Congress of the Latin American Studies Association, Atlanta, 1994.

28. According to the Supreme Electoral Council, the disputed votes are not enough to alter the final results. *Latin America Weekly Report,* January 13, 1994.

29. "Defense Minister Meets with Colombian Counterpart," *El Universal,* January 28, 1994, 2–19; reprinted in Foreign Broadcast Information Service (FBIS)-LAT-94–020, January 31, 1994, 68.

30. Michael Coppedge, "Parties and Society in Mexico and Venezuela: Why Competition Matters," *Comparative Politics* 25, no. 3 (1993): 253–74.

31. "Venezuelan Bank Collapse Threatens Nation's Future," *Los Angeles Times,* February 14, 1994, A1.

Chapter 2 Colombia: Building Democracy in the Midst of Violence and Drugs (Kline)

1. Archbishop Pedro Rubiano Saenz, quoted in *El Tiempo* (Bogotá), July 4, 1991.

2. Peter Wade, *Blackness and Race Mixture: The Dynamics of Racial Identity in Colombia* (Baltimore: Johns Hopkins University Press, 1993), 20.

3. María Jimena Duzán, "Colombia's Bloody War of Words," *Journal of Democracy* 2, no. 1 (1991): 105.

4. Ibid., 106.

5. Quoted in Douglas Farah, "Colombia's Culpables: Drug Corruption Probe Implicates Entrenched Ruling Class," *Washington Post*, August 23, 1995, A25.

6. Inter-American Commission on Human Rights, *Second Report on the Situation of Human Rights in Colombia* (Washington, D.C.: General Secretariat, Organization of American States, 1993), 36.

Chapter 3 Ecuador: Democracy Standing the Test of Time? (Isaacs)

I acknowledge the helpful comments of the anonymous reviewer and of Alan Angell, Jim Buchanan, and Joan Dassin, as well as the assistance of Pedro Armijos, Serena Hurralde, and Donna Lee Van Cott.

1. See Anita Isaacs, *Military Rule and Transition in Ecuador* (Pittsburgh: University of Pittsburgh Press, 1993), 117–43.

2. Ibid.

3. See Instituto de Estudios Sociales y de la Opinion Pública, *Informe Confidencial*, 1989 and 1993.

4. See, for instance, *Latin America Monitor*, February 1993.

5. See "Parto de los Montes," *Vistazo*, January 21, 1993, 610, and "Punto para Carlos Julio," *Vistazo*, February 4, 1993, 611.

6. For a thorough discussion of the Ecuadorian judicial system, see Laura Chinchilla and David Schodt, *The Administration of Justice in Ecuador* (Miami: Center for the Administration of Justice, Florida International University, 1993).

7. See, for example, *Latinamerica Press*, April 1, 1993.

8. Donna Lee Van Cott, "Modernization Alone Won't Save Ecuador," *Hemisphere* 5, no. 3 (1993): 16–17.

9. See, for instance, *Latin America Monitor*, January 1993, 1096; May 1993, 1144.

10. *Latin America Monitor*, July 1993, 1168.

11. See "45 mil burócratas se van," *Vistazo*, February 4, 1993, 611.

12. See *Latin America Special Report*, June 1993, 93–103.

13. See *Latin America Monitor*, July 1993, 1168. See also *Latin America Weekly Report*, June 17, 1993; December 2, 1993; and December 16, 1993.

14. *Latin America Weekly Report*, August 5, 1993; December 9, 1993.

15. Ibid., June 10, 1993.

16. *Constitución de la República* (Quito, 1982), 23–34. For a discussion of current military activity, see "El otoño del patriarca," *Vistazo*, March 4, 1993, 613, and "Defensores del estatismo," *Vistazo*, April 22, 1993, 616.

17. *Informe Confidencial*, 1993.

Chapter 4 Peru: The Rupture of Democratic Rule (Stokes)

1. We should resist the temptation to fuse the concept of democracy with that of the just society. We should retain a narrow definition of democracy as a system in which the holders of governmental office are chosen in fair elections

in which virtually the entire adult population is free to vote. Robert Dahl, *Polyarchy: Participation and Opposition* (New Haven: Yale University Press, 1971). Real state power, moreover, must reside in the offices thus filled. Philippe Schmitter and Terry Lynn Karl, "What Democracy Is . . . And What It Is Not," *Journal of Democracy* 2, no. 3 (1991): 75–88. Fair elections are ones in which citizens elect representatives whom they prefer, and, in forming their preferences, citizens have available to them information supplied by constitutionally guaranteed nongovernmental sources. See Dahl, *Polyarchy.* For elections to be fair in this sense, free association must also be constitutionally guaranteed.

2. John R. Londregan and Keith T. Poole, "Poverty, the Coup Trap, and the Seizure of Executive Power," *World Politics* 42, no. 2 (1990).

3. Again, for specific reasons the two other traditional party groupings could not offer viable candidates in 1990: APRA was the incumbent party that had presided over (and in part caused) a drastic economic crisis, and the United Left coalition had split into two smaller coalitions in 1989.

4. Quoted in *Latin American Regional Report, Andean Region,* December 1991.

5. Under the 1979 Constitution the president could adjourn Congress after three censure votes or votes of no confidence for the cabinet; new congressional elections would then be held. At the time of Fujimori's threat, the Congress had censured only one minister, and the president failed to accept his resignation, as the constitution required (see below).

6. This period was also one of conflict between the president and the judiciary. Fujimori objected to what he saw as the intimidation of judges by Sendero and corruption by drug traffickers. But there was also a more partisan conflict involved: in 1991 the Supreme Court found insufficient evidence of corruption against former president Alan García. In his televised speech the night of the coup, Fujimori gave as a justification the "covert plans of certain party leaders against the efforts by the people and the government" (quoted in *Latin America Weekly Reports, Andean Group,* May 1992). After the coup, Fujimori purged thirteen of thirty judges from the Supreme Court and appointed the prosecutor in the García case as comptroller-general [*fiscal*].

7. Some evidence suggests that the initial intention of the coup-makers was to install a civilian-military dictatorship that would persist into the foreseeable future. When in mid-April Fujimori announced a twelve-month timetable for the return to democracy, an intelligence officer was reported to have said, "it will be more like 18 years before he relinquishes power" (quoted in *Latin America Regional Report, Andean Group,* May 1992).

8. See *Situación Latinoamericana* 11 (October 1992). The World Bank and IDB initially announced suspension of loans. Days after the coup, Economic Minister Boloña traveled to Washington to try to convince the IFIs and U.S. Treasury to resume disbursements. He failed and returned to Lima to tender his resignation. Fujimori convinced Boloña to stay on (in part by firing his rival, central bank president Jorge Chávez). In explaining his decision to remain, Boloña told the Peruvian press that Enrique Iglesias, head of the IDB, was "looking for a way to support Peru so that our process of re-entry [into the international financial community] would not be blocked" (cited in *Latin America Regional Report, Andean Group,* May 1992).

9. In fact, Peru did not reach several of the goals established in the earlier Letter of Intent. The target for GNP growth, for example, had been 2.5 percent; in fact, GNP growth was –1 percent. Because the IMF and other IFIs frequently extend loans to countries that have not met conditionality, we cannot conclude that their motivations were explicitly political in this case; see, for example, Miles Kahler, "External Influence, Conditionality, and the Politics of Adjust-

ment," in Stephan Haggard and Robert R. Kaufman, eds., *The Politics of Economic Adjustment* (Princeton: Princeton University Press, 1992). Still, as I argue below, whatever their intentions, the IFIs played a critical role in the unfolding political situation in Peru, and that role did not contribute to the survival of democracy.

10. It is indicative of the peculiar quality of this constitution-writing process that the person who suspended the previous constitution was laying down specific rules on reelection in the future, new legal order, before the new constitutional assembly was even formed.

11. The 1979 Constitution allowed presidential reelection after one presidential term elapsed. The 1993 Constitution allows immediate reelection to a second term and then subsequent reelection after one term has elapsed.

12. In addition to drafting the new constitution, the CCD has acted as the legislature since the November 1992 elections and continued to act as such until the new legislature was elected.

13. The judge reasoned that if it were true, as the prosecutor claimed, that the officers had acted alone without the knowledge of their superiors, then they had acted as civilians.

14. See "After the Autogolpe: Human Rights in Peru and the U.S. Response" (Washington, D.C.: Washington Office on Latin America, July 1994), 12–15.

15. Pamela Constable, "Peru Coup Leaders Vow to Fight," *Boston Globe*, June 23, 1993.

16. Caleb Rossiter, *Washington Post*, April 12, 1992.

17. John Omicinski, *Gannett News Service*, April 13, 1992.

18. See the chapter by Jorge Castañeda in this collection.

19. Thomas L. Friedman, "Peru and U.S.: What Course to Take?" *New York Times*, April 15, 1992.

20. Thomas L. Friedman, "U.S. Is Shunning Sanctions against Peru," *New York Times*, April 14, 1992.

21. Presidential approval ratings fell from 64 percent in December 1993 to 54 percent in January 1994; see Imasen, cited in *Latin American Research Review, Andean Region*, February 1994.

22. I use the term *liberalization* here not in the sense of the first step toward a return to civilian rule, as fair elections would signal a return to democracy (as defined in note 1 above). But, as my analysis has made clear, the Peruvian political system is characterized by several authoritarian features, which, without remedying action, would persist even after a return to full democracy.

Chapter 5 Bolivia: Managing Democracy in the 1990s (Gamarra)

1. James M. Malloy and Eduardo A. Gamarra, *Revolution and Reaction: Bolivia, 1964–1985* (New Brunswick, N.J.: Transaction Press, 1988).

2. Ibid.

3. The best studies on these parties and their leaders can be found in Jorge Lazarte, "Partidos políticos, problemas de representación e informalización de la política: El caso de Bolivia," unpublished manuscript, 1992; Joaquín Saravia and Godofredo Sandoval, *Jach'a Uru: La esperanza de un pueblo?* (La Paz: ILDIS and CEP, 1991); and Fernando Mayorga, *La política del silencio* (La Paz: UMSS/ILDIS, 1991).

4. Lazarte, "Partidos políticos."

5. In one specific instance, for example, Fernández offered to build a *matadero frigorífico* (refrigerated slaughterhouse) in Santa Cruz at a cost of U.S.$800,000.

6. Author interview with Max Fernández, La Paz, March 3, 1989.

7. Author interview with U.S. embassy officials, July 1991.

8. Lazarte, "Partidos políticos."

9. Recently, for example, workers defended "Don Max" against charges of ties to the drug industry from Guillermo Lora, Bolivia's oldest Trotskyist leader. Lora was subsequently jailed following a lawsuit for defamation and libel brought against him by Max's lawyers.

10. For an excellent discussion of contemporary trends in the Bolivian party system, see Lazarte, "Partidos políticos."

11. Ibid.

12. For discussions of Bolivia's economic reforms, see Malloy and Gamarra, *Revolution and Reaction;* Juan Antonio Morales and Jeffrey Sachs, "The Bolivian Economic Crisis" (Cambridge, Mass.: National Bureau of Economic Research, Working Paper no. 2620, 1987); Juan Cariaga, "Hiperinflación, estabilidad, y crecimiento," unpublished manuscript, La Paz, 1993.

13. Since 1989 at least three such groups made their appearance in Bolivia. The first, Zárate Wilka, has all but disappeared owing to the government's crackdown following the May 1989 assassination of two young U.S. Mormon missionaries. A second group, the Ejército de Liberación Nacional-Nestor Paz Zamora, which boasted links to Peru's Tupac Amaru group, was also dismantled after the kidnapping and subsequent assassination of Jorge Londsdale, a prominent businessman. The third group, the Ejército Guerrillero Tupac Katari, has been more resilient; it has resorted only to occasional bombings of electric utility stations and the like.

14. Paz Zamora's speech was interpreted as the beginning of his campaign to return to office in 1997. His aim was to make a clear break with the MIR in an attempt to save himself from charges of corruption. Widespread rumors suggested that Paz Zamora intended to found a new party called Movimiento Ciudadano (Citizens Movement). These efforts, however, were soon nipped in the bud by revelations of alleged dealings with drug traffickers.

15. Under the terms of the MNR-UCS pact, Fernández' followers secured one ministry, two undersecretary posts, two embassies, the presidency of one regional development corporation, and the first vice-presidency of both the Chamber of Deputies and the Senate.

16. The MBL was promised one ministry, key congressional posts, and at least one embassy. Araníbar and the MBL extracted a high price, considering that his party won only 5 percent of the vote. Araníbar was later named minister of foreign affairs.

17. Responding to pressures from within his own party, in March 1994 Sánchez de Lozada replaced these entrepreneurs with members of the MNR.

18. Another common explanation given for the slow pace of the new administration is that Sánchez de Lozada prefers to involve himself in every last detail of nearly every policy.

19. MNR, *El Plan de Todos* (La Paz: April 1993), 19–20. Responding to the lack of interest by foreign capital, in January 1994 the government announced that foreign ownership would be increased to 50 percent.

20. In theory, these shares would be handled by pension fund administrators on behalf of the estimated 3.2 million Bolivians who would then apply their shares toward a retirement fund. The constitutional reform of August 1994 lowered the voting age from twenty-one to eighteen.

21. Goodwin Bennett and Dewey Ballantine, "Capitalization and Privatization: Successes and Pitfalls," paper presented at the seminar on "The Currents of Privatization and Capitalization," La Paz: ASOBAN, February 8, 1994.

22. The law was signed by President Gonzalo Sánchez de Lozada on April 20, 1994, and published in the Official Gazette of Bolivia as law no. 1551 on April 21, 1994. The law came into effect on the date of its publication.

23. "Otros 13 generales del Ejército pasarán al servicio pasivo," *Última Hora*, October 18, 1993, 6.

24. "Logias militares derribaron avión del LAB y mataron a Alexander y Otero Calderón," *Bolivian Times*, special edition, January 12, 1994, 1 and 4.

25. Malloy and Gamarra, *Revolution and Reaction*.

26. Indeed, since 1985 the principal political parties have revealed an extraordinary capacity to enter into and out of pacts and accords. The most relevant agreements are the February 5, 1991, and July 9, 1992, accords that encompassed every major political party.

27. The accusations detailed by the FELCN are reported in Eduardo Gamarra, *Entre la Droga y la Democracia* (La Paz: Instituto Latinoamericano de Investigaciones Sociales/ILDES, 1994).

28. In December 1994 Congress approved the law of majorities and minorities to regulate municipal elections. Until the approval of this law, the indirect election of a mayor mirrored the problems of electing a president at the national level. Under the new law, the party that attains even a slim plurality will be granted seven of the thirteen seats on the municipal council, thus ensuring the election of a mayor. In the long run, this mechanism could prove costly, especially in large urban centers such as La Paz where traditional parties fare poorly against populist candidates.

29. To secure congressional approval, the government proposed to amend article 230 of the constitution, which states: "This constitution can be partially reformed through the prior declaration of the need for reform. Reforms are to be determined by an ordinary law approved by two-thirds of the members present in each of the two chambers" (my translation). The MNR believes that the two-thirds requirement constitutes an "unnecessary obstacle" to constitutional reform. Opponents charge that the safeguards found in the constitution are deliberate to prevent any government from modifying the constitution to suit a temporary political trend.

30. In late January 1994 the government sponsored a seminar in which a number of European and Latin American legal scholars joined Bolivian colleagues to discuss the merits of constitutional tribunals. The government has been quite inspired by the sixteen-member constitutional tribunal in Germany. It has also been carefully examining the Spanish court.

31. The basic philosophy in Bolivia that the armed forces will take a leadership role in the fight against narcotics only if and when the police have been overrun by the traffickers may have been altered by the launching of the state of siege. Under the guidelines of these measures, troops have moved into coca-growing regions and have arrested union leaders including the best known and most controversial one, Evo Morales.

32. "Incertidumbre por estado de sitio en Bolivia," *El Nuevo Herald*, April 20, 1995, B2.

Chapter 6 Chile: The Political Underpinnings of Economic Liberalization (Scully)

I am very grateful to several colleagues and friends for their comments and suggestions for revising this chapter, especially E. William Beauchamp, C.S.C., David Collier, Abraham F. Lowenthal, Scott Mainwaring, Bill Maloney, Guillermo O'Donnell, and J. Samuel Valenzuela.

1. William F. Maloney argues persuasively that the set of policies adopted by the military regime during the first decades of authoritarian rule resulted in

unnecessary costs in Chile's transition to a market-oriented, high-growth economy. See "Getting There from Here: Second Thoughts on Chile's Economic Transition," unpublished monograph, Department of Economics, University of Illinois, September 1993.

2. A caveat is in order here. The expansion and diversification of the export sector under Pinochet resulted in little increase in high value-added products, being concentrated instead in (nontraditional) unfinished products. If this general orientation is not redressed, further sustained high growth is improbable over the long term.

3. A useful set of tables on economic performance during the Aylwin administration is available in the appendix to Alejandro Foxley, *Economía política de la transición* (Santiago: Ediciones Dolmen, 1993).

4. See Jaime Gatica, *Deindustrialization in Chile* (Boulder, Colo.: Westview Press, 1989); Eugenio Tironi, *Autoritarismo, modernización, y marginalidad: El caso de Chile 1973–1989* (Santiago: Ediciones Sur, 1990); Pilar Vergara, *Políticas hacia la extrema pobreza en Chile, 1973–1988* (Santiago: FLACSO, 1990); Larissa Lomnitz and Ana Melnick, *Chile's Middle Class: A Struggle for Survival in the Face of Neoliberalism* (Boulder, Colo.: Westview Press, 1991); Cristóbal Kay and Patricio Silva, eds., *Development and Social Change in the Chilean Countryside: From the Pre-Land Reform Period to the Democratic Transition* (Amsterdam: CEDLA, 1992), among others. For a very thorough and provocative review of ten contemporary books on the Chilean political and economic transition, see Gerardo L. Munck, "Authoritarianism, Modernization, and Democracy in Chile: Regime Dynamics and Social Change in Historical Perspective," *Latin American Research Review* 29, no. 2 (1994): 188–211.

5. Taken from "Una estimación de la magnitud de la pobreza en Chile, 1987," *Colecciones Estudios CIEPLAN* 31 (March 1993): 110.

6. Alan Angell, "What Remains of Pinochet's Chile?" *Occasional Paper No. 3*, Institute of Latin American Studies, University of London (1992), 4–5.

7. Tironi, *Autoritarismo, modernización, y marginalidad.*

8. Cited by Kurt Weyland, "Growth with Equity in Chile's New Democracy," Department of Political Science, Vanderbilt University, from *Estadísticas de las finanzas públicas, 1989–1992* (Santiago: Ministerio de Hacienda), 56, 71.

9. *El Mercurio*, July 23, 1993. The same article suggested that, in 1992, two-thirds of total government spending was directed toward social programs. This figure, however, seems inflated.

10. Angell, "What Remains of Pinochet's Chile?" 5.

11. Taken from a national poll administered by MIDEPLAN in November 1992. The Casen poll has been the government's standard social measurement since 1985. Also taken from the *Economist*, June 3, 1995, 17–19.

12. For an excellent discussion of the contemporary transformation of the Chilean state, see Oscar Muñoz, ed., *Después de las privatizaciones: Hacia el estado regulador* (Santiago: CIEPLAN, 1992).

13. Scott Mainwaring and I have discussed extensively in another place what we mean by an "institutionalized party system." We measure party system institutionalization in terms of four attributes: (1) stability in the patterns of interparty competition, (2) the existence of parties that have somewhat stable roots in society, (3) the acceptance of parties and elections as the legitimate institutions that determine who governs, and (4) the existence of party organizations that have reasonably stable rules and structures. Using these criteria, we label Chile as possessing an institutionalized party system (together with Costa Rica, Venezuela, Uruguay, Colombia, and Argentina). See Scott Mainwaring and Timothy R. Scully, eds., *Building Democratic Institutions: Party*

Systems in Latin America (Stanford: Stanford University Press, 1995), especially the Introduction.

14. It is worth reemphasizing here that, though the Aylwin government has not deviated from a basic reliance on free markets, some of its economic policy orientations do differ substantially from the Pinochet period. The most important changes focus on tax reform, labor legislation, and sharply increased social spending.

15. According to Garretón, this "backbone" was formed by "the interlocking of base-level social organizations with the political party structure, both in tension with the state as the focal point for political action." Manuel Antonio Garretón, "Introduction," in Marcelo Cavarozzi and Manuel Antonio Garretón, eds., *Muerte y resurrección: Los partidos políticos en el autoritarismo y las transiciones del Cono Sur* (Santiago: FLACSO, 1989), xvi.

16. As one indication of the moderation of social conflict in Chile, strike rates during the Aylwin administration have been extraordinarily low, both compared to historical rates as well as those of neighboring countries. See Angell, "What Remains of Pinochet's Chile?" 6–9.

17. Scott Mainwaring has shown quite convincingly that the combination of presidentialism with a multiparty format is problematic for maintaining democratic stability; see Mainwaring, "Presidentialism, Multipartism and Democracy: The Difficult Combination," *Comparative Political Studies* 28 (July 1993): 198–228. These notions are also developed in the Introduction to Mainwaring and Scully, *Building Democratic Institutions.*

18. For a more thorough discussion of continuities and changes in the Chilean party system, see Timothy R. Scully, *Rethinking the Center: Party Politics in Nineteenth and Twentieth Century Chile* (Stanford: Stanford University Press, 1992), especially chap. 5; Mainwaring and Scully, *Building Democratic Institutions*, especially chap. 5; also Timothy R. Scully and J. Samuel Valenzuela, "From Democracy to Democracy: Continuities and Changes of Electoral Choices and the Party System in Chile," in Arturo Valenzuela, ed., *Politics, Society, and Democracy: Latin America* (Boulder, Colo.: Westview Press, forthcoming). I take some of the discussion of the next several paragraphs from Scully and Valenzuela.

19. The reasons for this shift within the socialist party have been discussed amply elsewhere. Suffice it to say that it was partly a consequence of the experiences socialist leaders and militants had in both Eastern and Western Europe during their years of exile. See Ignacio Walker, *Socialismo y democracia en Chile: Chile y Europa en perspectiva comparada* (Santiago: CIEPLAN-Hachette, 1990); and Julio Faúndez, *Marxism and Democracy in Chile* (New Haven: Yale University Press, 1988).

20. See Giovanni Sartori, *Parties and Party Systems: A Framework for Analysis* (Cambridge: Cambridge University Press, 1976), 131–216.

21. Robert A. Packenham has written a very stimulating essay tracing the causes of economic liberalization in Argentina and Brazil. He suggests four pattern variables that explain economic liberalization in Argentina (and the absence of it in Brazil). I am indebted to him for his rich analysis. See Robert A. Packenham, "The Politics of Economic Liberalization: Brazil and Argentina in Comparative Perspective," *Kellogg Institute Working Paper* 206 (University of Notre Dame, 1993).

22. These changes are discussed more fully in Scully, *Rethinking the Center*, especially chap. 5.

23. This point should not be exaggerated. The Chilean state continues to play an important role in the economy. For example, the giant copper industry remains in state hands. The state continues to subsidize the forestry industry,

the automobile industry, and, most recently, the coal industry. Unions were also given more power under the Aylwin administration. Packenham ("The Politics of Economic Liberalization") refers to this as the Nixon in China syndrome: his impeccable anticommunist credentials strengthened his hand with potential domestic critics.

24. Issues relating to the process of democratic consolidation in comparative perspective are discussed in J. Samuel Valenzuela's chapter, "Democratic Consolidation in Post-Transitional Settings: Notion, Process, and Facilitating Conditions," in Scott Mainwaring, Guillermo O'Donnell, and J. Samuel Valenzuela, *Issues in Democratic Consolidation: The New South American Democracies in Comparative Perspective* (Notre Dame: University of Notre Dame Press, 1992), 57–104. The term "perverse institutionalization" is his. I have provided a full account of the constraining features of the 1980 Constitution in Timothy R. Scully and Alejandro Ferreiro Y., "Chile Recovers Its Democratic Past: Democratization by Installment," *Journal of Legislation* 18, no. 2 (1992): 317–29.

25. Rhoda Rabkin evaluates the prerogatives granted to the military by the 1980 Constitution: "The Aylwin Government and 'Tutelary' Democracy: A Concept in Search of a Case," *Journal of Interamerican Studies* 34, no. 4 (1992): 119–94.

26. J. Samuel Valenzuela, "Democratic Consolidation in Post-Transitional Settings: Notion, Process, and Facilitating Conditions," in Mainwaring, O'Donnell, and Valenzuela, *Issues in Democratic Consolidation*, 64.

27. *El Mercurio*, June 17, 1993.

28. The ease with which these provisions might be enacted should not be exaggerated, however. Any changes with respect to the armed forces (as well as the Constitutional Court and the National Security Council) require a two-thirds majority in both houses of Congress. To modify other features of the constitution requires a slightly lower majority of both houses, either three-fifths or four-sevenths, depending on the type of law to be modified.

29. For a full treatment of the electoral law and its multiple implications, see "El sistema electoral," Programa de asesoría legislativa, *Análisis de Actualidad* (June 1992). Also see Genaro Arriagada, "Después de los presidencialismos . . . ¿Qué?" in Oscar Godoy, ed., *Cambio de régimen político* (Santiago: Ediciones Universidad Católica de Chile, 1990), 57–91.

30. The overrepresentation of the rural sector was characteristic of pre-coup Chile as well. See Cesar Caviedes, *The Politics of Chile: A Sociographical Assessment* (Boulder, Colo.: Westview Press, 1979).

31. Caution should be exercised in interpreting these results, however, since parties ran in alliances, potentially producing some distortion in the results. Figures are taken from Arriagada, "Después de los presidencialismos," 78.

32. The 1980 Constitution originally provided for only twenty-six senators to be elected, in which case the nine designated would have represented more than one-fourth of that body's total. However, a constitutional reform in July 1989 raised the total number of elected senators to thirty-eight, lowering the relative importance of the designated senators to about one-fifth of the Senate.

33. Eduardo Silva notes his agreement with Brian Loveman; see Silva, "Capitalist Regime Loyalties and Redemocratization in Chile," *Journal of Interamerican Studies* 34, no. 4 (1992): 78.

34. President Aylwin's chief of staff, Edgardo Boeninger, stated two years into the transition that "the main threat is populism, by which I mean the danger of responding to widespread social demands by making promises that outstrip the resources available to fulfill them"; quoted in Rabkin, "The

Aylwin Government," 142. Alejandro Foxley, in an interview with the author, has suggested this to be the case.

35. Cited in Rabkin, "The Aylwin Government," 142.

36. The popularity enjoyed by President Patricio Aylwin's government was consistently high throughout the period of his administration, only once dipping below 50 percent approval. A poll in March 1993 gave Aylwin's government a 57.8 percent approval rating, compared with only 15.6 percent disapproving of the government. Longitudinal survey data covering the previous three years of the Aylwin presidency are provided in "Estudio social y opinion pública no. 19," Centro de Estudios Públicos (May 1993), 41. Eduardo Frei's popularity as president has been at least as high. According to a survey conducted by the Centro de Estudios Públicos, those who rated Frei's performance "positively" or "very positively" comprised 67 percent of the sample. See *Estudios Públicos,* Documento de Trabajo 236 (May–June, 1995).

37. Manuel Antonio Garretón ("La oposición política") argues forcefully that political learning among elites provides a principal explanation for the changed political arena. Nancy Bermeo provides a useful overview of the comparative literature in "Democracy and the Lessons of Dictatorship," *Comparative Politics* 24, no. 3 (1992): 273–91.

38. Acceptance speech made by Alejandro Foxley upon his induction into the Royal Academy of Moral and Political Sciences, Madrid, Spain, March 30, 1993.

39. Giovanni Sartori, *The Theory of Democracy Revisited* (Chatham, N.J.: Chatham House, 1987), 89–91.

Chapter 7 Paraguay: Transition from *Caudillo* Rule (Abente Brun)

1. The procedure for allocating seats in the party's primary was the D'Hondt proportional system. Consequently, Wasmosy's and Argaña's supporters won about an even share of the legislative candidacies. Upon taking office, Wasmosy was able to win the support of a number of former Argaña supporters.

2. The council is made up of eight members. Two are appointed by Congress (one by senators and the other by deputies), one by the executive, one by the Supreme Court, two by the law schools, and two by the lawyers. Of the six members already appointed, three belong to the Colorado Party and three are known as oppositionists. The proportional system is expected to ensure that of the two lawyers elected, one will belong to the Colorado Party and the other to the opposition, thus resulting in a 4–4 tie in the council, which will be forced to find consensus for major designations. The nominal system that the Colorado lawyers want to apply would give both seats to the Colorados, thus producing a 5–3 Colorado majority in the council.

3. According to the constitution, unconstitutionality actions do not have *erga omnes* effects, that is, they cannot result in the complete elimination of the law but only in the suspension of its effects on the individuals that have appealed. In such a context, the unconstitutionality awarded by the court was wholly inapplicable, for the court cannot legislate a different system of election. The most the court could do was to say: the proportional system is unconstitutional, you do not have to be ruled by it; but if you want to vote, you will have to use it because we cannot impose a different system. As the Brazilians would put it, "tem razao mas fica preso." Yet, by raising doubt over the issue, the court has opened the way for other legal actions that could further delay the reform of the judiciary.

4. The constitution excludes judicial acts from the realm of the *amparo,* but the lawyers argue that in calling the election the court has adopted a

merely administrative decision that is subject to a possible *amparo*. The discussion could be endless, but the bottom line is that, given the partiality of the judges, any conceivable recourse can stand, no matter how ridiculous.

Chapter 8 Uruguay: From Restoration to the Crisis of Governability (Rial)

1. This was considered the very essence of Batllismo, a current of thought and political action born and bred in the Colorado Party at the beginning of the century and deeply ingrained in the political culture of the country since then. Named after President José Batlle y Ordóñez (1856–1929) and deeply influenced by French Radicalism, German Krausism, and American Georgism, this ideological tendency postulated the presence of a strong state, conceived of as the great regulator of power relations within society and able to anticipate social demands in order to deflect and channel them. The judicious use of the law and of state intervention would then buffer conflicts, prevent injustice, and preempt revolutionary violence born of discontent. While many of the social and political advances of this small country can be attributed to this school of thought, its critics maintain that it also helped breed a sense of "entitlement to entitlement" in Uruguayan culture that ended by putting a brake on its later development. See Milton Vanger, *Model Country* (Brandeis: Brandeis University Press, 1980); Carlos Real de Azúa, *El impulso y su freno: Tres décadas de Batllismo* (Montevideo: EBO, 1964), and Real de Azúa, *La sociedad amortiguadora* (Montevideo: EBO, 1984).

2. See Fernando Filgueira, "Un estado social centenario: El crecimiento hasta el límite del estado social batllista," in *Peitho,* Documentos de Trabajo 81 (Montevideo: Peitho, 1991).

3. On clientelist practices in Uruguay, see Robert E. Biles, *Patronage Politics: Electoral Behavior in Uruguay* (Baltimore, Johns Hopkins University Press, 1975), and Juan Carlos Fá Robaina, *Cartas a un diputado* (Montevideo: Alfa, 1972).

4. See Oscar Botinelli, "El sistema electoral uruguayo: Descripción y análisis," in *Peitho,* Documentos de Trabajo 83 (Montevideo: Peitho, 1991), and Juan Rial and Jaime Klaczko, "Cómo se vota: El sistema electoral," in *Cuadernos de orientación electoral* 4 (Montevideo: Peitho/CAPEL, 1989).

5. Although the Broad Front, the coalition of parties from the Left, was born in 1971 within this framework, it could be created only by using the provisions of the existing electoral laws that permit accumulation of factions. In 1994 the Broad Front used the political name Encuentro Progresista (Progressive Confluence) but legally kept the designation Frente Amplio (Broad Front). On Uruguayan political parties, see Angel Cocchi, "Un sistema político centenario" and "Los partidos políticos y la historia reciente," in *Cuadernos de orientación electoral* 1, no. 2 (Montevideo: Peitho/CAPEL, 1989).

6. See Henry Finch, *A Political Economy of Uruguay since 1870* (New York: St. Martin's Press, 1981).

7. See Luis Costa Bonino, *Crisis de los partidos tradicionales y movimientos revolucionarios en el Uruguay* (Montevideo: EBO, 1985); Eddy Kauffman, *Uruguay in Transition* (New Brunswick, N.J.: Transaction Books, 1979); Arturo Porzecansky, *Uruguay's Tupamaros: The Urban Guerrilla* (New York: Praeger, 1973).

8. President Juan María Bordaberry, who had decreed the dissolution of the National Assembly on June 27, 1973, was in turn ousted by the military when he tried to institutionalize an authoritarian regime in 1976. See Charles Gillespie, "The Breakdown of Democracy in Uruguay: Alternative Political Models,"

in *Wilson Center for Scholars,* Working Papers 143 (Washington, D.C.: Woodrow Wilson Center, 1984).

9. I have borrowed this term from Carl Schmitt, *La dictadura* (Madrid: Revista de Occidente, 1968), 5ff (originally published in 1921). This idea was developed in Juan Rial, "Transitions in Latin America on the Threshold of the 1990s," *International Social Science Journal* 128 (May 1991), 285.

10. See Juan Corradi, Patricia Fagen, and Manuel A. Garretón, *The Culture of Fear in the Southern Cone* (Berkeley: University of California Press, 1994); Carina Perelli, "Settling Accounts with Blood Memory: The Case of Argentina," *Social Research* 50 (1992), 415–51; and Saul Sosnowski and Louise B. Popkin, eds., *Repression, Exile, and Democracy: Uruguayan Culture* (Durham, N.C.: Duke University Press, 1993).

11. On the transition process, see Charles Gillespie, *Negotiating Democracy: Politicians and Generals in Uruguay* (Cambridge: Cambridge University Press, 1991), and Luis E. González, *Political Structure and Democracy in Uruguay* (Notre Dame: University of Notre Dame Press, 1991).

12. See Juan Rial, *Elecciones de 1984: Sistema electoral y resultados* (San José: IIDH/CAPEL, 1986).

13. See Manuel Alcántara and Ismael Crespo, *Partidos y elecciones en Uruguay, 1971–1990* (Madrid: CEDEAL, 1992), and IIDH/CAPEL, *El referéndum uruguayo de 16 de abril de 1989* (San José: IIDH, 1989).

14. These are the reform measures recommended by the international organizations that monitor third world economies. See John Williamson, "What Washington Means by Political Reform," in John Williamson, ed., *Latin American Adjustment: How Much Has Happened?* (Washington, D.C.: Institute for International Economics, 1990).

15. In an interview with the author (May 1992), Dr. Sanguinetti admitted that this was the only way to prevent continual pressure to increase public expenditures, given the fragmentation of the party system.

16. The National Party obtained 38.87 percent of the vote and the faction of Luis Alberto Lacalle 22.57 percent. See Carina Perelli and Juan Rial, "Las elecciones uruguayas de noviembre de 1989," in Rodolfo Cerdas, Juan Rial, and Daniel Zovatto, *Elecciones y democracia en América Latina: Una tarea inconclusa* (San José: IIDH/CAPEL/Naumann, 1992).

17. Calculations made in 1995 indicate that each member of the active work force must pay an average of U.S.$3,600 dollars to the state in taxes or contributions to Social Security. This amount has been paid by Uruguayan workers since 1991. *Búsqueda 802,* July 27, 1994, 23.

18. The normal VAT rate was 22 percent, increased to 23 percent in 1995. It is one of the highest in the world.

19. It was 7.88 percent in 1992, 2.53 percent in 1993, and 5.08 percent in 1994 (data from the Central Bank of Uruguay). In 1995 the economic team forecasts a recession and 0 percent growth.

20. From 59 percent annual inflation in 1992 to 53 percent in 1993. In 1994 the figure was 44 percent, dropping to 37 percent in 1995.

21. In 1994, an election year, it was 2 percent.

22. In 1990, the Gini Index (which measures income distribution from 0–1, 0 being the most equal) was 0.37; in 1991, 0.43; in 1992, 0.44; in 1993, 0.42; and in 1994, 0.41.

23. If the population is divided into quintiles, the wealthiest 20 percent received 47.5 percent of total income in 1993. The poorest 20 percent received 5 percent of total income, the upper-middle-bracket (20%) received 23 percent of total income, the lower-middle bracket (20%) received 9.5 percent, and the middle bracket (20%) received 15 percent.

24. Carina Perelli and Juan Rial, "El referéndum sobre la Ley de empresas públicas del 13 de diciembre de 1992 en el Uruguay: Un plebiscito sobre la gestión del gobierno," in *Peitho*, Documentos de Trabajo 93 (Montevideo: Peitho, 1992).

25. The level of conflict was more important during Sanguinetti's term. Thus, according to data provided by CEALS (Centro de Estudios y Asesoramiento Laborales y Sociales), 2,139 days of work were lost in 1988 due to strikes; in 1992 there were 1,329 days lost, and in 1993 the number increased to 1,904. It decreased in 1994 and 1995. See Centro Uruguay Independiente, *Relaciones laborales y convenios en el Uruguay. Los sindicatos ante la reestructura* (Montevideo: CIU, 1995).

26. The inflated membership lists allow them to have more votes at the PIT-CNT congresses. The total number of affiliates is about 200,000 in a formal work force of 800,000.

27. In fact, this is what is beginning to occur in modern companies such as PepsiCo International and even some state companies such as UTE (electric company), ANTEL (telecommunications), and ANCAP (oil), where organized labor has negotiated productivity pacts and thus receives a share of the profits. See *Relaciones laborales y convenios*.

28. In 1993 an informant at a police station claimed that he was a Chilean named Berríos (he was investigated for human rights violations and was apparently connected to the Letelier case) and that he had been kidnapped by members of the Uruguayan military as part of an agreement with the Chilean armed forces. Police authorities tried to hush the scandal, and the informant disappeared. However, the press published the case, and some members of the police force and the army were sanctioned. In 1996 the scandal resurfaced. The corpse of a person believed to be Berríos appeared on a Uruguayan beach.

29. Uruguay had a UN battalion in Mozambique until January 1995; another battalion was part of the UN forces in Cambodia until May 1993; and a new battalion was deployed in Angola in 1995.

30. From 1934 to 1967, elections were held every four years.

31. A proposal to reform the constitution in order to allow voters to choose different *lemas* at the national and the municipal level was rejected in August 1994.

32. In 1994 the Congress approved a bill to pay U.S.$7 per vote, up from the previous U.S.$1 per vote.

33. The Electoral Court has proposed easing this rule by making voting voluntary for older citizens. While no resolution has yet been passed on this matter, Congress usually grants amnesty to older citizens who did not or could not vote at any given election.

34. In 1994, voter participation reached 89 percent.

35. The Colorado Party won the election with only 30,000 votes more than the National Party and 60,000 more than the Broad Front (Progressive Confluence). The Colorado Party will have thirty-one senators and thirty-two representatives in the house; the National Party ten senators and thirty-one representatives; the Broad Front nine senators and thirty-one representatives; and the Nuevo Espacio (New Space) Party, one senator and five representatives.

36. Robert Michels, *Los partidos políticos* (Buenos Aires: Amorrortu, 1969), 6ff.

37. Luis Eduardo González used this expression in a television public appearance in 1993.

38. See Carina Perelli, *Gobierno y política en Montevideo: La Intendencia Municipal de Montevideo y la formación de un nuevo liderazgo a comienzos de los años '90* (Montevideo: Peitho, 1991), and Carina Perelli: "La personaliza-

ción de la política: Nuevos caudillos, outsiders, política mediática y política informal," in Carina Perelli, Sonia Picado, and Daniel Zovatto, eds., *Partidos y clase política en América Latina en los 90* (San José: IIDH/CAPEL, 1995).

39. Rodney Arismendi was a member of parliament between 1949 and 1973, when his term of office was interrupted by the military dictatorship. Elected senator in 1989, he never occupied his seat as he died before his new term of office. He was secretary general of the Communist Party from 1955 until almost his death.

40. United Nations Development Program, *Human Development. Report 1994* (Cambridge: Oxford University Press/UNDP, 1995).

Chapter 9 Argentina: Democracy in Turmoil (De Riz)

1. See Mario Damill and Roberto Frenkel, "Restauración democrática y política económica: Argentina, 1984–1991," in Juan Antonio Morales and Gary McMahon, eds., *La política económica en la transición a la democracia: Lecciones de Argentina* (Santiago de Chile: CIEPLAN, 1993); Pablo Gerchunoff and José L. Machinea, "Un ensayo sobre la política económica después de la estabilización," in Pablo Bustos, ed., *Más allá de la estabilidad: Argentina en la época de la globalización y la regionalización* (Buenos Aires: Fundación FEBERT, 1995), 29–92; and Alberto Minujin and Gabriel Kessler, *La nueva pobreza en Argentina* (Buenos Aires: Editorial Planeta, 1995).

2. The best scholarly analysis of Menem's Argentina is Tulio Halperín Donghi, *La larga agonía de la Argentina peronista* (Buenos Aires: Espasa Calpe/Ariel, 1994). Some economists are now developing the concept of "modernización a la intemperie," as referred to by Halperín Donghi and Jose Nun, "Populismo, representación y menemismo," *Sociedad* 5 (October 1994): 93–121.

3. The Ministry of the Economy was initially assigned to the directors of the Bunge and Born group.

4. Shortly after taking office, President Menem obtained approval for the law of economic emergency with the consent of the Radicals. This law granted the executive full powers to modify legislation without the subsequent intervention of Congress and launched the privatization of the state-owned telephone and aviation companies. It must be remembered that President Menem's early assumption of power—a paraconstitutional solution to the governability crisis—opened up an anomalous period. The Menem administration began without the simultaneous renewal of Congress but with the tacit understanding that he would not encounter obstacles during that portion of his term on the part of an opposition that was on the defensive and considered responsible for the disarray and its premature relinquishing of power.

5. I refer to a number of factors: the removal of the deputy prosecutors and of the head of the National Prosecutor's Office for Administrative Investigations, without seeking the required approval by the Senate or submitting the accused officials to due process of political trials; the modification by decree of the statutes of the National Auditor's Office, the agency responsible for monitoring the legality of the administrative procedures for dispensing public funds; the suspension of four of the five members of this office without invoking due cause. The expansion of the number of members of the Supreme Court was one of a series of measures aimed at curtailing the independence of the powers of the state. By repeatedly resorting to *per saltum*, the court lost its character as an extraordinary tribunal and became an ordinary tribunal of the third instance, as cases were taken away from their rightful judges. The political role and resulting political commitment of the Supreme Court are blurred: the *per saltum* in the case of the privatization of Aerolíneas Argentinas is illustrative.

The majority of the members that comprise the court is in favor of the expansion of emergency powers, which have been virtually exempted from legislative controls. A documented analysis of the erosion of these controls is found in Horacio Verbitsky, *Hacer la corte* (Buenos Aires: Editorial Sudamericana, 1993).

6. The convertibility law requires that the money supply have an exact equivalent in foreign currency reserves in the central bank at the official exchange rate (10,000 australes per U.S. dollar). This prevents these reserves from being used for other purposes. In this way the government's hands are perceived to be "tied" and unable to alter the course that was established.

7. See Liliana De Riz, "El debate sobre la reforma electoral en Argentina," *Desarrollo Económico* 32, no. 126 (1992): 163–84. It should be noted that abstentions increased in the legislative elections of 1991, jumping from an average of 15 percent during the 1980s to 22 percent. The phenomenon of the growth of provincial parties to the detriment of the major national parties was accentuated. A new force to the right of the political spectrum, the Movement for National Dignity and Independence (MODIN), led by former colonel Aldo Rico (protagonist of the military rebellion of Easter Week, in April 1987), captured 10 percent of the vote in the province of Buenos Aires and three seats in the Chamber of Deputies. In Chaco a retired general became governor and in Salta, Captain Ulloa. Both men were former governors during the preceding military government. The triumph of Peronism in the elections for governor had the peculiarity of bringing nonparty candidates to power in provincial states. These candidates were chosen by the president without party consultation. They were something of a "new breed," for example, a singer (Ortega in Tucumán), a race car driver (Reuteman in Santa Fé), a businessman (Escobar in San Juan).

8. During the first four years of his term, President Menem issued three hundred eight Decrees of Necessity and Urgency, which sharply contrasts with the ten issued by President Alfonsín. See Delia Ferreira Rubio and Mateo Goretti, "El gobierno por decreto en la Argentina (1983–1993)," *El Derecho* 32, no. 8525 (June 27, 1994).

9. The New Country Alliance, in which historically antagonistic parties such as the PJ (Peronists), the UCEDE (Union of the Democratic Center), and the MID (Movement of Integration and Development) converged, obtained 32 percent of the vote. This figure coincides with that obtained by the FREJUPO (Popular Judicial Front) in the 1989 elections for senator of the federal capital. On that occasion, thanks to the votes of the UCEDE in the electoral college, the FREJUPO reached 52 percent (the UCEDE had obtained 20 percent of the vote). The corollary is the exodus in 1992 of allied votes toward the UCR (Radical Civic Union) and other parties such as the MODIN. The polls showed that 36 percent of those who held a positive image of Cavallo voted for the UCR and 26 percent of those who had a positive opinion of Menem also opted for the UCR. On the other hand, an analysis of the electoral results by electoral constituency shows that Avelino Porto, the candidate of the ruling party, defeated Fernando De la Rúa by a little more than 1 point in Villa Lugano, a district that in 1989 gave 55 percent of its vote to the PJ. Porto managed to win only in Villa Lugano and Socorro (two districts that represent the two extremes of the social scale). The performance of the UCR in 1992, compared with the results of the 1991 legislative elections, confirms the hypothesis that approximately 25 percent of the electorate that voted for Peronism in 1991 leaned toward the UCR, the MODIN, and the Frente del Sur (a leftist political group headed by Pino Solanas) in 1992. The senatorial elections in the capital (and, in particular, the 1992 elections in which De la Rúa ran and was the can-

didate who obtained the most votes in 1989, but did not take office because of the subsequent negotiations in the electoral college) are inconclusive about the volatility of the Peronist vote. These are, on the other hand, occasions when the candidate has greater "weight," and the opportunity exists for opinion votes that are less attached to partisan loyalties than is the case in elections for the partial renewal of the Chamber of Deputies.

10. The Yoma case refers to the trial of the president's sister-in-law—the former director of audiences of the presidency—and of her ex-husband, a fugitive from justice, for the laundering of drug money.

11. Within the framework of procedural reform, the control over the Judicial Federal Privilege was completed. The Judicial Federal Privilege decides which cases can be appealed to the Supreme Court, including the cases that involve officials of the executive branch. Carried out by promoting and transferring judges who ordered the prosecution of government officials, and replacing them with complacent judges, the control made possible a stay of proceedings in these types of cases. The continuance in power or the return of officials under suspicion—for instance, the former minister of public works, Roberto Dromi, was recently reappointed to the cabinet at the level of secretary of state—transformed the fight against corruption, defined by Menem as treason, into a parody.

12. The initiative included changes in the rules governing the party system: direct primaries for the election of party authorities, representation of minorities in the government and administration, the political-legal status of the parties at the municipal level, the establishment of time limits for interventions, setting the minimum age to vote in party primaries at sixteen years, simultaneous noncompulsory but open primaries, and the inclusion of independent candidates unless prohibited by the respective organizational charter of each party. The rules of party financing and municipal-government relations were also modified.

13. These figures suggest the formation of a Menemist electoral coalition that brings together those from the top and those from the bottom of the social scale. A large number of votes from the Right splintered toward Peronism. The Frente Grande (FG), a left-of-center political organization, benefited from the exodus of Radical votes and, to a lesser extent, of Peronist votes. With 13.6 percent of the vote, the FG became the third force in the district. See Liliana De Riz, "La coyuntura argentina," *Nueva Sociedad* 129 (1993): 6–14.

14. The PJ and the UCR represent two heterogeneous and contradictory political forces in their bases of social support. These forces compete on the same hunting grounds, located at the Center of the ideological spectrum. The logic of competition, stimulated by the bipartisan format that emerged in 1983, gradually blurred the traditional identities and profiles and accentuated the phenomenon of the personalization of politics. Given this context, the fluctuation of votes that is clearly evident since 1987 acquires greater sense. The emergence of ideological parties that embrace social protest, such as the FG in the capital and the MODIN in the province of Buenos Aires, creates a broader range of options toward both the Left and the Right. However, the MODIN obtained only 5.8 percent of the vote, and the FG, 3.6 percent (overall, the Left obtained 4.7 percent of the vote of the entire country). See De Riz, "La coyuntura argentina."

15. Article 30 of the constitution requires a two-thirds vote of members of both houses of Congress to declare the need for reform. The commission for Constitutional Affairs of the lower house approved a bill that sustains the interpretation of article 30 to mean that two-thirds of the members of each house present are needed to declare the need for reform.

16. It should be noted that, according to polls taken before the so-called Olivos Pact, the level of support for constitutional reform reached 50 percent. Likewise, data from surveys taken in ten provinces during September 1993 indicated that both the decision to participate in the plebiscite as well as the inclination to vote in support of the reform were about 70 percent. The lowest figure was recorded in Tucumán (64.1 percent) and the highest in Jujuy (74.6 percent expressed support for constitutional reform) (SOFRES [French polling association]–IBOPE [Brazilian Institute of Public Opinion]). The negotiation thus occurred within the framework of a diffuse reformist consensus throughout society. The sectors with the highest concentration of business owners were also in support of these reforms. Although traditionally reluctant to reform the constitution, the private sector ended by accepting the reform as a condition for the continuity of the economic model. Both the church and the armed forces also came to accept what appeared to them as a fait accompli. Even though important sectors of the establishment, represented in the editorials of the newspaper *La Nación,* maintained a stance of opposition toward reform and, in particular, toward presidential reelection, the crux of their position gradually changed. It shifted from challenging the necessity and opportunity for reform toward debating the constitutionality of the procedures followed by the government and the principal opposition, as well as criticizing the contents of the reform itself.

17. The content of the agreed text that was presented to the Congress establishes a nucleus of basic points of agreement, topics open for discussion by the Constituent Assembly, and guarantees for the enactment of what was agreed upon. Among the basic points of agreement are the direct election of the president and vice-president, the reduction of their term in office to four years, reelection for one term, the elimination of the confessional requirement in order to be president, ballotage, the creation of the position of chief of the Cabinet of Ministers, the direct election of three senators with a four-year term (one senator for the minority), the limiting of Decrees of Necessity and Urgency, the creation of the Council of Magistrates charged with proposing obligatory lists of two and three names for the appointment of judges, Senate approval of nominees to the Supreme Court by absolute majority, and the direct election of the intendant of the federal capital.

18. This is the lesson that was gained from the experience of the plebiscite held in the province of Buenos Aires to decide the reelection of the governor in the face of the opposition's refusal to endorse it at the Constituent Assembly. The opposition—in particular the UCR, in open contradiction to the party's position regarding presidential reelection—ended up a prisoner of its anti-reelectionist stand. The October 3, 1994, elections gave the victory to the PJ with 61 percent of the vote, securing the right of Governor Duhalde to run again for governor in that province. The opposition bungled the opportunity to negotiate the text of the constitution, contributed to making the elections into a national issue, and had to compete against the ruling party at a clear disadvantage in terms of resources.

19. Interview with Radio Mitre, February 2 and 5, 1994. Raúl Alfonsín justified his strategy in response to those who alleged that the opposition emerged from the negotiations weakened. He affirmed that "the opposition cannot reduce itself to declarations of principles and ideals; it should strive toward the achievement of objectives, a creation of a new type of dialogue with the government." (Radio Mitre, February 5, 1994). One of his main arguments was that, unlike what occurred in 1949 and 1957, this reform would be reached by consent.

20. The violence that erupted in that province took place within the framework of the approval of the law of adjustment of public employment and the amazing contrasts in salaries within the public administration. The mobilizations of protest that proliferated in the poorest provinces were toned-down replicas of what occurred in Santiago del Estero.

21. The PJ obtained 37.7 percent of the vote, a figure below its lowest historic record in 1983, and the UCR, 19.9 percent. With 13.6 percent of the vote, the FG became the third force at the national level. The MODIN went from 6 percent to 9 percent at the national level, achieving a more even distribution in various districts with respect to 1993. The FG prevailed in the federal capital with 37.6 percent of the vote, confirming the pattern of strong voting volatility in that district. In the province of Buenos Aires, the FG managed to become a second minority, slightly above the UCR, with 16.3 percent of the vote. It should be pointed out that the UCR was internally split over the legitimacy of the Olivos Pact and had slogans such as "better to vote for the original than for a copy." This may help explain the important loss of votes, which primarily benefited the FG.

22. The PJ was able to impose neither the clause related to the reelection of governors nor the ban on abortion, two issues over which the PJ encountered the joint resistance of the UCR and the FG.

23. The historic constitution did not consider the Office of Public Defender. Its creation and regulation originated in a law. Since the enactment of law 27, the president appoints the person who fills this office with the approval of the Senate. Political trial and resignation were the only conditions for premature termination of his or her functions. Nevertheless, President Menem removed the last public defender by means of a decree and appointed three attorneys general in his place.

24. Eleven provincial parties surpassed 1.5 million votes in the 1994 elections. Also, with the exception of the MODIN, Fuerza Republicana (the Tucumán Republican Force) of Tucumán, and Frente de la Esperanza (Front of Hope) (San Juan), the tendency toward the electoral strengthening of the provincial parties evident since 1983 is fueled by the discontent of the urban middle class, as confirmed by a demographic analysis of the data. In an indirect manner, this tendency is also shown by the lesser capacity of the UCR relative to the PJ to retain its social base. See Gerardo Adrogué, "Militares en las urnas: ¿a quienes representan?" *Desarrollo Económico* 33, no. 131 (1993): 425–42.

25. The FREPASO is a Center-Left coalition integrated by the FG, the Unidad Socialista (Socialist Union), the Democracia Cristiana (Christian Democrats), and the País (Country), a party created by Peronist senator José Octavio Bordón, former governor of Mendoza Province. Bordón was elected as their residential candidate in the FREPASO's February primaries. Much to everyone's surprise, five hundred thousand citizens cast their votes in the primaries to decide which of the two former Peronist leaders—Chacho Alvarez and Bordón—would be the presidential candidate in the May elections.

26. Under the new electoral rules, only positive votes were considered. The valid votes embrace not only the positive votes but also the annulled votes and the "votos en blanco" (the voter casts a ballot for none of the candidates). It must be kept in mind that voting is compulsory.

27. See Halperín Donghi, *La larga agonía de la Argentina*, and Juan Corradi, "Menem's Argentina, Act II," *Current History* (February 1995): 76–79. Since 1983, Peronist voters have remained steady, between 36 and 38 percent of the total.

28. The electoral results confirmed the evanescence of the two-party system. This was already obvious in the 1994 elections for the Constituent Assembly.

29. In the November 1994 primaries, the Radicals elected Horacio Massaccesi, governor of the Rio Negro province, as their presidential candidate. The fact that only 30 percent of registered Radicals voted in the primaries suggests that the candidate, close to the old guard, and more prone to compromising with President Menem, did not raise enough enthusiasm among many party members. The personal character of Massaccesi's electoral campaign prevented the party from establishing allies in the provincial parties.

30. The 1995 presidential electoral results were: Menem-Ruckauf, 47.7 percent; Bordón-Alvarez, 28.2 percent; Massaccesi-Hernández, 16.4 percent. The rest of the parties accounted for only 3.6 percent of the total. The MODIN did not reach 2 percent. The UCEDE lent its support to Menem's candidacy. The nine left-wing parties together did not reach 2 percent. Annulled and "en blanco" votes represented 4.1 percent of the total.

31. The electoral results for the renewal of the national Chamber of Deputies were: the Peronist Party, 43 percent; the Radical Party, 22 percent; and the FREPASO, 21 percent. The differences between votes for president and votes for deputies in the parties show the increasing tendency among voters to distribute their preferences between candidates belonging to different parties ("corte de boletas"). In the country as a whole, almost 20 percent of valid votes followed this pattern, while the historical median oscillated between 5 and 7 percent.

32. In the fourteen gubernatorial provincial elections, the UCR succeeded in retaining three of the provinces and winning in a new one (Catamarca). The FREPASO did not get any provincial governor (for this reason it is important to keep in mind that the central government established a sequential system of provincial elections). Elections for governor are scheduled in the remaining provinces for September and October 1995. It is also clear that in these elections for governor the UCR's and the PJ's candidates accumulated more votes than the presidential candidates from the same parties. This shows the weight of local politics in voting results. Only in two provinces did the votes for Menem outnumber the votes for Peronist gubernatorial candidates.

33. I refer to Congress' delay in sanctioning key executive legal programs, despite Menem's pressure for the support of Peronist legislators. Under the new constitutional rules, the lower house insisted on the amended executive programs despite Menem's veto, for example, in the case of the copyright law.

34. Since the convertibility plan, the unemployment rate has nearly doubled at the national level. In greater Buenos Aires, laboratory of the deepest, old-fashioned populist policies and led by Governor Eduardo Duhalde, it has nearly tripled.

35. The debate on the government privatization of the Yacyretá hydroelectric complex held in the upper house is a prime example. The Yacyretá case can be seen as an early indication that new constitutional rules will produce important changes in the exercise of presidential power. The minister of the economy is no longer able to impose his decisions on the Peronists. The debate on the privatization of the mail service is another case. Minister Cavallo himself is trying to prevent Peronist deputies from sanctioning it. Cavallo's accusations of corruption in the mail service privatization program brought this issue into the center of the political debates. Cavallo pointed out that if this program were approved by the lower house, a monopolistic mail system would be created that would be suitable for laundering drug money. In that case, Argentina would follow the Colombian pattern.

36. Eduardo Duhalde, former vice-president and current governor of the province of Buenos Aires, has positioned himself to succeed Menem as president in 1999. Elected to a second term as governor of the nation's most popu-

lous province under a new constitution changed to suit his ambitions, Duhalde challenges Cavallo, his rival in the race for the presidency.

37. Some observers have suggested that the former division of roles within the government is changing. As secretary of the presidency, Bauzá mediated in cabinet conflicts representing President Menem. Now, as chief of the cabinet, Bauzá has taken sides on various issues. As a result, Menem's role as mediator has become more clearly defined.

38. Gerchunoff and Machinea, "Un ensayo sobre la política económica." See also Adolfo Canitrot, "Navegamos a ultramar en carabela," *Página* 12 (July 23, 1995).

39. The financial crisis in the provinces is the result of a combination of factors: the provincial governments have been slow to privatize or have refused to do it, their banks are insolvent, their governments employ over half the labor force, and they rely on the central government for their revenues. The federal system in Argentina is such that the central government must regularly bribe the provinces in order to get their political support.

40. Natalio Botana has well described the present political weakness of the regime as a "republic of words," "a republic of suspicions" doomed to disintegrate as the result of both corruption and discord instead of the "modern Republic" that had inspired Mitre, Sarmiento, and Alberdi. *La Nación,* August 28, 1995. In the year that followed the enactment of the new constitution, Congress approved only three of the twenty-one laws that were to be passed. What is more, the deadline for three of the most crucial laws has expired.

41. According to the polls taken by Manuel Mora & Associates following Cavallo's accusations, 79 percent believe that the minister's accusations are true and 66 percent believe that it would be detrimental for Cavallo to resign. On the other hand, 29 percent consider that President Menem was weakened.

42. Stephan Haggard and Robert Kaufman, "The State in the Initiation and Consolidation of Market-oriented Reform," *Série política internacional e comparada* 4 (São Paulo: University of São Paulo, 1991).

43. A new type of relationship between the government and the armed forces was gradually forming throughout the course of the Menem administration. After suppressing the December 1990 Carapintada Rebellion and issuing a presidential pardon to the former commanders, Menem gave the military a function within the framework of the new international policy by sending troops abroad to participate in peacekeeping missions. This "exit into the world" places the military in a new position: it is now under the watchful eye of the rest of the world. At the same time, the emergence of parties of former military officers, such as the MODIN, Acción Chaqueña (Chaco Action), and Fuerza Republicana, synthesize the new type of link established between the military and politics. See Adrogué, "Militares en las urnas;" Argentina has become a successfully demilitarized state to a considerably greater degree than any other South American country. Its military expenses in relation to the gross domestic product have dropped significantly since the advent of the Menem administration. While it reached 3.5 percent in 1989, it represented only 1.9 percent in 1991. See Carlos Escudé and Andrés Fontana, "Divergencias estratégicas en el Cono Sur: Las políticas de seguridad de la Argentina frente a las de Brasil y Chile," in *Universidad Torcuato Di Tella,* Working Paper 20 (Buenos Aires, July 1995).

In this new situation, the armed forces' current demand that the government define its defense and security policy goals, and consequently the nature and scope of the role of the military, is a clear symptom of the unrest.

44. The General Confederation of Labor (CGT) resisted the policies of the Radical government by resorting to repeated general strikes. Today the CGT is no longer the "backbone" of Peronism as it was in the past, but rather one more component of the political system, obliged to lobby rather than stage general strikes. The breakup of the system of collective bargaining and its replacement by either a system of bargaining at individual firms or by salary freezes, and the increasing weakness of the retirement and public assistance systems, have stripped the CGT of its power resources. Its role is now confined to endorsing policies that are decided by the government without the participation of the CGT.

45. Gerchunoff and Machinea, "Un ensayo sobre la política económica."

46. It should be noted that the accumulated increase in gross national product between 1991 and 1994 was about 35 percent. At present, the unemployment and underemployment rates have reached 30 percent. On September 6, 1995, the CGT carried out its first general strike.

47. The September 3, 1995, gubernatorial election in the province of Santa Fé, one of the four main electoral districts, was transformed into another national scandal. The generalized suspicions of fraud raised by the unclear process of provisional scrutiny of the votes led political parties in the province to disavow the results and wait until the definitive count of votes was finished. Encotesa, the official mail service company in charge of the scrutiny, was either the supposed victim of sabotage (a hypothesis that Minister Cavallo himself suggested in an interview on Radio del Plata on September 7, 1995) or responsible for fraud. President Menem ordered Encotesa to publish the preliminary results on September 6. The PJ triumphed with a narrow margin of 4 points over the opposition. Under the current provincial electoral system (ley de lemas), the Peronist winner was the candidate backed by President Menem (a socialist and former mayor of Rosario City). According to the provisional scrutiny, Duhalde and Reuteman's candidate lost by the narrow margin of less than 1 percent. Governor Reuteman declared that he would investigate, despite his having received death threats if he did. He did not hesitate to hold the political sector of the government responsible.

Chapter 10 Brazil: The Hyperactive Paralysis Syndrome (Lamounier)

Support from the Mellon Foundation for background research is gratefully acknowledged.

1. On January 3, 1994, a prominent former ambassador, Paulo Nogueira Batista, wrote that Brazil's illness was "more political than economic" ("A Democracia Ameaçada," Folha de São Paulo); on January 13 the London-based Latin American Weekly Reports opened its Brazil report with the headline "Scale of Corruption Scandal Provokes New Fears of Military Intervention."

2. For an overview of Brazilian politics from the 1930s to 1964, see Thomas Skidmore, Politics in Brazil: An Experiment in Democracy (Oxford: Oxford University Press, 1967) on authoritarianism and democracy; Alfred Stepan, ed., Authoritarian Brazil: Origins, Policies and Future (New Haven: Yale University Press, 1973); and Bolívar Lamounier, "And Yet It Does Move: Formation and Evolution of the Democratic State in Brazil, 1930–1994," in Bolívar Lamounier et al., eds., Fifty Years of Brazil (Rio de Janeiro: Editora da Fundação Getúlio Vargas, 1994), 9–158.

3. On the ambivalent legitimacy of authoritarian rule, see Juan Linz, "The Future of an Authoritarian Situation or the Institutionalization of an Authoritarian Regime: The Case of Brazil," in Stepan, ed., Authoritarian Brazil, 233–

54, and Bolívar Lamounier, "Opening through Elections: Will the Brazilian Case Become a Paradigm?" *Government and Opposition* 19, no. 2 (1984): 167–77, and Lamounier, "Authoritarian Brazil Revisited: the Impact of Elections on the Brazilian 'Abertura,'" in Alfred Stepan, ed., *Democratizing Brazil: Problems of Transition and Consolidation* (New York: Oxford University Press, 1988), 43–79.

4. See Maria D'Alva G. Kinzo, *Legal Opposition Politics under Authoritarian Rule in Brazil* (Oxford: Macmillan, 1988); see also Lamounier, "Opening through Elections," and "Authoritarian Brazil Revisited."

5. This description of hyperactivism is limited to the political sphere; on its interaction with the formidable succession of anti-inflation shocks of this period, see Bolívar Lamounier and Edmar Bacha, "Democracy and Economic Reform in Brazil," in Joan Nelson, ed., *Precarious Balance: Democratic Consolidation and Economic Reform in Eastern Europe and Latin America* (Washington, D.C.: International Center for Economic Growth and the Overseas Development Council [ICEG/ODC], 1994). For a comparison of constitution-making experiences in Brazil, Spain, Portugal, and Chile, see Dieter Nohlen et al., "El proceso constituyente: Experiencias a partir de cuatro casos recientes—España, Portugal, Brasil y Chile," *Boletín electoral latinoamericano* (San José, Costa Rica: IIDH/CAPEL) 5 (Jan.–June 1991), In the Brazilian case, a drafting commission was to be announced by the president-elect, Tancredo Neves, in his inauguration speech (March 15, 1985), but he fell ill on that day and died on April 21. The commission was not appointed by President Sarney until late August. By then it had become an unwieldy fifty-member body, symptomatically entitled "Provisional Commission for Constitutional Studies." One year later, when the commission finished its draft, Sarney recognized it as a government document by having it published in the Diário Oficial, but refused to send it officially as an amendment to the Constitutional Congress.

6. This two-pronged depletion was at work since the 1970s but was bluntly symbolized after the 1982 gubernatorial elections. On one side, the last general, João Figueiredo, under the additional weight of serious health problems, found it clearly painful even to abide by the ceremonial duties of the presidential office; on the other, an angry crowd tried to break through the gates of the Bandeirantes Palace in São Paulo in an attempt to force the just inaugurated oppositionist Governor Franco Montoro to fulfill an alleged campaign promise of creating four hundred thousand jobs.

7. Lamounier and Bacha, "Democracy and Economic Reform in Brazil."

8. On the Workers' Party, see Rachel Meneguello, *PT: A Formação de um partido* (Rio de Janeiro: Editora Paz e Terra, 1989), and Margaret Keck, *The Workers Party and Democratization in Brazil* (New Haven: Yale University Press, 1992).

9. The model inherited from the 1930s was actually a tripod, with the corporatist regulation of capital/labor relations as the third leg; see Bolívar Lamounier, "Institutional Structure and Governability in the 1990s," in Maria D'Alva Kinzo, ed., *Brazil: The Challenges of the 1990s* (London: British Academic Press, 1992), 117–37. On the contrast between "consociational" and "majoritarian" democracies, see Arend Lijphart, *Democracies: Patterns of Majoritarian and Consensus Government in Twenty-One Countries* (New Haven: Yale University Press, 1984). It is worth remarking that Lijphart, a strong advocate of the consociational model, explicitly notes that it is incongruent with presidential government; see Arend Lijphart, "Presidencialismo e democracia majoritária," in Bolívar Lamounier, ed., *A Opção parlamentarista* (São Paulo: Editora Sumaré, 1991), 121–37.

10. Cited by Ralph Dahrendorf, *Essays in the Theory of Society* (Stanford: Stanford University Press, 1968), 178.

11. Data from Ibope polls analyzed in Bolívar Lamounier and Alexandre H. Marques, "A democracia brasileira no final da 'Década Perdida,'" in Bolívar Lamounier, ed., *Ouvindo o Brasil: Uma análise da opinião pública brasileira hoje* (São Paulo: Editora Sumaré, 1992), 139–58. President Clinton's loss of popularity during his first hundred days in office was the subject of a *Time* magazine cover story entitled "The Incredible Shrinking Man." Such an abrupt fall would probably have caused a serious crisis in any other presidentialist country. On plebiscitarian tendencies in the United States, see Theodore Lowi, *The Personal President: Power Invested, Promise Unfulfilled* (Ithaca: Cornell University Press, 1985), and Craig A. Rimmerman, *Presidency by Plebiscite: The Reagan-Bush Era in Institutional Perspective* (Boulder, Colo.: Westview Press, 1993).

12. On Collor's rise and fall, see Amaury Souza, "Collor's Impeachment and Institutional Reform in Brazil," paper prepared for the conference "Wither Brazil after Collor?" University of Miami, North-South Center, February 26–27, 1993; figures in the text are from Bolívar Lamounier and Amaury Souza, "O Congresso Nacional e a crise brasileira," *Research Report* (São Paulo: IDESP, 1991), table 13.

13. On Brazilian political parties, see Bolívar Lamounier and Rachel Meneguello, *Partidos políticos e consolidação democrática: O Caso brasileiro* (São Paulo: Editora Brasiliense, 1986); D'Alva G. Kinzo, *Legal Opposition Politics*; Antonio Lavareda, *A democracia nas urnas: O processo partidário-eleitoral brasileiro* (Rio de Janeiro: IUPERJ/Rio Fundo Editora, 1991); and Maria D'Alva G. Kinzo, *Radiografia do quadro partidário brasileiro* (São Paulo: Fundação Konrad Adenauer, 1994).

14. Arend Lijphart, *Democracies: Patterns of Majoritarian and Consensus Government in Twenty-One Countries* (New Haven: Yale University Press, 1984).

15. Equal representation of the states in the Senate obviously makes the upper house highly disproportionate in terms of the respective populations, but this is not a hotly contested issue. Such blatant deviation from proportionality is understandably supported by politicians from the overrepresented regions. Less understandable is that it also finds staunch supporters among intellectuals from other regions, who resort to the consociationalist argument that the "weaker" regions require a compensation in political power, even if this compensation amounts to a gross violation of the democratic principle "one person, one vote," which the 1988 Constitution also recognizes in article 14. It is also worth noting that some of the intellectuals who accept the disenfranchisement of almost half of the 22 million residents of the state of São Paulo on "consociational" grounds are extreme "proportionalists" when it comes to the electoral system, arguing that the Anglo-Saxon majoritarian and the German mixed models are bound to disenfranchise some worthy ideological minority.

16. In the crisis over salary readjustments of mid-March 1994, the Supreme Court made a decision in its own favor, and thus became directly involved in the continuing conflict between the executive and the legislature. Losing part of its authority to interpret the laws and act as a neutral umpire, the court itself made the crisis especially dangerous. But the underlying tension among all three branches of government can be gauged by the results of a survey conducted by IDESP among 570 judges. Asked to evaluate the performance of thirteen institutions, 23 percent said the federal executive was doing a good job, and 3 percent gave the same positive answer regarding the legislature. See

Maria Teresa Sadek, *O judiciário em debate* (São Paulo: Editora Sumaré, 1994), table 7.

17. On political culture and institutional utopias, see Bolívar Lamounier and Amaury Souza, "Changing Attitudes toward Democracy and Institutional Reform in Brazil," in Larry Diamond, ed., *Political Culture and Democracy in Developing Countries* (Boulder, Colo.: Lynne Rienner, 1993).

18. Commenting on the militants' frustrations over the lack of progress in the struggle to improve the workers' lot, a prominent PT intellectual says that "these hopes and frustrations . . . are the main determinant of internal party cleavages," but he explicitly recognizes that divisions also exist "with regard to key questions, such as the commitment to democracy (*compromisso com a democracia*), the dilemma of central planning versus market economy, and the possibility of resolving economic crises within the limits of the capitalist system." See Paul Singer, "Dilemas estratégicos do PT diante da crise econômica," *Carta Política* 20 (May 1993), 8.

19. See Amaury Souza and Bolívar Lamounier, "As elites brasileiras e a modernização do setor público," in *Seminários e debates* (São Paulo: IDESP, 1992), tables 4 and 5; Lamounier and Souza, "O Congresso Nacional e a crise brasileira," tables 6 and 7; also José Álvaro Moisés, "Democratization, Mass Political Culture, and Political Legitimacy in Brazil," *Working Paper* (Madrid: Juan March Institute, 1993).

20. See Amaury Souza and Bolívar Lamounier, "A feitura da Constituição: Um reexame da cultura política brasileira," in Bolívar Lamounier, ed., *De Geisel a Collor: O balanço da transição* (São Paulo: Editora Sumaré, 1990), 81–103.

Index

Acción Democrática (AD) (Venezuela),
10, 11, 12; Caldera and, 13–15, 16; con-
solidation and, 6–7; corruption and, 9;
labor organizations and, 17; loss of di-
rection in, 8; partyarchy and, 4–6
Acción Democrática y Nacionalista
(ADN) (Bolivia), 72, 74, 75, 80, 90–92
Accumulation system, 140
Acuerdo Patriótico (AP) (Bolivia), 72, 77,
78, 80, 88, 92
AD. See Acción Democrática; Alianza
Democrática M-19
Adecopeyano establishment, 4, 5, 6, 7, 9,
11, 13
ADN. See Acción Democrática y
Nacionalista
Afro-American Encounter (Colombia), 35
Agrarian reform: in Colombia, 39; in Ecu-
ador, 50
Alfaro Ucero, Luis, 14
Alfonsín, Raúl, 152–53, 154, 156, 157, 173
Aliança Renovadora Nacional (ARENA)
(Brazil), 169
Alianza Democrática M-19 (AD) (Colom-
bia), 23–24, 25, 37
Allende, Salvador, 15, 104, 112, 114
Alvarez, Carlos (Chacho), 155, 157
Alvarez Paz, Oswaldo, 12, 13
Amazon, 50
American Popular Revolutionary Alli-
ance (APRA) (Peru), 15, 58, 59, 60, 63,
70
Amnesty: in Brazil, 169; in Colombia, 37;
in Peru, 71; in Uruguay, 135, 142
ANDI. See National Association of Indus-
trialists
Angeloz, Eduardo, 161
ANIF. See National Association of Finan-
cial Institutions
ANR. See Colorado Party, in Paraguay
AP. See Acuerdo Patriótico; Popular
Action
APRA. See American Popular Revolution-
ary Alliance
Araníbar, Antonio, 80, 89, 90
Arce Gómez, Luis, 87
ARENA. See Aliança Renovadora Nacio-
nal
Argaña, Luis María, 119–20, 132
Argentina, 16, 17, 129, 132, 147–65; Bra-
zil compared with, 166, 173, 174, 176,
177, 181; bridge between Uruguay and,
144; constitution of, 151-159, 162; eco-
nomic crisis in, 148–59, 163, 164–65;
elections in, 158–59, 160–61; Left in,
150, 152; mafia in, 163; Plaza de Mayo
mothers in, 9
Arguedas, Antonio, 87
Arismendi, Rodney, 146
Armed Forces of the Colombian Revolu-
tion. See Fuerzas Armadas de la
Revolución Colombiana
Aronson, Bernard, 65
Arriagada, Genaro, 112
Arslanian, Ricardo, 151
Association of Producers and Exporters of
Sugarcane (Colombia), 31
Astori, Danilo, 145–46
Ayala, Carlos, 126
Aylwin, Patricio, 100, 101–2, 104, 105,
113, 116, 117; elections and, 110–11;
human rights and, 115; military and,
107–8; Right and, 111–12

Bacha, Edmar, 172–73
Baker, James, 65
Banco Latino, 18
Banking Association of Colombia, 31
Banzer Suárez, Hugo, 72, 74, 75, 80, 91
Barco, Virgilio, 22, 27, 36, 40
Basismo, 133
Belaúnde Terry, Fernando, 15, 60
Béliz, Gustavo, 151
Betancourt, Rómulo, 6–7, 12
Betancur, Belisario, 24, 27, 28, 29, 37
Blacks, 33–34, 35
Blanqueamiento, 34
Bolivia, 17, 18, 72–98; agenda for mid-
1990s in, 79–80; drug problem in, 78,
80, 91, 94–95, 96–97, 98; economic re-
form in, 72–75; emergence of new cau-
dillos in, 76–79; Left in, 77; legislative
successes in, 83–84; El Plan de Todos
in, 79, 81–83; political parties in, 90–
92; ruling coalitions in, 88–90
Bolivian Movement. See Movimiento
Boliviariano
Bolivian National Airways (LAB), 81
Bolivian Times, 87
Bolivian Worker Central. See Central Ob-
rera Boliviana
Boloña, Carlos, 64
Bordón, José Octavio, 160
Borja, Rodrigo, 51

Bravo, Leopoldo, 152
Brazil, 9, 16, 103, 130, 166–87; changing political culture in, 182–85; declining governability of, 170–72; drug problem in, 166; fragile institutional identity of, 175–82; historical background of, 168–70; hyperactive paralysis syndrome in (see Hyperactive paralysis syndrome); Left in, 174; state-led industrialization model in, 173, 186
Brazilian Democratic Movement. See Movimento Democrático Brasileiro
Brazilian Revolution, 181
Broad Front. See Frente Amplio; Frente Grande
Brown, Lee, 94
Business: in Bolivia, 74; in Chile, 100; in Colombia, 29–32. See also Entrepreneurship; Private sector
Bussi, Antonio, 161–62, 165

Caballero Vargas, Guillermo, 119, 120t
Cabinet restructuring law (Bolivia), 83–84
Caldera, Rafael, 3, 6, 7, 12–19; base of support for, 13–15; confidence in elections, 15–16; conflict with governors, 16; labor organizations and, 17; military and, 16–17; private sector and, 17–19
Cali drug group, 20, 25, 38
Camacho Leira, Luis Carlos, 28
CAMACOL. See Colombian Chamber of Commerce
Cambio de camisetas (shirt changing), 45, 54
Cambio '90 (Peru), 66
Camdessus, Michel, 64
Cano, Gabriel, 33
Capitalization law (Bolivia), 81–82, 83–84
Caracazo, 10
Cárdenas, Víctor Hugo, 72, 79–80
Cardoso, Fernando Henrique, 126, 160, 166–67, 168, 175, 185
Casella, Juan M., 153
Casso Michael, Carlos, 86
Castañeda, Jorge, 68–69
Castaño, Fidel, 38
Castro, Fidel, 87, 91
Catholic Church: in Bolivia, 96; in Colombia, 21, 32–33; in Ecuador, 54; in Uruguay, 133; in Venezuela, 6
Causa R, 12, 14, 15, 17
Cavallo, Domingo, 149, 151, 162–63
Cavallo Plan, 173
CBN. See Cervecería Boliviana Nacional
CCD. See Democratic Constitutional Congress
Center: in Argentina, 150, 152, 155; in Chile, 103, 104, 105, 112, 114, 117; in Ecuador, 48; in Peru, 58, 59

Center-Center Union. See Unión del Centro Centro
Central banks: in Argentina, 151; in Paraguay, 131
Central Obrera Boliviana (COB), 82, 83, 95–97
Central Workers Union (Colombia), 37
CEPAL. See Economic Commission for Latin America
Cervecería Boliviana Nacional (CBN), 77, 78
César, Julio, 38
CGT. See General Confederation of Labor
Chamber of Deputies: in Argentina, 150, 151, 152, 153; in Brazil, 171, 180, 182, 185–86
Chicago Boys, 101, 105
Chile, 4, 16, 17, 18, 99–117, 132; Brazil compared with, 176; democracy within constitutional framework, 105–11; democratic political institutions in, 102–5; growth with equity in, 100–102; Left in, 104, 109, 112, 114, 117; Peru compared with, 64
Christian Democratic Party (Chile), 104–5, 109, 114
Cisneros Vizquerra, Luis, 63
Civic organizations, in Colombia, 29–32
Civil society, 42
Clientelism, 76
Coalitions: in Bolivia, 88–90; congressional, 88; electoral, 88; ruling, 88–90
COB. See Central Obrera Boliviana
Coca, 37, 39, 40, 59, 94–95, 96–97, 98
Cocaine, 94–95
CODELCO. See National Copper Corporation
Collor de Mello, Fernando, 15, 171, 178–79; brother's accusations against, 174, 179; impeachment of, 170, 179
Collor de Mello, Pedro, 174, 179
Colombia, 16, 18, 20–41; drug problem in, 20, 22, 25, 26, 27, 29, 33, 37–38, 39, 40–41, 166; elections in, 22, 23–25, 34, 36; executive-legislative relations in, 26; gender discrimination in, 35–37; indigenous people in, 33–35; minority rights in, 33–35; reincorporation into democratic politics, 37–39; rule of law and judiciary in, 27–28; socioeconomic conditions in, 39–40; three models of governance in, 21–23
Colombian Agricultural Society (SAC), 31
Colombian Association of Automobile Parts Manufacturers, 31
Colombian Association of Plastic Industries, 31
Colombian Chamber of Commerce (CAMACOL), 30, 31

Colombian Federation of Metallurgical Industries (FEDEMETAL), 30, 31
Colorado Party: in Paraguay (ANR), 119, 120, 122, 123–24, 125, 130–32; in Uruguay, 133, 135, 137, 144–45
Comité de Organización Política Electoral Independiente (COPEI) (Venezuela), 10, 11, 12; Caldera and, 13–15, 16; consolidation and, 6–7; corruption and, 9; labor organizations and, 17; loss of direction in, 8; partyarchy and, 4–6
Commercial Council (CONSECOMERCIO), 6
Communist Party: in Brazil, 174, 180; in Chile, 103, 104, 105; in Colombia, 32; in Uruguay, 145, 146
Compañía Minera del Sur (COMSUR) (Bolivia), 75
COMSUR. See Compañía Minera del Sur
CONAIE. See Confederación de Nacionalidades Indígenas del Ecuador
Concertación: in Chile, 103, 113–15; in Ecuador, 45; in Venezuela, 5, 6, 8, 9
Concertación Democrática. See Concertation for Democracy
Concertation Alliance (Chile), 102, 104–5, 110, 111, 112, 114, 116–17
Concertation for Democracy (Chile), 108, 132
Conciencia de Patria (CONDEPA) (Bolivia), 76–77, 78, 80, 92
CONDEPA. See Conciencia de Patria
Confederación de Nacionalidades Indígenas del Ecuador (CONAIE), 42, 50
Confederation of Colombian Workers (CTC), 32
Confederation of Industry (CONINDUSTRIA), 6
Congress. See also Executive-legislative relations: of Argentina, 149, 158; of Bolivia, 89, 90, 92–93; of Brazil, 166, 171, 179, 181, 186; of Colombia, 22, 26; of Ecuador, 45, 46–47, 53, 54–55; of Paraguay, 122, 123, 124, 131; of Peru, 63–64, 66, 69, 70; of Uruguay, 140, 141–43; of Venezuela, 13–15
Congressional coalitions, 88
CONINDUSTRIA. See Confederation of Industry
Conscience of the Fatherland. See Conciencia de Patria
CONSECOMERCIO. See Commercial Council
Consejo de la Magistratura (Paraguay), 122–24
Consejo Político del Acuerdo Patriótico (COPAP) (Bolivia), 75
Consensus of Washington, 135
Consensus-seeking. See Concertación

Conservatives, in Colombia, 21–22, 23, 25, 33
Consociationalism: in Brazil, 175, 177, 178, 179, 181, 182, 184, 185; in Colombia, 21–22
Constituent Assembly: of Argentina, 156–57; of Colombia, 32, 33, 35, 36, 37
Constitution: of Argentina, 151-159, 162; of Bolivia, 92–94; of Brazil, 170, 171, 174, 179, 181, 182, 187; of Chile, 99, 105–13, 114, 116; of Colombia, 22, 26, 27, 32, 35, 36, 37; of Paraguay, 122–23; of Peru, 59–60, 65–68; of Uruguay, 141–43
Constitutional amendments law (Bolivia), 83
Constitutional Congress (Brazil), 176
Contreras, Manuel, 108
Convergencia Nacional (Venezuela), 12, 13, 14t
COPAP. See Consejo Político del Acuerdo Patriótico
COPEI. See Comité de Organización Política Electoral Independiente
Copper, 107
Correa, Enrique, 112
Corruption: in Argentina, 149; in Bolivia, 75, 86, 87, 90–92; in Brazil, 166, 186; in Ecuador, 49, 54; in Venezuela, 8–9, 10–11
Costa Rica, 4, 103
Cotton, 127
Council for Youth, Family, and Women (Colombia), 36–37
Council of Magistrates. See Consejo de la Magistratura
Coups: in Bolivia, 73; in Paraguay, 119, 128; in Peru, 60–61, 63–64, 65, 67, 68, 69, 70; in Venezuela, 11, 12
CRIC. See Regional Indigenous Council of the Cauca
Cruzado Plan (Brazil), 173–74, 175, 178
CSTC. See Syndical Confederation of Workers of Colombia
CTC. See Confederation of Colombian Workers
CTV. See Venezuelan Workers Confederation
Cuban Revolution, 7, 103
Curuchet, Juan C., 139

Dahik, Alberto, 49
Dahl, Robert, 122
Death penalty, 66
De Castro, Sergio, 105
Decompression, in Brazil, 169–70, 172, 176
Decrees of Necessity and Urgency (Argentina), 156, 158
Decree 21060 (Bolivia), 97

De la Rúa, Fernando, 150, 152–53
Delegative democracy, 76
Democratic Alliance. *See* Alianza Democrática
Democratic and Nationalist Action. *See* Acción Democrática y Nacionalista
Democratic Compromise (Paraguay), 123
Democratic Constitutional Congress (CCD) (Peru), 65–66, 68
Democratic governability. *See* Governability
Democratic Republican Union. *See* Unión Republicana Democrática
De Souza, Amaury, 184
D'Hondt formula, 60, 140
Diretas-Já campaign, 170, 171
Doctors, 127
Dollar, U.S., 136
Double minority system, 112
Double simultaneous vote, 133
Drugs: in Bolivia, 78, 80, 91, 94–95, 96–97, 98; in Brazil, 166; in Colombia, 20, 22, 25, 26, 27, 29, 33, 37–38, 39, 40–41, 166; in Paraguay, 129; in Peru, 63
Durán, Sixto, 45, 46, 48, 49, 51
Dutra, Eurico Gaspar, 178
Duzán, María Jimena, 40–41

Eastern Europe, 174
Economic Commission for Latin America (CEPAL), 136
Economic policy and development: in Argentina, 148–59, 163, 164–65; in Bolivia, 72–75; in Brazil, 169; in Chile, 99–117; in Mexico, 163; in Peru, 69
Ecuador, 42–57, 103; indigenous people in, 42, 47–48, 50, 53, 56; Left in, 47; political situation in, 43–48; possibilities for reform in, 53–57; socioeconomic conditions in, 48–53; Venezuelans exiled to, 16
Educational system: in Bolivia, 83–84; in Colombia, 40; in Uruguay, 143
Education reform law (Bolivia), 83–84
Ejército de Liberación Nacional (ELN) (Colombia), 37–38, 39
Ejército de Liberación Popular (ELP) (Colombia), 37
Elections: in Argentina, 158–59, 160–61; in Bolivia, 92–93; in Brazil, 168, 176, 185–86; in Chile, 108–11; in Colombia, 22, 23–25, 34, 36; in Ecuador, 43–45; in Paraguay, 118–20; in Uruguay, 140–43; in Venezuela, 5, 15–16
Electoral coalitions, 88
Elites: in Brazil, 183–84; in Paraguay, 121
ELN. *See* Ejército de Liberación Nacional
ELP. *See* Ejército de Liberación Popular
El Salvador, 16
EN. *See* Encuentro Nacional

Encuentro Nacional (EN) (Paraguay), 119, 122, 132
Encuentro Progresista (Uruguay), 145
Entrepreneurship: in Ecuador, 43; in Uruguay, 136–37. *See also* Business; Private sector
Errázuriz, Francisco Javier, 110
Erro, Enrique, 146
Escobar, Pablo, 25, 26, 29, 33, 38, 41
El Espectador, 33
Exchange rates: in Argentina, 149; in Peru, 62; in Venezuela, 18
Executions, 59, 66–67
Executive branch. *See* Presidency/executive branch
Executive-legislative relations: in Colombia, 26; in Ecuador, 46–47, 53, 55; in Paraguay, 123
Exports: Chile and, 100, 101, 104, 105; Peru and, 62

FA. *See* Frente Amplio
FARC. *See* Fuerzas Armadas de la Revolución Colombiana
Febres Cordero, León, 15, 47, 51
FEDECAFE. *See* National Federation of Coffee Growers
FEDECAMARAS. *See* Federation of Chambers of Commerce and Industry
FEDEMETAL. *See* Colombian Federation of Metallurgical Industries
Federación Unitaria de Trabajadores (FUT) (Ecuador), 50
Federation of Chambers of Commerce and Industry (FEDECAMARAS), 6
Federative balancing principle, 182
FEDESARROLLO. *See* Foundation for Higher Education and Development
FELCN. *See* Fuerza Especial de Lucha Contra el Narcotráfico
FENALCO. *See* National Federation of Merchants
Fermín, Claudio, 12
Fernández, Eduardo, 11, 12
Fernández, Max, 76, 77–79, 80, 90
Ferreira Aldunate, Wilson, 135
FG. *See* Frente Grande
Figueiredo, João, 170, 174–75
Foreign investments: in Bolivia, 81; in Chile, 101; in Ecuador, 49
Foro Batllista, 137
Foundation for Higher Education and Development (FEDESARROLLO) (Colombia), 40
Foxley, Alejandro, 105, 113
France, 139
Franco, Francisco, 175
Franco, Oscar Eid, 91
Free Bolivia Movement. *See* Movimiento Bolivia Libre

Free market. *See* Market-oriented reforms
Frei, Eduardo, 100, 102, 107, 110, 111–12, 113, 114, 117
Frente Amplio (FA) (Uruguay), 137, 145, 146
Frente Grande (FG) (Argentina), 155, 157
Frente Gremial (Colombia), 30, 31
FREPASO. *See* National Solidarity Front
Friedman, Thomas, 69
Fuerza Especial de Lucha Contra el Narcotráfico (FELCN) (Bolivia), 91
Fuerzas Armadas de la Revolución Colombiana (FARC), 24, 28, 37, 39
Fujimori, Alberto, 15, 60, 61–71; coups and, 63–64, 67, 68, 70; military and, 63, 67–68; public opinion of, 70; resolution of security and economic crisis, 69
FUT. *See* Federación Unitaria de Trabajadores

Galán, Luis Carlos, 24, 25
García, Alan, 59, 60, 64
García, Daniel, 139
García Meza, Luis, 87
Gaviria, César, 27, 28, 29, 31, 36, 38, 39, 40
Geisel, Ernesto, 169, 170, 172
Gender discrimination, 35–37
General Confederation of Labor (CGT) (Colombia), 32
General strikes: in Bolivia, 95–97; in Ecuador, 50–51; in Paraguay, 127
Gerchunoff, Pablo, 164
Germany, 139
Gómez, Alvaro, 23
Gómez, Laureano, 28, 34
González, Erman, 149
González Petit, Eduardo, 124
Governability: of Brazil, 170–72; of Paraguay, 121–22; of Uruguay, 135, 142–43; of Venezuela, 3–4, 12
Governability Pact (Bolivia). *See* Pacto de la Gobernabilidad
Governability Pact (Paraguay), 122
Gross domestic product (GDP): of Bolivia, 82; of Chile, 100
Gross national product (GNP): of Chile, 101; of Uruguay, 135, 138t
Guerrilla movements: in Bolivia, 79; in Colombia, 21, 22, 28–29, 37–38; in Peru, 71; in Uruguay, 140; in Venezuela, 7
Guevara, Che, 87
Guzmán, Abimael, 69
Guzmán, Jaime, 106

Haggard, Stephan, 164
Hauger, Deborah, 165
Hermoza, Nicolas de Bari, 67, 68
Herrera Campíns, Luis, 14

Honduras, 16
Human rights: in Bolivia, 93–94; in Brazil, 169; in Chile, 107, 115; in Peru, 67, 70–71; in Uruguay, 135
Hydrocarbons, 49
Hyperactive paralysis syndrome, 167–68, 170–72, 185; causes of, 172–75; defined, 170

Ibáñez, Blanca, 11
Iberian-legacy hypothesis, 182, 186
IESA Boys, 13
Illanes, Fernando, 81
Illia, Arturo, 15
IMF. *See* International Monetary Fund
Imports: Peru and, 62; Uruguay and, 136
Inacio da Silva, Luis (Lula), 170, 171, 178
Income distribution, in Chile, 101–2
Independent Democratic Union. *See* Unión Democrática Independiente
Indigenous people: in Colombia, 33–35; in Ecuador, 42, 47–48, 50, 53, 56
Inequality, in Uruguay, 137
Inflation: in Argentina, 148; in Bolivia, 83; in Brazil, 167, 175, 179; in Chile, 100; in Uruguay, 136, 138t; in Venezuela, 10, 14
Institutional Act number 5 (Brazil), 169
Inter-American Commission on Human Rights, 27, 41
Inter-American Development Bank (IDB), 65, 71
International financial institutions (IFIs), 65, 71
International Monetary Fund (IMF), 62, 64, 65, 71
Interunion Workers Council–Workers National Caucus (PIT-CNT) (Uruguay), 138
Itaipú dam, 119
IU. *See* United Left

Japan, 62
Jarrín Ampudia, Gustavo, 52–53
Judiciary: of Colombia, 27–28; of Paraguay, 122–24
Juicio político, 46, 49

Karl, Terry, 8
Kast, Miguel, 105
Kaufman, Robert, 164
Kidnapping, 22
Korean conflict, 134
Kubitscheck, Juscelino, 178

Laakso-Taagepera index, 180
Labor organizations: in Argentina, 17, 148; in Bolivia, 17, 82, 84, 87; in Chile, 17, 102; in Colombia, 29–32; in Ecuador, 49, 50–51, 53; in Paraguay, 127;

Labor organizations (*continued*)
in Peru, 17, 66; in Uruguay, 138–39; in
Venezuela, 5, 17
Lacalle, Luis Alberto, 135, 136, 137, 138,
139, 143, 146
Laíno, Domingo, 119, 120t, 122
Lamounier, Bolívar, 172–73
Land ownership, 50
Land reform. *See* Agrarian reform
Landazábal Reyes, Fernando, 28–29
Law-Bill of Amnesty for the Military
(Uruguay), 135
Lazarte, Jorge, 76, 78
Left: in Argentina, 150, 152; in Bolivia,
77; in Brazil, 174; in Chile, 104, 109,
112, 114, 117; in Ecuador, 47; in Peru,
58, 59, 63; in Uruguay, 143, 145; in Ven-
ezuela, 7
Letelier, Orlando, 108
Liberal Radical Authentic Party (PLRA)
(Paraguay), 119, 122, 132
Liberals, in Colombia, 21–22, 23, 24–25,
26, 33
Lijphart, Arend, 181
López Maya, Margarita, 15
López Michelsen, Alfonso, 20, 23, 24, 32, 36
López Pumarejo, Alfonso, 32
Lowenthal, Abraham F., 130
Lula. *See* Inacio da Silva
Lusinchi, Jaime, 11

M-19 (Colombia), 23, 27, 37. *See also* Al-
ianza Democrática M-19
Machinea, José, 164
Mafia, 163
Market-oriented reforms: in Brazil, 186;
in Chile, 102, 104
Marxism, 58, 177
MAS. *See* Movimiento al Socialismo
Massaccesi, Horacio, 160
MBL. *See* Movimiento Bolivia Libre
MDB. *See* Movimento Democrático
Brasileiro
Medellín group, 38
Media: in Colombia, 33; in Peru, 63; in
Venezuela, 10–11
Menem, Carlos, 147–48, 161–65, 173;
constitutional reform and, 153, 154,
155–57; construction of presidential au-
thority and, 148–50; May 1995 election
and, 160–61; problems in second term
of, 161–63
MEP. *See* People's Electoral Movement
Mercado Común del Sur (MERCOSUR),
126, 136, 143
MERCOSUR. *See* Mercado Común del
Sur
Mexico, 9, 18; economic crisis of, 163;
Peru compared with, 64
Michel, Robert, 145

Middle class, 137
Military: in Argentina, 17; in Bolivia, 17,
85–87; in Brazil, 167, 168–70, 173, 174,
176, 180; in Chile, 106–8, 115; in Co-
lombia, 28–29; in Ecuador, 42–43, 44,
52–53, 54; in Paraguay, 121, 124–26,
129, 131–32; in Peru, 17, 58–59, 63, 67–
68; in Uruguay, 134, 135, 139–40, 142;
in Venezuela, 5–6, 7, 16–17
Mineral Company of the South. *See*
Compañía Minera del Sur
Minority rights, 33–35
MIR. *See* Movimiento de Izquierda
Revolucionaria
MNR. *See* Movimiento Nacionalista
Revolucionario
Modernization law, in Ecuador, 48–49, 53
MODIN. *See* Movement for National Dig-
nity and Independence
Montesinos, Vladimiro, 63, 67
Movement for National Dignity and Inde-
pendence (MODIN) (Argentina), 155,
161
Movement to Socialism. *See* Movimiento
al Socialismo
Movimiento Democrático Brasileiro
(MDB), 169
Movimiento al Socialismo (MAS) (Vene-
zuela), 7, 12, 13, 14t, 17, 18
Movimiento Bolivia Libre (MBL), 80, 88,
89, 90
Movimiento Bolivariano, 86
Movimiento de Izquierda Revolucionaria
(MIR) (Bolivia), 72, 75, 80, 90–92
Movimiento Nacionalista Revolucionario
(MNR) (Bolivia), 72–73, 74, 75, 81, 89,
90; agenda for mid-1990s and, 79–80;
military and, 85–87
Movimiento Revolucionario Tupac Katari
(MRTK) (Bolivia), 79
MRTK. *See* Movimiento Revolucionario
Tupac Katari
MSN. *See* National Salvation Movement
Muñoz León, Radamés, 16–17

National Association of Exporters (Co-
lombia), 31
National Association of Financial Institu-
tions (ANIF) (Colombia), 30
National Association of Industrialists
(ANDI) (Colombia), 30, 31
National Confederation of Indigenous Na-
tionalities. *See* Confederación de
Nacionalidades Indígenas del Ecuador
National Convergence. *See* Convergencia
Nacional
National Copper Corporation
(CODELCO) (Chile), 107
National Electricity Company (ENDE)
(Bolivia), 81, 84

National Encounter. *See* Encuentro Nacional
National Federation of Coffee Growers (FEDECAFE) (Colombia), 30
National Federation of Livestock Raisers (Colombia), 31
National Federation of Merchants (FENALCO) (Colombia), 30, 31
National Front (Colombia), 21–22, 23, 25, 29
National Gremial Council (Colombia), 31
National Hydrocarbons Enterprises of Bolivia (YPFB), 81
National Indian Council (Colombia), 34
National Liberation Army. *See* Ejército de Liberación Nacional
National Liberation Movement (Tupamaros) (Uruguay), 134, 140
National Party (Uruguay), 133, 135, 144, 146
National Railroad Enterprises (ENFE) (Bolivia), 81
National Renovating Alliance. *See* Aliança Renovadora Nacional
National Renovation. *See* Renovación Nacional
National Revolutionary Movement. *See* Movimiento Nacionalista Revolucionario
National Salvation Movement (MSN) (Colombia), 23, 25
National Smelting Company (ENAF) (Bolivia), 81
National Solidarity Front (FREPASO) (Argentina), 132, 160–61
National Telecom Enterprises (ENTEL) (Bolivia), 81
Navarro, Antonio, 23–24
Neoliberalism, in Bolivia, 75
Neves, Tancredo, 170, 171, 172, 180
New Democratic Force (NFD) (Colombia), 23, 25
New Economic Policy. *See* Nueva Política Económica
New Liberalism movement (Colombia), 24
NFD. *See* New Democratic Force
Nicaragua, 16
Nongovernmental organizations (NGOs), 9
NPE. *See* Nueva Política Económica
Nueva Política Económica (NPE) (Bolivia), 73–75, 81
Nurses, 127

OAS. *See* Organization of American States
O'Donnell, Guillermo, 76
Odría, Manuel, 15
Odríist National Union (UNO) (Peru), 15

Oil revenues, in Venezuela, 7, 8, 10, 17
Olivos Pact (Argentina), 153, 157
Ominami, Carlos, 105
Operation Aries, 67
Option Zero (Bolivia), 94
Opus Dei (Uruguay), 133
Organization of American States (OAS), 64, 65
Ospina, Mariano, 32
Ossio, Luis, 93
Otero, Ariel, 38
Oviedo, Lino C., 119, 124–26, 129, 130, 131, 132

Pact for Change. *See* Pacto por el Cambio
Pact for Democracy. *See* Pacto por la Democracia
Pacto de la Gobernabilidad (Bolivia), 80, 88
Pact of Punto Fijo (Venezuela), 6, 8, 9, 12
Pacto por el Cambio (Bolivia), 80, 88
Pacto por la Democracia (Bolivia), 74, 75, 88
Pacts: in Argentina, 153, 157; in Bolivia, 74, 75, 80, 88; in Brazil, 182; in Paraguay, 122; in Uruguay, 133; in Venezuela, 6, 8, 9, 12
Páez, Helena, 36–37
Palenque, Carlos, 76–77, 78–79, 80, 92, 93
Panama, 21
Paraguay, 16, 118–32; challenges of transition in, 120–22; drug problems in, 129; elections in, 118–20; institutionalism in, 124–26; social demands in, 126–28, 129–30; struggle for independent judiciary in, 122–24
Paralelismo, 9
Paramilitary squads, 37, 38, 39, 40, 41
Parejo, Enrique, 40
Parliamentary system, 183
Participatory democracy, 22
Partido Justicialista (PJ) (Argentina), 151–52, 154, 159
Partido Social Cristiano. *See* Social Christian Party
Partido Unidad Republicana (PUR) (Ecuador), 45, 46
Partyarchy: corruption and, 8–9; formula for, 4–6; loss of direction and, 8; obsession with control and, 9–11; rise and decline of, 6–11; search for viable alternative to, 11–13
Party for Democracy (PPD) (Chile), 104, 114
Party of National Renovation (PRN) (Brazil), 178, 179
Pastrana, Andrés, 23
Pastrana, Misael, 29
Patriotic Accord. *See* Acuerdo Patriótico
Patriotic Union. *See* Unión Patriótica

Paz Estenssoro, Víctor, 72, 73–74, 92
Paz Zamora, Jaime, 72, 73, 75, 80, 86, 91–92
Peasants: in Paraguay, 127; in Venezuela, 7
Pensions: in Argentina, 150, 151; in Bolivia, 82, 84; in Uruguay, 135, 136
People's Electoral Movement (MEP) (Venezuela), 17
PEPES. *See* Persecuted by Pablo Escobar
Pérez, Carlos Andrés, 7
Pérez Jiménez, Marcos, 6, 7, 8, 13, 17; Caldera's attack on, 12; disillusionment with, 10; impeachment of, 11
Perón, Juan Domingo, 161
Peronism, 147, 149, 150, 165, 181; constitutional reform and, 151–55, 157; in May 1995 elections, 160, 161
Peronist Party, 162
Persecuted by Pablo Escobar (PEPES), 38
Peru, 15, 17, 58–71, 103; Brazil compared with, 166; constitutional rule in, 66–68; drug problem in, 63; fragilities in democratic system, 59–61; human rights in, 67, 70–71; Left in, 58, 59, 63; reconstitutionalization in, 65–66; resolution of security and economic crisis in, 69; trend toward redemocratization in, 64–68; Venezuelans exiled to, 16; war with Ecuador, 51, 52
Pinochet, Augusto, 100, 101, 102, 105, 106, 115–16, 117; electoral process influenced by, 108–9, 110–11; resignation requested, 107–8
PIT-CNT. *See* Interunion Workers Council–Workers National Caucus
PJ. *See* Partido Justicialista
El Plan de Todos, 79, 81–83
Plaza de Mayo mothers, 9
Plebiscites, 171, 175, 177, 178, 179, 180, 182, 183, 184, 186, 187
Plebiscito de los Jubilados, 135
PLRA. *See* Liberal Radical Authentic Party
Police force, in Bolivia, 86, 87
Political Council of the Patriotic Accord. *See* Consejo Político del Acuerdo Patriótico
Political parties: in Bolivia, 90–92; in Brazil, 169–70, 177, 180–81, 186; in Chile, 102–5; in Ecuador, 44–45; in Uruguay, 140–41; in Venezuela, 5
Poppies, 37, 40
Popular Action (AP) (Peru), 58, 60
Popular and Democratic Union. *See* Unidad Democrática y Popular
Popular Association of Industrialists, 31
Popular Christian Party (PPC) (Peru), 58
Popular Front (Chile), 104–5

Popular Liberation Army. *See* Ejército de Liberación Popular
Popular participation law (Bolivia), 83, 84–85
Popular Union. *See* Unión Popular
Popular Unity (Chile), 104
Por la Patria (Uruguay), 135
Potestad marital, 36
Poverty: in Bolivia, 83; in Chile, 101–2; in Colombia, 39; in Ecuador, 49–50, 56; in Uruguay, 137
PPC. *See* Popular Christian Party
PPD. *See* Party for Democracy
Presidency/executive branch: in Argentina, 148–50; in Brazil, 177–82, 183, 184, 186; in Chile, 112; in Peru, 59–60; in Uruguay, 140, 141–42. *See also* Executive-legislative relations
Presidential Summit of the Americas on Sustainable Development, 83–84
Press. *See* Media
Private sector, 5–6, 17–19. *See also* Business; Entrepreneurship
Privatization: in Argentina, 149, 150, 151; in Bolivia, 81; in Colombia, 30; in Ecuador, 48–49
PRN. *See* Party of National Renovation
Professional organizations, in Colombia, 29–32
Progressive Encounter. *See* Encuentro Progresista
Protestants, 32, 33
PSC. *See* Social Christian Party
PT. *See* Workers' Party
Public employees. *See* State enterprises
Puka Inti, 48
Punto final, 115
PUR. *See* Partido Unidad Republicana

Quintín Lame Armed Movement (Colombia), 35

Radical Civic Union (UCR) (Argentina), 151–55, 156, 159, 160–61
Radicals: in Argentina, 147, 150, 151–55, 156, 157, 160, 181; in Chile, 104, 105
Radio y Televisión Popular (RTP) (Bolivia), 76–77
Ramírez, Donald, 14
RECADI, 10
Reconstitutionalization, in Peru, 65–66
Redemocratization: in Chile, 99; in Peru, 64–68
Regional Indigenous Council of the Cauca (CRIC) (Colombia), 35
Renovación Nacional (RN) (Chile), 103, 109, 110
Revolutionary Movement of the Left. *See* Movimiento de Izquierda Revolucionaria

Rico, Aldo, 129
Right: in Argentina, 148, 150, 152; in
  Bolivia, 77; in Chile, 103, 104, 109,
  110, 111–13, 114, 115; in Ecuador, 47;
  in Peru, 58–59
Rio Group, 64
RN. *See* Renovación Nacional
Robles, Rodolfo, 68
Rodríguez, Ramón A., 119, 124, 129
Rodríguez Gacha, José Gonzalo, 38
Rodríguez Lara, Guillermo, 52–53
Rodríguez Orejuela group, 38
Rojas Pinilla, Gustavo, 28, 36
Rossiter, Caleb, 68, 69
Rossl Link, Enrique, 64
RTP. *See* Radio y Televisión Popular
Rubiano Sáenz, Pedro, 32
Rule of law, in Colombia, 27–28
Ruling coalitions, 88–90
Rural areas, 50, 83

Saadi, Vicente, 150
SAC. *See* Colombian Agricultural Society
Samper, Ernesto, 20, 26, 29, 31, 41
Sánchez de Lozada, Gonzalo, 72, 75, 78,
  84, 92, 93, 97; agenda for mid-1990s
  and, 79–80; coalition building by, 88,
  89, 90; drug problem and, 94–95; mili-
  tary and, 85–87; El Plan de Todos and,
  79, 81–83; strikes and, 96
Sanguinetti, Julio María, 134–35, 137,
  143–44, 146
Sanín, Noemí, 36
Sarney, José, 15, 171, 173–75, 178, 180
Sartori, Giovanni, 113–14
Sectarian democracy, 21
Seifart, Angel, 131, 132
Seineldin, Moisés, 129
Senate: of Argentina, 153, 161; of Brazil,
  171; of Chile, 108, 110–12, 115, 116
Sendero Luminoso movement (Peru), 59,
  69, 70, 166
Separatist movement, in Bolivia, 95–
  97
Shining Path. *See* Sendero Luminoso
Shirique, Moisés, 86
Siles Suazo, Hernán, 73
Single-shot anti-inflation strategy (Brazil),
  175, 179
Social Christian Party (PSC) (Ecuador),
  45
Socialism: in Chile, 103–4, 105, 114; in
  Peru, 58; in Uruguay, 146
Socioeconomic conditions: in Colombia,
  39–40; in Ecuador, 48–53
Solidarity Civic Union. *See* Unidad
  Cívica Solidaridad
Southern Cone Common Market. *See*
  Mercado Común del Sur
Soviet Union, 145, 174

Special Counternarcotics Force. *See*
  Fuerza Especial de Lucha Contra el
  Narcotráfico
State enterprises: in Bolivia, 82–83; in
  Uruguay, 136, 137–38
State-led industrialization model (Brazil),
  173, 186
States of exception: in Colombia, 26; in
  Peru, 66
States of siege: in Bolivia, 74, 87, 96; in
  Colombia, 22, 26, 33
Storani, Federico, 153
Strategic actors, 3–4
Strikes: in Bolivia, 82, 87, 95–97; in Co-
  lombia, 31–32; in Ecuador, 50–51; in
  Paraguay, 127; in Venezuela, 17
Stroessner, Alfredo, 118, 119, 125
Supreme Court: of Argentina, 151, 153; of
  Chile, 106; of Ecuador, 47; of Paraguay,
  123–24, 129, 130; of Peru, 66–67
Swiftgate, 149
Syndical Confederation of Workers of Co-
  lombia (CSTC), 32

Tariffs, 62
Tarija, separatist movement in, 95–
  97
Taxation: in Argentina, 149; in Brazil,
  174; in Chile, 101; in Uruguay, 136
Teachers, 84, 127, 150
Teachers' strikes, 50–51, 95–97
Technocrats, 13
Television, 142, 181
Territorial base communities, 85
Tironi, Eugenio, 101
Trade Association Front. *See* Frente
  Gremial
Tres Estrellas, 86
Tupac Katari Revolutionary Movement.
  See Movimiento Revolucionario Tupac
  Katari
Tupamaros. *See* National Liberation
  Movement
Turbay, Julio César, 28, 31
Turizo, Rosa, 36

UCC. *See* Unión del Centro Centro
UCEDE. *See* Union of the Democratic
  Center
UCR. *See* Radical Civic Union
UCS. *See* Unidad Cívica Solidaridad
UDI. *See* Unión Democrática In-
  dependiente
Unemployment: in Argentina, 162; in
  Bolivia, 83; in Chile, 100; in Uruguay,
  137, 138t
Unidad Cívica Solidaridad (UCS)
  (Bolivia), 76, 77–78, 80, 88, 89
Unidad Democrática y Popular (Bolivia),
  73

Unión del Centro Centro (UCC) (Chile), 103, 110
Unión Democrática Independiente (UDI) (Chile), 103, 109, 110
Union for the Progress of Chile, 114
Union of Colombian Workers (UTC), 32
Union of Insurers of Colombia, 31
Union of the Democratic Center (UCEDE) (Argentina), 152, 161
Unión Patriótica (UP) (Colombia), 24, 25
Unión Popular (Uruguay), 146
Unión Republicana Democrática (URD) (Venezuela), 6
United Federation of Workers. See Federación Unitaria de Trabajadores
United Left (IU) (Peru), 60, 70
United Nations (UN): Uruguay and, 139; on women's rights, 37
United Nations Development Program (UNDP): Argentina and, 165; Uruguay and, 146
United Republican Party. See Partido Unidad Republicana
United States, 16; Bolivia and, 73, 77, 80, 87, 91, 94–95, 97–98; Peru and, 62; Uruguay and, 139
UNO. See Odríist National Union
UP. See Unión Patriótica
Urban areas, 184
URD. See Unión Republicana Democrática
Uruguay, 103, 133–46; Brazil compared with, 176, 177; demographics of, 136; elections in, 140–43; human rights in, 135; inequality in, 137; Left in, 143, 145; new challenges faced by democracy of, 136–40; political scenario in, 140–46

UTC. See Union of Colombian Workers

Valenzuela, J. Samuel, 107
Value added tax, 136
Vargas, Getúlio, 173, 178, 183
Vargas Llosa, Mario, 61–62
Vázquez, Tabaré, 135, 145–46
Velasco Alvarado, Juan, 58
Velasco Ibarra, José María, 15
Velásquez, Andrés, 13, 16
Velásquez, Ramón J., 11–12
Venezuela, 3–19; Brazil compared with, 166, 177, 180–81; corruption in, 8–9, 10–11; governability of, 3–4, 12; Left in, 7; loss of direction in, 8; partyarchy in (see Partyarchy)
Venezuelan Workers Confederation (CTV), 17
Vigilance committees, 85
Violencia, la (Colombia), 21, 22, 33
Vivo Rojo, 86
Volonté, Alberto, 144, 146

Wade, Peter, 33–34, 35
Wages: in Ecuador, 49; in Uruguay, 136, 137, 138t
Wasmosy, Juan Carlos, 118–20, 128, 130–32; military and, 124, 125–26, 131–32; social demands on, 126–27
Weber, Max, 177
Women, 35–37
Workers' Party (PT) (Brazil), 174
World Bank, Peru and, 64, 65, 71

Yabrán, Alfredo, 163
Yacimientos Petrolíferos Fiscales (Argentina), 151
Yoma case, 150

III

Conclusion: Parties, Institutions, and Market Reforms in Constructing Democracies

Jorge I. Domínguez and Jeanne Kinney Giraldo

While discussing local events, some younger would-be reformers of Ilhéus (in Jorge Amado's novel *Gabriela: Cravo e canela*) observed that the traditional elites "support a state government that plunders us and then practically ignores us. While our local government does absolutely nothing . . . [and] in fact it actually places obstacles in the way of improvements." The reformers resolved to make changes; as one said to another, "you'll earn twice as much if you get into politics and change the existing situation."[1]

Though Amado wrote this forty years ago, his fictional characters still identify key themes in the political experience of a great many ordinary people in Latin America and the Caribbean in the mid-1990s. Government is unresponsive and at times an obstacle, traditional political leaders deserve no support, and political reform is an illusion because those who promise change are likely to change only the beneficiaries of corruption. The record reviewed in this book offers much justification for political cynicism and despair.

In the late 1980s and early 1990s, voters in many countries elected to office politicians who promised change but then disappointed the electorate. Elected on platforms committed to change, Fernando Collor de Mello in Brazil and Carlos Andrés Pérez in Venezuela were impeached for corruption and removed from office. Never before had a constitutionally elected president been removed from office in this manner and for this reason in either country.

More generally, the late 1980s and early 1990s was a time of troubles in many Latin American and Caribbean countries, a period when social, economic, and political circumstances were redefined. One sign of disaffection was the pattern of electoral outcomes. In those years, incumbent political parties were defeated at least once in Argentina, Uruguay, Brazil, Bolivia, Peru, Ecuador, Venezuela, Guyana, Barbados, Trinidad and Tobago, Jamaica, Panama, Costa Rica, Nicaragua, El Salvador, Honduras, and Guatemala, as were the incumbent politicians associated with the authoritarian government in Chile in 1989 and in Haiti in 1991.[2] The voters in these countries were unhappy with long-standing rulers and with would-be reformers.

Voters have blamed governing parties for the region's prolonged economic crisis. Dire living conditions still prevail years after the great depression that hit this region in the 1980s. By the end of 1994, on average and in real prices, the gross domestic product (GDP) per capita of the countries of Latin America and the Caribbean had yet to surpass the 1981 level. Among the Latin American countries, only Argentina, Chile, Colombia, Costa Rica, the Dominican Republic, Panama, and Uruguay had surpassed the 1981 level. In the Anglophone Caribbean, the record was better: the Bahamas, Belize, Guyana, Jamaica, and the countries that belong to the Organization of Eastern Caribbean States (OECS) had exceeded the 1981 level.[3]

Latin America and the Caribbean, in short, have been battered by the winds of change, anger, hope, and dissatisfaction. One might expect voter apathy and alienation from political parties to rise, politicians and civic leaders to redesign basic national institutions, market reforms to fail, and political regimes to fall.

In this chapter we advance four propositions that run somewhat counter to these expectations. Though there is much voter anger, new and many old parties have continued to mobilize support. Several new political parties have become credible opposition contenders even in countries where no "new" party has seriously challenged the political establishment in decades. In other cases, long-established political parties have "reinvented" themselves.

Second, while an orgy of constitutional reform-mongering designed to improve democratic governance has occurred, it has had little impact. Attempts have been made to redesign the relationship between executive and legislative branches, improve the performance of the judiciary, and decentralize certain tasks of government, but these attempts have either not gone far enough or proven counterproductive. In too many countries, the performance of state institutions remains poor and democratic governance is weak.

Third, contrary to the expectations of many in years past, democratic regimes in Latin America have proven more effective at introducing market reforms than had been the case with authoritarian regimes. Even more surprising to certain skeptics, in several cases these governments have effectively used the procedures of democracy to advance and secure such reforms.

And fourth, although the stability of constitutional government in the region is still a matter of concern—especially in view of the coup attempts that took place in the 1990s, some sponsored by constitutionally elected presidents—barriers against *successful* coup attempts have gradually been constructed. Since 1976, outside of Suriname, Haiti, and

Peru, all attempts to overthrow a constitutional government chosen through general fraud-free elections have failed. Important changes within the armed forces, in the relationships between the armed forces and the rest of the society, and in the international community have decreased the likelihood of successful military coups.

Crises and Opportunities for Representation

Latin American countries are facing a crisis of representation linked to the challenges of two major transitions: from authoritarian to constitutional governments, and from statist to more market-oriented economies. This second transition also affects most of the countries of the Anglophone Caribbean. Representative networks were battered by the authoritarian regimes; in some countries, they broke down. In nearly all new democracies, parties face a mass electorate that is larger, more urbanized, more educated, and more exposed to mass media than was the case under past constitutional governments. Moreover, the economic depression of the 1980s and the nearly simultaneous transition toward a more market-oriented economy strained old networks of representation and created demands for new forms of representation. Many parties have reconsidered their long-held adherence to statist ideologies. Labor union power has weakened nearly everywhere, while business and "liberal" ideologies have gathered strength. The cutbacks in government consumer subsidies and in funding for many public services have hurt the poor and weakened the political allegiances of many middle-class sectors.

As a result of these changes, organizations that seek to represent the interests of citizens have been simultaneously destroyed, created, and recreated. Many of these organizations have been political parties, but a wide array of social movements have also been involved, and many parties have drawn strength from such movements.[4]

This section examines four kinds of representational challenges facing countries undergoing the dual transition from authoritarianism and statist economies. In countries where the transition from authoritarian regimes to constitutional governments coincided with the end of civil war, new democracies face the challenge of incorporating parties that have been formed out of guerrilla and paramilitary groups. Second, in countries where parties have historically been strong, democratizing pressures and efforts to undertake economic reform have led to the creation of new parties that challenge the monopolies or oligopolies on representation that one or two parties have long held. In other countries where parties have been historically weak, such as Brazil, the major representational challenge is the construction of more programmatic and responsible parties. And fourth, older political parties in many countries have scrambled to adapt to changed circumstances, with varying degrees of success. On balance, the transformation of old parties and the appearance of new parties may improve the prospects of effective representation in the medium to long term.

Explaining the Defeat of Parties

One manifestation of the crisis of representation is the defeat of parties on election day. The most common reason for the defeat of parties at moments of transition from authoritarian rule has been the perception that they are "tainted." In elections that found a democratic regime, parties associated with, or conciliatory to, an outgoing military regime are punished at the voting booth. With the ambiguous exceptions of Mexico[5] and Paraguay, whose elections in the 1980s and early 1990s have been marred by irregularities that protected the incumbents from the full wrath of the voters, the parties most closely identified with an authoritarian regime lost the elections that marked the transition toward constitutional government. This fate befell parties as different as those of the Chilean Right, which lost the 1989 elections at the end of the dictatorship of Augusto Pinochet despite an excellent record of economic growth in the late 1980s, and the Sandinistas in Nicaragua in 1990.

In countries where no major parties supported the military regime, voters chose the opposition party most distant from the unpopular incumbents. This was one important reason why in 1983 Argentina's Radical Civic Union (UCR) beat the Peronistas for the first time since the latter political movement was founded in 1946; why in 1980 Fernando Belaúnde beat the APRA Party (American Popular Revolutionary Alliance) in Peru; and why in 1982 Hernán Siles Suazo became president of Bolivia at the head of a leftist political coalition.

Elections have also punished political parties that were elected as the standard-bearers of political reform but sinned through corruption once in power. The defeats of the Dominican Revolutionary Party (PRD) in 1986, the Christian Democrats (PDC) in El Salvador in 1989 and in Guatemala in 1990, APRA in Peru in 1990, and Acción Democrática (AD) in Venezuela in 1993 can be seen at least in part as voter retribution for such perceived failures.

A third source of electoral defeat for parties has been the response to bad economic conditions.[6] This was certainly a factor in the defeat of the Radical Party in Argentina in 1989, as well as in the defeats of the Christian Democrats in El Salvador in 1989 and in Guatemala in 1990, of APRA in Peru in 1990, and of Acción Democrática in Venezuela in 1993. The economic issue weakened every incumbent Brazilian president since the end of military government in 1985, though Itamar Franco's popularity rose at the very end of his presidency thanks partly to the successful inflation containment policies of his finance minister and eventual successor, Fernando Henrique Cardoso. It also weakened

Guillermo Endara's presidency in Panama, paving the way for the 1994 election victory of the Democratic Revolutionary Party (PRD) once associated with deposed General Manuel Antonio Noriega.

Given the overlap between these three explanations, which is most important to explain the defeat of parties? We believe that "association with authoritarian governments" has more explanatory power than the response to bad economic conditions. Except for the two ambiguous cases already noted (Paraguay and Mexico), no incumbent party tainted by association with prolonged authoritarian rule won an election during the transition from such rule. In contrast, some parties associated with incumbent governments have been defeated despite managing the economy well (in Chile and Jamaica in 1989 and in Uruguay and Costa Rica in 1994), and not every government that has mismanaged the economy has been defeated (Acción Democrática retained the presidency in the 1988 elections). Association with authoritarian rule has been punished more systematically than bad economic outcomes, while good economic management has not always been rewarded.

With the evidence available, however, it is more difficult to determine the relative importance of corruption and bad economic conditions. In Argentina in the early 1990s, for example, the positive economic results under President Carlos Saúl Menem meant more in the public opinion polls than the numerous charges of corruption leveled against people in or close to the administration. In Venezuela, in contrast, the positive performance of the economy under President Pérez during the same years did not bolster his popularity as much as Menem's. It did not save him from later impeachment and conviction on the grounds of corruption, nor did it save his party from election defeats that were also caused in part by the economy's eventual downturn.

The defeat of incumbent parties for any of these three reasons is understandable. Indeed, it is the essence of democratic politics that voters should turn out those officeholders of whose conduct or performance they disapprove. If the reasons why these parties have been defeated give cause to worry about the fate of constitutional government in the region, then the way these parties were defeated gives reason for hope that the instruments of constitutionalism can serve the people's needs.

However, another manifestation of the crisis of representation in the 1990s is the decline of electoral participation in the Anglophone Caribbean and in Venezuela, countries with well-established constitutional governments where such participation had been high historically. Citizens find no electoral vehicle that responds to their concerns to bring about meaningful change. In the early 1990s, as Trevor Munroe notes, voter turnout declined in ten of the thirteen Anglophone Caribbean countries in which general elections were held compared to the average for the 1980s. Voter turnout declined as well in Venezuela, a country with a once consistently high voting rate; its electoral abstention rate rose to 44 percent in 1993, a time of peril for its constitutional life.

Explaining the Birth of New Parties: From Warrior to Peacemaker

By definition, all new parties are born in dissent. Their leaders and followers claim that existing parties no longer represent them. The revolt against established parties has at times begun literally in rebellion. Never before in Latin America's twentieth-century history have so many political parties been spawned by paramilitary or guerrilla organizations. The new parties examined in this section differ in many ways but share one important trait: their founders once used violence to attempt to overthrow the government or dispose of their adversaries. The transformation of military movements into political parties is best explained as a slow, rational process in which exhausted leaders and followers conclude that politics is more cost-effective than war as a way to gain power.

On the Left, Venezuela's Movimiento al Socialismo (MAS) traces its origins in part to the Venezuelan Communist Party's decision to abandon the guerrilla warfare conducted against Venezuela's governments in the 1960s, after which some key leaders of that effort founded the MAS. By the 1980s and 1990s, as Alan Angell makes clear, the MAS had won a respected place among Venezuela's political parties, and it played an important role in Rafael Caldera's 1993 presidential election victory.

In Colombia the M-19 guerrilla group agreed to demobilize in 1989. Its leaders founded Alianza Democrática (AD) M-19, which won 12.5 percent of the vote in the 1990 presidential elections, the largest share of the vote for any party of the Left in Colombian history, as Harvey F. Kline notes. This party went on to win the second largest bloc of seats in the elections for the Constituent Assembly that met during the first half of 1991, though it had weakened greatly by the time of the 1994 national elections.

Revolutionary victory in Nicaragua in 1979 and the Sandinista defeat in 1990 gradually permitted and eventually required the transformation of the Sandinista Front for National Liberation (FSLN) from a military force into a political party. As Rose Spalding shows, the FSLN as a party has had a tumultuous history since 1990, but it has remained within the framework of constitutional politics.

In El Salvador the FMLN (Farabundo Martí National Liberation Front) began its transformation into a political party upon the signing of the peace agreement in 1992; allied with others on the political Left, as Ricardo Córdova Macías shows, it became the country's second-largest political force in the 1994 elections.

On the Right, it is only a slight exaggeration to argue that El Salvador's Nationalist Republican Alliance (ARENA) was born from a wedding between death squads and a segment of the business community. Roberto D'Aubuisson was the key figure in death squad activities in the late 1970s and early 1980s, and he would become ARENA's equally key leader until his death.

In Argentina, Colonel Aldo Rico led an unsuccessful military mutiny against the constitutional government in April 1987. When national congressional and gubernatorial elections were held in 1991, as Liliana De Riz shows, Rico's Movement for National Dignity and Independence (MODIN) won three seats in the Chamber of Deputies and 10 percent of the vote in the crucial province of Buenos Aires; its subsequent strength has varied but remained generally modest. Moreover, provincial parties in Chaco, Salta, and Tucumán nominated retired military officers who had served as governors during the previous military government; these candidates won the governorships.

The fate of these parties depends in part on their ability to resolve the often bitter internal debates over electoral strategy that occur frequently among new participants in the democratic process. In Colombia the M-19's decision to pursue electoral coalitions with traditional parties instead of focusing on party building seems to have backfired; by 1994 its electoral weight was insignificant. In El Salvador the FMLN split over these issues after the 1994 elections, as did the FSLN in Nicaragua in 1995. The importance of the new parties should not be underestimated, however. In the mid-1990s, the MAS was part of the governing coalition in Venezuela. The FSLN and the FMLN remained among the largest political forces in Nicaragua and El Salvador. And ARENA governed El Salvador.

Why did former military combatants lay down their arms to compete in elections? The general reason is *not* the end of the cold war, which had nothing to do with the creation of the MAS, ARENA, or MODIN, or the M-19's decision to end the armed struggle. Nonetheless, international factors did affect the costs and benefits of war for both the rebels and the government. The decision of some guerrillas in Venezuela in the late 1960s to abandon the armed struggle was part of a wider international debate within the political Left about the proper means to contest power. And the turn away from war by the FMLN and the FSLN was indeed framed by the end of the cold war in Europe.

Apart from these lesser considerations, a familiar but powerful explanation serves best.[7] In Thomas Hobbes' *Leviathan*, political order is established as exhausted individuals recoil from a state of war that is "nasty" and "brutish." In all the cases under review, terrible experiences of prolonged war eventually led the combatants to a rational decision to lay down their arms. Through prolonged war they learned that they could not win. The end of warfare in Latin America led, however, not to Leviathans but to constitutional governments. In the logic of stalemate, neither side could dictate its preferences to the other. Each settled for the second-best solution: to contest each other peacefully.[8] Putting something on the negotiating table became a more effective route to achieve their goals.

Latin America's warriors-turned-peacemakers stumbled unknowingly onto Robert A. Dahl's axiom that, from the government's perspective, "the more the costs of suppression exceed the costs of toleration, the greater the chance for a competitive regime."[9] From the perspective of the armed opposition, the axiom might be rewritten: "The more the costs of rebellion exceed the costs of participation, the greater the chance for a competitive regime."[10] Moreover, governments changed their strategies to provide institutional guarantees and other incentives for guerrillas to make peace and participate in politics. Lawful political space expanded; the insurgents responded rationally. Where the terms for peaceful participation remained insufficiently attractive, as in Guatemala and for some guerrilla forces in Colombia, the war staggers on.

Explaining the Birth of New Parties: A Protest against Partyarchy and Ideological Betrayal

In recent years, new parties have been more likely to be born and to attract nationwide support when two processes converged: (1) the preexisting party establishment gave signs of seeking to strengthen its ruling monopoly or duopoly, reducing the space for alternative political forces to express themselves within these parties; and (2) the key political party that had received support from the Left abandoned its prior policies and veered sharply toward promarket or other right-wing policies, seemingly "betraying the public trust" and generating a secession on its Left. Political entrepreneurs acted when space on the party spectrum was abdicated through ideological betrayal ("pull factor") and when they no longer found room to play a role within the existing parties ("push factor"). Facing blocked opportunities to voice dissent, the would-be founders of new parties and their followers exited.[11] The new parties gained electorally as citizens expressed their discontent with the status quo by voting against establishment parties.

Argentina, Mexico, Uruguay, and Venezuela exemplify these trends. In these four cases, the emergence of new parties has been in part a response to what some perceived as the arrogance of the national parties and the predominance within older parties of an apparently self-perpetuating leadership—a classic crisis of representation. Writing about Venezuela, Michael Coppedge uses the word *partyarchy* to describe this phenomenon. In Coppedge's analysis of partyarchy, parties fully penetrate organizations in civil society. We use the term a bit more loosely, simply to identify countries where the number of parties long perceived as capable of winning a presidential election is either one (Mexico) or just two (Argentina, Uruguay, and Venezuela), and where party leaders made use of this monopoly or duopoly to create a "cartel of party elites" (in Mexico, Uruguay, and Venezuela) or were perceived to be attempting to create such a cartel (in Argentina in 1994). Under partyarchy, party leaders and organizations seek to regulate electoral competition within each party and between the two dominant parties, to enforce party discipline in legislative assemblies and executive posts, and to rely on intra-elite negotiation to address various important issues.[12]

In Uruguay the constitution was modified in the late 1960s to concentrate greater powers in the presidency and to constrain political rights. Under President Jorge Pacheco Areco, the governing faction of the Colorado party turned to the Right. The government became generally repressive in response to the Tupamaro urban insurgency and began to adopt market-oriented economic policies. Because Uruguay's labor movement had been independent of the traditional parties, it served as a key vehicle to launch a third-party challenge to an entrenched duopoly (the Colorado and Blanco parties) long protected by the electoral law. In 1971 the law-abiding Left reorganized into a broad coalition, the Frente Amplio (FA), to capture 18 percent of the national vote, most of it from the city of Montevideo. By the 1994 national election, the Frente Amplio had made significant gains in the interior provinces; its share of the national vote rose to just under one-third, in a virtual three-way tie with the Blanco and Colorado parties.

In Argentina, President Menem led the governing Peronista Party toward promarket policies in the 1990s, dismantling the legacy of Juan Perón on which Menem had run for the presidency. Critics responded in various ways. Argentine provincial parties acquired a new lease on life.[13] Historically they had done well in gubernatorial and legislative elections, but in 1994 they also obtained important representation in the Constituent Assembly at the expense of both the Peronistas and the Radicals, as De Riz shows. Support for provincial parties, MODIN, and the left-leaning Frente Grande (FG) coalition blossomed in response to the 1994 agreement between President Menem and former president Raúl Alfonsín to modify the constitution, which was widely perceived as an effort to advance their own ambitions. To prevent the continuity of such a duopoly, many voters turned to third parties.

Something similar happened in Mexico, where national elections became much more competitive in the 1980s and 1990s, as Denise Dresser reminds us. After 1982 the long-ruling Institutional Revolutionary Party (PRI) abandoned decades of statist policies to shift toward promarket policies, but it was still reluctant to recognize opposition election victories. In response, the center-right National Action Party (PAN) ran on a platform calling for democratization and was able to increase its national appeal beyond its historic bases of support in various states of northern Mexico. Within the PRI, party elites raised the barriers to internal dissent even as they were abandoning decades of statist policies; denied a voice within the party they had called home, dissenters exited to form a new party. The new center-left Party of the Democratic Revolution (PRD), led by Cuauhtémoc Cárdenas, combined these dissidents from the PRI with supporters drawn from other small parties of the Left (including Mexico's communist party). The PRD considered itself a national party though it obtained disproportionate support from central and southern Mexico.[14] Both the reinvigoration of the PAN and the rise of the Cardenista opposition can be traced to protests against the PRI's monopoly on public office.

In Venezuela in 1989, President Carlos Andrés Pérez shifted away from his populist and statist past toward promarket policies markedly different from those that Acción Democrática had normally espoused. For the most part, the hitherto main opposition party, COPEI (Christian Democratic Party), supported the new economic orientation. In the early 1990s, opposition to these economic policies merged with a revolt against partyarchy that had been gathering strength during the previous decade. Opponents felt that they had no choice but to look outside the two long-dominant parties or to abstain; abstention rates in Venezuelan elections, historically very low, rose significantly. A plurality elected former president Rafael Caldera to the presidency in December 1993 after he had denounced the party establishment and its economic policies, broken with COPEI, and founded the National Convergence (CN), which aligned with the MAS and other parties. Another noteworthy result was the explosive growth of Causa R, a new political party that rose from a social and regional base and quickly became a national party. Causa R emerged in the labor movement of the State of Bolívar, led by union leader Andrés Velásquez, who was elected as state governor and served as the party's presidential candidate in 1993. By the 1993 national elections, Causa R had built a strong presence in the Venezuelan labor movement nationwide and drew support from other regions of the country to capture just under a fourth of the votes cast, a virtual tie with Acción Democrática and COPEI.

The combination of partyarchy and doctrinal abandonment set the stage for the rise of new parties. If partyarchy alone were the explanation, similar challenges should have developed in Colombia (see Kline's chapter) and Honduras (see the chapter by Mark B. Rosenberg and J. Mark Ruhl), where the Liberal and Conservative and the Liberal and National parties, respectively, enjoyed duopolies of representation and where party programs did not typically differ much in ideological content. In these countries, however, the question of "ideological betrayal" never arose. Parties remained reliable: once in office they did not change the behavior displayed in the pre-election campaign.[15] In these countries, despite discontent with the party establishment, no strong new parties emerged in the absence of ideological betrayal.

In the same vein, merely dropping previous programmatic commitments does not suffice to trigger the emergence of a third party seeking to represent interests within civil society. Third parties did not gain much support in Costa Rica in the 1980s, when Liberación Nacional (PLN) governments under presidents Luis Monge and Oscar Arias veered away from the party's historic statism toward freer market policies but did not seek simultaneously to increase barriers to representation. As Lowell Gudmundson tells us, court litigation became the channel for dissent from the new economic policies.

In Argentina, Carlos Menem ran for office without hinting that he planned to abandon decades of Peronista commitment to statist economic policies, but he did. In response, the Frente Grande coalition was formed on the Left to claim the political space that the Peronistas had ceded, but voting support for the Peronistas (though it declined slightly in 1991 relative to the 1989 elections) remained strong in the two nationwide congressional elections following his policy about-face. As De Riz shows, the Peronista share of the vote dropped only in response to the Menem-Alfonsín pact to modify the constitution. The Frente Grande had received only 3.6 percent of the vote in 1993 (before the Menem-Alfonsín pact), but it gained 13.6 percent in 1994 (after the pact), when it also carried the capital city of Buenos Aires; the MODIN's share of the vote rose from 6 percent before the pact to 9 percent after it. In the 1995 presidential elections, the Frente Grande transformed itself into the Frente País Solidario (FREPASO). Its candidate, former Peronista senator and governor José Octavio Bordón, won 28 percent of the votes, finishing second to Menem and ahead of the Radicals—the first time in a century that the Radical Civic Union had failed to come in first or second in a presidential election. (The MODIN's share of the votes fell below 2 percent.)

In short, neither a change in economic policy commitments nor the existence of partisan monopolies or duopolies suffices to trigger the emergence of new parties or party coalitions. Together, however, these two factors greatly increase the likelihood that such parties or coalitions will arise and grow.[16] A hypothesis to explore in the future is the following: when parties are formed around groups organized in civil society (Frente Amplio in Uruguay, PAN in Mexico, Causa R in Venezuela), they are more likely to endure and succeed than parties that are formed principally by dissidents who find their paths blocked within existing parties (Convergencia Nacional in Venezuela, FREPASO in Argentina), with Mexico's PRD exhibiting traits of both processes. There is preliminary support for this view in the December 1995 gubernatorial elections in Venezuela, in which Causa R received 13 percent of the votes cast, the MAS 10 percent, and Convergencia Nacional less than 9 percent.

Explaining the Birth of New Parties:
Constructing Political Society

In other countries, representation has suffered not because of the tight grip of one or two strong parties on public office but because of the predominance of many weak parties. Brazil, for example, has been bereft of "real" political parties. As Bolívar Lamounier and Frances Hagopian explain, the combination of powerful traditional elites, entrenched regional interests, the incentives created for politicians by the electoral laws, and the norms and habits of politics have left Brazil with weak, incoherent, unprogrammatic, undisciplined, and fractious parties. In contrast, as Lamounier put it at the Inter-American Dialogue's conference on democracy, "real" modern parties should be internally democratic, pragmatic, and able to recruit cadres and respond quickly to problems with well-defined initiatives.

Since the late 1970s, two real parties have been founded in Brazil. The PT (Workers' Party) grew out of the militant unionism developed in the late 1970s in the metallurgical industries of the highly urban state of São Paulo in protest against the ruling military dictatorship and in search of better economic conditions. It has become the largest explicitly socialist party in Latin America, incorporating a variety of small Brazilian left-wing parties within its midst and providing a partisan home for many social movements that arose in connection with Roman Catholic ecclesiastical base communities, neighborhood associations, and women's movements. In Brazil's 1990 and 1994 presidential elections, the PT's candidate, Lula (Luis Inácio da Silva), came in second. The PT's formal members have genuine opportunities to engage in internal party life and debate and choose party programs and policies. The PT has what Lamounier has called "a definite *esprit de corps.*" It is Brazil's first-ever large mass political party that does not depend on just the popularity of its leader or the efficacy of a patronage machine.

The second real party is the Brazilian Social Democratic Party (PSDB). Founded in 1988 from a schism in the Brazilian Democratic Movement Party (PMDB)—a classic incoherent combination of traditional clientelism, patronage, and factions—the PSDB sought to formulate a centrist "modern" alternative to other parties, with strong appeal to the urban middle class. The PSDB designed a program for effective democratic governance to which its officeholders were ordinarily bound. In 1994 PSDB founding leader Fernando Henrique Cardoso was elected president of Brazil in large part because of his previous success as finance minister. Like the PT, although to a lesser extent, the PSDB is characterized by programmatic coherence, officeholder discipline, and internal party life.

Since the 1994 elections, then, Brazil for the first time has had "real" parties in government and in opposition, in addition to the traditional clientelistic patronage machines. Nonetheless, the strength of those traditional machines was also evident in that election. In order to elect Cardoso to the presidency, the PSDB had to form an alliance with the Liberal Front Party (PFL), a classic patronage party. Thus it remains to be seen how much long-term impact the PT and the PSDB will have on the traditional style of politics in Brazil, especially because skewed electoral laws still limit their representation in Congress.

Explaining the Reinvention of Old Parties

The region's crisis of representation and its economic depression of the 1980s did not overwhelm every preexisting political party, nor was the creation of new parties the sole response to these problems, however. Many existing parties have made efforts to adapt to changed circumstances, a strategy of reinvention. In most cases, defeat—either of the party or of democracy as a whole—permitted challengers within the party to marginalize discredited factions and leaders, at times relieving them of their power. Defeat also made it easier to reexamine old dogmas and discard failed policies. Defeat alone is insufficient, of course, for the successful reinvention of parties. A reinvented party's programmatic reorientation can be consolidated only if the party is rewarded with electoral victory.

During the 1980s, as Timothy R. Scully demonstrates, the Chilean Christian Democrats and the socialists (including the socialist offshoot PPD, the Party for Democracy) rebuilt and repositioned themselves, and forged an alliance (the Concertación Democrática, CD) to win the 1988 plebiscite that ended the dictatorship and then to win the next two presidential elections in 1989 and 1993. The breakdown of democracy in 1973, the failure of the protests of the mid-1980s to unseat the military government, and the collapse of heterodox economic policies in neighboring countries affected the balance of forces within the parties of the Center and the Left and eventually resulted in the ascendance of new leaders who embraced a market-conforming political platform.

Also during the 1980s, the People's National Party (PNP) in Jamaica reconstructed its program and renewed its cadres, after the party's failed statist economic policies led to a crushing electoral defeat in 1980. The reinvented party won the parliamentary elections of 1989 and subsequently effected a transition of the prime ministership from Michael Manley to P. J. Patterson. The party recognized that its statist economic policies during the 1970s failed and had also resulted in its election defeat in 1980.

In Argentina, in response to their 1983 presidential election defeat, the Peronistas reinvented themselves. Founded in the mid-1940s by Juan Perón as what he called a "movement" more than a party, the Peronistas (Partido Justicialista, PJ) at last held internal party elections in the 1980s to choose candidates for office. These new internal procedures made it easier to remove many old-time leaders who had lost the support of the rank and file. In the early 1990s, in addition, the Menem government adopted an entirely new profile of economic policies.

In Panama in the early 1990s the PRD successfully recovered from its long cohabitation with General Noriega. As Richard L. Millett indicates, after its 1989 defeat the PRD modified its policies toward the United States, dropped its support for reestablishing the armed forces, adopted less confrontational stands toward other political forces, and adopted a market-friendly economic program. It won the 1994 presidential elections.

In Chile, Jamaica, Argentina, and Panama, the reinvention of the parties rested on a shift from statist to promarket economic policies, a shift made possible by the shock of defeat, which in turn permitted the removal of discredited leaders. In many cases a comfortable margin of victory for the reinvented parties in a later election facilitated the consolidation of the reinvention and the policies associated with it. Leaders who changed the historical policy commitments of their party were likely to lose some part of their previous constituency; the larger the victory, the less risky was this change. In Jamaica the margin of victory of the People's National Party in 1989 meant that the "renovating" leadership did not need to rely on the vote-mobilizing capabilities of the more radical wing of the party. In Chile the weakening of the Communist Party removed the incentive for leaders of the Center-Left to back away from their commitment to more market-oriented economic policies. In Argentina and Panama the Peronistas and the PRD, respectively, faced ineffectual opposition parties. In short, a significant victory over the opposition was as important to party renewal as the prior defeat of the party itself.

Representational Challenges to the Party System

Many of the new parties under review have been linked to social movements, but the relationship between political and civil society remains problematic in many countries. In Brazil, Chile, Mexico, Nicaragua, and Venezuela, for example, many groups in civil society have sought to increase their autonomy with regard to parties in order to avoid partisan manipulation. In Venezuela and Colombia, new social movements have pressed for the decentralization of the state as a way to weaken central party leaderships, and new local leaders have run for office successfully as independents. Though understandable, these combined trends may well make it more difficult to secure both effective political representation and sustained political cooperation on a nationwide basis.

In addition, there remain important representational voids that not even the new parties have begun to fill sufficiently and that are just as important for effective democratic governance. We call attention to three of them.

As Deborah J. Yashar points out, the representation of indigenous peoples has been woefully inadequate throughout the region. Organized ethnic protest has been emerging since the 1970s in countries with large indigenous populations. In Bolivia, new, small political parties have so far been able to channel these energies and provide some means for representation. But, as Eduardo A. Gamarra indicates, Víctor Hugo Cárdenas, the Aymara leader elected in 1993 as Bolivia's vice-president, may be more popular outside Bolivia than in his own country. He can obtain considerable international sympathy and support on behalf of those whom he claims to represent, but his actual backing within Bolivia, even among indigenous peoples, remains modest for a variety of reasons, including the internal diversity of the indigenous community and the limited accomplishments of his administration. Bolivia has also witnessed the phenomenon of Palenquismo, not organized ethnic protest but populist appeals to indigenous peoples by television and radio personality Carlos Palenque.

In the southern Mexican state of Chiapas, the Zapatista National Liberation Army (EZLN) combines ethnic and regional grievances with a larger national program and the disposition to use armed violence to advance its ends. Because of its reliance on violence, this insurgency has been the most worrisome example of ethnic protest.

In Ecuador the Confederation of Indigenous Nationalities (CONAIE) organized and spearheaded important nationwide protests in the 1990s in opposition to proposed land tenure law changes and other measures that, in its judgment, adversely affected the interests of indigenous peoples. CONAIE also learned to collaborate with some labor unions to organize general strikes. This may well be Latin America's strongest indigenous-based social movement independent of a political party.

Until the 1980s, nationwide political protest by indigenous peoples had been extremely rare in Latin America. To understand the change leading to the rise of such protest, Yashar highlights four features that apply with special force during the 1980s and 1990s: (1) the political opening associated with democratization; (2) the erosion of existing avenues of representation and the increase in material hardship that often accompany the implementation of neoliberal economic policies; (3) the nurturing and enabling effects of institutions such as the changed Roman Catholic Church and other religious communities; and (4) the growth of an international movement of foundations, scholars, and activists to provide support for indigenous organizations in Latin America. There is still the need to explain further, however, why Quechua speakers in Ecuador organize on behalf of the rights of indigenous peoples who happen to be poor, while Quechua speakers in Peru organize on behalf of the rights of poor people who happen to be indigenous.

Why does the likelihood of organized protest on behalf of ethnocultural and linguistic goals vary so much?

A second problem of inadequate representation is evident with regard to gender.[17] Universal suffrage came later to Latin America than to Western Europe and North America, and women's effective participation in politics has continued to lag. In the 1980s and 1990s, some women politicians have emerged on the national scene, but they are still rare. Some of the new and renovating political parties on the Left, such as Brazil's PT, the Chilean socialists, and Nicaragua's Sandinistas, consciously design their internal rules to attempt, with varying degrees of success, to create an active role for women in discussions and leadership.

A third problem of inadequate representation is the oldest and best known: the question of social class and democratic politics. In this collection, Jorge G. Castañeda examines the compatibility between new promarket economic policies and the distributive pressures that, he argues, inevitably emerge in democratic regimes. Latin American and Caribbean countries have not been good at meeting these goals in the past. The risk of neoliberal reforms is that the prospects for many people are likely to worsen unless there is a conscious commitment to address problems of absolute poverty so that "common folk" can become true "citizens." It is not just the troubles of the powerful, in other words, but the inattention to the troubles of the unempowered that has created a crisis of representation. Effective democratic governance demands that the voiceless be heard.

Reforming State Institutions

In response to the crisis of representation, the legacies of authoritarian rule, and the inefficacy of government economic management in all countries in the early 1980s, government institutions came in for close scrutiny after the demise of authoritarian rule. The result was a widespread and intensive effort to reform the institutions of the state. This section describes the strategies pursued and analyzes their limited success.

We focus on three major areas of attempted institutional redesign. One is the effort to break the gridlock between, and improve the democratic responsiveness of, the executive and the legislature. The second is the effort to reform the administration of justice: to combat crime and corruption, to depoliticize the courts, and to improve access to the court system. The third is the attempt to bring about territorial decentralization and to devolve responsibilities to subnational governments while seeking to improve their capacity to handle their new duties.

Reshaping Executive-Legislative Relations

With the return of constitutional government in Latin America, scholars and politicians advanced proposals for institutional reform designed to help solve the problems that they believed had contributed to the previous breakdown of democratic institutions. In many cases the nature of legislative-executive relations was blamed; in particular, fixed presidential terms and the stalemate between the legislature and the president in presidential systems were seen as crucial factors in democratic breakdown.

The most commonly heard prescription was parliamentarism. Its scholarly advocates believed that incentives for cooperation between the two branches would be increased by tying the legislators' tenure in office to the success of the executive.[18] Legislators who would face the prospect of losing their ballot positions in new elections called by a stymied prime minister would be more likely, the proponents of parliamentarism believed, to organize in disciplined parties and form effective government coalitions. Similarly, executives in parliamentary systems would face votes of no-confidence and thus would have more incentive to negotiate with legislators than would a president elected separately from the legislature and unaccountable to it. Despite these arguments, parliamentarism was not adopted in any Latin American country.

In the Anglophone Caribbean, the problems were different. In their existing parliamentary systems, the first-past-the-post electoral system and the small size of parliaments gravely weakened the capacity of the legislature to represent political minorities or to balance the executive. Elections produced large parliamentary majorities, denying even large minority parties adequate representation in parliament. Moreover, parliament was left with few means to check unbridled executive power. As Munroe reports, almost one-third of the region's members of parliament are also cabinet members. In effect, they are constitutionally debarred from independent and critical stances in relation to the executive because they are also in the executive. These problems remain unsolved for the most part.

Although politicians in Latin America and the Caribbean have been unwilling to undertake a wholesale change of state institutions (from presidentialism to parliamentarism, or vice versa), they did make a variety of institutional changes. Argentina (1994), Brazil (1988), Colombia (1991), and Peru (1978 and 1994) convened constituent assemblies to rewrite their basic charter. In Bolivia, Chile, Nicaragua, Paraguay, and Venezuela, legislators undertook constitutional reforms. In Ecuador a commission of experts drafted a new constitution based on widespread consultation and subsequent submission to a referendum.

There have been two waves of constitutional reforms. The first wave accompanied the transition to democracy and was aimed at solving the problems that were believed to have plagued previous experiences with democracy, especially gridlock and exclusionary practices such as the effective disenfranchisement of large numbers of citizens. Exclusionary

practices also came in for sharp criticism in the long-established constitutional polities of Colombia, Venezuela, and the Anglophone Caribbean, where the most widely voiced demand was for an opening of the
political system to greater participation (a cry heard also in Mexico).
The second wave of constitutional reforms responded to long-standing
problems of democratic governance that came to public attention as
governments attempted to implement market reforms: corruption, excessive concentration of power in the presidency, and irresponsible behavior by legislators.

The goals for reform advanced by the two waves were broad and potentially contradictory: (1) to break the stalemate between the executive and the legislature; (2) to encourage the democratic responsiveness
of the executive by checking its unbridled powers; and (3) to increase
the democratic responsiveness of the legislature. This third point had
two aspects: to encourage responsible, programmatic behavior by legislators and to increase the effective representation of voting minorities.

In order to break the stalemate between the executive and the
legislature, several kinds of reforms were passed to strengthen the executive. The most widely adopted reform was the ballotage, that is, a
"second round" in presidential elections in order to ensure that the
president would be elected by a majority. Since the late 1970s, this has
been introduced in Argentina and Nicaragua (where a candidate needs
only 45 percent of the vote to avoid a second round), and also in Brazil,
Chile, Colombia, the Dominican Republic, Ecuador, El Salvador, Guatemala, and Peru. A second reform was to give special powers to the
executive to make macroeconomic policy. Such reforms first occurred
in gridlocked democracies: Uruguay in 1967, Colombia in 1968, and
Chile in 1970. They would be introduced in Peru in 1979 and 1993,
Brazil in 1988, and passed by plebiscite in Ecuador in 1994.

A third change, introduced in Peru in 1993 and in Argentina in 1994,
was to permit the president's immediate reelection, ostensibly to
strengthen the incumbent's capacity to govern. The fact that incumbent presidents Fujimori and Menem benefited from the reform, however, led many to see this change as a resurgence of personalism in
contexts where partisan, judicial, and legislative checks on the executive remain weak.

A different approach to breaking stalemates between the president
and the legislature focused on the electoral law and the incentives it
provides to legislators. The electoral law is often cited as an explanation for the stable governmental coalition in Congress in Chile and for
unstable coalitions in Congress in Brazil. Brazilianists point to electoral law incentives that hinder cooperation, foster party indiscipline
and disloyalty, and induce preferential attention to pork-barrel politics
over policy issues. In contrast, Scully calls attention to Chile's quite
different electoral law of the early 1990s, whose "almost inexorable bi-

polar logic" has provided strong incentives for interparty cooperation at the polls and in the legislature.

In order to check the president's powers, politicians in various countries have granted greater prerogatives to legislatures. In Colombia, the Congress was authorized to censure ministers. In Nicaragua in 1994, the Assembly acquired greater authority over tax policy. In Argentina the 1994 constitutional reform created a cabinet chief accountable to the legislature and curbed the president's power to rule by decree. Bans on presidential reelection, already in place in most countries, have been added to several constitutions. In 1994 Nicaragua and the Dominican Republic banned immediate reelection; in 1991 Colombia banned reelection at any time. This strengthening of congressional prerogatives is largely a reaction against the abuse of presidential power that occurred as chief executives attempted to stabilize and reform the economies of these countries. (This happened only to a limited degree in Brazil, where the 1988 Constitution increased a great many of the legislature's powers but at the same time made the president's decree powers, established in the prior authoritarian constitution, even more arbitrary.)

Meanwhile, some reformers tried to end exclusionary practices and foster the legislature's democratic responsiveness by increasing representational pluralism. In many countries, expansion of the suffrage was expected to provide a constituency for reformist parties of the Center and Left. The ballotage in Argentina and Colombia was designed to encourage the proliferation of presidential candidates, and consequently of parties as representative vehicles, by permitting "sincere" voting (in which voters support the candidate they truly prefer) in the first round. Colombia's use of national districts for the election of senators allows voting minorities not concentrated in a particular region to gain representation in this chamber. Venezuela's shift to voting in part for individual candidates, not just for party slates, seeks to promote greater pluralism and weaken control by party leaders as well.

The most striking characteristic of these reform processes as a whole, however, has been their failure to improve the quality of democratic governance. Constitutional reform has proceeded the least in the Anglophone Caribbean, but the Latin Americans, frankly, have relatively little to show for their efforts, either. The greatest disappointments are evident in Brazil, Colombia, Ecuador, and Honduras, where little seems to have changed, and in Chile, where the electoral laws and the standing and structure of Congress remain well below acceptable levels for democratic constitutionalism. There, executive powers are excessive, one-fifth of the Senate is unelected, and the electoral law overrepresents conservative rural districts and impedes the effective representation of voting minorities.

How can this failure be explained? Some of the problems are genuinely intractable. Even if "smart people" were omnipotent in implementing reforms, they would still find it extraordinarily hard to determine how to balance the trade-off between accountability and effectiveness. The somewhat contradictory goals present early in the reform process were just as evident at the end.

In some cases, the diagnoses and prescriptions advanced by reforming elites turned out to be faulty. Ecuadorian academics, Anita Isaacs reminds us, expected radical changes even though the modifications enacted in 1979 were for the most part limited to the extension of the suffrage, party registration, and ballotage, stopping well short of reforming the institutional relations between the executive and the legislature. Ecuadorian elites erroneously focused their attention on creating incentives for short-term *electoral* coalitions (such as the ballotage), failing to realize that these incentives did not facilitate longer-term *governing* coalitions. Similarly flawed was the exercise in Brazil. Brazilian constitutionalists in 1988 did not address the electoral law's incentives for politicians to focus on pork-barrel politics and its disincentives for party discipline. Lamounier argues that this neglect can be traced to the mistaken notion that fragmented ("pluralist") representation in the legislature and concentrated power in the executive are the best ways to reconcile democratic government and effectiveness. (Although Brazil has long suffered from representational imbalance and electoral fragmentation, the 1988 Constitution continued to over-represent the northeast while failing to establish a minimum vote threshold that parties must meet to win representation in Congress.) In both Ecuador and Brazil, constitutional reform did little to solve the problem of governmental gridlock; president and congress continued to confront each other, the former often resorting to rule by decree.

In many cases, necessary reforms were not passed because they threatened the interests of elites. Munroe shows that the first-past-the-post electoral laws common throughout the Anglophone Caribbean protect the interests of the dominant parties best because they exclude third parties from ever gaining significant parliamentary membership.

More generally in Latin America, Hagopian's study of traditional elites shows that the interests of such elites are best served by existing electoral arrangements that reinforce the clientelistic nature of parties. Clientelistic party systems are characterized by fragmentation, personalism, a patronage or rent-seeking approach to the state and public policy, and a lack of party loyalty on the part of legislators and voters. Party indiscipline is especially evident when politicians desert the parties on whose tickets they ran, as a majority of Brazilian members of Congress have done since the restoration of civilian government in 1985 and as a comparable proportion of Ecuadorian members of Congress have done since a similar transition in 1979; in each of these two countries, as many as a third of the members of the legislature change parties during one term of office.

In clientelistic party systems, parties fail to articulate the interests of their constituents at a programmatic level, which fuels voter apathy and, in some cases, social violence. Collective action is difficult when power is dispersed among many parties (as in Brazil and Ecuador, for example); even where parties are fewer (as in Colombia and Honduras), internal factionalization and lack of discipline within large parties frequently results in an equally paralyzing de facto multipartyism. Members of congress pursue pork-barrel objectives at the expense of legislation or administrative oversight, permitting the excessive concentration of powers in the presidency. Traditional elites can make such conditions work well for them.

In clientelistic systems, presidents can employ patronage to co-opt the opposition, weaken congressional supervision over executive policies, and lull legislators into permitting the use of presidential decree powers. For these reasons, presidents, too, often prefer the constitutional status quo, therefore. For example, as Kline notes, Colombian presidents since 1946 have routinely ruled under "state of siege" provisions authorized by the constitution, relying on decrees rather than laws for the governance of the economy.

In this book, Hagopian argues that traditional elites are less predisposed to respect democratic institutions and processes and more likely to abuse the state for ends that are both antidemocratic and antimarket. Lamounier, Kline, Isaacs, Edelberto Torres-Rivas, Rosario Espinal, and Rosenberg and Ruhl document the long-standing clientelistic features of party systems in Brazil, Colombia, Ecuador, Guatemala, the Dominican Republic, and Honduras, which have had the effects summarized above. As Rosenberg and Ruhl put it, the two principal parties in Honduras have offered little effective leadership because their interest is largely directed at meeting the needs of their respective clienteles. Power is rarely exercised to effect a larger vision of the common good. In all such cases, democratic representativeness suffers, and effective constitutional reform to improve governance becomes highly unlikely.

Nevertheless, there have been some modest improvements, especially in countries with little experience of congressional assertiveness or efficacy. Ironically these improvements have resulted less from constitutional changes than from a more even balance of power between executive and legislature. For the first time ever, the Congress of El Salvador plays a role of oversight and legislation in the 1990s, with all of the country's political forces represented in its midst. During these same years, the Mexican Congress began to question the executive more systematically. Also in the 1990s, albeit (as Spalding shows) after excruciating difficulties, Nicaragua's Assembly began to legislate to address some of the country's ills. After the 1993 national elections, as Diego Abente Brun points out, Paraguay found itself with a divided government for the first time in its history; at issue was the capacity of president and congress to deepen a still-incipient process of constitutionalizing the government while maintaining acceptable levels of governability.

History also shows the importance of political learning in improving democratic governance. Consider the problem of resolving executive-legislative gridlock. The cases of Costa Rica in the 1950s and El Salvador in the 1990s exemplify the capacity of politicians to learn to cooperate for the purpose of fostering civil peace and establishing constitutional government. In each of those cases, civil wars came to an end and constitutional governments were installed. Venezuela in the 1950s and Chile in the 1990s provide related examples: various parties were able to cooperate to end dictatorship, install constitutional government, and fashion effective relations between president and congress.

Bolivia in the mid-1980s is equally remarkable. As Gamarra shows, Bolivia had had a textbook example of a weak, fragmented party system that permitted the military and, later on, drug traffickers to influence the exercise of power. In 1985, Bolivian politicians responded with inventiveness and creativity to a runaway hyperinflation. They have been able to form three kinds of partisan coalitions: one to contest elections, another in Congress to identify the next president (in the past three elections, the winner of the plurality of votes became president only once), and a third also in Congress to fashion reliable congressional governing majorities. The very same parties that had brought the country near its grave made possible its resurrection.

Each of these five countries was in the midst of effecting an epochal transition from economic chaos (Bolivia), civil war (Costa Rica and El Salvador), or dictatorship (Chile and Venezuela). In each case, politicians successfully responded to the problems of their times. These examples suggest that institutional changes are most effective and lasting when they are backed by strong political coalitions and serve the interests of the dominant political forces at a critical juncture.

Reforming the Court System

Judiciaries throughout Latin America are in dire need of reform, but little headway is being made. The problems with the court system occur at nearly every level, for four general reasons: (1) the corruption of judges; (2) the politicization of the courts; (3) the gutting of judicial independence by the president; and (4) the operational incapacities of the court system itself. In the 1980s and 1990s, reform efforts have attempted to expedite the administration of justice to combat crime and corruption, depoliticize the courts, and improve societal access to the court system. This section looks first at the four explanations for the malperformance of the court system and then turns to reform efforts.

In some countries, especially Bolivia and Colombia, the judiciary has been corrupted by drug traffickers. In Colombia, Kline recalls, drug leaders have been convicted infrequently because they have bribed, threatened, or killed judges. In response, the Colombian judicial system acknowledged its incapacity and came to rely more on plea bargaining: any person could receive a reduced sentence upon surrendering and confessing one crime. The problem of judicial corruption from drug trafficking has spread to other countries.

Meanwhile, the extent of politicization of judicial appointments by political parties is a threat to impartiality. In Ecuador in 1983 and again in 1993, Isaacs reports, congressional majorities deeply politicized the appointments to the Supreme Court, gutting its independence and threatening constitutional order.[19]

The threat to judicial independence comes not only from the legislature but, even more frequently, from an executive eager to reduce all obstacles to the implementation of presidential policies. In Argentina in the early 1990s, De Riz reminds us, President Menem increased the size of the Supreme Court to add his appointees and at the same time reduced the scope of Supreme Court jurisdiction over cases bearing on the "economic emergency." The Supreme Court's deference to the executive seriously compromised its legitimacy in the eyes of much of the public and the legal community. In other places—such as the Dominican Republic, as Espinal tells us—presidentialist personalism in the appointment of judges is routine and has greatly weakened the independence of the judiciary.

Presidents have also meddled with the courts to avert the politically costly prosecution of their allies. In February 1994 President Fujimori used his legislative majority to prevent the Peruvian Supreme Court from trying military officers accused of extrajudicial executions, the killings of nine students and a professor from La Cantuta national teachers' university.[20] In Argentina, President Menem replaced the independent judges who were slated to try some of his associates on corruption charges with more compliant court officers.

Finally, the operation of the courts is itself defective. In Bolivia, for example, Gamarra notes that the most serious problem facing the judicial system is the non-Spanish-speaking population's lack of access to the courts. By law, all proceedings must be conducted in Spanish, even though this is not the primary language of a substantial proportion of the population. As a result, many people look for justice outside the courts.

Operative deficiencies are also apparent in Colombia, according to Kline: in the early 1980s, only one in ten reported crimes ever led to a verdict, and in the early 1990s that figure had dropped to one of twenty. Similar statistics, regrettably, are common throughout the region. In many countries the court system is severely underfinanced, as Millett and Isaacs point out for the cases of Panama and Ecuador, respectively.

Despite these enduring and serious problems, there are glimmers of reform. In many cases, sustained efforts are under way to allocate greater resources to the courts, to improve the training of judges, and to professionalize the circumstances of their work. Colombia's 1991 Constitution created a National Prosecutor's Office (Fiscalía Nacional) with the authority to investigate and prosecute cases and to coordinate the activities of all military and civilian agencies gathering evidence on crimes. Thus the new constitution broke with the Napoleonic Code tradition in which some judges investigate crimes and others adjudicate them; the reforms freed the court system from investigative responsibilities. During the first two years, the judicial system processed 50 percent more cases than under the old system. This change holds promise for expediting the administration of justice.

Argentina's constitutional reform of 1994 also holds promise. In the so-called Olivos Pact between Alfonsín and Menem, a new council was created to nominate all judges prior to their appointment. The constitutional reform created a new General Accounting Office to audit the government's accounts and thus combat corruption. These agreements enhanced the independence and professionalism of the judiciary system, created more effective means to combat corruption, and attempted to depoliticize the judiciary. Parties in El Salvador, Nicaragua, and Paraguay have also been able to reach agreements and appoint balanced supreme courts. The willingness of political actors to compromise raises the hope that one of the root causes of judicial politicization, legislative-executive conflict, might be reduced.

Most ambitious has been Costa Rica's experiment with judicial activism to facilitate societal access to the court system, as described by Gudmundson. Since the 1980s the Fourth or Constitutional Chamber (Sala IV) of the Supreme Court has become involved in an ever-widening number of disputes. Nongovernmental organizations (NGOs) have gone to the Fourth Chamber to challenge the neoliberal economic policies implemented by Congress and the executive. The Chamber has also become involved in tourist, coastal, and national park development projects and in disputes about the rights of indigenous peoples, labor unions, and prisoners. Virtually all important economic interest groups have litigated to oppose the elimination of protection or subsidies. Plaintiffs often try to generate publicity and controversy to provoke the executive to modify its policies. Although effective at channeling discontent in the short run, this approach could lead to the atrophy of legitimate political channels for interest articulation and conflict resolution, and a heightened sense of popular cynicism regarding the judiciary.

The Territorial Decentralization of State Powers

In the 1980s and 1990s most Latin American countries placed territorial decentralization on their national agendas.[21] Many see it as a way to unburden the national government by turning over some of its responsibilities to local entities that may understand local conditions better and, reformers hope, may be more effective; at times, it is but one way to cut the national budget.

For others, decentralization is widely regarded as a means to increase the participatory nature of regimes, especially in countries that have come to elect local officials only in the 1980s or 1990s, such as Colombia and Venezuela. For many groups in civil society which have had trouble articulating their interests at the national level because of a reluctance to form close ties with political parties, local government holds hope for meaningful participation in community affairs. Parties of the Left, as Angell notes, hope that territorial decentralization will allow their officeholders to prove their competence in government at the local level, paving the way for a claim to national office; Causa R in Venezuela's Bolívar State, the Frente Amplio in the city of Montevideo, and the PT in São Paulo exemplify this strategy. Finally, local governments can provide new participatory opportunities for the informally disenfranchised, including indigenous groups and the poor; their increased participation at the local level might have positive implications for democratization at the national level.

Government and opposition may have contradictory objectives with regard to decentralization, however. The example of Chiapas illustrates this tension. For the Mexican government, territorial decentralization in Chiapas is a means to pacify the region and co-opt some indigenous elites. For the Zapatistas who began an insurgency in January 1994, the objective is to establish bases from which to launch wider political challenges, as they did in 1994 and 1995.

Despite these high (and somewhat contradictory) hopes, the results are discouraging. In most countries, local governments possess neither the funds nor the technical expertise to assume the new responsibilities assigned to them. Under these circumstances, subnational governments can undermine the efforts of national executives to carry out economic reforms. In Argentina and Brazil, for example, fiscal powers and prerogatives were extended to states and municipalities without corresponding responsibilities; the resulting deficits and debt contracted by subnational governments have hampered the consolidation of economic reforms.

Decentralization can also undermine democratization by reinforcing the power of local elites, their practices of clientelism (to which Hagopian calls attention), and the power of their military or paramilitary allies, as in Brazil, Colombia, El Salvador, and Mexico. Especially in the rural areas, these countries suffer from the inability of the central state to enforce the law equitably throughout its national territory. Instead of increasing the accountability of local elites to civil society, decentralization would decrease even further their accountability to national authority, and it might permit the consolidation of petty tyrannies. Decentralization is also likely to remove certain issues from the national agenda, which has been more likely to be hospitable to initiatives from the political Left. Decentralization may some day empower ordinary citizens to take better charge of their government, and permit a wider range of innovation at the local level, but there is still a long way to go before these promises are realized.

Economic Reforms, the Market, and Democratic Consolidation

Free markets and free politics are celebrated throughout much of the region, and thoughtful arguments are advanced about why they "go together" in Latin America and the Caribbean in the 1990s. Yet many scholars and political activists also argue that the rapid implementation of "neoliberal" market reforms has disrupted democratic representation, hurt the poor, and increased social conflict.[22]

Market reforms (especially deregulation, privatization, and the termination of business subsidies) can serve the goals of democratic politics. Statist economic arrangements often permit and foster close connections between economic and political elites, reducing the prospects for wider participation and fair contestation. Statist economics privilege business groups whose profits depend on political connections, not necessarily on efficiency or quality. Market reforms can break the ties between political and economic elites, reduce the opportunities for corruption and rent-seeking behavior, and create a level playing field for economic actors. Insertion into international markets provides external actors with the leverage needed to defend constitutional government in the region; such leverage helped to thwart Guatemalan president Jorge Serrano's attempt to overturn the constitution in 1993. In the 1990s, external actors have also used their economic leverage to prevent authoritarian reversals and to widen political openings in the Dominican Republic, Mexico, and Peru.

Some governments—most notably in Argentina, Chile, and Costa Rica—are establishing a "happy partnership" between market reforms and nationalism, replacing the historic alliance of populism and nationalism, as a means to consolidate both constitutional government and a market economy. In Chile, for example, defenders of constitutionalism and market openings appeal to nationalist sentiments suggesting that a proud nation would surely wish to meet these standards of "civilized" peoples; similar arguments are made for the integration of the poorest sectors into the national economy.

Democracy, in turn, can help to consolidate a market economy. In countries where levels of societal contestation and political instability have often been very high and organized opposition forces have been strong, democracy can reduce many transaction costs. There may be fewer disruptions from labor strikes or insurgencies if the would-be supporters of these strategies can find more cost-effective alternatives to advance their interests within democratic politics. In addition, democratic regimes can involve the political opposition in support of a market economy more effectively than can authoritarian regimes. In Argentina and Chile in the 1990s, for example, key decisions— Argentina's convertibility law governing monetary and exchange rate policies and Chile's tax laws—have resulted from negotiation between executive and Congress. By giving the opposition a voice and vote in the creation of fundamental long-term market-conforming policies, democratic regimes can set the foundations for credible and stable long-term rules. In these circumstances, rational investors can expect that today's rules will endure tomorrow even if the opposition wins the general elections. The procedures of democracy help to consolidate the market economy.

But the connection between democracy and the market is complex. Many of the devices designed to maintain fiscal discipline barely meet the test of democracy. For example, a closed and technocratic style of decision making reinforces the unresponsiveness of the state to societal demands and may well be authoritarian. At times presidents rule by decree, deliberately bypassing the legislature. These concerns were raised most often in Argentina and Bolivia in the 1990s. Even strong parties such as those in Chile, which have adapted well to the challenges of governance, must still prove their ability to articulate societal interests; there is so much "consensus" in Chile that dissenting interests and values may be neglected.

The turn toward a market opening has coincided with spectacular cases of corruption that led to the impeachments of presidents Collor in Brazil and Pérez in Venezuela. Concern about corruption also looms high in nearly all other countries. During the early stages of the privatization of state enterprises, for example, there are substantial opportunities for government officials to favor certain business groups. Mexico illustrates a related problem: because PRI politicians can no longer rely as much on state resources to pay for their campaigns, they resort to private funds in a political environment where rules governing campaign financing are weak and often unenforced.[23]

In the short run, moreover, the shift in economic models has contributed to the crisis of representation discussed earlier because parties must overhaul their economic programs and find new ways to gain support from their often surprised constituents. New parties and social movements have arisen to protest these policies, invigorating democratic contestation, to be sure, but also challenging the scope and durability of market reforms. Populist parties and corporatist forms of interest representation had in years past tied labor and other groups to the political system, but in the 1990s these forces have weakened precisely at the moment when public support must be found to help guarantee the stability of economic reforms and constitutional government, especially in Brazil, Mexico, and Venezuela. And, as noted earlier, Yashar traces the rise of indigenous mobilization throughout the hemisphere in part to grievances exacerbated by neoliberal reforms and left unarticulated by eroded representational networks.

The change in economic models has also altered the roles of the political Right, the political Left, and the traditional elites, shaping the quality of politics and the stability of constitutional government. The political Right has increased its participation in party politics in many countries, as Edward L. Gibson demonstrates. Parties of the Right, or parties with strong support from the Right, have proven far stronger than some eminent scholars had thought as recently as the early 1980s that they would be.[24] As the 1990s opened, for instance, elected parties or coalitions with strong support from the Right governed in every Central American country. This development portends well for the stability of constitutional rule, at least in the short term, because conservative interests (most often those of business) are well represented through the party system.

The marriage between democracy and the market also makes it possible for many economic actors to pledge their allegiance to constitutional government. Few incentives now exist for business to knock on the barracks door to alter national economic policy. The military is often judged to be too incompetent to manage the economy, given its generally poor record in government in the 1970s and early 1980s. Labor unions are weak, and macroeconomic policies benefit property owners. Business participates in politics, often supporting parties of the Right (though sometimes also other parties), mainly through the deployment of resources at election time (such as purchasing television time during campaigns), not through party building. The connection between business and parties may be close in El Salvador (with regard to ARENA) and in Mexico (with regard to the PRI), but it is tactical at best in most countries.

One obstacle to building parties of the Right has been the tendency of formerly populist parties in Argentina, Bolivia, Mexico, and Venezuela to usurp neoliberal platforms. One question for these parties is whether they can incorporate the Right as leaders and as constituents and still retain lower-class support. In the mid-1990s, perhaps surprisingly, the answer (except in Venezuela) seemed to be yes—a true feat of partisan skill.

The stability of constitutional government in the short term depends on the representation of the Right, but the long-run consolidation of democracy depends on the representation of nonelite interests, often by parties of the Left as Hagopian argues in her chapter. The development of a social democratic Left in Latin America, as Angell shows, has been encouraged by the same events that have weakened the Left in general: authoritarian repression, the collapse of communism, the decline of labor unions, and the narrowing of economic options. Widespread corruption and inattention to social needs have become key issues for these parties. The parties of the social democratic Left are very strong in Brazil, the Dominican Republic, Nicaragua, Panama, Uruguay, and Venezuela, and strong in Chile and El Salvador. For them, constitutional government holds the only route to national power in the 1990s. The Left's lack of governing experience in most countries and the absence of a clear economic alternative are liabilities, however.

Finally, as Hagopian notes, most traditional elites have opposed market reforms because such reforms threaten their control of resources and their access to government policymakers. To the extent that reforms succeed in shifting control over clientelistic resources from traditional elites to the executive, or reduce the salience of such resources by means of privatization and deregulation, the reforms are likely to advance the cause of both freer markets and freer politics. Traditional elites undermine democracy and markets by skewing electoral laws in order to block the emergence of political rivals who articulate mass interests, by placing limits on market and other policy reforms as a condition of their support for constitutional government, and by deforming the mechanisms of political representation with clientelism. These practices have pernicious effects on the extent and effectiveness of democratic governance. The alienation of citizens from the political system and the obstacles to market reforms are greatest where traditional elites are the strongest, as in Brazil, Ecuador, and Guatemala.

In sum, market reforms in many countries have strengthened the Right's allegiance to constitutional government[25] (especially evident in the export business sectors), while they have revivified the prospects for parties of the Left[26] that can channel some of the discontent aroused by such policies. Traditional elites, in contrast, are the enemies of both markets and democracy.

Empirically, in the mid-1990s voters signaled their preliminary approval of the shift toward a market economy. They abandoned the punitive electoral behavior noted at the beginning of this chapter. They began to reward officeholders who had managed the economy and other fundamental tasks well. Colombia's Liberal Party won three consecutive presidential elections in the 1980s and 1990s, in part in response to good economic management. Chile's Concertación Democrática coalition (including Christian Democratic, socialist, and other parties) won a second consecutive presidential election in 1993 thanks to its consolidation of a transition to a democratic regime and its excellent economic management. El Salvador's ARENA party, credited with securing internal peace and reactivating the economy, won a second consecutive presidential election in 1994. Ernesto Zedillo won the fairest-ever Mexican presidential election in 1994 in part because his party, the PRI, was perceived to have rescued Mexico from the economic depression of the 1980s. Fernando Henrique Cardoso was elected Brazil's president in 1994 mainly because of his successful control of inflation during his term as finance minister. Alberto Fujimori was reelected president of Peru in 1995 because he was credited with taming inflation, reactivating the economy, and controlling a virulent insurgency. And Carlos Menem, having presided over the termination of hyperinflation and the revival of economic growth, was reelected president of Argentina. In these and other instances, rational voters supported new market-oriented policies, thereby wedding the future of constitutional government to the success of the market economy.

For the "happy partnership" between democracy and markets to prosper, however, more needs to happen. Poverty must be reduced if citizens are to have the needed resources for effective participation; only with a widespread capacity to participate is democratic consolidation achieved. The reform of social services—their financing, organization, and effectiveness—awaits attention throughout the region. And the capacity of the state to raise revenues to rebuild infrastructure, and to improve the quality of health and education, requires ongoing effort. Special care must be taken to ensure that privatization decisions and implementation are transparent, not opportunities for corruption. Other issues include the balance between direct and indirect taxation, as well as the efforts of middle-class groups to resist reforms that hurt their interests (most notably in Uruguay, as Juan Rial points out, to protect and increase middle-class pensions through the use of a plebiscite). Successful defense of past rent-seeking achievements limits the resources available for other urgent needs.

The worry, best expressed by Castañeda, is that the political system will be unable to handle the pent-up demands that are bound to be expressed as the memories of authoritarian governments and hyperinflationary crises recede. Creating the understanding that democracy cannot solve everything is essential for a democratic culture, but it is not sufficient for stability; sooner or later constitutional government must provide some answers to the material problems of the poor. To justify his authoritarian methods, former Peruvian strongman Manuel Odría used to argue that people cannot eat democracy. For democracy to be consolidated and for the poor to resist the temptation of would-be authoritarians, democratic polities with market economies must make it possible for the poor to eat.

The Armed Forces and the Consolidation of Democracy

Since the mid-1980s there have been three types of military assault on constitutional government; they are discussed here in increasing order of concern. One, evident in the early 1990s in Haiti, as Anthony P. Maingot notes, is for the high command of the armed forces to overthrow the civilian government. In the 1980s this was the principal means to rotate rulers under authoritarian regimes, as in the case of Panama throughout the Noriega years. As Abente Brun notes, it was also used to terminate General Alfredo Stroessner's regime in Paraguay. This practice had been common in much of South and Central America from the mid-1960s to the early 1980s, but no successful military coup led by the high command has occurred in other South or Central American countries since 1982, when one group of Guatemalan military officers overthrew another. In the 1980s and early 1990s, the less professional the military, the more likely that its high command would publicly lead an overthrow of the government—the opposite of the pattern that prevailed in the 1960s and 1970s.[27]

In several countries with professional armed forces, however, there have been military mutinies against constitutional governments in the late 1980s and early 1990s. These revolts were led by disgruntled middle-ranking officers in Argentina, Ecuador, Guatemala, Panama, and Venezuela;[28] each of these countries except Panama has seen at least two coup attempts in these years. The motivations for the coups varied. In Argentina and Panama, they were related to the downsizing of the security forces, and in Argentina to the prospect of trials for human rights violations. In Argentina, Ecuador, and Venezuela, ambitious and popular officers led the coup effort. In Guatemala, opposition from some business elites to tax and other economic policies played a role. A common aspect of these mutinies was that the military chain of command broke down; the mutinies were aimed at the high command as much as at the constitutional government. Consequently, the capacity to maintain civilian control was shaken because the generals could no longer ensure the loyalty of the lower ranks of the armed forces. Military deprofessionalization was associated with the increased likelihood of coup attempts. All of these attempts failed in the end because they were opposed by the military high command and because civilian politicians, for the most part, closed ranks in support of constitutional government. But will the high command and the civilians be able to retain control in the future?

Finally, a grave threat to constitutional government may come from a coup led by an elected civilian president supported by the high command of the armed forces against the congress, the courts, the political parties, and all vehicles that help civil society seek advocacy and representation for its interests. Pioneered in Uruguay in the early 1930s and repeated in Uruguay in the early 1970s, this pattern is associated in the 1990s with Peru's president Fujimori. Thus far only Guatemalan president Jorge Serrano has attempted to emulate him, without success. (Susan Stokes discusses Fujimori's case in detail.) In these cases, presidents have claimed that extensive corruption in congress generates gridlock as well as the pursuit of illicit objectives at the expense of the public interest. Presidents thus call on the military to establish a temporary civilian dictatorship. This pattern of coup-making is particularly worrisome, even if it has succeeded just in one country, because the problems of corruption and gridlock are real, and the disenchantment with the performance of constitutional government has been considerable in many countries.

The aftermath of Fujimori's coup in Peru has made his suspension of constitutional government especially appealing to antidemocrats. The economic reforms initiated in Peru in the early 1990s before the coup finally began to bear fruit, while good police work led to the capture of Abigael Guzmán, the founder and longtime leader of the Sendero Luminoso insurgency. Though both outcomes could have occurred without a coup, Fujimori claimed that his decisive anticonstitutional act brought them about. Right after the coup, the Organization of American States (with strong backing from the U.S. government) pressured Fujimori into calling internationally supervised elections for a constituent assembly (which would double as a parliament) and to agree not to prolong his presidential term without a free election. In April 1995 Fujimori was reelected president by a strong majority. Despite some irregularities, the election was fair enough.

This combination of circumstances recalls the potentially great appeal of a Caesar who proclaims the need for a temporary interruption of constitutional government to save the country and constitutionalism in the long run. The problem, of course, is that such interruptions often last for a longer time. Fujimori's economic and military policies, together with his acquiescence to international pressure in returning to the procedures of constitutional government, may have had the paradoxical effect of making a "Fujimorazo" much more appealing than either Fujimori or the international community ever imagined: he seemed to have fulfilled the promise of a short and effective dictatorship.

On balance, however, the barriers against *successful* military coups did rise in Latin America in the 1980s and 1990s and remain high in the Anglophone Caribbean. In general, the "demand" for coups has been constrained by the generally disastrous performance of military rulers in the late 1970s and early 1980s. The economies of Latin American countries collapsed when military presidents governed. The military lost the reputation for competence beyond its specific professional sphere, though the Pinochet government in Chile regained such a reputation during the second half of the 1980s. The demand for coups has also been reduced by the strength of parties of the Right, as noted above; many business elites no longer rely on military coups to advance their objectives because they are effective under civilian rule. The "supply" of coup-makers has also been limited because military officers recall their frustration, their unpreparedness, and the loss of their own military professionalism when they attempted to run the government. If the memories of military misgovernment fade and the performance of constitutional governments remains weak, however, the prospects for such coups might increase again.

Another reason for the decline in the frequency of coups is that in many cases the armed forces can have their demands met without resorting to such tactics. The military retains significant prerogatives in countries as different as Chile and Nicaragua, Cuba and Honduras, Brazil and Peru, Colombia and Guatemala. Military courts defy civilian jurisdiction over the criminal activities of some military personnel. The military continues to control police forces and intelligence agencies in a great many countries, without significant civilian oversight. Retired and, at times, active duty military officers continue to control important state enterprises directly or indirectly; in Chile a portion of earnings from copper exports is explicitly reserved for military use. In these ways, the armed forces in many countries retain an independent source of revenue to shield them from budget austerity. In some countries, military commanders also maintain significant subnational influence through their alliance with local power elites. In countries where civil violence is particularly high, the armed forces exercise even greater power; despite transitions to constitutional government and despite elections, much of Colombia, Guatemala, and Peru has remained under direct military rule. For the rural citizens of these countries, no "democratic transition" has taken place. Such military prerogatives remain important obstacles to the realization of democratic practice.[29]

There is considerable debate about the appropriate roles of the armed forces in contemporary Latin America. In Argentina and Uruguay, civilian governments have eagerly promoted military participation in international peacekeeping and peace-enforcing operations under the auspices of the United Nations in order to focus the armed forces on these new professional issues. The hope is that the military will be less likely to interfere in domestic politics if so occupied.

One persistent concern about any military operation, including military involvement in combating drug trafficking, is the need for effective means of civilian control. For the most part, such mechanisms remain insufficiently developed, and in some countries they have yet to exist because too many civilian "defense experts" have been specialists not in controlling the military but in aligning with them to make coups.

There is a related concern about military involvement in the development of infrastructure or the improvement of public health. Such normally praiseworthy activities may blur civilian and military lines of authority, reviving the notion (proven false during the economic crises of the late 1970s and early 1980s) that military officers can handle the routine affairs of government more effectively than civilians. In short, the task of establishing civilian supremacy over the military remains daunting, and the likelihood of coup attempts remains high. Nonetheless, the prospects for continued constitutional government are better than at any time since the great depression of the 1930s.

The International Defense and Promotion of Democracy

Never before has there been such a strong international commitment to the defense and promotion of constitutional government in Latin America and the Caribbean. Such a new commitment is yet another barrier to successful coup attempts. Propelling the international activity on behalf of constitutional government is a change in the attitude of many Latin American governments toward intervention. This shift is best exemplified by Resolution 1080 of the Organization of American States, enacted in Santiago, Chile, in June 1991; it requires OAS member governments to address the interruption of constitutional government, should it occur.

There is also a marked change in the behavior of the U.S. government. Twice since the end of the cold war in Europe, the United States has deployed tens of thousands of troops to a near neighbor, motivated at least in part by the need to establish or restore viable constitutional government. In Panama in 1989 and in Haiti in 1994, U.S. troops deposed a military ruler and installed a civilian president. In Panama, international observers found that Guillermo Endara had won the 1989 presidential elections but was prevented from taking office because the military government stopped counting the ballots when it became evident that its candidate would lose. In Haiti, Jean-Bertrand Aristide was duly elected and took office, but was subsequently overthrown.[30] While the renewed commitment to constitutional government is encouraging, the lowering of barriers to the use of force across international boundaries is a source of concern.

The U.S. and other governments in Latin America, the Caribbean, Canada, and Western Europe, as well as the United Nations and the OAS, have also played valuable roles in ending wars in Nicaragua, El Salvador, and Suriname, making possible a transition toward more open politics. Through election observation, moreover, foreign governments and transnational NGOs have fostered a climate for freer elections in the Dominican Republic, Guyana, Paraguay, Peru, and Mexico. These international actors have supported trends away from electoral abuse and fraud, assisted with the logistics that permit freer and fairer elections, and denounced violations of the electoral process where they occurred. In Guatemala the international community played a decisive role in foiling President Jorge Serrano's attempted coup against constitutional government. And in the early to mid-1990s, the international community, including the Clinton administration, helped advance peace and constitutionalism in Guatemala, El Salvador, and Nicaragua, as well as defending constitutional government in Venezuela.

The defense of constitutional government has had some noteworthy limitations. Transition to civilian rule in Haiti was not accomplished without military force. And Peruvian president Fujimori's coup against constitutional government was not reversed; its thrust was mitigated through international pressure and negotiation in ways that, inadvertently, may have increased its appeal. On balance, however, the international community has had a good record defending constitutional government in the 1990s.

There is also the hope that the increased international engagement of certain countries will promote constitutional government within them. Mexico's participation in the North American Free Trade Agreement (NAFTA) may help consolidate the economic reforms enacted in the late 1980s and early 1990s, assist the country's recovery from the late 1994 and early 1995 currency devaluation shock, and foster a more open political climate. As Dresser's chapter shows, the administrations of presidents Carlos Salinas and Ernesto Zedillo were required to change many undemocratic political practices in order to safeguard Mexico's participation in NAFTA. Under international scrutiny, Mexico created mechanisms to protect human rights, reduce the likelihood of election fraud, and recognize opposition victories for subnational offices. Similarly, Paraguay's engagement in international trade and other economic relations through MERCOSUR (with Argentina, Brazil, and Uruguay) may help to open the political system further, years after the end of Alfredo Stroessner's dictatorship. Freer markets in the global economy, as in domestic economies, may contribute to the consolidation of freer politics in the long run.

By the same token, however, international factors may also create pressures that destabilize domestic politics. NAFTA, for example, is making it very difficult for Mexican maize producers to compete with imports from the United States, fueling discontent in already volatile rural areas and giving credence to the enemies of NAFTA (and of the government) within Mexico.

These perspectives offer a window into the future of Cuba, which Marifeli Pérez-Stable reviews in this collection. Will the future of Cuba be like the past in Panama in the 1980s and Haiti in the early 1990s, where massive U.S. military intervention occurred after unarticulated civil societies and weak and fragmented opposition movements within and outside the country were unable to launch a successful process of democratization? Will it be like Nicaragua and El Salvador in the 1980s, where extensive civil war with external participation lingered for years? Or will the future of Cuba be like the 1980s and 1990s in much of Central America, Mexico, and Paraguay, where an engaged international community aided a peaceful transition toward more open politics? The third scenario would require, of course, that Cuban leaders be more willing than they have been in the past to negotiate new rules of governance with the domestic opposition. From the perspective of democratization, the prospects are not good; the current political regime seems likely to endure, though it has already become much friendlier to international market forces. For the reasons Pérez-Stable reviews, however, we believe that the third scenario has the better chance of achieving Cuba's successful transition to democracy because it would impose the lowest costs on its people and its neighbors.

Conclusion

"Like all men in Babylon," Jorge Luis Borges wrote, "I have been a proconsul; like all, a slave. I have also known omnipotence, opprobrium, imprisonment."[31] In many ways, this characterizes the experience of many prominent Latin American politicians in the 1990s. Some, like Argentine president Carlos Saúl Menem, spent years in prison under military government. Others, like President Fernando Henrique Cardoso of Brazil, spent years under official opprobrium and exile during his country's period of military rule. As Latin America and the Caribbean approach a new millennium, the task is to banish forever slavery, opprobrium, and imprisonment without succumbing to the temptations of the omnipotent proconsul. The power of presidents and ministers to govern is at times vast and injurious to democratic practice, for it presumes falsely that the executive alone has been elected by the people.

In this work we call attention to the importance of institutions and procedures that remain fundamental for democratic practice. In particular, we have focused on parties and their key role as bridges between state and society. And we have pondered the issues and concerns that arise within governments regarding executive, legislative, judiciary, and military institutions. These institutions and relationships are at the heart of the future of constitutional government in the Americas.

With regard to the prospects for military intervention in politics, we have echoed the alarm of others and have noted the extent to which the military may remain involved in politics short of staging a coup. Nonetheless, we are heartened by the decreased frequency of successful overthrows of constitutional government.

Thus the task at hand is to improve effective democratic governance. We are especially encouraged by the capacity of many to organize peacefully to participate in political life, but we are discouraged by continuing evidence that the design and redesign of the institutions of constitutional government have fallen well short of the needs of these countries. Between these two trends lies the future of democracy in the region.

Notes

This is not a freestanding chapter. Instead, it calls attention to, and to some degree summarizes, themes that emerge in the chapters in this collection and in other work that has been part of the Inter-American Dialogue project on democratic governance. Because the introductory chapter by Jorge Domínguez and Abraham F. Lowenthal highlights certain policy issues, this chapter concentrates on more scholarly questions. This chapter relies occasionally on textual references to other chapters, but our debt to the authors in this collection is much greater than these citations suggest. The views expressed here are ours alone. The Inter-American Dialogue and the authors are at liberty to claim that all the errors in this chapter are ours and all the insights are theirs. We are also grateful for comments on an earlier version from Alan Angell, Michael Coppedge, Rosario Espinal, Peter Hakim, Harvey F. Kline, Abraham F. Lowenthal, Marifeli Pérez-Stable, Rose J. Spalding, Michael Shifter, and Deborah J. Yashar. An earlier version was presented at meetings of the Harvard University comparative politics faculty group and of the University's Sawyer Seminar, sponsored by the Mellon Foundation; we are also grateful for the comments from the participants, Eva Bellin, Daniel Goldhagen, Torben Iversen, Stanley Hoffmann, Stephen Krasner, Anthony Pereira, Theda Skocpol, and Deborah J. Yashar. We thank Linda Lowenthal for very fine editing. All mistakes are ours alone.

1. Jorge Amado, *Gabriela: Clove and Cinnamon*, trans. James L. Taylor and William L. Grossman (New York: Crest Books, 1964), 75, 80.

2. Reelections had occurred uninterruptedly only where there had been no competition (Cuba), or where doubts have existed about the fairness of electoral procedures (Antigua, the Dominican Republic, Mexico, and Paraguay). Only in Colombia (except in 1982) and elsewhere in the eastern Caribbean have fair elections resulting in repeated incumbent party victories been the norm.

3. United Nations, Economic Commission for Latin America and the Caribbean, *Preliminary Overview of the Economy of Latin America and the Caribbean, 1994*, LC/G.1846 (December 20, 1994), 39.

4. On this linkage function of social movements, see Kay Lawson and Peter Merkl, eds., *When Parties Fail* (Princeton: Princeton University Press, 1988).

5. The Mexican case is complex for two other reasons. Civilians have ruled in Mexico, and, despite important irregularities in Mexican elections, the evidence from public opinion polls shows that a plurality of voters have preferred to vote for the Institutional Revolutionary Party (PRI) than for any of the opposition parties. See Jorge I. Domínguez and James A. McCann, "Shaping Mexico's Electoral Arena: The Construction of Partisan Cleavages in the 1988 and 1991 National Elections," *American Political Science Review* 89, no. 1 (1995): 34–48.

6. See also Karen Remmer, "The Political Economy of Elections in Latin America, 1980–1991," *American Political Science Review* 87, no. 2 (1993): 393–407.

7. This and the next two paragraphs draw on Jorge I. Domínguez, "Transiciones democráticas en Centro América y Panamá," in Jorge I. Domínguez and Marc Lindenberg, eds., *Transiciones democráticas en Centro América* (San José, Costa Rica: Editorial Instituto Centroamericano de Administración de Empresas, 1994), 19–62.

8. For a discussion of bargains that may lead to democratic outcomes, see also Adam Przeworski, *Democracy and the Market: Political and Economic Reforms in Eastern Europe and Latin America* (Cambridge: Cambridge University Press, 1991), chaps. 1–2.

9. Robert A. Dahl, *Polyarchy: Participation and Opposition* (New Haven: Yale University Press, 1971), 15.

10. For a more elaborate discussion of the costs and benefits facing guerrillas and governments, see Matthew Soberg Shugart, "Guerrillas and Elections: An Institutionalist Perspective on the Costs of Conflict and Competition," *International Studies Quarterly* 36, no. 2 (1992): 121–51.

11. For the general concepts, see Albert Hirschman, *Exit, Voice, and Loyalty* (New Haven: Yale University Press, 1970).

12. Barriers to entry by new parties in the electoral law are, however, often low; in some cases, they have been lowered in recent years. This is why dissident politicians can form new parties instead of seeking to overthrow the government by force.

13. For a discussion of the historic role of Argentina's provincial parties, see Edward Gibson, *Conservative Parties and Democratic Politics: Argentina in Comparative Perspective* (Baltimore: Johns Hopkins University Press, 1996).

14. See Domínguez and McCann, "Shaping Mexico's Electoral Arena."

15. For a classic discussion of the utility of "reliability" and "responsibility" in parties, see Anthony Downs, *An Economic Theory of Democracy* (New York: Harper & Row, 1957), 96–113.

16. We recognize an anomaly. If this argument were right in every instance, a major third party should have emerged in Jamaica in the early 1990s in response to the People's National Party's turn from statism toward promarket policies and the continued resistance of the two dominant parties to changing the electoral law to lower the threshold for third-party membership in parliament. Our argument with regard to the Latin American cases requires, therefore, permissive electoral laws—proportional representation. This is exactly what the Anglophone Caribbean does not have.

17. For further discussion, see Jane S. Jaquette, "Rewriting the Scripts: Gender in the Comparative Study of Latin American Politics," in Peter H. Smith, ed., *Latin America in Comparative Perspective: New Approaches to Methods and Analysis* (Boulder, Colo.: Westview Press, 1995), 111–33.

18. See Juan J. Linz and Arturo Valenzuela, eds., *The Failure of Presidential Democracy* (Baltimore: Johns Hopkins University Press, 1994); Juan J. Linz, Arend Lijphart, and Arturo Valenzuela, eds., *Hacia una democracia moderna: La opción parlamentaria* (Santiago: Ediciones Universidad Católica de Chile, 1990).

19. For an overview of supreme courts, see Joel G. Verner, "The Independence of Supreme Courts in Latin America: A Review of the Literature," *Journal of Latin American Studies* 16, no. 2 (1984): 463–506.

20. For a general discussion of human rights issues during democratic transitions, see Manuel Antonio Garretón, "Human Rights in Processes of Democratization," *Journal of Latin American Studies* 26, no. 1 (1994): 221–34.

21. For a general discussion, see R. Andrew Nickson, *Local Government in Latin America* (Boulder, Colo.: Lynne Rienner, 1995); Jonathan Fox, "Latin America's Emerging Local Politics," *Journal of Democracy* 5, no. 2 (1994): 105–16.

22. For a theoretical argument about the economic advantages of democracy over autocracy, see Mancur Olson, "Dictatorship, Democracy and Development," *American Political Science Review* 87, no. 3 (1993): 567–76. See also the special issues on "Economic Liberalization and Democratization: Explorations of the Linkages" in *World Development* 21, no. 8 (1993), and on "Economic Reform and Democracy" in *Journal of Democracy* 5, no. 4 (1994).

23. For a related argument, see Barbara Geddes and Artur Ribeiro, "Institutional Sources of Corruption in Brazil," *Third World Quarterly* 13 (1992): 641–61.

24. See, for example, Guillermo O'Donnell and Philippe Schmitter, *Tentative Conclusions about Uncertain Democracies: Transitions from Authoritarian Rule* (Baltimore: Johns Hopkins University Press, 1986), 62–63.

25. The greater allegiance of the Right to democracy can be found to varying degrees (listing from south to north) in Argentina, Chile, Colombia, Panama, Costa Rica, Nicaragua, El Salvador, and Mexico.

26. Opposition to some of the negative consequences of market reforms has strengthened the long-term prospects for parties of the Left to varying degrees. Listing from south to north, this is evident in Argentina, Uruguay, Brazil, Panama, Nicaragua, El Salvador, and Mexico.

27. For discussion of the earlier pattern, see Alfred Stepan, "The New Professionalism of Internal Warfare and Military Role Expansion," in Abraham F. Lowenthal and J. Samuel Fitch, eds., *Armies and Politics in Latin America,* (New York: Holmes and Meier, 1986), 134–47.

28. This pattern has been common elsewhere as well. See Samuel P. Huntington, *The Third Wave: Democratization in the Late Twentieth Century* (Norman: University of Oklahoma Press, 1991), 234.

29. A number of scholars stress the prerogatives retained by the military after the transition to constitutional government and the threat that this poses to democracy. See Alfred Stepan, *Rethinking Military Politics* (Princeton: Princeton University Press, 1988), 68–127. See also Brian Loveman, "'Protected Democracies' and Military Guardianship: Political Transition in Latin America, 1978–1993," *Journal of Interamerican Studies and World Affairs* 36, no. 2 (1994): 105–89; and Felipe Agüero, "The Military and the Limits to Democratization in South America," in Scott Mainwaring, Guillermo O'Donnell, and J. Samuel Valenzuela, eds., *Issues in Democratic Consolidation: The New South American Democracies in Comparative Perspective* (Notre Dame: University of Notre Dame Press, 1992). In contrast, Wendy Hunter shows how democracy has helped to limit military prerogatives in Brazil. See her "Politicians against Soldiers: Contesting the Military in Postauthoritarian Brazil," *Comparative Politics* 27, no. 4 (1995): 425–43.

30. To be sure, the main U.S. motivation for intervention has not always been the promotion of democracy. In Panama the main motivation was to curtail drug trafficking and financial laundering, while in Haiti it was to make it easier to stop the flow of immigration and to return undocumented immigrants. Another important difference between the two interventions is that in Haiti the United States had sought and obtained prior authorization from the United Nations Security Council and a commitment that other countries would eventually join a peacekeeping effort; in Panama the United States acted unilaterally.

31. Jorge Luis Borges, "The Lottery in Babylon," in his *Labyrinths: Selected Stories and Other Writings,* ed. Donald A. Yates and James E. Irby (New York: New Directions Books, 1964), 30.